Fodor's 2008

ALASKA PORTS OF CALL

Where to Stay and Eat
for All Budgets

Must-See Sights
and Local Secrets

Ratings You Can Trust

Fodor's Travel Publications   New York, Toronto, London, Sydney, Auckland
www.fodors.com

FODOR'S ALASKA PORTS OF CALL 2008
Editor: Adam Taplin

Editorial Production: Evangelos Vasilakis, Astrid deRidder
Editorial Contributors: Linda Coffman, Sue Kernaghan, Ken Marsh, Emily Wilder
Maps & Illustrations: David Lindroth Inc.; Mark Stroud, Moon Street Cartography, *cartographers;* Bob Blake and Rebecca Baer, *map editors*
Design: Fabrizio LaRocca, *creative director;* Guido Caroti, Siobhan O'Hare, *art directors;* Tina Malaney, Chie Ushio, Ann McBride, *designers;* Melanie Marin, *senior picture editor;* Moon Sun Kim, *cover designer*
Cover Photo: (Leconte Glacier): Douglas Peebles Photography/Alamy
Production/Manufacturing: Steve Slawsky

COPYRIGHT

ISBN 978–1–4000–1819–2

ISSN 1520–0205

SPECIAL SALES

This book is available at special discounts for bulk purchases for sales promotions or premiums. Special editions, including personalized covers, excerpts of existing books, and corporate imprints, can be created in large quantities for special needs. For more information, write to Special Markets/Premium Sales, 1745 Broadway, MD 6-2, New York, New York 10019, or e-mail specialmarkets@randomhouse.com.

AN IMPORTANT TIP & AN INVITATION

Although all prices, opening times, and other details in this book are based on information supplied to us at press time, changes occur all the time in the travel world, and Fodor's cannot accept responsibility for facts that become outdated or for inadvertent errors or omissions. So **always confirm information when it matters,** especially if you're making a detour to visit a specific place. Your experiences—positive and negative—matter to us. If we have missed or misstated something, **please write to us.** We follow up on all suggestions. Contact the Alaska Ports of Call editor at editors@fodors.com or c/o Fodor's at 1745 Broadway, New York, NY 10019.

PRINTED IN THE UNITED STATES OF AMERICA
10 9 8 7 6 5 4 3 2 1

Be a Fodor's Correspondent

Your opinion matters. It matters to us. It matters to your fellow Fodor's travelers, too. And we'd like to hear it. In fact, we need to hear it.

When you share your experiences and opinions, you become an active member of the Fodor's community. That means we'll not only use your feedback to make our books better, but we'll publish your names and comments whenever possible. Throughout our guides, look for "Word of Mouth," excerpts of your unvarnished feedback.

Here's how you can help improve Fodor's for all of us.

Tell us when we're right. We rely on local writers to give you an insider's perspective. But our writers and staff editors—who are the best in the business—depend on you. Your positive feedback is a vote to renew our recommendations for the next edition.

Tell us when we're wrong. We're proud that we update most of our guides every year. But we're not perfect. Things change. Hotels cut services. Museums change hours. Charming cafés lose charm. If our writer didn't quite capture the essence of a place, tell us how you'd do it differently. If any of our descriptions are inaccurate or inadequate, we'll incorporate your changes in the next edition and will correct factual errors at fodors.com immediately.

Tell us what to include. You probably have had fantastic travel experiences that aren't yet in Fodor's. Why not share them with a community of like-minded travelers? Maybe you chanced upon a beach or bistro or B&B that you don't want to keep to yourself. Tell us why we should include it. And share your discoveries and experiences with everyone directly at fodors.com. Your input may lead us to add a new listing or highlight a place we cover with a "Highly Recommended" star or with our highest rating, "Fodor's Choice."

Give us your opinion instantly at our feedback center at www.fodors.com/feedback. You may also e-mail editors@fodors.com with the subject line "Alaska Ports of Call Editor." Or send your nominations, comments, and complaints by mail to Alaska Ports of Call Editor, Fodor's, 1745 Broadway, New York, NY 10019.

You and travelers like you are the heart of the Fodor's community. Make our community richer by sharing your experiences. Be a Fodor's correspondent.

Tim Jarrell, Publisher

CONTENTS

ALASKA IN FOCUS

CLOSEUPS

ABOUT
THIS BOOK

Up front you'll find a **Cruise Primer,** with some basic information about cruising and what to expect.

Choosing Your Cruise gives you the lowdown on the cruise lines and cruise ships that regularly ply the waters of Alaska. This section will help you sort through the various lines, ships, and itineraries available.

Ports of Embarkation gives you background on the most important ports for joining a cruise, including suggestions on where to stay and eat, and what you might want to do if you spend an extra day or two there before or after.

Ports of Call gives you our best advice on what to do in each major Alaska cruise port if you want to go your own way, as well as a rundown of our favorite shore excursions offered by most ships if you don't.

Disagree with any of our choices? Care to nominate a place or suggest that we rate one more highly? Visit our feedback center at www. fodors.com/feedback.

Budget Well
Hotel and restaurant price categories from ¢ to $$$$ are defined in the opening pages of chapters 3 and 4. For attractions, we always give standard adult admission fees; reductions are usually available for children, students, and senior citizens. Want to pay with plastic? **AE, D, DC, MC, V** following restaurant and hotel listings indicate whether American Express, Discover, Diner's Club, MasterCard, and Visa are accepted.

Restaurants
Unless we state otherwise, restaurants are open for lunch and dinner daily. We mention dress only when there's a specific requirement and reservations only when they're essential or not accepted—it's always best to book ahead.

Hotels
Hotels have private bath, phone, TV, and air-conditioning and operate on the European Plan (aka EP, meaning without meals), unless we specify that they use the Continental Plan (CP, with a Continental breakfast), Breakfast Plan (BP, with a full breakfast), or Modified American Plan (MAP, with breakfast and dinner) or are all-inclusive (including all meals and most activities). We always list facilities but not whether you'll be charged an extra fee to use them, so when pricing accommodations, find out what's included.

Many Listings	
★	Fodor's Choice
★	Highly recommended
⊠	Physical address
↔	Directions
⌂	Mailing address
☎	Telephone
🖷	Fax
⊕	On the Web
✑	E-mail
🖃	Admission fee
☉	Open/closed times
Ⓜ	Metro stations
▭	Credit cards

Hotels & Restaurants	
🏨	Hotel
⌥	Number of rooms
⚐	Facilities
⑩	Meal plans
✕	Restaurant
⚲	Reservations
⚘	Smoking
ᵠᵠ	BYOB
✕🏨	Hotel with restaurant that warrants a visit

Outdoors	
⚑	Golf
⛺	Camping

Other	
☾	Family-friendly
⇨	See also
⊠	Branch address
☞	Take note

Cruise Primer

WORD OF MOUTH

"Do your homework, shopping isn't a priority for most, but what is outside the ship is. Tours are costly and excellent, budget fully, you get only half a trip without them. In your cruise selection consider ports, time in ports, route, glacier, ship naturalist, price. THEN find a ship."

—BudgetQueen

"Cruising has a lot of detail that first-timers aren't aware of. There are tons of choices for Alaska cruising and it's difficult to get your arms around all of it. Airfares can be very expensive for one-way cruises, too. If you plan on doing the land tour, there's another set of options to choose from."

—Crowsie

BEFORE YOU GO

DOCUMENTS

By Linda
Coffman

TICKETS

After you make the final payment to your travel agent, the cruise line will issue your cruise tickets and vouchers for airport-to-ship transfers. Depending on the airline, and whether you have purchased an air-sea package, you may receive your plane tickets or charter-flight vouchers at the same time; you may also receive vouchers for any shore excursions, although most cruise lines issue these aboard ship. Should your travel documents not arrive when promised, contact your travel agent or call the cruise line directly. If you book late, tickets may be delivered directly to the ship.

> ### PREBOARDING TIP
>
> To expedite preboarding paper-work, some cruise lines have convenient forms on their Web sites. As long as you have your reservation number, you can provide the required immigration information, reserve shore excursions, and even indicate any creature-comfort special requests. Be sure to print copies of any forms you fill out and bring them with you to the pier.

PASSPORTS & VISAS

Whether they embark in the United States or Canada, American and Canadian citizens on Alaska cruises are required to bring proper identification and proof of citizenship. If you arrive at the port without it, you may not be allowed to board, and the line won't issue a fare refund. Most travel agents know the requirements and can guide you to the proper agency to obtain what you need if you don't have it.

As a result of laws enacted in early 2007, all American citizens must have a passport for travel by air or sea to or from Canada. Permanent residents of the United States and Canada who are not citizens should also carry their Green Card or Permanent Resident Card.

If you're a citizen of another country, you may be required to obtain visas in advance. Check with your travel agent or cruise line about specific requirements. If you do need a visa for your cruise, your travel agent should be able to help you obtain it, but there may be a charge for this service, in addition to the visa charge. Read your cruise documents carefully to see what documents you'll need for embarkation. You don't want to be turned away at the pier.

Immigration regulations require every passenger boarding a cruise ship from a U.S. port to provide additional personal data, such as your current mailing address and telephone number, to the cruise operator in advance of embarkation. Failure to provide this information may result in denial of boarding.

PERMISSION LETTERS

Often, single parents or grandparents want to take their children or grandchildren on a cruise; it's also not uncommon for parents to invite their teenager's friend to sail along. An often-overlooked requirement

Dress Codes Decoded

Although no two cruises are quite the same, evening dress tends to fall into three categories.

■ **Casual.** Daytime wear is always casual. A casual evening may call for no jeans or shorts in the dining room, but otherwise anything goes.

■ **Informal.** Informal for women is a dressier dress, pants outfit, or a nice skirt and top; for men it almost always includes a sport coat and often a tie.

Check your documents carefully for a specific definition.

■ **Formal.** Formal nights, which are optional on some cruises and absent entirely on others, are the highlight of the week for people who like to dress up. You'll see women in everything from simple cocktail dresses to elaborate glittering gowns. Jackets and ties for men are the rule at dinner, and tuxedos are not uncommon. For children, Sunday-best is appropriate.

is a notarized letter of permission, which is usually required any time a child under 18 travels to a foreign country with anyone other than both of his or her parents. Airlines, cruise lines, and immigration agents can deny minors initial boarding or entry to Canada without proper proof of identification and citizenship *and* the permission letter. Your travel agent or cruise line can help with the wording of such a letter.

WHAT TO PACK

CRUISE WARDROBE

Certain packing rules apply to all Alaska cruises. It's often misty or rainy, so rain gear is essential—many travelers who plan on indulging in some of the more active shore excursions should pack a complete rain suit. Fleece jackets are ubiquitous in Alaska because they're light, warm, and fast-drying. Alaska summer temperatures can change from shorts-and-T-shirt balmy to jeans-and-jacket chilly within hours, so pack for both extremes and be prepared to dress in layers. Make sure you take at least one pair of comfortable walking shoes for exploring port towns; waterproof footwear is also useful. Some shore excursions (whale-watching in an open boat, for example) call for special equipment or all-weather gear, but this is usually supplied. Your shore excursion pamphlet will tell you what you need to bring.

Onboard wear depends on the style of cruise; you'll receive information telling you what the dress codes are. On most small ships and on some of the less-traditional cruise lines, such as Norwegian Cruise Lines, there are no dress codes and casual attire is always appropriate. Some small ships may have one "dress-up" night when men don a jacket and women wear a dress or pants outfit; informal large ships may have one optional formal night.

On a more traditional cruise with, for example, Holland America, cruise wear falls into three categories: casual, informal, and formal. Cruise documents should include information indicating how many evenings fall into each category. You will know when to wear what by

CLOSE UP

Things You'll Wish You Had Packed

■ **Eye covers for sleeping:** the 24-hour light may disrupt your sleep patterns.

■ **Bug spray:** mosquitoes in Alaska can be huge!

■ **Film:** bring twice as much film as you think you'll need.

■ **Sunscreen:** you can still get burned, even in Alaska.

■ **Clothes for all temperatures:** you can go from boiling to freezing within hours.

■ **Supply of one-dollar bills:** they'll come in handy for tipping shore excursion guides and porters at the pier.

■ **Germicidal hand cleaner:** a must-have for adventure excursions or for where soap and water might be hard to find.

■ **Short extension cord:** since most cabins have only one or two electrical outlets, an extension cord will allow you to use more than one appliance at a time, and give you more flexibility to move around.

■ **Travel alarm clock:** if you don't want to rely on shipboard wake-up calls, bring your own alarm, as most staterooms don't have them.

reading your ship's daily newsletter—each evening's dress code will be prominently announced.

Men can usually rent their formal attire from the cruise line, and if they do so, it will be waiting when they board. Be sure to make these arrangements in advance; your travel agent can get the details from the cruise line. But if you're renting a tux, buy your own studs: a sure-fire way to spot a rented tuxedo is by the inexpensive studs that come with it.

In general, one outfit for each two days of cruising should suffice. Ships may have laundry service (though it will be pricey) and many have self-serve laundry facilities. Cabin amenities typically include soap and often shampoo and conditioner; other toiletries are available in port shops or the ship's gift shop (though usually at a premium price).

APPLIANCES

Outlets are usually compatible with U.S.-purchased appliances. This may not be the case on older ships or those with European registries; call ahead if this is a concern for you. Most cabin bathrooms are equipped with low-voltage outlets for electric shavers, and many newer ships have built-in hair dryers.

EXTRAS

Other items to pack include swimwear so you can take advantage of the hot tub or indoor pool, workout or yoga gear, and film or an extra memory card for digital cameras. Some families bring walkie-talkies so they can keep track of each other on a big ship. Binoculars are invaluable for spotting wildlife and admiring scenery (your ship may provide them, so don't hesitate to ask).

ACCESSIBILITY ISSUES

ON BOARD

More than the usual amount of preplanning is necessary for smooth sailing if you have special needs. All major cruise lines offer a limited number of wheelchair- and scooter-accessible staterooms. Booking a newer vessel will generally assure more choices. On newer ships, public rooms are generally more accessible, and more facilities have been planned with wheelchair users in mind. Auxiliary aids, such as flashers for the hearing impaired and buzzers for visually impaired passengers, as well as lifts for swimming pools and hot tubs, are available upon request.

> **CAUTION**
>
> Small ships are generally not wheelchair accessible, although the *Clipper Odyssey* has an elevator and one wheelchair-accessible cabin.

AT THE DOCK

When a ship is unable to dock, passengers are taken ashore on tenders that are sometimes hard even for the able-bodied to negotiate under adverse conditions. Some people with limited mobility may even find it difficult to embark or disembark the ship when docked due to the steep angle of gangways during high or low tide at certain times of day. In some situations, crew members may offer assistance that involves carrying guests, but if the sea is choppy, that might not be an option.

SPECIAL EQUIPMENT

Passengers who require continuous oxygen or have service animals can bring both aboard a cruise ship; be sure to bring proof of your animal's vaccinations for entry into Canada.

INSURANCE

It's a good idea to purchase travel insurance, which covers a variety of possible hazards and mishaps, when you book a cruise. One concern for cruise passengers is being delayed en route to the port of embarkation and missing the ship. Another major consideration is lost luggage—or even the delay of luggage. These should be covered. You may miss the first day or two of your cruise, but all will not be lost financially. A travel policy will ensure you can replace delayed necessities (toothbrush, basic clothing, etc.), secure in the knowledge you'll be reimbursed for those unexpected expenditures. Save your receipts for all out-of-pocket expenses to file your claim and be sure to get an incident report from the airline at fault.

No one wants their cruise vacation spoiled by a broken arm, heart attack, or worse, but if one of life's tragedies occurs, you want to be covered. The medical insurance program you depend on at home might not extend coverage beyond the borders of the United States. It's worth noting that all ships of foreign registry are considered to be "outside the United States" by Medicare. U.S. residents should consider purchasing additional insurance to cover them during the cruise; non-U.S. residents

Crime on Ships

Crime aboard cruise ships has occasionally become headline news, thanks in large part to a few well-publicized cases. Most people never have any type of problem, but you should exercise the same precautions aboard ship that you would at home. Keep your valuables out of sight—on big ships virtually every cabin has a small safe in the cabin. Don't carry too much cash ashore, use your credit card whenever possible, and keep your money in a secure place, such as a front pocket that's harder to pick. Single women traveling with friends should stick together, especially when returning to their cabins late at night. Be careful about whom you befriend, as you would anywhere, whether it's a fellow passenger or a member of the crew. With normal precautions, a cruise, especially an Alaska cruise, is one of the safest ways to travel.

will need travel medical insurance that specifically covers travel to the United States. Either way, look for a policy that will cover a ship-to-shore evacuation. Ships have medical facilities, but in a life-or-death situation, you're better off in a shoreside hospital.

Some independent insurers such as Travel Guard or CSA offer comprehensive policies at attractive rates. Nearly all cruise lines offer their own line of insurance. Compare the coverage and rates to determine which is best for you. Keep in mind that insurance purchased from an independent carrier is more likely to include coverage if the cruise line goes out of business before or during your trip.

ARRIVING & EMBARKING

GETTING TO THE PORT

Most cruise-ship passengers fly to the port of embarkation. If you book your cruise far enough in advance, you'll be given the opportunity to purchase an air-and-sea package, which can save you money on your flight.

If you buy an air-and-sea package, a uniformed cruise-line agent will meet you at the airport to smooth your way to the pier. You'll need to claim your own bags and give them to the transfer driver so they can be loaded on the bus. Upon arrival at the pier, luggage is automatically transferred to the ship for delivery to your cabin. The cruise-line ground-transfer system can also be available to independent fliers. However, be sure to ask your travel agent how much it costs; you may find that a taxi or shuttle service is less expensive and more convenient.

BOARDING

CHECKING IN

The lines for check-in can be long, particularly at peak times. Be prepared to wait for several hours. Some, but not all, cruise lines provide snacks for waiting passengers. If check-in starts at noon but continues to 4 PM, you can expect lines to trail off as the boarding deadline approaches. You'll be asked to produce your documents and any forms you were sent to complete ahead of time, plus proof of citizenship and a credit card (to cover onboard charges). You'll be issued a boarding card that often doubles as your stateroom "key" and shipboard charge card. At some point—either before you enter the check-in area or before proceeding to the ship—you and your hand luggage will pass through a security procedure similar to those at airports.

FIRST THINGS FIRST

Do your plans for the cruise include booking shore excursions and indulging in spa treatments? The most popular tours sometimes sell out, and spas can be very busy during sea days, so if you haven't prebooked, your next stops should be the Shore Excursion Desk to book tours and the spa to make appointments.

Procedures vary somewhat once you're greeted by staff members lined up just inside the ship's hull; however, once again you'll have to produce your boarding card for the security officer and, possibly, a picture ID before heading to your cabin.

SMALL SHIPS

On a small-ship cruise, embarkation is much more relaxed. Passengers usually rendezvous at a hotel for check-in, and are then taken to the ship, where they'll usually be greeted personally by the captain and crew. Although documents are checked, you won't face much of a line.

SETTLING IN

Check out your cabin to make sure that everything is in order. Try the plumbing and set the air-conditioning to the temperature you prefer—your cabin may feel warm while docked but will cool off when the ship is underway. You should find a copy of the ship's daily schedule in the cabin telling you about meals, activities, and other entertainment.

Rented tuxedoes are either hanging in the closet or will be delivered sometime during the afternoon; bon voyage gifts sent by your friends or travel agent usually appear as well. Be patient if you're expecting deliveries, particularly on megaships. Cabin stewards participate in the ship's turnaround and are extremely busy, although yours will no doubt introduce himself at the first available opportunity. It will also be a while before your checked luggage arrives, so your initial order of business is usually the buffet and a cocktail.

Dining room seating arrangements are another matter for consideration. Some people like to check the main dining room to determine where their table is located. If it isn't to your liking, or if you requested a large table and find yourself assigned to a small one, you'll want to see the head waiter. The daily schedule will indicate where and when to meet with him.

SMALL SHIPS

On a small-ship cruise, there's much less business to attend to. After checking out your cabin, you can simply head to the lounge to meet the other passengers, to hear directly from the crew what to expect on the cruise, and perhaps even to enjoy a complimentary embarkation cocktail.

CRAVING ALONE TIME?

If there's a port call that doesn't particularly interest you, you may choose to spend some time on the ship while almost everyone else is in town. Although the number of activities is somewhat curtailed, onboard programs don't cease entirely. There are still exercise classes, spa treatments, and games and movies are sometimes planned.

ON BOARD

PORT CALLS

Traveling by cruise ship presents an opportunity to visit many places in a short time. The flip side is that your stay in each port of call will be brief. If your ship anchors in the harbor, you will have to take a small boat—called a launch or tender—to get ashore.

ARRIVING IN PORT

When your ship arrives in a port, it will either tie up alongside a dock or anchor out in a harbor. If the ship is docked, passengers walk down the gangway to go ashore. Docking makes it easy to go back and forth between the shore and the ship.

TENDERING

Tendering is a nuisance. Passengers wishing to disembark may be required to gather in a public room, get sequenced boarding passes, and wait until their numbers are called. The ride to shore may take as long as 20 minutes. If you don't like waiting, plan to go ashore an hour or so after the ship drops its anchor. Because tenders can be difficult to board, passengers with mobility problems may not be able to visit certain ports. Larger ships are more likely to use tenders. It's usually possible to learn before booking a cruise whether the ship will dock or anchor at its ports of call.

RETURNING TO THE SHIP

Cruise lines are strict about sailing times, which are posted at the gangway and elsewhere and announced in the daily schedule of activities. Be sure to be back on board at least a half-hour before the announced sailing time or you may be stranded.

SHORE EXCURSIONS

Cruise lines offer shore excursions that appeal to a wide variety of tastes: sightseeing, hiking, biking, kayaking, and a host of other activities. These excursions are tried and tested, and as a rule, provide a good experience for the money. If you prefer to do your own tour-

ing, you're naturally free to book
a private guide or taxi, rent a vehicle, or use public transportation,
and delve into whatever interests
you. A cautionary rule of thumb
is that it's often better to take a
ship's tour if you want to explore
an area some distance from where
the ship is docked. In case of any
delay, your ship will wait for you
if you've booked a ship-sponsored
excursion. On the other hand, if
you're on your own, the ship will
depart without you if you haven't
returned by the announced departure time.

> **MISSING THE BOAT**
>
> If the ship sails without you,
> immediately contact the cruise
> line's port representative, whose
> phone number is often listed on
> the daily schedule of activities.
> You may be able to hitch a ride
> on a pilot boat, although that is
> unlikely. Passengers who miss the
> boat must pay their own way to
> the next port.

To make the most of your hours ashore, research your options ahead
of time. Before your cruise, you'll receive a booklet describing the shore
excursions your cruise line offers. A few lines let you book excursions
in advance; all sell them on board during the cruise. Canceling your
excursion may incur penalties, and the amount varies with the number
of days remaining until the tour. These trips have limited capacity and
are sold on a first-come, first-served basis.

Cruise-line shore-excursion booklets present a variety of options, and
many companies provide detailed descriptions of tours on their Web
sites. In each port-of-call section, we have compiled a selection of the
most worthwhile excursions to help you make your choices. Not all
those listed below are offered by all cruise lines. Prices will vary.

You can also arrange many of these tours through the visitor-infor-
mation counter in each port. These counters are usually close to the
pier. *See Coming Ashore in each port of call section in Chapter 4 for
exact locations.*

DAYS AT SEA

All days at sea are not identical, but they do follow a certain rhythm.
Most ships schedule activities, port talks, lectures, games, and fitness
programs on a nonstop basis. This is the time to personalize your
cruise experience—you can participate in scheduled activities, enjoy
the scenery from the deck, or read a book in your stateroom. Sea days
on Alaska cruises are usually reserved for spectacular scenery, such as
Glacier Bay National Park, sailings in Misty Fiord, or glacier-viewing in
Prince William Sound. If seeing glaciers is a priority for you, you might
not want to plan too many onboard activities during these days.

DINING

All food, all the time? Not quite, but it's possible to literally eat the day
and most of the night away on a large cruise ship. A popular cruise
director's joke is, "You came on as passengers, and you will be leaving

as cargo." Although it's meant in fun, it does contain a ring of truth. Food is available 24 hours a day on most cruise ships, and the dining experience at sea has reached almost mythical proportions.

RESTAURANTS

Every large ship has at least one main restaurant and a casual buffet alternative. Increasingly important are specialty restaurants. Meals in the primary and buffet restaurants are included in the cruise fare, as are round-the-clock room service, midday tea and snacks, and late-night buffets. Most mainstream cruise lines levy a surcharge for dining in alternative restaurants that may, or may not, also include a gratuity, although there generally is no additional charge on luxury cruise lines.

KNOTS

The bridge announces you're making 21 knots, an efficient service speed for modern cruise ships. So how fast are you really going? Nautical miles differ from statute miles (the unit of measure on your road map) in that a nautical mile represents a minute of a degree of latitude, or about 6,000 feet. (Who knows where we came up with 5,280 feet for a land mile?) To relate that to how fast your car passes highway mile markers, a knot at sea is equivalent to 1.151 mi per hour ashore. If you feel compelled to convert from one measure to another, at 21 knots your ship is cruising at 24.171 sedate land miles per hour.

You may also find a pizzeria or a specialty coffee bar on your ship. Although pizza is complimentary, expect an additional charge for specialty coffees at the coffee bar and, quite likely, in the dining room as well. You'll also likely be charged for any drinks during meals other than iced tea, regular coffee, tap water, and fruit juice; this includes soft drinks.

There is often a direct relationship between the cost of a cruise and the quality of its cuisine. The food is very sophisticated on some (mostly expensive) lines, but on most mainstream cruise lines, the food is what you would find in any good hotel dining room—perfectly acceptable but certainly not great.

SMALL SHIPS

Food on small ships is often less ubiquitous, but also very good. It tends to be fresh and wholesome, but not elaborate, with a home-cooking, rather than restaurant-style, presentation. There's usually just one dining room with set dining times, but drinks and snacks are generally available. On very small ships, passengers eat together family-style at one table, though many meals are served as picnics on shore excursions.

SEATINGS

If your cruise ship has traditional seatings for dinner, your seating choices may set the tone for your entire trip. Which is best? Early dinner seating is generally scheduled between 6 and 6:30 PM, while late seating can begin from 8:15 to 8:45 PM. So the "best" seating depends on you, your lifestyle, and your personal preference.

Drinking on Board

1

It's hard to avoid the ship's bars since they are social centers, but alcoholic drinks are not usually included in your cruise fare, and bar bills can add up quickly. You should expect to pay about the same for a drink on board a cruise ship as you would pay in a bar at home: $3 to $4 for a domestic beer, $4 to $9 for a cocktail, $5 to $7 for a glass of wine, $1 to $1.50 for a soft drink. To save money on your bar bill, follow a few simple strategies. In lounges, request the less-expensive bar brands or the reduced-price drink-of-the-day. On some ships, discounted "beverage cards" for unlimited fountain soft drinks and/or a set number of mixed drinks are available.

WINE
Wine by the bottle is a more economical choice at dinner than ordering it by the glass. Any wine you don't finish will be kept for you and served the next night. Gifts of wine or champagne ordered from the cruise line (either by you, a friend, or your travel agent) can be taken to the dining room. Wine from any other source will incur a corkage fee of approximately $8 to $10 per bottle.

UNDERAGE DRINKING
In international waters there are, technically, no laws against teenage drinking, but almost all ships require passengers to be over either 18 or 21 to purchase alcoholic beverages.

Families with young children and older passengers often choose an early seating. Early-seating diners are encouraged not to linger too long over dessert and coffee because the dining room has to be readied for late seating. Late seating is viewed by some passengers as more romantic and less rushed.

Open seating is primarily associated with more upscale lines; it allows you the flexibility to dine any time during restaurant hours and be seated with whomever you please. Led by Norwegian Cruise Line and Princess Cruises, more contemporary and premium cruise lines are exploring open seating to offer variety and a more personalized experience for their passengers. More mainstream Carnival Cruise Line and Holland America Line have added a twist with four seating times instead of the usual two, plus casual evening dining in the Lido buffet.

Cruise lines understand that strict schedules no longer satisfy the desires of all modern cruise passengers. Many cruise lines now include alternatives to the set schedules in the dining room, including à la carte restaurants and casual dinner menus in their buffet facilities where more flexibility is allowed in dress and mealtimes.

SPECIAL DIETS
If you have special dietary considerations—such as low-salt, kosher, or food allergies—be sure to indicate them well ahead of time and check to be certain your needs are known by your waiter once on board. In addition to the usual menu items, "spa," low-calorie, low-carbohydrate, or low-fat selections, as well as children's menus, are usually available. Requests for dishes not featured on the menu can often be granted if you ask in advance.

THE CAPTAIN'S TABLE

You'll know if you have been included in this exclusive coterie when an embossed invitation arrives in your stateroom on the day of a formal dinner. RSVP as soon as possible; many people covet this special experience, and if you're unable to attend, someone else will be invited in your place. Who is invited to the captain's table? If you're a frequent repeat cruiser, the occupant of an Owner's Suite, or hail from the captain's hometown, you may be considered. Honeymoon couples are sometimes selected at random, as are couples celebrating a golden wedding anniversary. Attractive, unattached female passengers often round out an uneven number of guests. Requests made by travel agents on behalf of their clients sometimes do the trick.

> **CHANGING TABLES**
>
> While dining preferences may be requested by your travel agent, no requests are guaranteed, and table assignments are generally not confirmed until embarkation. If there's a problem, see the maître d' for assistance. Changes after the first evening are generally discouraged, so make sure to go to the designated place to iron out seating problems on embarkation day.

ENTERTAINMENT

Seven-night cruises on large cruise ships usually include two original production shows. One of these might be a Las Vegas–style extravaganza and the other a best-of-Broadway show featuring old and new favorites from the Great White Way. Other shows highlight the talents of individual singers, dancers, magicians, comedians, and even acrobats. Don't be surprised if you're plucked from the audience to take the brunt of a comedian's jokes or act as the magician's temporary assistant.

Enrichment programs have become a popular pastime at sea, but lecturers on many large cruise ships often offer more information on shore excursions and shopping than insight into the ports of call. If more cerebral presentations are important to you, consider a cruise on a line that features stimulating enrichment programs and seminars at sea. Speakers can include destination-oriented historians, popular authors, business leaders, radio or television personalities, and even movie stars.

SMALL SHIPS

Small ships may lack big Broadway-style productions, but usually have interesting lectures by onboard naturalists or historians. Many will invite local experts or First Nations performers on board or show videos of local wildlife. Passengers on these ships tend to seek quieter amusements, and spend time getting to know one another.

LOUNGES & NIGHTCLUBS

Karaoke and singing along in a piano bar are shipboard favorites for would-be crooners. Some passengers even take the place of the ship's pianist during breaks to demonstrate their skills. Smaller onboard

1

lounges might feature easy-listening music or jazz for pre- and post-dinner dancing. Later in the evening, lounges pick up the pace with music from the 1950s and '60s; clubs aimed at a younger crowd usually have more contemporary dance music during the late-night hours.

CASINOS & GAMBLING

A sure sign that your ship is in international waters is the opening of the casino. In addition to slot machines, these casinos might feature roulette, craps, and a variety of poker games. Cruise lines strive to provide fair and professional gambling entertainment and supply gaming guides that set out the rules of play and betting limits for each game.

Casino hours vary based on the itinerary or location of the ship; most are required to close while in port, while others may simply close table games while offering 24-hour slot machines. Every casino has a cashier, and you may be able to charge a cash advance to your onboard account.

OTHER ENTERTAINMENT

Most vessels have a room for screening movies, either in a genuine cinema-style movie theater, or in a simple multipurpose room. Over the course of a weeklong voyage a dozen films may be screened, each repeated several times. Theaters are also used for lectures, religious services, and private meetings. Most medium-size and large ships have video arcades, and nearly all ships now have computer centers.

With a few exceptions, ocean liners equip their cabins with closed-circuit TVs showing movies (continuously on some newer ships), shipboard lectures, and regular programs (thanks to satellite reception). Ships with in-cabin VCRs or DVDs usually provide a selection of movies at no charge (a deposit is sometimes required).

HEALTH & FITNESS

Onboard sports facilities might include a court for basketball, volleyball, tennis—or all three—a jogging track, or an in-line skating track. Some ships are even offering innovative features, such as the rock-climbing walls and bungee trampolines on some Royal Caribbean ships. For the less adventurous, there's always table tennis and shuffleboard.

Although virtually all large cruise ships have an outdoor swimming pool on board, only some keep them open in Alaska. If swimming is important to you, look for a ship with an indoor pool, or one with a retractable roof. Princess Grand-class ships have challenging, freshwater "swim against the current" pools for swimming enthusiasts who want to get their low-impact exercise while on board.

Golf is a perennial seagoing favorite of players who want to take their games to the next level. Shipboard programs can include clinics, use of full-motion golf cages, and even individual instruction from resident pros using state-of-the-art computer analysis.

Health & Safety at Sea

CLOSE UP

FIRE SAFETY

The greatest danger facing cruise-ship passengers is fire. All cruise lines must meet international standards for fire safety, which require sprinkler systems, smoke detectors, and other safety features. These rules are designed to protect against loss of life, but they don't guarantee against fire.

Once settled into your cabin, locate life vests and review posted emergency instructions. Make certain the ship's purser knows of any physical infirmities that may hamper a speedy exit from your cabin. If you're traveling with children, be sure that child-size life jackets are placed in your cabin. Within 24 hours of embarkation, you will be asked to attend a mandatory lifeboat drill. Do so and listen carefully. If you are unsure of how to use your vest, now is the time to ask. Only in the most extreme circumstances will you need to abandon ship—but it has happened.

HEALTH CARE

All large ships have an infirmary to deal with minor medical emergencies, and the ship's doctor or a clinic ashore should be able to treat you for minor problems. For complicated medical conditions, such as a heart attack or appendicitis, the ship's medical team evacuates passengers to the nearest hospital ashore. While at sea, evacuation expenses can rise as fast as the helicopter that whisks the patient away. You'll need supplementary insurance to cover these costs.

NOROVIRUSES

Noroviruses are a group of related viruses that cause acute gastroenteritis in humans. Norovirus infection usually causes vomiting, diarrhea with abdominal cramps, and nausea. Low-grade fever also occasionally occurs and vomiting is more common in children. Dehydration is the most common complication, especially among the young and elderly, and may require medical attention. Symptoms generally last 24 to 60 hours. To avoid illness, first and foremost: wash your hands thoroughly and often. The Centers for Disease Control (CDC) also advise the use of an alcohol-based hand sanitizer (they come in travel-size bottles) along with hand washing. If you become ill, the ship's doctor will probably quarantine you in your cabin.

FITNESS CENTERS

Cruise vacations can be hazardous to your waistline if you aren't careful. But shipboard fitness centers have become ever more elaborate, offering state-of-the-art exercise machines, treadmills, and stair steppers, not to mention weights and weight machines. As a bonus, many fitness centers with floor-to-ceiling windows have the world's most inspiring sea views.

If you prefer a more social atmosphere as you burn off sinful chocolate desserts, there are specialized fitness classes for all levels of ability. High-impact, energetic aerobics are not for everyone, but any class that raises the heart rate can be toned down and tailored to individual capabilities. Stretching classes help you warm up for a light jog or brisk walk on deck, and there are even sit-for-fitness classes for mature passengers or those with delicate joints. Fees are sometimes charged

1

for specialty classes, such as Pilates, spinning, and yoga. Personal trainers are usually on board to get you off on the right foot, also for a fee.

SMALL SHIPS

Some small ships have exercise equipment on board, but, for the most part, the great outdoors is your gym. Passengers keep fit with kayaking and hiking trips into the Alaskan wilderness.

SPAS

With the pampering and service in luxurious surroundings, simply being on a cruise can be a stress-reducing experience. Add to that the menu of spa and salon services at your fingertips and you have a recipe for total sensory pleasure. They have also become among the most popular of shipboard areas.

> ### SHIP SHAPE
>
> You don't have to return from your cruise with extra weight. Even if you don't want to take time out to hit the gym, you can walk on the ship's promenade deck or turn your back on the elevators and use the stairs. And you can always control calories by requesting that any sauces be served on the side. Have no fear; it's actually possible to return home from a cruise more buff than buffet.

PRACTICALITIES

TIPPING

One of the most delicate—yet frequently debated—topics of conversation among cruise passengers involves the matter of tipping. Like their land contemporaries, cruise-ship service personnel depend on gratuities for a major portion of their compensation. Educate yourself about gratuities by reading your cruise-line brochure, where suggested tipping levels are usually listed on the back with the rest of the fine print or the small booklet that comes with your cruise documents for up-to-the-minute information.

When transfers to and from your ship are a part of your air-and-sea program, gratuities are generally included for luggage handling. In that case, don't worry about the interim tipping. However, if you take a taxi to the pier and hand over your bags to a stevedore, be sure to tip him at least $5.

During your cruise, room-service waiters generally receive a cash tip of $1 to $3 per delivery. A 15% gratuity will automatically be added to each bar bill during the cruise. If you use salon and spa services, a similar percentage is generally added to the bills there. If you dine in a specialty restaurant, you will usually be asked to provide a onetime gratuity for the service staff.

There will be a "Disembarkation Talk" on the last day of the cruise that explains tipping procedures. If you're expected to tip in cash, small white "tip" envelopes will appear in your stateroom that day. If you tip in cash, you usually give the tip envelope directly to each person on the last night of the cruise. Tips generally add up to about $10 to $12 per person per day. You tip the same amount for each person who shares the cabin, including children, unless otherwise indicated.

Will I Get Seasick?

Many first-time passengers are anxious about whether they'll be stricken by seasickness, but there is no way to tell until you actually sail. Modern vessels are equipped with stabilizers that eliminate much of the motion responsible for seasickness. On an Alaska cruise you will spend most of your time in calm, sheltered waters, so, unless your cruise includes time in the open sea (say, between San Francisco and Vancouver), you may not even feel the ship's movement—particularly if your ship is a megaliner. You may feel slightly more movement on a small ship, but even on these ships, seasickness is not usually a problem as they keep, for the most part, to the shelter of the Inside Passage.

If you have a history of motion sickness, don't book an inside cabin. For the terminally seasick, it will begin to resemble a movable coffin in short order. If you do become seasick, you can use common drugs such as Dramamine and Bonine. Some people find anti-seasickness wristbands helpful; these apply gentle pressure to the wrist in lieu of drugs. Worn behind the ear, the Transderm Scop "patch" is a remedy that dispenses a continuous metered dose of medication, which is absorbed into the skin and enters the bloodstream. Apply the patch four hours before sailing and it will continue to be effective for three days. You'll need a prescription from your physician for the patch and, while wearing it, be vigilant for possible side effects including blurred vision, dry mouth, and drowsiness.

Most lines now either automatically add gratuities to passengers' onboard charge accounts or offer the option. If that suits you, then do nothing further. However, you're free to adjust the amounts up or down to more appropriate levels or ask that the charge be removed altogether if you prefer distributing cash gratuities.

PAYING FOR THINGS ON BOARD

Because a cashless society prevails on cruise ships, during booking or check-in, an imprint is made of your credit card or you place a cash deposit for use against your onboard charges. Then you're issued a charge card that usually doubles as your stateroom "key." Most onboard expenditures are charged to your shipboard account with your signature as verification, with the exception of casino gaming—even so, you can often get "cash advances" against your account from the casino cashier.

An itemized bill listing your purchases is provided at the end of the voyage. In order to avoid surprises, it's a good idea to set aside your charge slips and request an interim printout of your bill from the purser to ensure accuracy. Any discrepancies in your account should be taken care of before leaving the ship, usually at the Purser's Desk. Should you change your mind about charging onboard purchases, you can always inform the purser and pay in cash or traveler's checks instead. If your cash deposit was more than you spent, you'll receive a refund.

SMALL SHIPS

Small ships may also have shipboard accounts, but as there are fewer opportunities to spend money, the process is much more relaxed. When signing up for shore excursions or ordering alcoholic drinks, simply tell the bartender or exploration leader your room number. Before disembarking the ship on the last day, stop by the bar to settle your bill with a credit card, cash, or a check. On some ships, everything is included, so there's nothing for you to worry about.

> **TIP**
>
> Check the balance of your shipboard account before the end of your cruise. You can avoid a long line at the purser's desk that last morning after the final bill arrives.

SHIPBOARD SERVICES

Laundry & Dry Cleaning: Most cruise ships offer valet laundry and pressing (and some also dry-cleaning) services. Expenses can add up fast, especially for laundry, as charges are per item and the rates are similar to those charged in hotels. If you book one of the top-dollar suites, laundry service may be included for no additional cost. Most cruise ships also have a low-cost or free self-service laundry room (they usually feature an iron and ironing board in addition to washer and dryer), where you can do your own laundry for about $3 or less per load. None of the vessels in the Royal Caribbean or Celebrity Cruises fleets have self-service laundry facilities. A few small ships have laundry service; none have self-serve laundry facilities on board.

Library: Cruise ship libraries run the gamut from a few shelves of relatively uninspiring titles to huge rooms crammed with volumes of travel guides, classics, and the latest best sellers. As a rule, the smaller the ship, the more likely you are to find a well-stocked library. The space allotted to the library falls in proportion to the emphasis on glitzy stage shows: on small ships the passengers generally favor quiet diversions.

Photo Shop: Alaskan cruises are a series of photo opportunities, and ships' photographers are on hand to capture boarding, departure, port arrivals, and other highlights. Photographers seem to pop up everywhere and take far more pictures than you could ever want; however, they are a unique souvenir, and there's no obligation to purchase them. Prices for the prints, which are put on display, range from $6 to $20, depending on size. Film, batteries, single-use cameras, and related merchandise may be available in the Photo Shop. Some ships' photography staffers can process your film or your digital prints right on board as well.

Shore Excursion Desk: Manned by a knowledgeable staff, the Shore Excursion Desk can not only offer the sale of ship-sponsored tours, but may also be the place to learn more about ports of call and garner information to tour independently. Although staff members and the focus of their positions vary widely, the least you can expect are basic information and port maps. Happily, some shore excursion staff members possess a wealth of information and share it without reservation. Others may emphasize shopping and "recommended" merchants,

Keeping in Touch

IN-ROOM PHONES

Most cruise-ship cabins contain a direct-dial telephone. Rates vary from $5 to as much as $15 *per minute,* so most passengers reserve their cabin phone for emergency use only.

CELL PHONES

Some cruise ships can act as a cell "tower" so you may be able to use your own phone and number at sea. Depending on the agreements your mobile service provider has established, you may be able to connect to local networks when in port. Rates for using the maritime service, as well as any roaming charges, are established by your provider and are worth checking into before you leave home.

ONBOARD INTERNET

Connection charges on board range from 50¢ to $1 per minute. There may also be a small one-time account acti-
vation charge. Cruise-ship computer systems vary widely, and the connection speed can be maddeningly slow. Most ships have an Internet center where you can go online using the ship's computers; some ships have in-cabin data ports or wireless systems that allow you to use your own laptop or a rented one.

CUTTING COSTS

Using the Internet and making calls is usually less expensive on land. There are often Internet cafés with high-speed connections near the pier; almost any crew member can point the way to them. Some towns, such as Petersburg and Haines, have public libraries that allow you to connect to the Internet for free. To make calls without worrying about roaming charges, use a phone card with an 800 number at pay phones in town.

with little to impart regarding sightseeing or the history and culture of ports.

DISEMBARKATION

All cruises come to an end eventually. The disembarkation process actually begins the day before you arrive at your ship's home port. During that day your cabin steward delivers special luggage tags to your stateroom, along with customs forms and instructions.

Room service is not available on most ships on the last day; however, after breakfast is served, there isn't much to do but wait comfortably in a lounge or on deck for your tag color or number to be called. All passengers must meet with customs and immigration officials before disembarkation, either on the ship or in the terminal. Procedures vary and are outlined in your instructions.

CUSTOMS & DUTIES

U.S. CUSTOMS

Before a ship lands, each individual or family must fill out a customs declaration. If your purchases total less than the limit for your destination, you won't need to itemize them. Be prepared to pay whatever duties are owed directly to the customs inspector, with cash or check. Be sure to keep receipts for all purchases, and be ready to show curious officials what you've bought.

SHIP SALES

If you find prices on board too much to bear, shop the ship's boutiques on the last day of your cruise, when they're likely to run special sales.

U.S. Customs pre-clears some ships—it's done on the ship before you disembark. In other ports you must collect your luggage from the dock, then stand in line to pass through the inspection point. This can take up to an hour.

ALLOWANCES
U.S. residents who have been out of the country for at least 48 hours may bring home, for personal use, $800 worth of foreign goods duty-free, as long as they haven't used the $800 allowance or any part of it in the past 30 days.

Travelers 21 and older may bring home 1 liter of alcohol. Travelers of any age may also bring back 200 cigarettes, and 100 non-Cuban cigars. Family members from the same household who are traveling together may pool their $800 personal exemptions.

Note that goods bought in duty-free shops are still subject to duty when you return home. Unless they fall within the above allowances, you will still have to pay duty on them.

SENDING PACKAGES HOME
Although you probably won't want to spend your time looking for a post office, you can send packages home duty-free, with a limit of one parcel per addressee per day (except alcohol or tobacco products or perfume worth more than $5). You can mail up to $200 worth of goods for personal use; label the package "personal use" and attach a list of the contents and their retail value. If the package contains your used personal belongings, mark it "personal goods returned" to avoid paying duty on your laundry. You may also send up to $100 worth of goods as a gift (except alcohol or tobacco products or perfume worth more than $5); mark the package "unsolicited gift." Items you mailed do not affect your duty-free allowance on your return.

NON-U.S. CITIZENS
Non–U.S. citizens returning home within hours of docking may be exempt from all U.S. Customs duties. Everything you bring into the United States must leave with you when you return home, though. When you reach your own country, you'll have to pay duties there.

CANADIAN CUSTOMS
Canadian residents who have been out of Canada for at least seven days may bring in C$750 worth of goods duty-free. If you've been away fewer than seven days but more than 48 hours, the duty-free allowance drops to C$200. If your trip lasts 24 to 48 hours, the allowance is C$50; if the goods are worth more than C$50, you must pay

full duty on all of the goods. You may not pool allowances with family members. Goods claimed under the C$750 exemption may follow you by mail; those claimed under the lesser exemptions must accompany you. Alcohol and tobacco products may be included in the seven-day and 48-hour exemptions but not in the 24-hour exemption. If you meet the age requirements of the province or territory through which you reenter Canada, you may bring in, duty-free, 1.5 liters of wine *or* 1.14 liters (40 imperial ounces) of liquor *or* 24 12-ounce cans or bottles of beer or ale. Also, if you meet the local age requirement for tobacco products, you may bring in, duty-free, 200 cigarettes, 50 cigars or cigarillos, and 200 grams of tobacco. You may have to pay a minimum duty on tobacco products, regardless of whether you exceed your personal exemption. Check ahead of time with the Canada Customs and Revenue Agency or Agriculture Canada for policies regarding meat products, seeds, plants, and fruits.

You may send an unlimited number of gifts (only one gift per recipient, however) worth up to C$60 each duty-free to Canada. Label the package UNSOLICITED GIFT—VALUE UNDER $60. Alcohol and tobacco are excluded.

U.K. CUSTOMS
From countries outside the European Union, including the United States and Canada, you may bring home, duty-free, 200 cigarettes or 50 cigars; 1 liter of spirits or 2 liters of fortified or sparkling wine or liqueurs; 2 liters of still table wine; 60 milliliters of perfume; 250 milliliters of toilet water; plus £145 worth of other goods, including gifts and souvenirs. Prohibited items include meat products, seeds, plants, and fruits. You cannot pool your allowances with other family members.

Choosing Your Cruise

By Linda
Coffman

ALASKA IS ONE OF CRUISING'S showcase destinations. Itineraries give passengers more choices than ever before—from traditional loop cruises of the Inside Passage, round-trips from Vancouver or Seattle, to one-way Inside Passage–Gulf of Alaska cruises. A number of smaller ships sail only in the Inside Passage and Prince William Sound, away from big-ship traffic.

Though Alaska generally attracts an older group of travelers than the Caribbean, more and more young people and families are setting sail for the 49th state. In peak summer season, children are a common sight aboard ship. Cruise lines have responded with children's programs and with some discount shore excursions for youngsters under 12. Shore excursions have become more active, too, often incorporating activities families can enjoy together, such as bicycling, kayaking, and hiking. For adults, too, most lines offer pre- or post-cruise land tours as an optional part of a package trip, and onboard entertainment and learning programs are extensive. Some lines hire celebrity or native speakers, naturalists, or local personalities to lead discussions stimulated by the local environment.

Cruise ships may seem like floating resorts, but you can't check out and go someplace else if you don't like your ship. The one you choose will be your home. The ship determines the type of accommodations you have, what kind of food you eat, what style of entertainment you see, and even the destinations you visit. If you don't enjoy your ship, you probably won't enjoy your cruise. That is why the most important choice you'll make when booking a cruise is the combined selection of cruise line and cruise ship.

CRUISING IN ALASKA

Which cruise is right for you depends on a number of factors, notably the size and style of ship you opt for, the itinerary you choose, and how much you're willing to spend.

ITINERARIES

Ocean liners typically follow one of two itineraries in Alaska: round-trip Inside Passage loops starting and finishing in Vancouver, British Columbia, or Seattle; and one-way Inside Passage–Gulf of Alaska cruises sailing between Vancouver or Seattle and Whittier or Seward, the ports for Anchorage. Both itineraries are usually seven days, though some lines offer longer trips.

The most popular Alaskan ports of call are Haines, Juneau, Skagway, Ketchikan, and Sitka. Lesser-known ports in British Columbia, such as Victoria and the charming fishing port of Prince Rupert, have begun to see more cruise traffic.

SMALL SHIPS
Small ships typically sail within Alaska, setting out from Juneau or other Alaskan ports, and follow a flexible itinerary, stopping at the

popular ports as well as smaller, less-visited villages. Some expedition vessels focus on remote beaches and fjords, with few, if any, port calls.

ROUND-TRIP INSIDE PASSAGE LOOPS

A seven-day trip typically starts and finishes in Vancouver, British Columbia, or Seattle, Washington. The first and last days are spent at sea, traveling to and from Alaska along the mountainous coast of British Columbia. Once in Alaska, most ships call at a different port on each of four days, and reserve one day for cruising in or near Glacier Bay National Park or another glacier-rich fjord. Ports of call include: Haines, Juneau, Skagway, Ketchikan, and Sitka.

WHICH GLACIER?

As you research, you'll notice that some itineraries include stops at Tracy Arm and Sawyer glaciers, and others spend a day sailing in Glacier Bay National Park. If you're undecided about which ship and itinerary to book, pick the one that goes to Glacier Bay. The glaciers here are bigger and more dramatic, and you'll see much more wildlife here than in Tracy Arm.

ONE-WAY INSIDE PASSAGE–GULF OF ALASKA ITINERARIES

These cruises depart from Vancouver, Seattle or, occasionally, San Francisco or Los Angeles, and finish at Seward or Whittier, the seaports for Anchorage (or vice versa). They're a good choice if you want to explore Alaska by land, either before or after your cruise. For this itinerary, you'll need to fly into and out of different cities (into Vancouver and out of Anchorage, for example) which can be pricier than a regular return flight.

SMALL-SHIP ALASKA-ONLY ITINERARIES

Most small ships and yachts homeport in Juneau or other Alaskan ports and offer a variety of one-way and round-trip cruises entirely within Alaska. A typical small-ship cruise is a seven-day, one-way or round-trip from Juneau stopping at several Inside Passage ports—including smaller ports skipped by the liners.

SMALL-SHIP INSIDE PASSAGE REPOSITIONING CRUISES

Most of Alaska's small cruise ships and yachts are based in Juneau throughout summer, but twice a year, usually in May and September, they sail between their winter homes in the Pacific Northwest through the Inside Passage to Alaska. These trips are usually about 11 days, and are often heavily discounted because they take place during the shoulder season.

FERRY TRAVEL

The cruise-ship season is over by October, but for independent, off-season ferry travel November is the best month. After the stormy month of October, it's still relatively warm on the Inside Passage (temperatures will average about 40°F). It's a good month for wildlife-watching as well. Some animals show themselves in greater numbers during November. In particular, humpback whales are abundant off Sitka, and bald eagles congregate by the thousands near Haines.

OTHER ITINERARIES

Although the mainstream lines stick to the popular seven-day Alaskan itineraries, some of the smaller excursion lines are adding more exotic options. Cruise West, for example, offers voyages across the Bering Sea to Japan and Asia. You can also create your own itinerary by taking an Alaska Marine Highway System ferry to ports of your choosing.

> **TIP**
>
> If you choose to travel by rail independently, the Alaska Railroad cars also have onboard guides and glass-dome observation cars, and make the trip between Anchorage and Fairbanks hooked up to the same engines as the cruise-line cars. Alaska Railroad's Web site ⊕ *www.akrr.com* has details.

CRUISE TOURS

Most cruise lines give you the option of an independent, hosted, or fully escorted land tour before or after your cruise. On an independent tour you have a preplanned itinerary with confirmed hotel reservations and transportation arrangements, but you're free to follow your interests and whims in each town. A hosted tour is similar, but tour-company representatives are available along the route for assistance. On fully escorted tours, you travel with a group, led by a tour director. Activities are preplanned (and typically prepaid), so you have a good idea of how much your trip will cost (not counting incidentals) before you depart. Most cruise lines offer a cruise tour itinerary that includes a ride aboard the Alaska Railroad in a glass-dome railcar.

SMALL SHIP LINES

Most of the small-ship lines offer hotel add-ons, but not land tours. Exceptions are American Safari Cruises, which offers fishing in southeast Alaska and helicopter-accessed hiking in British Columbia, and Cruise West, which offers fully escorted land tours by rail and bus from Anchorage to Denali and Fairbanks.

DO-IT-YOURSELF LAND SEGMENTS

Independent travel by rental car or RV before or after the cruise segment is another option. Passengers generally begin or end their cruise in Anchorage, the most practical port city to use as a base for exploring the state. Almost any type of car or recreational vehicle, from a small, two-person RV to a large, luxurious motor home, can be rented here.

WHEN TO GO

Cruise season runs from mid-May to late September. The most popular sailing dates are from late June through August, when warm days are apt to be most plentiful. In spring, wildflowers are abundant, and you'll likely see more wildlife along the shore because the animals haven't yet gone up to higher elevations. May and June are traditionally drier than July and August. Alaska's early fall brings the splendor of autumn hues and the first snowfalls in the mountains. The animals return to low ground, and shorter days bring the possibility of seeing the northern lights. Daytime temperatures along the cruise routes in May, June, and

September are in the 50s and 60s. July and August averages are in the 60s and 70s, with occasional days in the 80s. Cruising in the low seasons provides other advantages besides discounted fares. Availability of ships and particular cabins is greater in the low and shoulder seasons, and the ports are almost completely free of tourists.

BOOKING YOUR CRUISE

According to the Cruise Line International Association (CLIA), the majority of cruisers plan their trips four to six months ahead of time. It follows then, that a four- to six-month window should give you the pick of sailing dates, ships, itineraries, cabins, and flights to the port city. You'll need more time if you're planning to sail on a small adventure vessel, because their more popular itineraries can be fully booked six to eight months ahead of time. If you're looking for a standard itinerary and aren't choosy about the

> **TIMING TIP**
>
> Keep in mind that the landscape along the Inside Passage changes dramatically over the course of the summer. You'll see snow-capped mountains and dramatic waterfalls that are made by the melting process cascading down the cliff faces in May and June, but by July and August, most of the snow and waterfalls will be gone.

vessel or dates, you could wait for a last-minute discount, but industry experts warn that these are harder to find than they used to be.

If a particular shore excursion is important to you, consider booking it when you book your cruise to avoid disappointment later. You can even book your spa services precruise on some cruise lines' Web sites so you can have your pick of popular times, such as sea days or the afternoon before a formal night.

If you cruise regularly with the same line, it may be easiest to book directly with them, by phone or Web. Most cruises (90% according to CLIA) are, however, booked through a travel agent. Your best bet is a larger agency that specializes in cruises. They can sort through the myriad options for you, and often have the buying clout to purchase blocks of cabins at a discount. Cruise Lines International Association ⊕*www.cruising.org* lists recognized agents throughout the United States.

CRUISE COSTS

The average daily price for Alaskan itineraries varies dramatically depending on when you sail, which ship and grade of cabin you choose, and when you book. At the bargain end, cruising remains one of the best travel deals around: a weeklong cruise on an older ship, for example, with an interior stateroom, in the off-season, can still be had at a basic fare of less than $100 per day (before airfare, taxes, and other costs); or about $150 per day in the high-season. At the other end of the scale, a voyage on a luxury line such as Regent Seven Seas or a small luxury yacht may cost more than four times as

10 Questions to Answer Before Visiting a Travel Agent

If you've decided to use a travel agent, ask yourself these 10 simple questions, and you'll be better prepared to help the agent do his or her job:

1. Who will be going on the cruise?

2. What can you afford to spend for the entire trip?

3. Where would you like to go?

4. How much vacation time do you have?

5. When can you get away?

6. What are your interests?

7. Do you prefer a casual or structured vacation?

8. What kind of accommodations do you want?

9. What are your dining preferences?

10. How will you get to the embarkation port?

much as a cruise on a mainstream line such as Carnival or Holland America. Cruises on small adventure vessels tend to be pricier than trips on mainstream lines because there are fewer passengers to cover the fixed costs of the cruise.

When you sail also affects your costs: published brochure rates are highest during July and August; you'll pay less, and have more space on ship and ashore, if you sail in May, June, or September. Some of the best deals on small ships are their positioning cruises, when the vessels are moved between their winter homes in the Pacific Northwest to Alaska at the beginning and end of each summer sailing season. You'll find these trips offered mostly by small-ship lines, although some large ships also offer positioning cruises from Los Angeles or San Francisco to Seattle or Vancouver.

Whenever you choose to sail, remember that the brochure price is the highest fare the line can charge for a given cruise. Most lines offer early-booking discounts. Although these vary tremendously, many lines will offer at least 10% off if you book several months ahead of time, usually by the end of January for a summer cruise; this may require early payment as well. Sometimes you can book a discounted last-minute cruise if the ship hasn't filled all its cabins, but you won't get your pick of ships, cabins, or sailing dates. However, since most cruise lines will, if asked, refund the difference in fare if it drops after you've paid, there's little advantage in last-minute booking. Some other deals to watch for are "kids sail free" deals, where children under 12 sail free in the same cabin as their parents; free upgrades rather than discounts; or special deals for home port residents. Frequent cruisers also get discounts from their preferred cruise lines.

SOLO TRAVELERS
Solo travelers should be aware that single cabins are nonexistent on most ships; taking a double cabin for yourself can cost as much as twice the advertised per-person rates (which are based on two people shar-

ing a room). Some cruise lines will find roommates of the same sex for singles so that each can travel at the regular per-person, double-occupancy rate.

EXTRAS

Your cruise fare typically includes accommodation, onboard meals and snacks, and most onboard activities. It does not normally include airfare to the port city, shore excursions, tips, soft drinks, alcoholic drinks, or spa treatments. In addition, you may be levied fees for port handling, security and fuel surcharges, or sales taxes, all of which will be added to your cruise fare when you book.

> **TIP**
>
> Although most other kinds of travel are booked over the Internet nowadays, cruises are a different story. Your best bet is still to work with a travel agent who specializes in cruises to Alaska. Agents have built strong relationships with the lines, and have a much better chance of getting you the cabin you want, and possibly even a free upgrade.

OTHER CONSIDERATIONS

Children's programs: Virtually every line sailing to Alaska has children's programs, but some lines only offer them during school holidays. Small ships are less likely to offer kids' programs, though the *Safari Quest* has educational nature programs for school-age kids and teens in summer. Check also whether the available shore excursions include activities that will appeal to kids.

Dining: Some cruise lines offer traditional assigned dining, meaning that you will dine each evening at the same table with the same companions. Others offer open seating, allowing you to dine whenever and with whomever you like; still others offer a choice between the two systems. Cruise ships also vary in the number of dining alternatives they offer. Most have at least one restaurant in addition to the main dining room; some have multiple choices. Most ships offer vegetarian options, and many now sport heart-healthy or low-carb options. Check ahead if you need to follow a special diet while on board.

Ports of call: You'll want to know where and when you will be stopping. Will there be enough time in port to do what you want to do there? Will it be the right time of day for your chosen activity? Will you tender to shore by boat or moor up at the dock? This is important as tendering can take some time away from your port visit. Note also that just because a port is on the itinerary doesn't guarantee that passengers will be allowed to disembark. Be sure to ask when you book, especially if the time allowed at a given port seems brief.

Onboard activities: Your cruise will likely include two full days at sea. Think about how you'd like to fill the time. Do you want great workout facilities or a top-of-the-line spa? What about educational opportunities or shopping? If seeing Alaska itself is your priority, choose a ship with lots of outdoor *and* indoor viewing space.

ABOUT THESE REVIEWS

In this chapter, large and luxury cruise lines and their ships are presented first, in alphabetical order, followed by small-ship cruise lines, also in alphabetical order. Ships for each cruise line are listed individually or by "class." When ships belong to the same class—or are basically similar—they're listed together with their names separated by commas. Some ships owned by the cruise lines listed do not include regularly scheduled Alaska cruises on their published itineraries as of this writing and are not reviewed in this book. *For a complete listing of the ships and the itineraries they are scheduled to follow in the 2008 cruising season, see ⇨ Cruise Ships at a Glance.*

CRUISE SHIPS

Large cruise lines account for the vast majority of passengers sailing to Alaska. These typically have both larger cruise ships and megaships in their fleets. Cruise ships have plentiful outdoor deck space, and most have a wraparound outdoor promenade deck that allows you to stroll or jog the ship's perimeter. In the newest vessels, traditional meets trendy, but for all their resort-style innovations, they still feature cruise-ship classics—afternoon tea, complimentary room service, and lavish pampering. The smallest cruise ships carry 500 passengers, while larger vessels accommodate 1,500 passengers and offer a wide variety of diversions. Megaships boast even more amenities and amusements, and carry between 1,500 and 3,000 passengers—enough people to outnumber the residents of many Alaskan port towns. Megaships are a good choice if you're looking for nonstop activity and lots of options; they're especially appealing for groups traveling together and families with older kids. If you prefer a gentler pace and a chance to get to know your shipmates, try a smaller ship.

SMALL SHIPS

Compact expedition-type vessels bring you right up to the shoreline to skirt the face of a glacier and pull through narrow channels where big ships don't fit. Alaska, not casinos or spa treatments, is the focus of these cruises. You'll see more wildlife and call into smaller ports, as well as some of the larger, better-known towns. Lectures and talks—conducted daily by naturalists, Native Alaskans, and other experts in the Great Land's natural history and native cultures—are the norm. But in comparison with those on traditional cruise ships, cabins on expedition ships can be quite tiny, usually with no phone or TV, and some bathrooms are no bigger than cubbyholes. Often, the dining room and the lounge are the only common public areas on these vessels. Other small ships, however, are luxurious yachts with cushy cabins, comfy lounges and libraries, and hot tubs on deck. You won't find any nightlife or even movie theaters aboard, but what you trade for space and onboard diversions is a unique and detailed glimpse of Alaska that you're unlikely to forget.

CLOSE UP

Cabin Cruising

INSIDE CABINS

An inside cabin is just that: a stateroom that's inside the ship with no window or porthole. These are always the least expensive cabins and are ideal for passengers who would rather spend their vacation funds on excursions or other incidentals than on upgraded accommodations. Inside cabins are generally just as spacious as outside cabins, and decor and amenities are similar. Many ships locate triple and quad cabins (accommodating three or more passengers) on the inside. ■TIP➜**For passengers who want a very dark room for sleeping, an inside cabin is ideal.**

OUTSIDE CABINS

A standard outside cabin has either a picture window or porthole. To give the illusion of more space, these cabins might rely on the generous use of mirrors for an even airier feeling. ■TIP➜**If you pick an outside cabin, check to make sure your view of the sea is not obstructed by a lifeboat. The ship's deck plan will help you figure it out.**

BALCONY CABINS

A balcony—or veranda—cabin is an outside cabin with floor-to-ceiling glass doors that open onto a private deck. Although the cabin may have large expanses of glass, the balcony is sometimes cut out of the cabin's square footage (depending on the ship). To give the illusion of even more space, a balcony cabin might also rely on the liberal use of mirrors. ■TIP➜**If you have small children, a veranda cabin isn't the best choice. Accidents can happen, even on balconies with solid barriers beneath the railing.**

SUITES

Suites are the most lavish accommodations afloat, and although they're always larger than regular cabins, they don't always have separate rooms for sleeping. Some luxury ships designate all accommodations as suites, and they can range in size from about 250 to 1,500 square feet. The most expansive (and expensive) have large living rooms and separate bedrooms and may also have huge private outdoor sundecks equipped with hot tubs, changing rooms, and dining areas.

Most small ships are based in Juneau or another Alaska port in summer and sail entirely within Alaska. Twice a year, however, usually in May and September, most offer an Inside Passage cruise as they move the ships to and from their winter homes in the Pacific Northwest.

Small-ship cruising can be pricey as costs are spread over a few dozen, rather than hundreds of, passengers. Fares tend to be inclusive (except for airfare), with few onboard charges, and, given the size of ship and style of cruise, fewer opportunities to spend money on board. Small ships typically offer the same kinds of early-booking and other discounts as the major cruise lines.

CARNIVAL CRUISES

The world's largest cruise line originated the "Fun Ship" concept in 1972 with the relaunch of an aging ocean liner that got stuck on a sandbar during its maiden voyage. In true entrepreneurial spirit, founder Ted Arison shrugged off an inauspicious beginning and introduced "superliners" a decade later. Sporting red-white-and-blue flared funnels, which are easily recognized from afar, new ships are continuously added to the fleet and rarely deviate from a successful pattern.

Food. Carnival ships have both flexible dining options and casual alternative restaurants. Although the upscale supper clubs on certain ships serve cuisine comparable to high-end steak houses and seafood restaurants ashore, the main dining room menus were uninspired until the line partnered with world-renowned chef–restaurateur Georges Blanc. Carnival already served the best food of the mainstream cruise lines and the inclusion of "Georges Blanc Signature Selections" improves menus with a variety of gourmet-quality appetizers, entrées, and desserts now served in main dining rooms and Lido restaurants, as well as the supper clubs. In addition to the regular menu, vegetarian, low-calorie, low-carbohydrate, low-salt, no-sugar, and children's selections are available. If you don't feel like dressing up for dinner, the Lido buffet serves full meals and excellent pizza.

Fitness & Recreation. Carnival's trademark spas and fitness centers are some of the largest and best equipped at sea. State-of-the-art cardiovascular and strength-training equipment, a jogging track, and basic exercise classes are available at no charge in the fitness centers. There's a fee for personal training and specialized classes such as yoga and Pilates.

Dress Code. Two formal nights are standard on seven-night cruises. Although men are encouraged to wear tuxedoes, dark suits or sport coats and ties are more prevalent. All other evenings are casual, although jeans are discouraged in restaurants.

Kids. "Camp Carnival" earns high marks for keeping young cruisers busy and content. Run year-round by trained professionals, dedicated children's areas include great playrooms with separate splash pools. There are specialized activities for toddlers, ages 6 to 8, and 9 to 11. Teens (12 to 14) particularly appreciate social events, parties, and sports. Every night they have access to the ships' discos from 9:30 until 10:45 PM, followed by late-night movies, karaoke, or pizza. Games, parties, and dances are just some of the organized activities for the 15- to 17-year-old teen set. The Club O2 program, designed specifically for their age group, promises a dedicated lounge where they can catch a movie or meet new friends.

Tipping. Gratuities of $10 per passenger, per day, are automatically added to onboard accounts and are distributed to stewards and waitstaff. Passengers may adjust the amount based on the level of service experienced. A 15% gratuity is automatically added to bar and beverage tabs.

Service. Service on Carnival ships is friendly but not polished. State-room attendants are not only recognized for their attention to cleanliness, but also for their expertise in creating "towel animals"—cute critters fashioned from bath towels that appear most nights during turn-down service.

Your Shipmates. Carnival's passengers are overwhelmingly active Americans, mostly couples in their mid-thirties to mid-fifties. Holidays and school vacation periods are very popular with families, and there are lots of kids on Alaska cruises.

Contacts. *Carnival Cruise Lines, 3655 N.W. 87th Ave., Miami, FL33178-2428 305/599–2600, 800/438–6744, or 800/327–9501 www.carnival.com.*

CARNIVAL SPIRIT

Itineraries. In 2008 Carnival will offer seven-day, one-way cruises between Vancouver and Whittier, which call at Ketchikan, Juneau Skagway, and Sitka, and cruise through College Fjord and Lynn Canal; and round-trip loop cruises from Vancouver that stop at Juneau, Skagway, and Ketchikan, and cruise through Glacier Bay.

Public Areas & Facilities. While newer ships grow bigger and bigger, *Carnival Spirit* is a classic vessel from a more modest era, though this sleek and fast ship includes all the trademark characteristics of its larger fleetmates. It has plenty of nooks and crannies for relaxation as well as expansive lounges. This is a long ship—a really long ship—and you may want to consider any mobility issues when selecting a cabin. Thankfully, there are three banks of well-placed elevators.

Restaurants. One two-deck formal restaurant serves open-seating breakfast and lunch; it also serves dinner in two assigned evening seatings. The casual Lido buffet with numerous serving stations offers a variety of food choices; at night it becomes the Seaview Bistro for casual diners. There's also a pizzeria, outdoor grills, and a patisserie.

Accommodations. Cabins on Carnival ships are generally more spacious than industry standard, and these are no exception. Nearly 80% have an ocean view, and of those, more than 80% have balconies. Suites and some ocean-view cabins have private balconies outfitted with chairs and tables. Every cabin has adequate closet and drawer-shelf storage. Ocean-view cabins have small sitting areas and suites also have a whirlpool tub, VCR, and walk-in closet. Inside cabins have ample room, but no sitting areas. Decks 5, 6, and 7 each have a pair of balcony staterooms that connect to adjoining "interior" staterooms, ideal for families because of their close proximity to children and teen areas.

CELEBRITY CRUISES

Founded in 1989 Celebrity has gained a reputation for fine food and professional service. The cruise line has built premium, sophisticated ships and developed signature amenities, including a specialty coffee shop, martini bar, large standard staterooms with generous storage, spas, and butler service for passengers booking the top suites. While spacious accommodations in every category are a Celebrity standard, the addition of ConciergeClass makes certain premium ocean-view and balcony staterooms almost the equivalent of suites in terms of amenities and service.

A lineup of lavish, though somewhat uninspired, revues is presented in the main show lounges by production companies of singers and dancers. Bands also play a wide range of musical styles for dancing and listening in smaller lounges. Guest lecturers in the Enrichment Series program lecture on topics ranging from financial strategies, astronomy, wine appreciation, and politics to the history and culture of ports of call. Culinary demonstrations, Bingo, and art auctions are additional diversions throughout the fleet.

Food. Every ship in the fleet has a highly experienced team headed by executive chefs and food and beverage managers who developed their skills in some of the world's finest restaurants. Alternative restaurants on *Infinity* and *Millennium* offer fine dining in classic ocean-liner splendor. There is no alternative restaurant on the Mercury.

Fitness & Recreation. Celebrity's fitness centers and spas are some of the most tranquil and nicely equipped at sea. Each AquaSpa has a large thallassotherapy pool; it's complimentary on *Infinity* and *Millennium,* but there's a charge to use it on *Mercury.* State-of-the-art exercise equipment, a jogging track, and some fitness classes are available at no charge. Spa treatments include a variety of massages, body wraps, and facials. Each ship has an Acupuncture at Sea program administered by a specialist in Chinese medicine. Hair and nail services are offered in the salons.

Dress Code. Two formal nights are standard on seven-night cruises. Men are encouraged to wear tuxedoes, but dark suits or sport coats and ties are more prevalent. Two evenings are designated informal, and other evenings are casual, although jeans are discouraged in restaurants. The line requests that no shorts be worn in public areas after 6 PM, and most people observe the dress code, unlike on some other cruise lines.

Kids. Each Celebrity vessel has a dedicated playroom and offers a five-tiered program of activities designed for children aged 3 to 6, 7 to 9, 10 to 12, and 13 to 17, plus Toddler Time for children under age 3, which allows parents to participate and toddlers to interact with other children their age. Younger children must be toilet-trained to participate in the programs and use the facilities; however, families are welcome to borrow toys for their untoilet-trained kids. A nominal fee may be assessed for participation in children's dinner parties, the Late-Night Slumber Party, and Afternoon Get-Togethers while parents are ashore in ports of call. Evening in-cabin babysitting can be arranged for a fee.

Tipping. Gratuities can be added to shipboard accounts or personally distributed in cash by passengers on the last night of the cruise.

Suggested guidelines are per person, per day: waiter and cabin steward–butler $3.50; assistant waiter $2; assistant chief housekeeper and maitre d' 75¢; cabin attendant in ConciergeClass $4. Passengers may adjust the amount based on the level of service experienced. For children under 12 who accompany adults as third or fourth occupants of a stateroom, half the suggested amount is recommended. An automatic gratuity of 15% is added to all beverage tabs.

Service. Service on Celebrity ships is unobtrusive and polished. If you care to spend some extra money, guests in the ConciergeClass staterooms are given more personalized service and amenities, including priority check-in, preferential treatment on shore excursions, and many other luxuries.

Your Shipmates. Celebrity caters to American cruise passengers, primarily couples from their mid-thirties to mid-fifties. Many families cruise on Celebrity's fleet during summer months and holiday periods.

Contacts. ✉ *1050 Caribbean Way, Miami, FL33132* ☎ *305/539–6000 or 800/437–3111* ⊕ *www.celebrity.com.*

INFINITY, MILLENNIUM

Itineraries. In 2008 *Millennium* will make seven-day, one-way Gulf of Alaska cruises between Vancouver and Seward calling at Ketchikan, Juneau, Skagway, and Icy Strait Point and cruising Hubbard Glacier; the *Infinity* will sail the Inside Passage round-trip from Seattle with stops at Ketchikan, Juneau, Icy Strait Point, and cruising Hubbard Glacier.

Public Areas & Facilities. Dramatic exterior glass elevators, a glass-domed pool area, and a window-wrapped ship-top observation lounge keep the magnificence of Alaska well within view aboard Millennium-class ships. These are the newest and largest in Celebrity's fleet, and each stocks plenty of premium amenities, including a flower-filled conservatory, roomy library, Internet café, golf simulator, and an expansive spa.

Restaurants. The formal two-deck restaurant serves evening meals in two assigned seatings and is supplemented by a casual Lido buffet. An upscale, reservations-only alternative restaurant houses a demonstration kitchen and wine cellar and features table-side meal preparation. Other dining options include a luncheon grill, Cova Café patisserie, a spa café, and 24-hour room service.

Accommodations. Cabins are spacious, well appointed, and 80% have an ocean view (74% of those have private verandas). Thoughtfully designed, closet and storage space is ample and a sitting area with sofa, chair, and table add comfort to the space. Extras include toiletries, refrigerators, and robes, which are provided for use during the cruise. Former "premium" balcony cabins on four decks are now categorized as ConciergeClass staterooms. Most cabins and suites have convertible sofa beds, and many categories are capable of accommodating third and fourth occupants. Family staterooms feature huge balconies and some have not one, but two sofa beds. Suite luxuries vary, but most include a whirlpool tub and walk-in closet, while all have butler service.

MERCURY

Itineraries. The *Mercury* will cruise the Inside Passage from Vancouver in 2008, with stops at Juneau, Ketchikan, and Sitka or Prince Rupert, BC, as well as Hubbard Glacier.

Public Areas & Facilities. With features such as a golf simulator, video walls, and interactive television systems in cabins, this ship is a high-tech pioneer yet warm and elegant at the same time. Many large windows—including a dramatic two-story wall of glass in the dining room and wraparound windows in the Navigator Club, the gym, and the beauty salon—bathe the ship in natural light and afford excellent views of Alaska's natural beauty. There's also a retractable glass sunroof over the aft pool for perfect swimming conditions in any weather.

Restaurants. The formal two-deck restaurant serves evening meals in two assigned seatings and is supplemented by a casual Lido restaurant, two poolside luncheon grills, Cova Café patisserie, and 24-hour room service.

Accommodations. Standard cabins are intelligently appointed, with few frills; space is well used, making for maximum elbow room in the bathrooms and good storage space in the closets. Extras include refrigerators, toiletries, and robes for use during the cruise. The availability of balcony accommodations isn't as generous as on newer and larger ships; however, an additional 14 balconies were added to aft-facing staterooms during a 2007 drydock. Standard balcony cabins on Penthouse and Sky decks have been reclassified as ConciergeClass accommodations.

HOLLAND AMERICA LINE

Holland America Line has enjoyed a distinguished record of traditional cruises, world exploration, and transatlantic crossings since 1873. Even the ships' names follow a pattern set long ago: all end in the suffix "dam" and are derived from the names of various dams that cross Holland's rivers, important Dutch landmarks, or points of the compass.

Entertainment tends to be more Broadway-stylish than Las Vegas–brash. Colorful revues are presented in main show lounges by the ships' companies of singers and dancers. Other performances might include a variety of cabaret acts: comedians, magicians, jugglers, and acrobats. Live bands play a wide range of musical styles for dancing and listening in smaller lounges and piano bars. Movies are shown daily in cinemas that double as the Culinary Arts Centers.

Noted for focusing on passenger comfort, Holland America Line (HAL) cruises are classic in design and style; however, with an infusion of younger adults and families on board, they remain refined without being stuffy or stodgy. In 2006 HAL completed its "Signature of Excellence" program to raise product and service standards throughout the fleet. An interactive Culinary Arts Center offers cooking demonstrations and wine-tasting sessions; Explorations Café is a coffeehouse-style library and Internet center; and the Explorations Guest Speakers Series is supported by in-cabin televised programming on flat-screen TVs in all cabins; the traditional Crow's Nest observation lounge has a new nightclub layout, video wall, and sound-and-light systems; and facilities for children and teens have been greatly expanded.

Food. The quality, taste, and selection of food have all improved in recent years. A case in point are the reservations-required, $20 per person Pinnacle Grill alternative restaurants. Dining is further enhanced by Alaskan specialties such as king crab legs and salmon. Other delicious onboard traditions are afternoon tea, a late-night Dutch Chocolate treat, and Holland America Line's signature bread pudding. Vegetarian options as well as healthy "Inbalance Spa Cuisine" are available, and special dietary requests can be handled with advance notice.

Fitness & Recreation. Fitness facilities are well-equipped and fully staffed. Basic fitness classes are available at no charge. There's a fee for personal training and specialized classes such as yoga and Pilates. The Greenhouse Spa offers a variety of treatments. Hair styling and nail services are offered in the salons. All ships have a jogging track, multiple swimming pools, and sports courts.

Dress Code. Evenings on Holland America Line cruises fall into three categories: casual, informal, and formal. Ties are optional, but men are asked to wear a sport coat on one informal night. For the two formal nights standard on seven-night cruises, men are encouraged to wear tuxedoes, but dark suits or sport coats and ties are acceptable, and you'll certainly see them. Other nights are casual. It's requested that no T-shirts, jeans, swimsuits, tank tops, or shorts be worn in public areas after 6 PM.

Kids. Club HAL is Holland America Line's professionally staffed youth and teen program. Activities planned for children ages 3 to 7 include storytelling, arts and crafts, ice-cream or pizza parties, and games; for children ages 8 to 12 there are arcade games, Sony Play Stations, theme parties, on-deck sports events, and scavenger hunts. Club HAL After Hours offers late-night activities from 10 PM until midnight for an hourly fee. Baby food, diapers, cribs, high chairs, and booster seats may be requested in advance of boarding. Private in-cabin babysitting is sometimes available if a staff member is willing. Teens ages 13 to 17 have their own lounge with activities including dance contests, arcade games, sports tournaments, movies, and an exclusive sun deck on some ships.

Tipping. $10 per passenger, per day, is automatically added to shipboard accounts, and gratuities are distributed to stewards and waitstaff. Passengers may adjust the amount based on the level of service experienced. Room-service tips are usually given in cash (it's at the passenger's discretion here). An automatic 15% gratuity is added to bar-service tabs.

Service. Professional, unobtrusive service is a fleetwide standard on Holland America Line. Crew members are trained in Indonesia at a custom-built facility called the Nieuw Jakarta, where employees polish their English-language skills and learn housekeeping in mock cabins.

Your Shipmates. No longer just your grandparents' cruise line, today's Holland America sailings attract families and couples, mostly from their late thirties on up. Holidays and summer months are peak Alaska periods when you can find more children in the mix. Retirees are often still in the majority, particularly on longer cruises.

Contacts. ✉ *300 Elliott Ave. W, Seattle, WA 98119* ☎ *206/281–3535 or 800/577–1728* ⊕ *www.hollandamerica.com.*

AMSTERDAM

Itineraries. Round-trips from Seattle stopping in Juneau, Sitka, Ketchikan, and Victoria, BC, and scenic cruising in either Glacier Bay or Tracy Arm.

Public Areas & Facilities. *Amsterdam* is one of Holland America Line's "flagships." One of the most traditional ships in the fleet, *Amsterdam* is fitted with wood appointments in the interior public areas on Promenade and Lower Promenade decks and displays priceless works of art throughout. Additions include a thermal suite in the spa, a culinary-arts demonstration center in the theater, and expansive areas for children and teens.

Restaurants. Flexible scheduling includes a selection of two fixed dinner seatings or "As You Wish" open seating in the two-deck formal restaurant. Pinnacle Grill, the reservations-only restaurant, serves steak and fresh seafood. Entrées made to order and tableside waiter service enhance the Lido's evening casual dining alternative. The Lido restaurant and poolside buffets supplement formal restaurants for breakfast and lunch. Servers circulate throughout lounges with canapés before dinner and during late-night hours. Room service is available 24 hours.

Accommodations. Staterooms are spacious and comfortable, although fewer have private balconies than on newer fleetmates. Every cabin has adequate closet and drawer–shelf storage, as well as bathroom shelves. Some suites also have a whirlpool tub, powder room, and walk-in closet. All staterooms and suites are appointed with flat-panel TVs and DVD players. Bathrooms have bathrobes to use during the cruise. Penthouse Verandah and Deluxe Verandah suites have exclusive use of the private Neptune Lounge, personal concierge service, canapés before dinner on request, binoculars and umbrellas for use during the cruise, an invitation to a VIP party with the captain, and complimentary laundry services. Connecting cabins are available in a range of categories. Although there are a number of triple cabins to choose from, there are not as many that accommodate four. Twenty-one staterooms are designed for wheelchair accessibility.

OOSTERDAM, WESTERDAM

Itineraries. *Oosterdam*: Round-trips from Seattle stop at Juneau, Sitka, Ketchikan, and cruise Hubbard Glacier; *Westerdam*: Round-trips from Seattle stop at Juneau, Sitka, and Ketchikan, and cruise through Glacier Bay.

Public Areas & Facilities. These Vista-class vessels successfully integrate new youthful and family-friendly elements into Holland America Line's classic fleet. Although several decks are termed "promenade," the exterior teak promenade actually encircles public rooms, not cabins. As a result, there are numerous outside accommodations with views of the sea restricted by lifeboats on the Upper Promenade Deck. Veterans of cruises on other Holland America class ships will find the layout of public spaces somewhat different; however, some lounges are still high atop the ships and continue to be some of the best observation lounges at sea.

Restaurants. Flexible scheduling includes a selection of two dinner seatings or "As You Wish" open seating in the two-deck formal restaurants. Pinnacle Grill, the reservations-required specialty restaurant overlooking the atrium, serves steak and fresh seafood. Made-to-order entrées and tableside waiter service enhance the Lido's evening casual dining alternative. The Lido restaurant, Terrace Grill, Java Corner, and Windstar Café supplement formal dining rooms. Servers circulate throughout lounges with canapés before dinner and during late-night hours. Room service is available 24 hours.

Accommodations. At least 85% of all Vista-class accommodations have an ocean view, and almost 80% of those also have a private balcony furnished with chairs, loungers, and tables. All staterooms and suites are appointed flat-panel TVs and DVD players and some suites have a whirlpool tub, powder room, and walk-in closet. Penthouse Verandah and Deluxe Verandah suites have exclusive use of the private Neptune Lounge, personal concierge service, canapés before dinner on request, binoculars and umbrellas for use during the cruise, an invitation to a VIP party with the captain, and complimentary laundry, pressing, and dry-cleaning services. Connecting cabins are featured in a wide range of categories; however, the ships fall somewhat short of family friendliness: although there are a number of triple cabins to choose from, there are not many that accommodate four. Twenty-eight staterooms are designed for wheelchair accessibility.

VOLENDAM, ZAANDAM

Itineraries. *Volendam*: One-way from Anchorage or Vancouver stopping at Skagway or Haines, Juneau, and Ketchikan, with scenic cruising through College Fjord and Glacier Bay; *Zaandam*: one-way from Anchorage or Vancouver stopping at Juneau, Ketchikan, Skagway, or Haines, with scenic cruising through College Fjord and Glacier Bay; or round-trip from Vancouver with stops in Juneau, Skagway, and Ketchikan and scenic cruising in Glacier Bay.

Public Areas & Facilities. Similar in layout to Statendam-class vessels *(below)*, these slightly larger sister ships introduced playful art and interior design elements to Holland America Line's classic vessels, and the extra space allows for a larger specialty restaurant and a roomier feel throughout. Atriums open onto three "Promenade" decks. The lowest contains staterooms encircled by a wide, teak outdoor deck furnished with padded steamer chairs; the other two promenades include only interior passageways lined with lounges, bars, libraries, and card rooms in traditional Holland America style. The interior decor and much of the artwork found in each vessel has a predominant theme—*Volendam* centers around flowers, and *Zaandam*, music.

Restaurants. Dining rooms on both ships are particularly stunning, with grand staircases and delicate spidery chandeliers overhead. There are two dinner seatings or "As You Wish" open seating in the two-deck formal restaurant. Pinnacle Grill, the reservations-only restaurant, serves steak and fresh seafood. The Lido buffet becomes a more casual dining alternative by night, with made-to-order entrées and waiter service. The Lido restaurant and poolside buffets supplement formal restaurants for breakfast and lunch, and an outdoor barbecue dinner buffet is usually offered one evening. Tea is served in the afternoon. Servers circulate throughout lounges with canapés before dinner and during late-night hours. Room service is available 24 hours.

Accommodations. Staterooms are spacious and comfortable. Every cabin has adequate closet and drawer–shelf storage, as well as bathroom shelves. Some suites have a whirlpool tub, powder room, and walk-in closet. All staterooms and suites are appointed with flat-panel TVs and DVD players and deluxe bathrobes to use during the cruise. Penthouse Verandah and Deluxe Verandah suites have exclusive use of the private Neptune Lounge, personal concierge service, canapés before dinner on request, binoculars and umbrellas for use during the cruise, an invitation to a VIP party with the captain, and complimentary laundry, pressing, and dry-cleaning services. As a nod to families, connecting cabins are featured in a range of categories. However, although the number of triple cabins is generous, there are not many that accommodate four. Twenty-two staterooms are designed for wheelchair accessibility.

STATENDAM, RYNDAM & VEENDAM

Itineraries. *Statendam*: Round-trip from Vancouver stopping at Skagway, Juneau, and Ketchikan, with cruising through Tracy Arm and Glacier Bay; *Ryndam*: Round-trip from Vancouver with stops at Juneau, Skagway, and Ketchikan, and cruising through Glacier Bay and Tracy Arm; *Veendam*: Round-trip from Vancouver with stops at Juneau, Skagway, and Ketchikan, and cruising through Glacier Bay; or one-way from Vancouver or Anchorage stopping at Ketchikan, Juneau, Skagway, and Icy Strait Point with scenic cruising at Hubbard Glacier.

Public Areas & Facilities. These sister ships retain the most classic and traditional characteristics of Holland America Line vessels. Routinely updated with innovative features, they combine all the advantages of intimate, mid-size vessels with high-tech and stylish details. At the heart of the ships, triple-deck atriums graced by suspended glass sculptures open onto three so-called "promenade" decks; the lowest contains staterooms encircled by a wide, teak outdoor deck furnished with padded steamer chairs, while interior art-filled passageways flow past lounges and public rooms on the two decks above. It's easy to find just about any area on board, with the possible exception of the main level of the dining room. Either reach the lower dining room floor via the aft elevator, or enter one deck above and make a grand entrance down the sweeping staircase.

Restaurants. Passengers are assigned to one of two dinner seatings or may choose "As You Wish" open seating in the two-deck formal restaurant. Pinnacle Grill, the reservations-only restaurant, serves steak and fresh seafood. The Lido restaurant is a casual dinner alternative with waiter service and made-to-order entrées. The Lido restaurant and poolside buffets supplement formal restaurants for breakfast and lunch. Tea is served in the late afternoon. Servers circulate throughout lounges with canapés before dinner seatings and during late-night hours. Room service is available 24 hours.

Accommodations. Staterooms are spacious and comfortable, although fewer of them have private balconies than on newer fleetmates. Some suites have a whirlpool tub, powder room, and walk-in closet. New touches include flat-panel TVs, DVD players, and deluxe bathrobes to use during the cruise. Penthouse Verandah and Deluxe Verandah suites have exclusive use of the private Neptune Lounge, personal concierge service, canapés before dinner on request, binoculars and umbrellas for use during the cruise, an invitation to a VIP party with the captain, and complimentary laundry service. Dozens of connecting cabins are featured in a range of categories. Although there are a number of triple cabins to choose from, few of them accommodate four. Six staterooms are designed for wheelchair accessibility; nine staterooms are modified with ramps although doors are standard width.

NORWEGIAN CRUISE LINE

Noted for top-quality, high-energy entertainment and emphasis on fitness facilities and programs, NCL combines action, activities, and a variety of dining options in a casual, free-flowing atmosphere. "Freestyle" cruising was born when Asian shipping giant Star Cruises acquired NCL—the new owners were confounded that Americans meekly conformed to rigid dining schedules and dress codes. All that changed with NCL's introduction of a host of flexible dining options that allow you to choose open seating in the main dining rooms or dine in any of a number of à la carte and specialty restaurants at any time and with whom you please.

More high jinks than high-brow, entertainment after dark features some of the best Broadway and Las Vegas–style revues at sea. You can get into the act by taking part in talent shows or step up to the karaoke microphone. Live bands play for dancing and listening in smaller lounges, and each ship has a lively disco. Casinos, Bingo sessions, and art auctions are well attended. Goofy poolside games are an NCL staple, and the ships' bands crank up the volume during afternoon and evening deck parties. It's lively and enjoyable, even if you just watch the action from the sidelines.

Food. Main dining rooms serve what is traditionally deemed Continental fare, although it's about what you would expect at a really good hotel banquet. Where NCL really shines is the specialty restaurants, especially the French-Mediterranean Le Bistro (on all ships), the pan-Asian restaurants, and steak houses (on the newer ships). As a rule of thumb, the newer the ship, the wider the variety. You may find Spanish tapas, an Italian trattoria, a steak house, and a pan-Asian restaurant complete with a sushi and sashimi bar and Teppanyaki room. Some, but not all, carry a cover charge or are priced à la carte and require reservations. An NCL staple, the late-night Chocoholic Buffet continues to be a favorite event.

Fitness & Recreation. Mandara Spa offers a long list of unique and exotic spa treatments fleetwide on NCL, although facilities vary widely. State-of-the-art exercise equipment, jogging tracks, and basic fitness classes are available at no charge. There's a fee for personal training, and specialized classes such as yoga and Pilates.

Dress Code. Resort casual attire is appropriate at all times; however, the option of one formal evening is available on all cruises of seven nights and longer. Most passengers actually raise the casual dress code a notch to what could be called casual chic attire.

Kids. For children and teens, each NCL vessel offers the "Kid's Crew" program of supervised entertainment for young cruisers ages 2 to 17. Younger children are split into three groups from ages 2 to 5, 6 to 9, and 10 to 12; activities range from storytelling, games, and arts and crafts to dinner with counselors, pajama parties, and treasure hunts. Evening group and private babysitting services are available for a fee. Parents whose children are not toilet trained are issued a beeper to alert them when diaper changing is necessary. Children under age two cruise free with their parents, and there's no minimum age for infants. For teens ages 13 to 17, options include sports, parties, teen disco, movies, and video games. Some ships have special clubs where teens hang out in adult-free zones.

Tipping. A fixed service charge of $10 per person, per day, is added to shipboard accounts. For children ages 3 to 12, a $5 per person per day charge is added; there's no charge for children under age three. An automatic 15% gratuity is added to bar tabs. Staff members are encouraged to go the extra mile for passengers and are permitted to accept cash gratuities. Passengers in suites are asked to offer a cash gratuity to concierge and butlers at their own discretion.

Service. Although somewhat inconsistent, service is congenial.

Your Shipmates. NCL's mostly American cruise passengers are active couples ranging from their mid-thirties to mid-fifties. Many families cruise on NCL ships during summer months on Alaska itineraries. Longer cruises and more exotic itineraries attract passengers in the over-55 age group.

Contacts. ✉ *7665 Corporate Center Dr., Miami, FL 33126* ☎ *305/436–4000 or 800/327–7030* ⊕ *www.ncl.com.*

NORWEGIAN PEARL

Itineraries. In 2008 *Norwegian Pearl* offers round-trip cruises from Seattle that stop in Juneau, Skagway, Ketchikan, and Victoria, BC, as well as scenic cruising through Glacier Bay.

Public Areas & Facilities. *Norwegian Pearl* is the next step up in the continuing evolution of Norwegian's ship design—the interior location of some public rooms and restaurants has been tweaked, and Courtyard Villas, the latest category of deluxe accommodations, have been added. In addition, the "Bar Central" concept features a Martini bar, a wine and champagne bar, and a beer and whiskey pub. All new on *Norwegian Pearl* are a rock-climbing wall and a four-lane, 10-pin bowling alley, the latter in an entertainment, sports bar, and nightclub complex called Bliss.

Restaurants. Ten dining rooms and ethnic restaurants with open seating and flexible hours offer continental and specialty dining. Two are complimentary; specialty restaurants, including NCL's signature Le Bistro, carry a cover charge and require reservations. Other dining choices include La Cucina Italian Restaurant, Lotus Garden Asian Restaurant, Cagney's Steakhouse, Mambos Latin Tapas Restaurant, and Blue Lagoon for 24-hour fast food. Casual daytime options are the Lido buffet, the outdoor grill, an ice-cream bar, a home-style eatery, and room service, which is available around the clock.

Cabins. Cherrywood cabinetry, tropical patterns, a refrigerator, Internet connection, bathrobes for use during the cruise, and a sitting area with sofa, chair, and table are typical standard features in all accommodations. Most bathrooms are compartmentalized with sink area, shower, and toilet separated by sliding glass doors. Family-friendly staterooms interconnect in most categories, enabling families of nearly any size to find suitable accommodations. Nearly every stateroom has a third or fourth berth and some even sleep as many as five and six. *Norwegian Pearl* has Garden Villas, among the largest suites at sea, as well as posh Courtyard Villas with access to an exclusive concierge lounge and a private courtyard with pool, hot tub, sundeck, and small gym. Other suites include such luxuries as whirlpool tubs, entertainment centers with CD/DVD players, and walk-in closets. Twenty-four staterooms are designed for wheelchair accessibility.

NORWEGIAN STAR

Itineraries. In 2008 *Norwegian Star* offers round-trip cruises from Seattle that stop in Ketchikan, Juneau, Skagway, and Prince Rupert, BC, with scenic cruising at Sawyer Glacier.

Public Areas & Facilities. Built specifically to accommodate NCL's Freestyle Cruising concept, Norwegian Star introduced innovations to the fleet, including Garden Villas and sprawling children's facilities (there's even a miniature water park). Bright colors are playful in the disco/karaoke lounge, yet throughout the ship there are plenty of choices to appeal to a broad range of tastes, including a sporty pub, a forward-facing observation lounge, and an intimate piano bar overlooking the pool deck. The highlight of the spa is one of the largest indoor swimming pools at sea. The European-style Stardust Theater is one of the most beautiful show lounges afloat.

Restaurants. Offering more dining choices than most ships in Alaska, *Norwegian Star* has 10 different eateries. Two main complimentary dining rooms are open seating and resort casual. Specialty restaurants are by reservation only and cost extra. Additional casual options are a lobby coffee bar, a diner-style café, the Lido buffet, La Trattoria serving Italian specialties for dinner, and an ice-cream bar. Room service is available 24 hours.

Accommodations. While NCL ships aren't noted for large staterooms, *Norwegian Star*'s standard cabins take their cue from high-end hotel rooms, with rich cherrywood cabinetry and small sitting areas with sofa, chair, and table. Storage and closets are somewhat tight, but adequate for a one-week cruise. Relatively large bathrooms are compartmentalized with sliding doors separating the toilet and shower areas from the central vanity. Small luxuries include toiletries and robes for use during the cruise. All suites have concierge and butler service and Garden Villas, the top-of-the-line three-bedroom suites, have private rooftop terraces. Most staterooms can accommodate a third guest, and many cabins in a variety of categories can be linked to create suites for larger groups. Nearly half of all accommodations include a private balcony. Twenty staterooms are designed for wheelchair accessibility.

NORWEGIAN SUN

Itineraries. In 2008 *Norwegian Sun* sails round-trip from Vancouver with stops at Ketchikan, Juneau, and Skagway, and scenic cruising at Sawyer Glacier.

Public Areas & Facilities. Norwegian Cruise Line hadn't introduced many new ships in a while at the time *Norwegian Sun* was on the drawing board, but with Freestyle Cruising instituted and growing in popularity, the vessel moved into the forefront of the fleet with nine restaurants, an expansive casino, trendy spa, and more family- and kid-friendly facilities.

The observation lounge with floor-to-ceiling windows is a subdued and tasteful spot for relaxation, for afternoon tea, or for dancing into the late-night hours. An Internet café encircles one atrium level, and the Java Café is a welcoming delight on the main atrium floor. Sunshine pours into the atrium through an overhead skylight by day, while at night it's the ship's glamorous hub of activity. A single exception to the understated furnishings is found in the two-deck-high Stardust Lounge showroom, but its flamboyant color scheme can be forgiven: it offers comfortable seating, good sight lines, and lavish productions.

Restaurants. This is a freestyle ship, so all seating is open; dress is always resort casual. The two main dining rooms are complimentary; some specialty restaurants carry a cover charge and require reservations. Casual daytime choices are a lobby coffee bar, the Lido buffet, an ice-cream bar, pizzeria, and room service, which is available around the clock.

Accommodations. Staterooms are a bit more generous in size than on the older vessels in the NCL fleet and contain more than adequate closet and drawer space for a one-week cruise. More than two-thirds have an ocean view, and nearly two-thirds of those have a private balcony. Clever use of primary colors and strategically placed mirrors make them feel spacious. All have a sitting area with sofa, chair, and table. Suites have walk-in closets. Refrigerators, broadband Internet connections, and bathrobes for use during the cruise are typical standard amenities. Suites include such luxuries as whirlpool tubs and entertainment centers, and there's butler and concierge service. Connecting staterooms are available in several categories, including those with balconies. Oddly sandwiched between Deck 6 and Deck 7 forward is Deck 6A. Take care when selecting a cabin on that truncated deck, as it has no direct access to elevators. Sixteen staterooms are designed for wheelchair accessibility.

PRINCESS CRUISES

Princess Cruises may be best known for introducing cruise travel to millions of viewers when its flagship became the setting for *The Love Boat* television series in 1977. Since that heady time of small-screen stardom, the Princess fleet has grown both in the number and the size of ships. Although most are large in scale, Princess vessels manage to create the illusion of intimacy in lovely public rooms graced by multi-million-dollar art collections.

Princess has become more flexible lately; "Personal Choice Cruising" offers alternatives for open-seating dining (when you wish and with whom you please) and entertainment options as diverse as those found in resorts ashore. Welcome additions to Princess's roster of adult activities, which still includes standbys like Bingo and art auctions, are enrichment programs featuring guest lecturers, cooking classes, wine-tasting seminars, pottery workshops, and computer and digital photography classes. Nighttime production shows tend toward Broadway-style revues presented in the main show lounge. Live bands play a wide range of musical styles for dancing and listening in smaller lounges throughout the ships, and each large ship has a dance club.

Food. Personal choices regarding where and what to eat abound, but there's no getting around the fact that most Princess ships are large and carry a great many passengers. Unless you opt for traditional assigned seating, you could experience a brief wait for a table in one of the open-seating dining rooms. Menus are varied and extensive in the main restaurants, and the results are good to excellent considering how much work is going on in the galleys. A special menu is designed especially for children. Alternative restaurants are a staple throughout the fleet, but vary by ship class. With a few breaks in service, Lido buffets on all ships are almost always open, and a pizzeria and grill offer casual daytime snack choices. The fleet's patisseries and ice-cream bars charge for specialty coffee, pastries, and ice-cream treats. If you can, try the "Ultimate Balcony Dining" meal for breakfast or dinner one day. Both come with champagne, and during dinner, a server is on duty throughout the four-course meal.

Fitness & Recreation. Spa and salon options include massages, body wraps, facials, and numerous hair and nail services, as well as a menu of special pampering treatments designed specifically for men, teens, and couples. Modern exercise equipment, a jogging track, and basic fitness classes are available at no charge. There's a nominal fee for personal training and specialized classes such as yoga and Pilates. Grand-class ships have a resistance pool so you can get your "laps" in effortlessly.

Dress Code. Two formal nights are standard on seven-night cruises; an additional formal night may be scheduled on longer sailings. Men are encouraged to wear tuxedoes, but dark suits are appropriate. All other evenings are casual, although jeans are discouraged in restaurants, and it's requested that no shorts be worn in public areas after 6 PM.

Kids. Infants under six months are not permitted; private in-cabin babysitting is not available on any Princess vessel. Children under age three are welcome in the playrooms if supervised by a parent. For young passengers ages 3 to 17, each Princess vessel has a playroom, teen center, and programs of supervised activities designed for different age groups: 3 to 7, 8 to 12, and 13 to 17. Activities to engage youngsters include arts and crafts, scavenger hunts, deck parties, backstage and galley tours, games, and videos. Events such as dance parties in their own disco, theme parties, athletic contests, karaoke, pizza parties, and movie fests occupy teenage passengers. Children also participate in learning programs focused on the environment and wildlife in areas where the ships sail. The National Park Service Junior Ranger Program teaches kids about glaciers, endangered wildlife and other native animals during Alaska cruises. Park Rangers give children and teens the opportunity to earn a Jr. Ranger badge for participation in activities and special presentations. To afford parents independent time ashore, youth centers operate as usual during port days, including lunch with counselors. For a nominal charge, group babysitting is available nightly from 10 PM until 1 AM.

Tipping. A gratuity of $10 per person, per day, is added to shipboard accounts for distribution to stewards and waitstaff. Passengers may adjust the amount based on the level of service experienced. An automatic 15% is added to all bar tabs for bartenders and drink servers; gratuities to other staff members may be extended at passengers' discretion.

Service. Professional service by an international staff is efficient and friendly. It's not uncommon to be greeted in passageways by smiling stewards who know your name.

Your Shipmates. Princess Cruises attract mostly American passengers ranging from their mid-thirties to mid-fifties. Families cruise together on the Princess fleet, particularly during holiday seasons and summer months, when many children are on board. Longer cruises appeal to well-traveled retirees and couples who have the time.

Contacts. ✉24305 *Town Center Dr., Santa Clarita, CA91355-4999* ☎*661/753–0000 or 800/774-6237* ⊕*www.princess.com.*

DAWN PRINCESS

Itineraries. In 2008 *Dawn Princess* offers round-trip 10-night cruises from San Francisco stopping at Sitka, Haines, Icy Strait Point, or Skagway, plus Juneau, Ketchikan, and Victoria, BC, and scenic cruising in Tracy Arm Fjord.

Public Areas & Facilities. Refined and graceful, *Dawn Princess* offers choices available on larger Grand-class ships without sacrificing the smaller-ship atmosphere for which it is noted. The spectacular four-story atrium is an ideal setting for relaxation, people-watching, and making a grand entrance. The main public rooms are on four lower decks and, with the exception of Promenade Deck, cabins are forward and aft. In a nice design twist, the casino is somewhat isolated, and passengers aren't forced to use it as a passageway to reach dining rooms or the art deco main show lounge.

Restaurants. *Dawn Princess* has one dining room with two traditional assigned dinner seatings and one open-seating dining room for Personal Choice cruisers. Alternatives are the reservations-only Sterling Steakhouse specialty restaurant (actually a section of the Lido buffet that's dressed up for the evening and for which there's a charge) and the complimentary pizzeria, which becomes a trattoria-style setting for dinner with traditional Italian menu items. The pizzeria, grill, patisserie, and ice-cream bar offer casual daytime snack options, and the Lido buffet and room service are available 24 hours. "Ultimate Balcony Dining" is available to passengers with balcony accommodations.

Accommodations. Princess Cruises' trademark is an abundance of staterooms with private balconies, yet even the least expensive inside categories have ample storage and a small sitting area with a chair and table. Suites have two TVs, a separate sitting area, a dining-height table with chairs, walk-in closets, double-sink vanities, and a separate shower and whirlpool tub. Minisuites have a separate sitting area, two TVs, walk-in closet, and separate shower and whirlpool tub. Decorated in pastel colors, staterooms typically have mirrored accents, a personal safe, a refrigerator, a hair dryer, and bathrobes for use during the cruise. All suite passengers receive complimentary Internet access, dry cleaning, and shoe polishing, afternoon tea, evening canapés delivered to their suites, and priority embarkation, disembarkation, and tendering privileges. An extended room-service menu is also available for them as are priority reservations for dining and shore excursions. Cabins that sleep third and fourth passengers aren't as numerous as on other Princess ships, and no staterooms have interconnecting interior doors. Adjacent cabins with balconies can be interconnected by unlocking doors in the balcony dividers. Nineteen staterooms are designed for wheelchair accessibility.

CORAL PRINCESS, ISLAND PRINCESS

Itineraries. In 2008 *Coral Princess* and *Island Princess* sail one-way cruises from Vancouver or Anchorage, stopping at Ketchikan, Juneau, and Skagway, and cruising Glacier Bay and College Fjord.

Public Areas & Facilities. Although Princess includes *Coral Princess* and *Island Princess* in the Sun-class category, which also includes *Dawn Princess,* they're actually larger ships with a similar capacity, which results in more space per passenger. All the personal choice features of the larger Grand-class ships were incorporated in this new ship design with a few unique additions, such as a demonstration kitchen and ceramics lab where enrichment programs are presented. While signature rooms such as the Wheelhouse Bar are more traditional, the casinos have subtle London- (*Coral Princess*) and Paris-style (*Island Princess*) themes that extend to the slot machines. Crooner's Bar is a retro '60s Vegas-style martini and piano bar. In addition to the stately Princess Theater showroom, a second entertainment venue, the Universe Lounge, has three stages for shows and flexible seating on two levels, making it a multipurpose space.

Restaurants. Each ship has one dining room with two traditional assigned dinner seatings and a second dining room for open-seating Personal Choice cruisers. Alternative dining options are the two specialty restaurants, Sabatini's and Bayou Café and Steakhouse, which have a surcharge and require reservations. The pizzeria, grill, patisserie, and ice-cream bar offer casual daytime dining and snack options and the Lido buffet and complimentary room service are available 24 hours. Ultimate Balcony Dining is available to passengers with balcony accommodations.

Accommodations. More than 83% of ocean-view staterooms include private balconies. Even the least expensive inside categories have plentiful storage and a small sitting area with chair and table. Suites have two televisions, a sitting area, wet bar, large walk-in closet, and separate bathtub and shower. Minisuites have a separate sitting area, two televisions, walk-in closet, and a combination bathtub–shower. Other typical stateroom features include refrigerators and bathrobes for use during the cruise. Cabins that sleep third and fourth passengers are numerous, but the best for families are interconnecting balcony staterooms on Aloha Deck (A624–A631 and A704–A722), which are adjacent to facilities dedicated to children and teens. Twenty staterooms are designed for wheelchair accessibility.

DIAMOND PRINCESS, SAPPHIRE PRINCESS

Itineraries. In 2008 *Diamond Princess* and *Sapphire Princess* offer one-way cruises from Vancouver or Anchorage and stop at Ketchikan, Juneau, and Skagway, with scenic cruising at Glacier Bay and College Fjord.

Public Areas & Facilities. These sister-ships include all the features traditionally enjoyed on Princess's Grand-class vessels, but with a twist. They're larger than their Grand-class fleetmates, yet carry fewer passengers relative to their size. As a result, they have sleeker profiles, a higher ratio of space per person and feel much roomier. The disco overlooks the ships' sterns, and is a perfect spot for romantic stargazing. Inside, the arrangement of public rooms is a bit different, with the signature Wheelhouse Bar moved forward of its position on other Grand-class ships and an expanded Internet Café, where beverages and snacks are actually served, in its place. All the elements of a Princess ship are included, particularly the small-ship atmosphere and sparkling, yet understated, interior decoration.

Restaurants. Princess is all about choice and *Diamond Princess* and *Sapphire Princess* offer expanded dining choices. In addition to a dining room with two traditional assigned dinner seatings, these ships have four additional dining rooms for open-seating Personal Choice cruisers. Each is smaller than those on other Princess Grand-class ships, but all offer the same menus with a few additional selections that reflect the "theme" of each dining room. Alternative dining options are the two specialty restaurants, Sabatini's and Sterling Steakhouse, which have a surcharge and require reservations. The pizzeria, grill, patisserie, and ice-cream bar offer casual daytime dining and snack options. The Lido buffet and complimentary room service are available 24 hours. Ultimate Balcony Dining is offered to passengers with balcony accommodations.

Accommodations. More than 78% of ocean-view staterooms include private balconies. Even the least expensive inside categories have ample storage and a small sitting area with chair and table. Typical stateroom features are personal safes, refrigerators, and bathrobes for use during the cruise. Suites have two televisions, a sitting area, wet bar, large walk-in closet, and separate bathtub and shower. Minisuites have a separate sitting area, two televisions, walk-in closet, and a combination bathtub–shower. Cabins that sleep third and fourth passengers are numerous. The best for families are Family Suites with interconnecting balcony staterooms on Dolphin Deck. Twenty-seven staterooms are designed for wheelchair accessibility.

GOLDEN PRINCESS, STAR PRINCESS

Itineraries. For 2008 *Golden Princess* and *Star Princess* offer round-trip cruises from Seattle with stops at Juneau, Skagway, Ketchikan, and Victoria, BC, and scenic cruising through Tracy Arm Fjord.

Public Areas & Facilities. Sister-ships in Princess Cruises' lineup are the Grand-class *Golden Princess* and *Star Princess*. Interiors feature soothing pastel hues with splashes of glamour in the sweeping staircases and marble-floored atriums, and the Skywalkers Disco hovers futuristically approximately 150 feet above the water line. Surprisingly intimate for such large ships, the large public lounges are subdivided with unobtrusive furniture.

Restaurants. Passengers have the choice between two traditional dinner seatings in an assigned dining room, or open seating in the ships' other two formal dining rooms. Alternative evening dining options include reservations-required and extra-charge Sabatini's Italian Trattoria and Sterling Steakhouse specialty restaurants. A pizzeria, grill, patisserie, and ice-cream bar offer casual daytime snack options and the Lido buffet and complimentary room service are available 24 hours. Ultimate Balcony Dining is an option available to passengers with balcony accommodations.

Accommodations. *Golden Princess* and *Star Princess* have a large number of staterooms with balconies—80% of all outside accommodations have private balconies. Standard in all categories are refrigerators, ample storage space, and the use of bathrobes. Typical stateroom features are sitting areas with chair and table. Two family "suites" are interconnecting staterooms that each sleep up to eight people. Other adjacent cabins can be connected by unlocking doors in the balcony dividers. Minisuites have a separate sitting area, two televisions, walk-in closet, and combination shower–bathtub. Grand Suites have a separate sitting room and dining room, two televisions, personal computer, refrigerator and wet bar, walk-in closet, and separate shower and whirlpool tub. Owner's, Penthouse, Premium, and Vista suites include a separate sitting room with desk, two televisions, wet bar, walk-in closet, and separate shower and tub. Twenty-eight staterooms are designed for wheelchair accessibility.

TAHITIAN PRINCESS
Itineraries. In 2008 *Tahitian Princess* will offer 14-night round-trip sailings from Vancouver with calls at Ketchikan, Skagway, Valdez, Seward, Kodiak, Juneau, Sitka, and Victoria, BC, and scenic cruising of Glacier Bay.

Public Areas & Facilities. At 30,277 tons, *Tahitian Princess* appears positively diminutive beside her megaship fleetmates, but it provides a true alternative for passengers who prefer the clubby feel of a smaller "boutique"-style ship without skimping on big-ship features. *Tahitian Princess* has cozy public spaces, a stunning observation lounge where you can take in the Alaska scenery through floor-to-ceiling windows on three sides, and a lovely library with a domed trompe l'oeil painted ceiling, faux fireplace, comfortable seating, and, most importantly, well-stocked bookshelves. The most photographed spot on the ship has to be the dramatic grand staircase, reminiscent of those found on transatlantic liners at the height of the Gilded Age of ocean travel.

Restaurants. The only disappointment on *Tahitian Princess* is the lack of a Personal Choice dining room. The lone formal dining room has two scheduled seatings with assigned tables for dinner, but there are other options. Sabatini's Italian Trattoria and Sterling Steakhouse specialty restaurants are reservations-required and extra-charge selections for dinner. The Lido buffet–bistro and complimentary room service are available 24 hours at no charge. A pizzeria and poolside grill offer casual daytime lunch and snack options. Ultimate Balcony Dining for breakfast or dinner is available to passengers with balcony accommodations.

Accommodations. Designed for longer cruises, all staterooms have ample closet and storage space, although bathrooms in lower categories are somewhat tight. In keeping with the rest of the fleet, 73% of all outside cabins and suites have a balcony and interiors are similar in size. Amenities in standard cabins are a bit spartan compared to other Princess ships, yet all have at least a small sitting area. Bath toiletries, personal safes, and robes for use during the cruise are all included, but you must move up to a minisuite or suite to have a bathtub. Full suites are particularly nice, with living–dining rooms, entertainment centers, separate bedrooms, whirlpool bathtubs, a guest powder room, and large balconies overlooking the bow or stern. Four staterooms are designed for wheelchair accessibility.

REGENT SEVEN SEAS CRUISES

Regent Seven Seas Cruises (formerly Radisson Seven Seas Cruises) sails an elegant fleet of vessels that offer a nearly all-inclusive cruise experience in sumptuous, contemporary surroundings. Ships feature exquisite service, generous staterooms with abundant amenities, a variety of dining options, and superior lecture and enrichment programs, including cooking classes taught by renowned Cordon Bleu–trained chefs. Cruises are destination-focused, and most sailings host guest lecturers—historians, anthropologists, naturalists, and diplomats. Certain "Spotlight" cruises center around popular pastimes and themes, such as photography. Production revues, cabaret acts, solo performers, and comedians may be featured in show lounges, with combos playing for listening and dancing in lounges and bars throughout the ships. Casinos are more akin to Monaco than Las Vegas. All ships display tasteful and varied art collections, including pieces that are for sale. Guests are greeted with champagne upon boarding and, as part of Regent's all-inclusive fare, select wines and spirits, soft drinks, and bottled water are complimentary in all bars and restaurants.

Food. Menus may appear to include the usual beef Wellington and Maine lobster, but in the capable hands of Regent Seven Seas chefs, the results are outstanding. Specialty dining varies within the fleet, but the newest ships, including Seven Seas Mariner, have the sophisticated Signatures restaurant, which features the cuisine of Le Cordon Bleu of Paris, and Latitudes, which offers menus either inspired by regional American favorites or nouveau international cuisine. In addition, Mediterranean-inspired bistro dinners are served in the venues that are the daytime casual Lido buffet restaurants. Although special dietary requirements should be relayed to the cruise line before sailing, general considerations such as vegetarian, low-salt, or low-cholesterol food requests can be satisfied on board the ships simply by speaking with the dining room staff. Wines chosen to complement dinner menus are poured freely each evening.

Fitness & Recreation. Although gyms and exercise areas are well-equipped, these are not large ships, so the facilities tend to be on the small side. Each ship has a jogging track, and the larger ones feature a variety of sports courts. Exclusive to Regent Seven Seas, the spa and salon are operated by high-end Carita of Paris.

Dress Code. When sailing in Alaska, the nightly dress code is somewhat relaxed compared to typical Regent cruises. Country-club casual prevails in Alaska, meaning most men tend to wear a sport coat to dinner and ties are optional. One evening may be designated as informal. Women select their evening wardrobes accordingly. While casual wear is appropriate all day, it's requested that dress codes be observed in public areas after 6 PM.

Kids. Regent Seven Seas' vessels are adult-oriented and do not have dedicated children's facilities. However, a "Club Mariner" youth program for children ages 5 to 9, 10 to 13, and 14 to 17 is offered on selected sailings, including during summer months in Alaska. Supervised by counselors, the organized, educational activities focus on nature and the heritage of destinations the ship will visit. Activities, including games, craft projects, movies, and "food fun," are organized to ensure that every child has a memorable experience. Teens are encouraged to help counselors select the activities they prefer.

Tipping. Gratuities are included in the fare, and none are expected. To show their appreciation, passengers may elect to make a contribution to a crew welfare fund that benefits the ship's staff.

Service. The efforts of a polished European staff go almost unnoticed, yet special requests are handled with ease. Butlers provide an additional layer of personal service to guests in the top-category suites.

Your Shipmates. Regent Seven Seas Cruises are inviting to active, affluent, well-traveled couples ranging from their late thirties to retirees who enjoy the ships' elegance and destination-rich itineraries. Longer cruises attract veteran passengers in the over-sixty age group.

Contacts. ✉ *1000 Corporate Dr., Suite 500, Fort Lauderdale, FL 33334* ☎ *954/776–6123 or 877/505–5370* ⊕ *www.rssc.com.*

SEVEN SEAS MARINER
Itineraries. For 2008 *Mariner* will sail one-way from Vancouver or Seward, including stops at Sitka, Juneau, Skagway, Ketchikan, or Campbell River, BC, and scenic cruising at Hubbard Glacier and Tracy Arm Fjord.

Public Areas & Facilities. The world's first all-balcony, all-suite ship introduced the innovative Regent Seven Seas concept of luxury while retaining the tradition of stylish accommodations on a vessel with exceptionally generous space per passenger throughout. Lounges feature large expanses of glass to bring the sea views inside and fill interiors with sunlight. Mariner Lounge serves as a piano bar and a delightful spot to meet for predinner cocktails and conversation. A spiral staircase provides a grand entrance from the casino to Stars Nightclub, a late-night dance club.

Restaurants. Four restaurants function on an open-seating basis with no dining assignments. In addition to Compass Rose, the main dining room, choices include Signatures, Le Cordon Bleu restaurant (reservations required); Latitudes (reservations required); and La Veranda, the daytime buffet that's converted to an evening bistro serving Mediterranean cuisine. A poolside grill and Lido buffet serve casual daytime meals, afternoon tea is offered daily, and room service is available 24 hours. Passengers can select items from the full Compass Rose dining room menu during dinner hours to be served in their suites or on their balconies, a particularly pleasant option during a late port departure.

Accommodations. Rich, textured fabrics and warm-wood finishes add a touch of coziness to the larger-than-usual suite accommodations in all categories. Every suite is furnished with an entertainment center with CD/DVD player, stocked refrigerator and bar, and personal safe. Marble bathrooms have a combination tub–shower. Master suites have two bedrooms and a separate sitting–dining room, as well as a guest powder room and two full baths, not to mention two balconies. Other suites have a single bedroom. The top three suite categories have Bose Wave Music Systems; butler service is available for passengers in Master, Grand, Navigator, Penthouse, and Horizon suites. Depending on location, the dimensions of upper-category suites may vary; those located aft are larger than those located mid-ship and have considerably larger balconies. A dozen aft-facing Horizon Suites have extended balconies that almost double the usable space. Although some suites accommodate three people, none have interior adjoining doors. Six suites are designed for wheelchair accessibility and are equipped with showers only.

ROYAL CARIBBEAN INTERNATIONAL

Big, bigger, biggest! More than a decade ago, Royal Caribbean launched the first of the modern megacruise liners for passengers who enjoy traditional cruising with a touch of daring and whimsy tossed in. All Royal Caribbean ships are topped by the company's distinctive signature Viking Crown Lounge, and expansive multideck atriums and the generous use of floor-to-ceiling glass windows give each vessel a sense of spaciousness and style.

A variety of lounges and high-energy stage shows draws passengers of all ages out to mingle and dance the night away. Comedians, acrobats, magicians, jugglers, and solo entertainers fill show lounges on nights when the ships' singing and dancing companies aren't performing. The action is nonstop in casinos and dance clubs after dark, although daytime hours are filled with games and traditional cruise activities. Port "talks" tend to lean heavily on shopping recommendations and the sale of shore excursions.

Food. Dining is an international experience with nightly changing themes and cuisines from around the world. Passenger preference for casual attire and a resortlike atmosphere has prompted the cruise line to add laid-back alternatives to the formal dining rooms in the Windjammer Café and, on certain ships, the sunny Seaview Café evokes an island beachside stand. Royal Caribbean doesn't place emphasis on celebrity chefs or specialty alternative restaurants, although they have introduced a more upscale and intimate dinner experience in the form of Portofino, an Italian-specialty restaurant, and Chops Grille, a steak house, on Radiance-class ships.

Fitness & Recreation. Royal Caribbean has pioneered such new and unheard-of features as rock-climbing walls, ice-skating rinks, bungee trampolines, and even the first self-leveling pool tables on a cruise ship. Exercise facilities vary by ship class but all Royal Caribbean ships have state-of-the-art exercise equipment and jogging tracks, and passengers can work out independently or participate in a variety of basic exercise classes. Most classes are included in the fare, but there's a fee for specialized spinning, yoga, and Pilates classes, as well as the services of a personal trainer. Spas and salons are top-notch, with full menus of day spa–style treatments and services to pamper and relax adults and teens.

Dress Code. Two formal nights are standard on seven-night cruises; one formal night is the norm on shorter sailings. Men are encouraged to wear tuxedoes, but dark suits or sport coats and ties are more prevalent. All other evenings are casual, although jeans are discouraged in restaurants. It's requested that no shorts be worn in public areas after 6 PM, although there are passengers who can't wait to change into them after dinner.

Kids. Supervised age-appropriate activities are designed for children ages 3 through 17; babysitting services are available as well (either group sitting or individual in-stateroom babysitting, but sitters will not change diapers). Children are assigned to the Adventure Ocean youth program by age. For infants and toddlers 6 to 36 months of age, interactive playgroup sessions combine fun and learning time in the company of other tots and parents. A teen center with a disco is an adult-free gathering spot that will satisfy even the pickiest teenagers. A flat-rate soda card program is a bonus for family budgets—children can have all the fountain soft drinks they desire for a single charge. Pluses are "family-size" staterooms on all ships currently sailing in Alaska; drawbacks are the small standard cabins in the older vessels and the lack of self-service laundry facilities.

Tipping. Tips can be prepaid when the cruise is booked, added onto shipboard accounts, or given in cash on the last night of the cruise. Suggested gratuities per passenger, per day, are: $3.50 for the cabin steward (or $5.75 for suite attendant); $3.50 for the waiter; $2 for the assistant waiter; and $0.75 for the head waiter. Passengers may adjust the amounts based on the level of service experienced. An automatic 15% gratuity is automatically added to all bar tabs.

Service. Service on Royal Caribbean ships is friendly, but not consistent. Assigned meal seatings assure that most passengers get to know the waiters and their assistants, who in turn get to know the passengers' likes and dislikes; however, that can lead to a level of familiarity that some find uncomfortable.

Your Shipmates. Royal Caribbean cruises have a broad appeal for active couples and singles, mostly in their thirties to fifties. Families are partial to the newer vessels that have larger staterooms, huge facilities for children and teens, and plenty of choices for activities and dining options.

Contacts. ⊠ *1050 Royal Caribbean Way, Miami, FL 33132–2096* ☎ *305/ 539–6000 or 800/327–6700* ⊕ *www.royalcaribbean.com.*

RADIANCE OF THE SEAS, SERENADE OF THE SEAS

Itineraries. In 2008 *Radiance of the Seas* will sail one-way from either Anchorage or Vancouver and stop at Ketchikan, Juneau, Skagway, and Icy Strait Point and cruise Hubbard Glacier; *Serenade of the Seas* will sail round-trip from Vancouver, stopping at Juneau, Skagway, and Icy Strait Point or Ketchikan and cruising Hubbard Glacier.

Public Areas & Facilities. Considered by many people to be the most beautiful vessels in the Royal Caribbean fleet, these Radiance-class ships are large but sleek and swift, with sun-filled interiors and panoramic elevators that span 10 decks along the ships' exteriors. High-energy and glamorous spaces are abundant throughout these sister-ships. From the rock-climbing wall, children's pool with water slide, and golf area, to the columned dining room, sweeping staircases, and the tropical garden of the solarium, these ships have something to offer to a wide range of interests and tastes.

Restaurants. The double-deck formal dining room serves meals in two evening seatings and is supplemented by Portofino Italian restaurant and Chops Grill steak house, each of which requires reservations and a supplemental charge. The casual Lido buffet serves three meals a day, and the Seaview Café is open for quick lunches and dinners. A pizzeria in the Solarium serves pizza by the slice; Latte-Tudes patisserie sells specialty coffees, pastries, and ice cream. Room service is available 24 hours.

Accommodations. With the line's highest percentage of outside cabins, standard staterooms are bright and cheery as well as roomy. Nearly three-quarters of the outside cabins have private balconies. Every cabin has adequate closet and drawer–shelf storage, as well as bathroom shelves. Particularly spacious family ocean-view cabins, which sleep up to six people and can accommodate a rollaway bed and/or crib, have two twin beds (convertible into queen-size), additional bunk beds in a separate area, a sitting-room space with sofa bed, a vanity area, and bathroom with shower. All full suites and family suites have private balconies; full suites include concierge service. Nineteen staterooms are designed for wheelchair accessibility.

RHAPSODY OF THE SEAS

Itineraries. In 2008 *Rhapsody of the Seas* will sail round-trip from Seattle with stops at Juneau, Skagway, Vancouver, and Prince Rupert, BC, and cruising Tracy Arm Fjord.

Public Areas & Facilities. The first Royal Caribbean ships to offer private balconies in a number of categories, Vision-class vessels, which includes *Rhapsody of the Seas,* have acres of glass skylights that allow sunlight to flood in and windows that offer wide sea vistas. The soaring central atrium at the heart of each ship is anchored by champagne bars and fills with music after dark. Entertainment is the focus of a variety of lounges and cozy bars spread throughout mid-level decks and in Viking Crown Lounges, which overlook the Lido deck and the horizon beyond. Vision-class ships were the first in Royal Caribbean's fleet to include indoor-outdoor solarium pools with adjacent fitness centers and spas.

Restaurants. The double-deck-high formal dining room serves meals in two assigned evening seatings. Windjammer, the casual Lido buffet, serves three meals a day, including a laid-back dinner. Room service is available 24 hours.

Accommodations. Cabins are airy and comfortable, but the smaller categories are a tight squeeze for more than two adults. Every cabin has adequate closet and drawer–shelf storage, as well as bathroom shelves. Family ocean-view cabins, which sleep up to six people, have two twin beds, additional bunk beds in a separate area, separate sitting area with sofa bed, and one bathroom with a shower. The number of staterooms that contain third- and fourth-passenger berths or have connecting doors to adjacent cabins varies, but nearly all balcony rooms have a sofa bed. Fourteen staterooms are designed for wheelchair accessibility.

SILVERSEA CRUISES

Intimate ships are the hallmarks of Silversea luxury cruises. All-inclusive fares include not just all beverages on board, but gratuities as well. Personalization is a Silversea maxim. Their ships offer more activities than other comparably sized luxury vessels, although you can also opt to read in any number of quiet spots.

Guest lecturers are featured on nearly every cruise; language, dance, and culinary lessons and excellent wine-appreciation sessions are always on the schedule of events. During afternoon tea, ladies gather for conversation over needlepoint, and the ranks of highly competitive trivia teams increase every successive afternoon. After dark the bar is a predinner gathering spot and the late-night place for dancing to a live band. A multitiered show lounge is the setting for spirited production shows, classical concerts, magic shows, big-screen movies, and folkloric entertainers from ashore. A small casino offers slot machines and gaming tables.

Food. Dishes from the galleys of Silversea's master chefs are complemented by those of La Collection du Monde, created by Silversea's culinary partner, the chefs of Relais & Châteaux. Special off-menu orders are prepared whenever possible, provided that the ingredients are available on board. A highlight of every cruise is the Galley Brunch, when passengers are invited into the galley to select from a feast decorated with imaginative ice and vegetable sculptures. Even when meals are served buffet-style in the Terrace Café, you'll seldom have to carry your own plate as waiters are at hand to assist you to your table. Wines are chosen to complement each day's luncheon and dinner menus.

Fitness & Recreation. The small gym is equipped with cardiovascular and weight-training equipment, and fitness classes are held in the mirror-lined, but somewhat confining, exercise room. South Pacific–inspired Mandara Spa offers numerous treatments including exotic sounding massages, facials, and body wraps. A plus is that appointments for spa and beauty salon treatments can be made online from 60 days until 48 hours prior to sailing. Golfers can sign up with the pro on board for individual lessons utilizing a high-tech swing analyzer and attend complimentary golf clinics or participate in a putting contest.

Dress Code. Two formal nights are standard on seven-night cruises and three to four nights, depending on the itinerary, on longer sailings. Men are required to wear tuxedos or dark suits after 6 PM. All other evenings are either informal, when a jacket is called for (a tie is optional, but most men wear them), or casual, when slacks with a jacket over an open-collar shirt for men and sporty dresses or skirts or pants with a sweater or blouse for women are suggested.

Kids. Silversea Cruises is adult-oriented and unable to accommodate children less than one year of age, and the cruise line limits the number of children under the age of three on board. No dedicated children's facilities are available, so parents are responsible for the behavior and entertainment of their children.

Tipping. Tipping is neither required nor expected.

Service. Personalized service is carried out with precision; the staff strive for perfection and often achieve it. The attitude is decidedly European and begins with a welcome-aboard flute of champagne, then continues throughout as personal preferences are remembered and satisfied.

Your Shipmates. Silversea Cruises appeal to sophisticated, affluent couples who enjoy the country-clublike atmosphere, exquisite cuisine, and polished service.

Contacts. ✉ *110 E. Broward Blvd., Fort Lauderdale, FL 33301* ☎ *954/ 522–4477 or 800/722–9955* ⊕ *www.silversea.com.*

SILVER SHADOW

Itineraries. In 2008 *Silver Shadow* will make 9-day round-trip voyages from Vancouver, 10-day cruises between Anchorage and Vancouver or Vancouver and San Francisco, and one 12-day San Francisco round-trip sailing. Port calls vary by sailing and include Ketchikan, Juneau, Skagway, Wrangell, Sitka, Haines, Valdez, Prince Rupert, BC, or Victoria, BC, and scenic cruising in College Fjord, Hubbard Glacier, or Sawyer Glacier.

Public Areas & Facilities. The logical layout of this ship, with suites in the forward two-thirds of the ship and public rooms aft, makes orientation simple. Large expanses of glass for sunshine and sea views in public areas enhance passenger comfort. Silversea ships boast unbeatable libraries stocked with books and movies for in-suite viewing. Extremely wide passageways in public areas are lined with glass-front display cabinets full of interesting and unusual artifacts from the places the ship visits. The Humidor by Davidoff is a clubby cigar smoking room with overstuffed leather seating and a ventilation system that even non-smokers can appreciate.

Restaurants. The formal restaurant offers open-seating during scheduled hours and is more than large enough to seat all passengers at once. For a more casual setting, the Terrace Café has indoor and outdoor seating for buffet-style breakfast and lunch and is transformed nightly into a reservations-only alternative dining room with theme menus. A gourmet alternative for dinner (by reservation only) is intimate Le Champagne—unlike other dining venues, there's a charge for the exclusive dinners served with vintage wines in Le Champagne. The ultracasual poolside grill offers an alternative luncheon option. Always available are extensive selections from the room-service menu. The full restaurant menu may also be used for room-service orders that can be served course by course in your suite during dining hours.

Accommodations. Every suite is outside with an ocean view, and more than 80% have a private teak-floor balcony. Standard suites have a sitting area that can be curtained off from the bed for more privacy and an entertainment center with a TV and DVD or VCR, hair dryer, a cocktail cabinet, personal safe, and a refrigerator stocked with complimentary beer, soft drinks, and bottled water. Marble bathrooms come with huge towels and terry robes for use during the cruise, and have double sinks and a separate, glass-enclosed shower as well as a tub. In addition to the regular suite amenities, Grand, Royal, and Owner's suites have either one or two separate bedrooms, living room, dining area, CD player, flat-screen TV, as well as a second TV and dressing table in the bedrooms, bidet and whirlpool tub in the master bathroom, and a guest powder room. Even more perks include complimentary laundry service and a butler to help you pack and unpack suitcases, draw your bubble bath, or plan a private cocktail party; all are certified by the Guild of Professional English Butlers. Two suites are designed for wheelchair accessibility.

CRUISE SHIPS AT A GLANCE

	Cabins	Double Occupancy	Decks	Restaurants	In-Cabin VCR/DVD Players	Wi-Fi	Pool	Hot Tubs	Bars	Cinema	Library	Showroom	Children's Programs	Dance Clubs
Carnival														
Spirit	1062	2124	12	2	VCR (some)	yes	3	4	7	no	yes	1	ages 2–17	2
Celebrity														
Infinity/Millennium	975	1950	11	2	VCR (some)	yes	3	6	7	yes	yes	1	ages 3–17	1
Mercury	943	1886	10	1	VCR (some)	yes	3	5	7	yes	yes	1	ages 3–17	1
Holland America														
Amsterdam	680	1380	9	2	DVD	yes	2	2	6	yes	yes	1	ages 3–17	1
Oosterdam, Westerdam	924	1848	11	2	DVD	yes	2	5	9	yes	yes	1	ages 3–17	2
Volendam, Zaandam	720	1440	10	2	DVD	yes	2	2	6	yes	yes	1	ages 3–17	1
Ryndam, Statendam, Veendam	633	1258	10	2	DVD	yes	2	2	9	yes	yes	1	ages 3–17	1
Norwegian														
Pearl	1197	2394	15	8	DVD (some)	yes	2	4	9	yes	yes	1	ages 2–17	2
Star	1120	2240	11	10	DVD (some)	yes	3	6	9	yes	yes	1	ages 2–17	2
Sun	968	1936	10	6	DVD (some)	yes	3	5	8	yes	yes	1	ages 2–17	1
Princess														
Sun, Dawn	975	1950	10	3	no	yes	3	5	7	no	yes	2	ages 3–17	1
Coral, Island	985	1970	11	4	no	yes	3	5	7	no	yes	2	ages 3–17	2
Diamond, Sapphire	1337	2670	13	7	DVD (some)	yes	4	8	11	no	yes	2	ages 3–17	2
Golden	1300	2600	14	5	no	yes	4	9	9	no	yes	2	ages 3–17	2
Pacific	335	670	9	3	no	yes	1	2	8	no	yes	1	ages 3–17	1
Regent														
Mariner	350	700	8	3	DVD	yes	1	2	5	no	yes	1	ages 5–17	1
Royal Caribbean														
Radiance, Serenade	1056	2112	12	3	VCR (some)	yes	2	3	11	yes	yes	1	ages 3–17	1
Vision	999	1998	11	1	VCR (some)	yes	2	6	6	no	yes	1	ages 3–17	1
Silversea Cruises														
Silver Shadow	141	382	7	3	DVD	yes	1	3	3	no	yes	1	no	1

**all ships on this list have in-cabin safes, in-cabin refrigerators, laundry service and dry cleaning, hair salons, gyms and fitness classes, spas, saunas, steam rooms, and casinos, dance clubs, and showrooms

AMERICAN SAFARI CRUISES

NEW VESSELS FOR 2008

American Safari Cruises plans to double its Alaska capacity in 2008 when the 150-foot, 39-passenger yacht *Safari Explorer*, and a 108-foot, six-passenger, charter-only boat *Safari Legacy* join the fleet. While details were sketchy at press time, both vessels are scheduled to begin cruising Alaska waters in May 2008.

"Luxury in pursuit of adventure" is the tagline for this high-end yacht-cruise line, which operates some of the smallest vessels in Alaska. With just 12 to 21 passengers and such decadent amenities as ocean-view hot tubs, American Safari's yachts are among the most comfortable small ships cruising Alaska.

Shallow drafts mean these little ships and their landing craft can reach hidden inlets and remote beaches and slip in for close-up looks at glaciers and wildlife. Itineraries are usually flexible; there's no rush to move on if the group spots a pod of whales or a family of bears. All sailing is in daylight, with nights spent at anchor in secluded coves, and the yachts stop daily to let you kayak, hike, or beachcomb. An onboard naturalist offers informal lectures and guides you on shore expeditions. Guests on all ships have access to the bridge, so they can sip coffee and chat with the captain during the day. All three ships carry exercise equipment, kayaks, mountain bikes, Zodiac landing crafts, and insulated Mustang suits for Zodiac excursions. All shore excursions and activities are included in the price.

Food. The chefs serve a choice of nicely presented dinner entrées, featuring fresh local ingredients and plenty of seafood. All cruises are offered as all-inclusives, so premium wines and liquors are available at every meal.

Tipping. All shore excursions and alcoholic drinks are included in the fare. Tips are discretionary, but 5% to 10% of the fare is suggested. A lump sum is pooled among the crew at the end of the cruise.

Your Shipmates. Unlike most other yachts, which have to be chartered, American Safari's vessels sail on a regular schedule and sell tickets to individuals: there's no need to charter the whole ship, though that is an option. Many people charter the entire ship for family reunions and other group events.

Contacts. ✑ *American Safari Cruises, 19221 36th Ave. W, Suite 208, Lynnwood, WA 98036* ☎ *206/284–0300 or 888/862–8881* ⊕ *www.amsafari.com.*

SAFARI QUEST

Itineraries. *Quest* will make weeklong, one-way Inside Passage sailings between Juneau and Sitka. There are two two-week repositioning cruises between Seattle and Juneau.

Public Areas & Facilities. American Safari's largest vessel, this luxurious yacht has warm wood trim throughout. There's plenty of outer deck space for taking in the views, and a lounge on the top deck is a pleasant hideaway from which to take in the views while relaxing.

Accommodations. The four higher-end Admiral staterooms have sliding glass doors leading to a balcony. Five rooms have elevated portlights rather than picture windows. One stateroom is reserved for single travelers; the rest have king or queen beds.

Fast Facts. ⚓*11 cabins, 21 passengers, 4 passenger decks ᓚ Dining room, in-cabin DVDs, in-cabin VCRs, gym, outdoor hot tub, bar, library; no smoking.*

SAFARI ESCAPE

Itineraries. *Escape* offers eight-night cruises, May through August, one-way between Juneau and Prince Rupert, BC. There are two two-week repositioning cruises between Seattle and Juneau.

Public Areas & Facilities. Although *Escape* is one of Alaska's smallest cruise ships, it comes with all kinds of creature comforts usually associated with bigger ships, including exercise equipment, mountain bikes, and, in one cabin, a private sauna. An enclosed flybridge at the top of the yacht offers 360-degree views of the passing scenery and wildlife. Everyone dines together at one large table; lunch might be a gourmet picnic on a secluded beach.

Accommodations. Mariner staterooms have queen or twin beds and portholes rather than windows. The higher-end staterooms have a king- or queen-size bed and a window. All have rich fabrics and wood paneling.

Fast Facts. ⚓*6 cabins, 12 passengers, 3 decks ᓚ Dining room, in-cabin DVDs, in-cabin VCRs, gym, outdoor hot tub; no smoking.*

SAFARI SPIRIT

Itineraries. *Spirit* makes weeklong, one-way Inside Passage cruises between May and August. There are two two-week repositioning cruises between Seattle and Juneau.

Public Areas & Facilities The *Safari Spirit* is one of Alaska's most luxurious yachts. A forward-facing library with a 180-degree view, covered outside deck space, an on-deck hot tub, and even a sauna–steam bath are part of the pampering. Excellent meals are served at one grand table.

Accommodations. The bright, cheerful cabins, all with plush bedding, Jacuzzi bathtubs, and heated bathroom floors, are among the roomiest in the American Safari fleet. Three have king-size beds and balconies, and the other three have queen- or twin-size beds.

Fast Facts. ⚓*6 cabins, 12 passengers, 4 decks ᓚ Dining room, in-cabin DVDs, in-cabin VCRs, gym, outdoor hot tub, sauna, bar; no smoking.*

MAJESTIC AMERICA LINE

In the 19th century, paddle wheelers were a key part of Alaska's coastal transport, taking adventurers and gold seekers north. In 2003 *Empress of the North* became the first overnight stern-wheeler to ply these waters in 100 years. This faithful re-creation recalls the grand coastal paddle wheelers of the past, from the lavish interior to the paddle wheel powering the ship. A naturalist and historian give lectures on local history and culture. Gold-rush follies, Russian-American dances, and Native American songs and dances bring the region's past to life. Variety shows, ranging from golden oldies and big bands to country-and-western, play nightly. A shore excursion is included at each port of call, including a trip on the White Pass and Yukon Railroad. Adding yet another dimension to Alaska small-ship cruising, Majestic America introduced *Contessa* in 2007. The intimate yachtlike ship accommodates 48 passengers on three decks. With an unusual catamaran hull and excellent viewing platform, *Contessa* affords close-up access to Alaska's most breathtaking sights. A jet boat tour of the Stikine River, one of America's last wild waterways, is included.

Because the ships are highly maneuverable and have shallow drafts, they are able to explore intriguing places larger ships are unable to reach. In Alaska, that makes small inlets and narrow fjords open to their access. Additionally, their captains have latitude when it comes to the day's itinerary and, depending on weather conditions, can take the vessels to the day's best viewing options.

Food. A gourmet chef prepares five-star cuisine, featuring Pacific Northwest beef and fish, although the staff easily caters to vegetarians and special diets, too. The Captain's farewell dinner is a special—and informal—occasion to savor truly exceptional food.

Tipping. As with most small ships, tips are pooled by the crew at the end of the cruise. A tip of $12 to $14 per person per night is suggested.

Your Shipmates. These novel small ships attract passengers from all over the world—Italy, Spain, Australia—with an average age of about sixty-plus, and include a few families.

Contacts. ⌕ *Majestic America Line, 2101 4th Ave., Suite 1150, Seattle, WA98121* ☎*206/292–9606 or 800/434–1232* ⊕*www.majesticamericaline.com.*

CONTESSA

Itineraries. In developments at press time, it appears that Majestic America Line's *Contessa* is unlikely to sail in Alaska in 2008, although no definitive announcement has been made. If it does sail in 2008, from May through September, *Contessa* will make seven-night, one-way sailings between Ketchikan and Sitka, with calls at Wrangell and Juneau and cruising in Thomas Bay, Le Conte Glacier, Silver Bay, or Dawes Glacier. All sailings include scenic cruising in Glacier Bay National Park.

Public Areas & Facilities. There are only two public rooms—the Explorer Dining Room aft and Vista View Lounge forward on Main Deck. Outside, open areas on Observation Deck and Main Deck are the best spots to view wildlife and calving glaciers. Dining is small-ship casual, with open seating and no need to dress formally. *Contessa* has no elevators and is not recommended for the physically challenged.

Accommodations. All cabins have large windows with either queen-size beds or twins that can be converted to a queen. Only the two President's Suites have a television, DVD player, small refrigerator, and sitting area.

Fast Facts. ⤳*24 cabins, 48 passengers, 3 passenger decks* ⌂*Dining room, some in-cabin DVDs, 1 bar.*

EMPRESS OF THE NORTH

Itineraries. In 2008, May through September, the *Empress* will make seven-night, round-trip sailings from Juneau, with stops at Skagway, Sitka, Petersburg, Wrangell, and Dawes Glacier. All cruises include a visit to Glacier Bay National Park. In April and September the *Empress* will offer 12-night Inside Passage cruises between Seattle and Juneau.

Public Areas & Facilities. Alaskan art and historical artifacts enrich the public areas, and the staterooms mimic Victorian opulence, with lush fabrics and rich colors. The chandelier-lighted dining room looks formal, but is actually small-ship casual, with open seating and no need to dress up. There are two elevators that go to all four decks.

Accommodations. All cabins have big picture windows, and most have balconies. There are lavish two-room suites, as well as singles and triples. Two wheelchair-accessible cabins are available.

Fast Facts. ⤳*112 cabins, 235 passengers, 4 passenger decks* ⌂*Dining room, café, 2 elevators, in-cabin DVDs, 3 bars, showroom.*

CRUISE WEST

A big player in small ships, Seattle-based Cruise West is family-owned, and this is reflected in the ships' homey atmosphere. Alaskan wilderness, wildlife, and culture take precedence over shipboard diversions. Ports of call include small fishing villages and native settlements as well as major towns. An exploration leader, who is both a naturalist and cruise coordinator, offers evening lectures and joins passengers on many of the shore activities—at least one of which is included at each port of call. At some stops local guides come on board to add their insights, and schedules are flexible to make the most of wildlife sightings. Binoculars in every cabin, a library stocked with books of local interest (as well as movies on some ships), and crew members as keen to explore Alaska as the passengers all enhance the experience.

Food. The lounge feels like a living room, wholesome meals include bread baked on board, seating is open, and jeans are as formal as it gets.

Tipping. Tips are included in most Cruise West fares. For shore excursions and land extension, $2 to $3 for drivers and $5 per day for shore exploration leaders is suggested. All ships prohibit smoking indoors, and there is limited smoking space outdoors.

Your Shipmates. The passengers, who inevitably get to know one another during the cruise, are typically active, well-traveled over-fifties. They come from all regions of the United States, as well as from Australia, Canada, and the United Kingdom.

Contacts. ⌓ *Cruise West, 2301 5th Ave., Suite 401, Seattle, WA98121* ☎*206/441–8687 or 888/851–8133* ⊕*www.cruisewest.com.*

SPIRIT OF GLACIER BAY
Itineraries. From May through August *Nantucket* offers three- and four-night getaway cruises from Juneau featuring two nights in Glacier Bay; in May and September, 10-night sailings between Juneau and Seattle.

Public Areas & Facilities. The Observation Lounge features expansive picture windows, a video and lending library, plus cozy banquettes and conversation circles for getting to know your fellow travelers.

Accommodations. Every stateroom features a wide picture window or porthole, private facilities, a writing desk and ample storage.

Fast Facts. ⤳*51 cabins, 102 passengers, 2 decks* ⌓ *Dining room, in cabin DVDs, in-cabin VCRs, gym, outdoor hot tub, sauna, bar; no smoking.*

SPIRIT OF OCEANUS
Itineraries. The *Oceanus* sails one-way cruises between Vancouver and Whittier for 12 nights via Metlakatla, Misty Fjords, Petersburg, Skagway, Glacier Bay, Sitka, Tracy Arm, and Prince William Sound. Also available in July is a 13-night voyage to the Bering Sea, from Whittier to Nome via Kodiak, Katmai National Park, Shumagin Islands, Dutch Harbor, Pribilof Islands, remote islands in the Yukon Delta National Wildlife Refuge and Russia's Chukotka Peninsula, Arctic Circle, Bering Sea. The Bering Sea cruise can be combined with a 12-night cruise for a 24-night sailing called In Harriman's Wake.

Public Areas & Facilities. Cruise West's flagship vessel is also its most luxurious, with marble and polished wood in the dining room, lounges, game room and library, and cabins. Four of the five decks have outside viewing areas and there's an elevator on board. The ship, equipped with stabilizers for open-ocean cruising, also carries a fleet of inflatable excursion craft for close-up visits to glaciers, waterfalls, and icebergs. Breakfast and lunch are served on deck when the weather permits.

Accommodations. All staterooms are outside suites and have large marble bathrooms, a lounge area, and walk-in closets. They can either be configured with twin beds or a king-size bed. Fifteen of them have teak-floor private balconies.

Fast Facts. ⤴*59 cabins, 120 passengers, 5 decks* ♿*Dining room, in-cabin safes, refrigerators, in-cabin VCRs, in-cabin phones, Wi-Fi, gym, Internet terminal, outdoor hot tub, bar, laundry service; no smoking.*

SPIRIT OF ENDEAVOUR

Itineraries. The *Spirit of Endeavour* sails Inside Passage cruises for eight nights between Juneau and Ketchikan via Misty Fjords, Metlakatla, Petersburg, Frederick Sound, Tracy Arm, Sitka, Glacier Bay, Skagway, and Haines and 10-night Inside Passage cruises between Juneau and Seattle.

Public Areas & Facilities. One of Cruise West's largest and fastest ships, the *Endeavour* has a roomy lounge with large picture windows for superb views. There's ample deck space both on the stern where everyone gathers to observe wildlife, and also on the upper decks, which are good for watching sunsets or walking a few minilaps before dinner (to burn off the cookies the chef might bake during cocktail hour). Passengers can head out on Zodiacs to get closer to the water and touch icebergs. As with Cruise West's other ships, itineraries are flexible: the captain can linger to let passengers watch a group of whales, and still make the next stop on time.

Accommodations. Most of the cabins have picture windows, and some have connecting doors, which make them convenient for families traveling together. Most cabins have twin beds, although a couple have queens. Bathrooms are small, but comfortable.

Fast Facts. ⤴*51 cabins, 102 passengers, 4 passenger decks* ♿*Dining room, some refrigerators, in-cabin VCRs, Wi-Fi, bar; no smoking.*

SPIRIT OF '98

Itineraries. This ship offers one-way Inside Passage cruises between Juneau and Ketchikan that include Misty Fjords, Metlakatla, Petersburg, Frederick Sound, Tracy Arm, Sitka, Glacier Bay, Skagway, and Haines. There are also repositioning cruises between Juneau and Seattle.

Public Areas & Facilities. With rounded stern and wheelhouse, old-fashioned smokestack, and Victorian decor, the *Spirit of '98* evokes a turn-of-the-20th-century steamer, although she is actually a modern ship, built in 1984. Mahogany trim inside and out, overstuffed chairs with plush floral upholstery, and an old-world bar and player piano in the grand salon add to the gold-rush-era motif. For private moments, you can find plenty of nooks and crannies aboard the ship, including the cozy Soapy's Parlor bar at the stern.

Accommodations. All cabins, including the two single cabins on board, have picture windows. The Owner's Suite has a living room and a whirlpool tub. Some of the cabins are wheelchair accessible and there's an elevator between the main and upper decks. Bed sizes vary from twin to queen.

Fast Facts. ⤴*48 cabins, 96 passengers, 4 passenger decks* ♿*Dining room, some refrigerators, in-cabin VCRs, Wi-Fi, bar; no smoking.*

SPIRIT OF DISCOVERY

Itineraries. The *Spirit of Discovery* sails an eight-day Inside Passage route round-trip from Juneau to Gastineau Channel, Tracy Arm, Sitka, Frederick Sound, Icy Strait, Elfin Cove, Glacier Bay National Park, and a port call at a remote Alaskan Village. Ten-night repositioning cruises are scheduled between Juneau and Seattle in May and September.

Public Areas & Facilities. Floor-to-ceiling windows in the main lounge provide stunning views aboard this snazzy cruiser. From here, passengers have direct access to a large outdoor viewing deck, one of two aboard.

Accommodations. The *Spirit of Discovery* has six classes of cabins, including two cabins reserved for single travelers. All cabins have large picture windows, and most of them have twin beds.

Fast Facts. *43 cabins, 84 passengers, 3 decks ♿ Dining room, some in-cabin VCRs, bar; no smoking.*

SPIRIT OF ALASKA

Itineraries. *Spirit of Alaska* sails eight-night Inside Passage journeys round-trip from Juneau to Gastineau Channel, Tracy Arm, Sitka, Frederick Sound, Icy Strait, Elfin Cove, Glacier Bay National Park, and a port call at a remote Alaskan Village. Ten-night repositioning cruises are scheduled between Juneau and Seattle in May and September.

Public Areas & Facilities. The sleek *Spirit of Alaska* carries a fleet of inflatable excursion craft for impromptu stops at isolated beaches and close-up looks at glaciers. She's also able to do bow landings, enabling passengers to go ashore at isolated spots without docks.

Accommodations. Most cabins are small but cheerfully decorated with light wood paneling and bright checkered bedspreads. Toilets and showers are a combined unit (the toilet is inside the shower). Top-deck cabins have windows on two sides, so you can sample both port and starboard views. Solo travelers can book a lower-deck cabin with no single supplement.

Fast Facts. *39 cabins, 78 passengers, 4 passenger decks ♿ Dining room, some refrigerators, some in-cabin VCRs, bar; no TV in some cabins, no smoking.*

SPIRIT OF COLUMBIA

Itineraries. *Spirit of Columbia* will sail three- and four-night round-trip cruises from Anchorage/Whittier to College Fjord and Esther Passage, Icy Strait, Cordova (on four-day only), Change Glacier, and Knight Island. Ten-night repositioning cruises are scheduled between Juneau and Seattle in May and September.

Public Areas & Facilities. The *Columbia*'s interior is inspired by the national park lodges of the American West, with muted shades of evergreen, rust, and sand. Like the *Spirit of Alaska,* the *Columbia* can land at isolated spots without docks.

Accommodations. Cabins range from windowless inside units (which solo travelers can book with no single supplement) to comfortable staterooms with chairs and picture windows. The Columbia Deluxe cabin stretches the width of the vessel; just under the bridge, its row of forward-facing windows gives a captain's-eye view of the ship's progress.

Fast Facts. *38 cabins, 78 passengers, 4 passenger decks ☆ Dining room, some refrigerators, some in-cabin VCRs, bar; no TV in some cabins, no smoking.*

SPIRIT OF YORKTOWN

Itineraries. The *Yorktown* makes eight-night round-trip Inside Passage trips between Juneau and Ketchikan that include Skagway, Haines, Glacier Bay, Sitka, Tracy Arm, Frederick Sound, Petersburg, Metlakatla, and Misty Fjords. Ten-night repositioning cruises between Juneau and Seattle are scheduled for May and September.

Public Areas & Facilities. The *Spirit of Yorktown* looks more like a box yacht than a cruise ship. Its signature design is dominated by a large bridge and picture windows that ensure bright interior public spaces. In keeping with its small size, there are only two public rooms and deck space is limited. The glass-walled observation lounge does triple duty as the ship's bar, lecture room, and occasional movie "theater." A fleet of inflatable landing craft takes passengers ashore for independent exploration.

Accommodations. Most cabins have a picture window, but a few have portholes; none have televisions. Toilets and showers are a combined unit (the toilet is inside the shower). Although the larger top-deck staterooms are quite spacious, there are only eight of them. For 2007 cabins will be refurbished in keeping with the ship's new owner, Cruise West.

Fast Facts. *69 cabins, 138 passengers, 4 decks ☆ Dining room, in-cabin safes, bar, movies; no TV in cabins.*

LINDBLAD EXPEDITIONS

The ships of Lindblad Expeditions spend time looking for wildlife, exploring out-of-the-way inlets, and making Zodiac landings (on inflatable boats) at isolated beaches. Each ship has a fleet of kayaks as well as a video-microphone: a hydrophone (an underwater microphone that picks up whale calls) is combined with an underwater camera so passengers can listen to whale songs and watch live video of what's going on beneath the waves. In the evening, the ships' naturalists recap the day's sights and adventures over cocktails in the lounge. A video chronicler makes a film of the whole cruise for you to purchase. In July and August some family expeditions are offered. These follow the same itinerary as Lindblad's other trips, but include a crew member dedicated to running educational programs for school-age kids. All

Lindblad cruises offer substantial discounts for young people up to 21 traveling with their parents.

Food. Lindblad prides itself on serving fresh Alaska seafood, including Dungeness crab, halibut, and Alaska King salmon, but there are also plenty of meat and vegetarian options. Breakfast is buffet-style, and lunch is served family-style. The recently launched "Seafood for Thought" program is meant to ensure that sustainable seafood is being served.

Tipping. All shore excursions except flightseeing are included. Tips of $12–$15 per person per day are suggested; these are pooled among the crew at journey's end.

Your Shipmates. Lindblad attracts active, adventurous, well-traveled over-forties, and quite a few singles, as the line charges one of the industry's lowest single supplements. They are making a push, however, to be more family-friendly, and staff members have undergone extensive training to tailor activities toward children. Smoking is not permitted on board.

Contacts. ⌂ *Lindblad Expeditions, 96 Morton St., New York, NY10014* ☎ *212/765–7740 or 800/397–3348* ⊕ *www.expeditions.com.*

SEA BIRD, SEA LION

Itineraries. These ships sail eight-day one-way cruises from Juneau to Seattle, stopping in Tracy Arm, Petersburg, Frederick Sound, Glacier Bay, and Sitka (passengers disembark and fly together from Sitka to Seattle).

Public Areas & Facilities. These small, shallow-draft sister-ships can tuck into nooks and crannies that bigger ships can't reach. An open-top sundeck, forward observation lounge, and viewing deck at the bow offer plenty of room to take in the scenery. The ships are also equipped with bowcams (underwater cameras that monitor activity) and you can navigate the camera using a joystick to observe sea life. The ship's Internet kiosk provides e-mail access. Fitness equipment is set up on the bridge deck, and the LEX Wellness room offers massages, body treatments, and a morning stretching program on deck. A fleet of Zodiacs and kayaks can take you closer to the water.

Accommodations. These ships are comfortable, but public spaces and cabins are proportionally small. All staterooms are outside, and upper-category cabins have picture windows that open; the lowest category cabins have portholes that admit light, but do not open or afford a view. Most of the cabins have single beds that can convert to a double, and a few on the upper deck have pull-out beds to accommodate a third person. A functional in-cabin sink has good lighting over a square mirror and vanity that contains a hair dryer. A curtain separates the toilet and shower compartment in the "head"-style bathroom.

Fast Facts. ⟿ *31 cabins, 62 passengers, 3 passenger decks* ⚓ *Dining room, bar, library; no TV in cabins, no smoking.*

Ports of Embarkation

WORD OF MOUTH

"One of my most memorable meals, anywhere, was at the Granville Island Market. I bought smoked salmon from one retailer, buns from another, cream cheese, blueberries, etc. The only downside was that I ended up with lots of leftovers!"

—BAK

"Anchorage is home to the largest float plane fleet in the world. We have booked a float plane trip and when we told them we were only there one day and had no rental car, they said, no problem, we'll come pick you up!"

—peggi

MANY NORTHBOUND CRUISES BEGIN IN Vancouver, British Columbia, but Seattle has become an important port as well, with some cruise lines even setting up their own facilities at SeaTac airport. A few ships sail out of San Francisco or Los Angeles. Anchorage is the primary starting point for cruise passengers heading south, but ships don't actually dock there. Instead, travelers fly into and may overnight in Anchorage before being transported by bus or train to the ports of Seward or Whittier for southbound departures.

Cruise travelers frequently opt for combination packages that include an Inside Passage cruise plus a tour by bus or train through interior Alaska (and sometimes the Yukon). Denali National Park, located too far inland to be included on Inside Passage cruises, is a particular focus of these trips. Before or after the cruise, travelers with a more independent streak may want to rent a car, and strike out on their own to places not often visited by cruise ships, such as Homer or Valdez.

PORT ESSENTIALS

RESTAURANTS & CUISINE
Given the seaside location of the embarkation towns, it's no surprise that fresh fish and other seafood are especially popular. Fresh halibut and salmon are available throughout summer, along with specialties such as shrimp, oysters, and crab. Seafood meals can be simply prepared fast food, like beer-battered fish-and-chips, or more elaborate dinners of halibut baked in a macadamia nut crust with fresh mango chutney. If seafood isn't your first choice, rest assured that all the staples—including restaurants serving steaks, burgers, pizza, Mexican, or Chinese food—can also be found.

WHAT IT COSTS					
	¢	$	$$	$$$	$$$$
ANCHORAGE	under $10	$10–$15	$15–$20	$20–$25	over $25
SEATTLE	under $8	$8–$16	$16–$24	$24–$32	over $32
VANCOUVER	under C$8	C$8–C$12	C$12–C$20	C$20–C$30	over C$30

Restaurant prices are for a main course at dinner, excluding tip, taxes, service charges, and liquor charges.

ABOUT THE HOTELS
Whether you're driving or flying into your port of embarkation, it's often more convenient to arrive the day before or to stay for a day (or longer) after your cruise. Cruise travelers typically stay in one of the larger downtown hotels booked by the cruise lines in order to be closer to the ports, but you might like to make your own arrangements for a pre- or post-cruise sojourn. Therefore, we offer lodging suggestions for each port.

The hotels we list are convenient to the cruise port and the cream of the crop in each price category. Properties are assigned price categories based on the range between their least and most expensive standard double room at high season (excluding holidays).

Assume that all hotel rooms have air-conditioning and cable TV unless otherwise noted, and that hotels operate on the **European Plan** (EP, with no meals) unless we specify that they use either the **Continental Plan** (CP, with a continental breakfast), **Breakfast Plan** (BP, with a full breakfast), or the **Modified American Plan** (MAP, with breakfast and dinner). The following price categories are used in this book.

3

WHAT IS COSTS					
	¢	$	$$	$$$	$$$$
ANCHORAGE	under $100	$100–$150	$150–$200	$200–$250	over $250
SEATTLE	under $100	$100–$150	$150–$200	$200–$250	over $250
VANCOUVER	under C$100	C$100–C$150	C$150–C$200	C$200–C$250	over C$250

Prices are for two people in a standard double room in high season, excluding tax and service.

ANCHORAGE

Anchorage today is Alaska at its most urban. Nearly half of all Alaskans, 278,000 people, live in Anchorage, the state's only true metropolis. Superficially, Anchorage looks much like any other sprawling western American city, with Wal-Marts, espresso stands, and shopping malls, but here sled-dog racing is as popular as surfing is in California, and moose frequently roam city bike trails. The Chugach Mountains rise around the city in a striking, spiky frame, and the spectacular Alaskan wilderness is found just out the back door. Downtown Anchorage is famous for the colorful flowers that spill from hanging baskets and window boxes all summer long. There's a performing-arts center, a diversity of museums and shops, and scores of restaurants and brewpubs for you to sample.

Anchorage took shape with the construction of the federally funded Alaska Railroad, completed in 1923. With the tracks laid, the town's pioneer settlers actively sought expansion by hook and—not infrequently—by crook. City founders delighted in telling how they tricked a visiting U.S. congressman into dedicating the site for a federal hospital that had not yet been approved.

Boom and bust periods followed major events: an influx of military bases during World War II; a massive buildup of Arctic missile-warning stations early in the Cold War; and the construction of the trans-Alaska pipeline with the discovery of oil at Prudhoe Bay. Nearly all the city's buildings postdate the massive 1964 earthquake—one of the largest in recorded history.

VISITOR INFORMATION

Behind the sod-roof **Log Cabin Visitor Information Center** is a larger visitor center stocked with brochures. Fourth Avenue sustained heavy damage in the great 1964 earthquake. The businesses on this block withstood the destruction, but those a block east fell into the ground as the earth under them slid toward Ship Creek. ⊠ *4th Ave. and F St., Downtown* ☎ *907/274–3531* ⊕ *www.anchorage.net* ☾ *June–Aug., daily 7:30–7; May and Sept., daily 8–6; Oct.–Apr., daily 9–4.*

ON THE MOVE

GETTING TO THE PORT

Anchorage is the starting (or ending) point for many Alaskan cruises, but most passengers actually board or disembark their ships from Seward (125 mi south on Resurrection Bay). Seward is a three-hour bus ride or a four-hour train ride from Anchorage. The train station is a few blocks away from downtown Anchorage. Princess Cruises now stops at Whittier (59 mi southeast of Anchorage), on the western shore of Prince William Sound. Access between Anchorage and these ports is by bus or train, and is generally included as part of your cruise. You'll spend virtually no shore time there before you embark or after disembarkation—the buses and train also offer dock-to-airport service in both places. The few ships that do dock at Anchorage proper dock just north of downtown. There's an information booth on the pier. It's only a 15- or 20-minute walk from the town to the dock, but this is through an industrial area with heavy traffic, so it's best to take a taxi.

ARRIVING BY AIR

Ted Stevens Anchorage International Airport is 6 mi from downtown. Airport redevelopment has brought a new air terminal as well as an Alaska Railroad station. Trains stop downtown, in addition to direct service for cruise-ship companies transporting their passengers to Seward or Whittier. Taxis queue up outside baggage-claim. A ride downtown runs about $17, not including tip. Alaska Shuttle offers transport from the airport to downtown for $12 for one to three people; they also offer standard, taxi-type service around town.

🖫**Ted Stevens Anchorage International Airport** (☎ *907/266–2529* ⊕ *www.anchorageairport.com*). **Alaska Shuttle** (☎ *907/338–8888*) **Checker Cab** (☎ *907/276–1234*).

SEWARD OR WHITTIER?

For friendly information and to arrange reservations on major cruise lines operating in Alaska, contact the Cruise Web at ⊕ *www.cruiseweb.com* or phone (☎ 800/377–9383). Here's an easy rundown of which large cruise lines use Seward, Whittier, or both:

■ Carnival: Whittier

■ Celebrity: Seward

■ Holland America: Seward

■ Norwegian: neither

■ Princess: Whittier

■ Regent: Seward

ARRIVING BY CAR

The Glenn Highway enters Anchorage from the north and becomes 5th Avenue near Merrill Field; this route leads directly into downtown. Gambell Street leads out of town to the south, becoming New Seward Highway at about 20th Avenue. South of town, it becomes the Seward Highway.

RENTAL CARS

Anchorage is the ideal place to rent a car and explore sites farther afield before or after your cruise. National Car Rental has a downtown office. All the major companies (and several local operators) have airport desks and free shuttle service to the airport to pick up cars.

🚗Arctic Rent-a-Car (☎907/561–2990). **Budget** (☎907/243–0150). **Denali Car Rental** (☎907/276–1230). **National Car Rental** (✉1300 E. 5th Ave., Downtown ☎907/265–7553 ✉Ted Stevens International Airport ☎907/243–3406).

TAXIS

Downtown Anchorage is easy to navigate on foot. If you want to see some of the outlying attractions, such as Lake Hood, you'll need to hire a taxi. Taxis are on a meter system; rates start at $2 for pickup and $2 for each mile. Most people call for a cab, although it's possible to hail one.

🚗Alaska Yellow Cab (☎907/222–2222).

EXPLORING ANCHORAGE

❺ Anchorage's centerpiece is its distinctively modern **Alaska Center for the Performing Arts,** where musical, theatrical, and dance groups perform throughout the year. In summer, IMAX films are shown inside. Out front is flower-packed **Town Square,** a delightful place to relax on a sunny day. ✉621 W. 6th Ave., at G St. ☎907/263–2900, 800/478–7328 tickets ⊕www.alaskapac.org ⊗Daily 8–5. Free tours Wed. at 1 PM.

❶ Displays about Alaska's national parks, forests, and wildlife refuges can be seen at the **Alaska Public Lands Information Center.** The center also shows films highlighting different regions of the state and sells natural-history books. Guided walks to historic downtown sights depart daily. The Log Cabin Visitor Information Center is directly across the street. ✉605 W. 4th Ave., at F St. ☎907/271–2737 ⊕www.nps.gov/aplic ⊗Memorial Day–Labor Day, daily 9–5:30; day after Labor Day–Memorial Day, weekdays 10–5:30.

❻
♥
Fodor'sChoice
★
The **Anchorage Museum of History and Art** occupies the entire block at 6th Avenue and A Street, with an entrance on 7th Avenue. It houses a fine collection of historical and contemporary Alaskan art, displays on Alaskan history, and a special section for children. One gallery is devoted to views of Alaska, as seen by early explorers, painters, and contemporary artists. Informative 45-minute tours are given several times a day, and the café is an excellent lunch option. ✉121 W. 7th Ave.

Downtown

W. 2nd Ave.

❷

❸

W. 3rd Ave.

❶

◆ Eisenhower
Memorial

◆ Egan
Convention
Center

W. 4th Ave.

❹

◆ Log Cabin Visitor
Information Center

W. 5th Ave.

Central
Bus Depot

❺

W. 6th Ave.

L St.   K St.   J St.   H St.   G St.   F St.   E St.   D St.   C St.   B St.   A St.

W. 7th Ave.

❻

0   1/8 mile

0   200 meters

W. 8th Ave.

Elderberry
Park

N St.   K St.

W. 9th Ave.

Delaney Park

W. 10th Ave.

W. 11th Ave.

W. 13th Ave.

W. 15th Ave.

0   1/2 mile

0   800 meters

KEY

······ Coastal Trail

⊢——⊢ Rail Lines

Knik Arm

Cook Inlet

*Westchester
Lagoon*

W. Marston Dr.

Fish Creek

Hillcrest Dr.

Forest Park Dr.

Arlington Dr.

Turnagain Pkwy.

Northern Lights Blvd. W.

W. 29th St.

W. 30th Ave.

W. 31st Ave.

W. 32nd Ave.

Turnagain St.

Barbara St.

Benson Blvd.

Spenard Rd.

W. 34th Ave.

W. 35th Ave.

McRae Dr.

Lois Dr.

Minnesota Dr.

Spenard Rd.

Aero Ave.

Wisconsin Dr.

W. 40th Ave.

Northwood Dr.

Lois Dr.

*Lake
Hood*

44th Ave.

**Spenard
Beach**

↙ TO
AIRPORT

Lake Spenard

←❽

Anchorage

3

☎907/343–4326, 907/343–6173 *recorded information* ⊕*www.anchoragemuseum.org* ✉*$8* ⊙*Mid-May–mid-Sept., daily 9–6, Thurs. 9–9; mid-Sept.–mid-May, Tues.–Sat. 10–6, Sun. 1–5.*

② **Resolution Park,** a cantilevered viewing platform dominated by a monument to British explorer Captain Cook, looks out toward Cook Inlet and the mountains beyond. Mt. Susitna (locally called the Sleeping Lady) is the prominent low mountain to the northwest, and mounts Spurr and Redoubt, both active volcanoes, are just south of Mt. Susitna. To her north, Mt. McKinley, Mt. Foraker, and other peaks of the Alaska range are often visible more than 100 mi away. (Most Alaskans prefer the traditional, native name for this peak, Denali.) ⊠*3rd Ave. and L St.*

③ The paved Tony Knowles Coastal Trail runs along Cook Inlet for about 11 mi and is accessible from the west end of 2nd Avenue. This is a wonderful place to take in the view or to join the throngs of folks walking, running, biking, or skating. Next to the trail at the north end of tiny Elderberry Park is the **Oscar Anderson House Museum.** It was Anchorage's first permanent frame house, built in 1915. Tours are included in your admission. In late summer the park is a good place to watch for porpoise-size beluga whales in Cook Inlet. ⊠*420 M St.* ☎*907/274–2336* ✉*$3* ⊙*June–mid-Sept., weekdays noon–5.*

④ A fun stop for both children and adults is the **Imaginarium,** an interactive ☪ science museum that lets kids stand inside a giant soap bubble, hold a starfish in the marine exhibit, or take a galaxy tour in the planetarium. There's also a great gift shop. ⊠*737 W. 5th Ave.* ☎*907/276–3179* ⊕*www.imaginarium.org* ✉*$5.50* ⊙*Mon.–Sat. 10–6, Sun. noon–5.*

OUTSIDE DOWNTOWN

⑧ The **Alaska Aviation Heritage Museum** at Lake Hood offers an excellent ☪ overview of Alaska's long love affair with the airplane. In addition to Fodor's Choice photos and artifacts from the past, there's a gallery of meticulously ★ restored and maintained vintage aircraft, true works of art in metal, wood, and canvas. There's also a workshop on the premises where you can watch dedicated volunteers busily re-creating and refurbishing the museum's backlog of classic planes, including a 1931 Pilgrim. ⊠*4721 Aircraft Dr.* ☎*907/248–5325* ✉*$10* ⊙*May 15–Sept. 15 open daily 9–5.*

⑦ On a 26-acre site facing the Chugach Mountains, the extraordinary Fodor's Choice **Alaska Native Heritage Center** introduces you to Alaska's native peoples ★ through displays, artifacts, photographs, demonstrations, performances, and films. Outside, you can explore five village exhibits, which circle a small lake. At each of these you can see traditional structures and Alaska natives demonstrating their heritage. A café and gift shop are on-site. ■TIP→ **The Heritage Center provides a free shuttle from the downtown Log Cabin Visitor Information Center several times a day in summer.** ⊠*8800 Heritage Center Dr., Glenn Hwy. at Muldoon Rd., 5 mi east of downtown* ☎*907/330–8000 or 800/315–6608* ⊕*www.alaskanative.net* ⊡*$23.50* ⊙*Mid-May–Sept., daily 9–5; Oct.–mid-May, Sat. noon–5.*

WHERE TO EAT

Smoking has been banned in all Anchorage restaurants, except for bars that also serve meals. Most local restaurants are open daily in summer, with reduced hours in winter. Only a few places require reservations, but it's always best to call ahead, especially for dinner. *(For price categories, see About the Restaurants, above.)*

$$$$
Fodor'sChoice
★
✕**Marx Brothers' Café.** Inside a little frame house built in 1916, this elegant and nationally recognized 46-seat café opened in 1979 and is still going strong. The menu changes weekly, and the wine list encompasses more than 400 international choices. The outstanding Caesar salad is a superb opener for the macadamia-encrusted baked halibut. If your schedule permits, sign up for one of the Caesar salad classes, given on select Saturdays—they're educational, delicious, and great fun. A second Marx Brothers' Café, housed in the Anchorage Museum of History and Art, provides casual dining for lunch and dinner. ⊠*627 W. 3rd Ave., Downtown* ☎*907/278–2133* ⊕*www.marxcafe.com* ⌂*Reservations essential* ▤*AE, DC, MC, V* ⊙*Closed Mon. Sept.–May. No lunch.*

$$$–$$$$
✕**Club Paris.** Alaska's oldest steak house has barely changed since opening in 1957, and most of the friendly staff have been here since the 1980s. The restaurant has dark woods and an old-fashioned feel and serves tender, flavorful steaks of all kinds, including a 4-inch-thick filet mignon. If you have to wait for a table, have a martini at the bar and order the hors d'oeuvres platter ($28)—a sampler of top sirloin steak, cheese, and prawns that could be a meal for two. Dinner reservations are advised. ⊠*417 W. 5th Ave., Downtown* ☎*907/277–6332* ⊕*www.clubparisrestaurant.com* ▤*AE, D, DC, MC, V* ⊙*No lunch Sun.*

$$–$$$$
✕**Kumagoro.** Stop at the take-out deli, which has such specialties as herring roe on kelp, or the sleek sushi bar (open evenings only). The best items on the dinner menu are the sizzling salmon and beef teriyaki, both served with miso soup and salad. With the *shabu-shabu* dinner ($52 for two people), you cook your own meats and vegetables in a stockpot of boiling broth. All entrée prices include a 10% gratuity. ⊠*533 W. 4th Ave., Downtown* ☎*907/272–9905* ▤*AE, D, DC, MC, V.*

> **"THE PLANE! THE PLANE!"**
>
> If you have the time, take a taxi to the **Lake Hood floatplane base,** where colorful aircraft come and go almost constantly in summer.
>
> The best vantage point is from the patio of the lounge at the **Millennium Anchorage Hotel** (⊠*4800 Spenard Rd., Lake Spenard* ☎*907/243–2300 or 800/544–0553*).

$$–$$$$ ✕**Orso.** One of Anchorage's culinary stars, Orso ("bear" in Italian) evokes the earthiness of a Tuscan villa. Alaskan touches flavor the rustic Italian dishes and locally famous desserts—most notably the molten chocolate cake. If you can't get a table at dinner (reservations are advised), you can select from the same menu at the large, open bar. The upstairs is quiet and cozy. ⊠*737 W. 5th Ave., Downtown* ☎*907/222–3232* ⊕*www.orsoalaska.com* ⊟*AE, D, DC, MC, V.*

$$–$$$$ ✕**Sacks Café.** This bright and colorful restaurant serves light American cuisine such as capellini primavera; chicken and scallops over udon noodles; and penne pasta. For the oenophile, wines are available to taste in flights that rotate monthly. Be sure to ask about the daily specials, particularly the fresh king salmon and halibut. Flowers adorn the tables, and singles congregate along a small bar, sampling wines. The café is especially crowded at lunch, served 11–2:30. ⊠*328 G St., Downtown* ☎*907/276–3546 or 907/274–4022* ⚐*Reservations essential* ⊟*AE, MC, V.*

$$–$$$$ ✕**Simon & Seafort's Saloon & Grill.** Big windows overlooking Cook Inlet vistas, high ceilings, and a classy brass-and-wood interior have made this an Anchorage favorite since 1978. The diverse menu includes prime rib (aged 28 days), pasta, and salads, but the main attraction here is seafood—fish is prepared any way you like. Try the king crab legs or the grilled ahi tuna with ginger and mango salsa. The Brandy Ice—vanilla ice cream whipped with brandy, Kahlúa, and crème de cacao—is deliciously decadent. The bar is a great spot for microbrews, single-malt scotch, and martinis; the best tables are adjacent to tall windows facing the water. ⊠*420 L St., Downtown* ☎*907/274–3502* ⊕*www.r-u-i.com/sim* ⚐*Reservations essential* ⊟*AE, DC, MC, V* ☾*No lunch weekends.*

$–$$$$ ✕**Glacier BrewHouse.** The scent of hops permeates the air in the cavernous, wood-beam BrewHouse where a dozen or so ales, stouts, lagers, and pilsners are brewed on the premises. Locals mingle with visitors in this noisy, always-busy heart-of-town restaurant where dinner selections include thin-crust, 10-inch pizzas, seafood chowder, whiskey barbecue pork ribs, and jambalaya fettuccine. For dessert, don't miss the wood-oven roasted apple and currant bread pudding. You can watch the hardworking chefs in the open kitchen. The brewery sits behind a glass wall, and the same owners operate the equally popular Orso, next door. ⊠*737 W. 5th Ave., Downtown* ☎*907/274–2739* ⊟*AE, D, DC, MC, V.*

$–$$$$ ✕**Snow Goose Restaurant.** Although you can dine indoors at this comfortable edge-of-downtown eatery, the real attraction at Snow Goose is alfresco dining on the back deck and rooftop. On clear days you can see Mt. McKinley on the northern horizon and the Chugach Mountains to the east of the city. The menu emphasizes Alaskan fare, but the beer and the view are the best reasons to visit. To sample the specialty beers, gather around oak tables in the upstairs bar for a brewed-on-the-premises ale, India Pale Ale, stout, barley wine, or porter. ⊠*717 W. 3rd Ave., Downtown* ☎*907/277–7727* ⊕*www.alaskabeers.com* ⊟*AE, D, DC, MC, V.*

¢–$$ ✕**F Street Station.** Space is at a premium in this minuscule downtown bar where the business crowd heads for a light meal. It isn't for kids, but the food is always delicious. The steak sandwich and cheeseburgers are good bets, but also look over the board's daily seafood specials. A giant block of cheese occupies one corner of the bar, and TVs are usually tuned to sports in this *Cheers*-type gathering place. ⊠*325 F St., Downtown* ☎*907/272–5196* ▭*AE, DC, MC, V.*

¢–$ ✕**Downtown Deli.** This popular café is across the street from the Log Cabin Visitor Information Center. Chow on familiar sandwiches or Alaskan favorites, like grilled halibut and reindeer stew. The rich chicken soup comes with noodles or homemade matzo balls; breakfasts range from omelets and homemade granola to cheese blintzes. Sit in one of the wooden booths or out front at the sidewalk tables for summertime people-watching. ⊠*525 W. 4th Ave., Downtown* ☎*907/276–7116* ⌂*Reservations not accepted* ▭*AE, D, DC, MC, V.*

¢–$ ✕**Snow City Cafe.** You'll find dependably good and reasonably priced breakfasts and lunches at this unassuming café along "lawyer row." Service is fast and the setting is a funky mix of mismatched chairs, Formica tables, and families and singles enjoying some of Anchorage's best breakfasts. A recent remodel has opened up the space considerably without sacrificing the original feel of the place. Breakfast is served all day, but arrive early on the weekend or be prepared to wait. Snow City's lunch menu consists of hot or cold sandwiches, fresh soups, and salads. The kitchen closes at 3 PM on weekdays and 4 PM on weekends. ⊠*4th Ave. and L St., Downtown* ☎*907/272–2489* ▭*AE, D, DC, MC, V* ⊗*No dinner.*

¢–$ ✕**Sweet Basil Café.** Lunchtime sandwiches (hot or cold) on freshly baked sweet basil bread are a hit at this small and earthy juice bar accented by lavender walls and a big map of the planet. Fresh pastas, salads, wraps, fish tacos, smoothies, pastries, and light breakfasts fill out the menu, but the daily specials are often your best bet. The juice bar is one of a handful in Anchorage, and the lattes may be the best downtown. ⊠*335 E St., Downtown* ☎*907/274–0070* ▭*AE, D, MC, V* ⊗*Closed weekends. No dinner.*

WHERE TO STAY

Lodging for most cruise-ship travelers is typically included in package tours set up through a travel agency, an online site, or directly from the cruise line. If you prefer to pick your own hotel or bed-and-breakfast, make your reservations well ahead of time since many central hotels fill up months in advance for the peak summer season. Fortunately, quite a few new hotels have been added to the Anchorage market in the past few years, so rooms are generally available, though you may be staying in midtown, 2 mi from downtown.

Several hotels in Anchorage have top-drawer amenities, with summertime rates to match. Smaller inns and 175 or so B&Bs offer character and quaint amenities at more modest prices. A complete source for lodging options is the Anchorage Convention & Visitors

Bureau's annual visitors guide; it's also available online at ⊕ *www. anchorage.net.*

For price categories, see About the Hotels at the beginning of this chapter.

$$$$ ⛱ **Anchorage Hilton.** Alaska's largest hotel is a block from the city center and fills with cruise-ship passengers all summer long. An inviting and ample lobby includes Alaskan touches and is flanked by a café and a classy sports bar. The hotel's premier restaurant, Top of the World, occupies the 15th floor of the west tower. Well-maintained rooms, decorated in a contemporary style with oak and maple furnishings, are in two towers, one of which is 22 stories high. Request a corner north-facing suite on the upper levels for Mt. McKinley vistas. ⊠ *500 W. 3rd Ave., Downtown* ☎ *907/272–7411 or 800/245–2527* ⊕ *www. hilton.com* ↩ *572 rooms, 23 suites* ⚼ *In-hotel: 3 restaurants, indoor pool, gym, in-room Ethernet, room service, concierge* ▤ *AE, D, DC, MC, V.*

$$$$ ⛱ **Anchorage Marriott Downtown.** One of Anchorage's biggest lodgings, the brightly decorated Marriott appeals to both business travelers and tourists. The hotel's Café Promenade serves American cuisine with an Alaskan flair. All guest rooms have huge windows and well-designed furnishings. If you stay on one of the top three levels of this 20-story hotel, you have access to a concierge lounge and are served a light breakfast as well as evening hors d'oeuvres and desserts. Wireless Internet is available in the lobby. ⊠ *820 W. 7th Ave., Downtown* ☎ *907/279–8000 or 800/228–9290* ⊕ *www.marriott.com* ↩ *392 rooms, 3 suites* ⚼ *In-hotel: restaurant, room service, bar, pool, gym, concierge* ▤ *AE, D, DC, MC, V.*

$$$$ ⛱ **Hotel Captain Cook.** This classy Anchorage hotel recalls Captain Cook's voyages to Alaska and the South Pacific, with dark teak paneling lining the interior and a nautical theme that continues into the remodeled guest rooms. All rooms have ceiling fans, and guests can use the full gym, business center, and other facilities, including four restaurants and a coffee bar. The hotel occupies an entire city block with three towers, the tallest of which is capped by the Crow's Nest Restaurant. ⊠ *4th Ave. and K St., Downtown* ☎ *907/276–6000 or 800/843–1950* ⊕ *www.captaincook.com* ↩ *451 rooms, 96 suites* ⚼ *In-room: no a/c Wi-Fi. In-hotel: 4 restaurants, room service, pool, gym, concierge, public Internet* ▤ *AE, D, DC, MC, V.*

$$$–$$$$ ⛱ **Millennium Hotel Anchorage.** Perched on the shore of Lake Spenard, the Millennium Anchorage is one of the city's best places to watch planes come and go—the outdoor deck is right under the floatplane base's final approach. The lobby resembles a hunting lodge with its stone fireplace, trophy heads, and mounted fish. The luxuriously appointed rooms continue the inviting Alaska theme. The Flying Machine Restaurant here is locally famous for its enormous Sunday brunch buffet. ⊠ *4800 Spenard Rd., Midtown* ☎ *907/243–2300 or 866/866–8086* ⊕ *www.millenniumhotels.com* ↩ *243 rooms, 5 suites* ⚼ *In-room: refrigerator. In-hotel: restaurant, room service, bar, gym, laundry serv-*

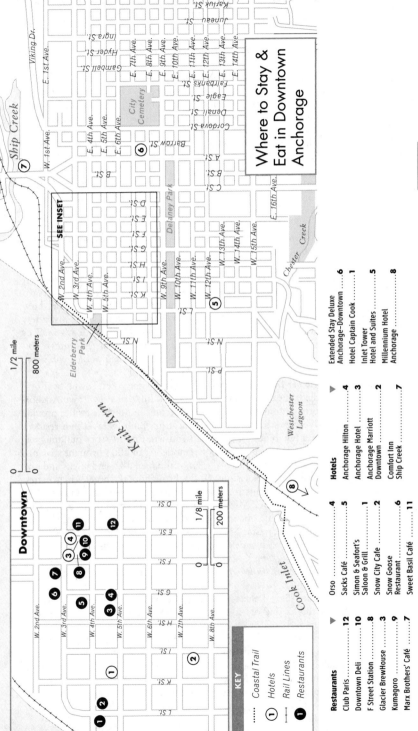

Where to Stay & Eat in Downtown Anchorage

3

KEY

····· Coastal Trail
① Hotels
├─┤ Rail Lines
● Restaurants

Restaurants

▶
Club Paris **12**
Downtown Deli **10**
F Street Station **8**
Glacier BrewHouse **3**
Kumagoro **9**
Marx Brothers' Café **7**
Orso **4**
Sacks Café **5**
Simon & Seafort's
Saloon & Grill **1**
Snow City Cafe **2**
Snow Goose
Restaurant **6**
Sweet Basil Café **11**

Hotels

▶
Anchorage Hilton **4**
Anchorage Hotel **3**
Anchorage Marriott
Downtown **2**
Comfort Inn
Ship Creek **7**
Extended Stay Deluxe
Anchorage–Downtown **6**
Hotel Captain Cook **1**
Inlet Tower
Hotel and Suites **5**
Millennium Hotel
Anchorage **8**

ice, airport shuttle, some pets allowed, public Internet ⊟*AE, D, DC, MC, V.*

$$$ 🏨**Anchorage Hotel.** This little building has been around since 1916. Experienced travelers call it the only hotel in Anchorage with charm: the original sinks and tubs have been restored, and upstairs hallways are lined with old Anchorage photos. The rooms are nicely updated with dark cherrywood furnishings. The small lobby, its fireplace crackling in chilly weather, has a quaint European feel, and the staff is adept at meeting your needs. Request a corner room if possible; rooms facing the street may have some traffic noise. The junior suites include comfortable sitting areas. ✉*330 E St., Downtown* 🕾*907/272–4553 or 800/544–0988* ⊕*www.historicanchoragehotel.com* 🖅*16 rooms, 10 junior suites* ♿*In-room: refrigerators, Wi-Fi. In-hotel: no-smoking rooms* ⊟*AE, D, DC, MC, V* ⍩*CP.*

$$–$$$ 🏨**Comfort Inn Ship Creek.** Ship Creek gurgles past this popular family hotel, a short walk northeast of the Alaska Railroad depot. Rooms, which can be a bit noisy at times, come in a variety of configurations, including kitchenette and two-room suites. A continental breakfast is served each morning, and the lobby features an enormous brown bear. The hotel stocks a limited number of fishing poles for those who want to try their luck catching salmon in Ship Creek, just a few steps away. ✉*111 Ship Creek Ave., Downtown* 🕾*907/277–6887 or 800/362–6887* ⊕*www.comfortinn.com* 🖅*88 rooms, 12 suites* ♿*In-room: kitchen (some), refrigerator, Wi-Fi. In-hotel: pool, gym, some pets allowed (fee)* ⊟*AE, D, DC, MC, V* ⍩*CP.*

$$–$$$ 🏨**Inlet Tower Hotel and Suites.** Windows in the Inlet Tower overlook either the Chugach Mountains, the Cook Inlet, or downtown Anchorage. Corner rooms, particularly those on the northeast side, provide expansive views from the hilltop location. Built in 1952 in a residential area a few blocks south of downtown, this 14-story building was Alaska's first high-rise. A major remodeling in 2003 brought spacious rooms and suites, uniquely Alaskan wallpaper, high-end linens and luxurious beds, large televisions, Wi-Fi throughout the hotel, kitchenettes, and blackout curtains for summer mornings when the sun comes up at 3 AM. Downstairs, Mick's at the Inlet serves three meals a day, with a dinner menu that encompasses roasted duck, king salmon, elk ribs, and walnut sage pasta. ✉*1200 L St., Downtown* 🕾*907/276–0110 or 800/544–0786* ⊕*www.inlettower.com* 🖅*154 rooms, 26 suites* ♿*In-room: kitchen (some), refrigerator. In-hotel: restaurant, gym, laundry facilities, airport shuttle, parking (no fee), public Wi-Fi* ⊟*AE, D, DC, MC, V.*

$$ 🏨**Extended Stay Deluxe Anchorage–Downtown.** Formerly the Aspen Hotel, this is one of Anchorage's newest downtown hotels. Rooms are large and comfortably furnished with a single king or two queen beds, a writing table, 27-inch TV, DVD player, mini-refrigerator, and microwave. Two-room suites include a larger refrigerator, stovetop, and pull-out sofa; some also have in-room Jacuzzis. The hotel is a block from the Anchorage Museum of History and Art and Delaney Park Strip, and has limited off-street parking plus a pool and Jacuzzi downstairs. Nightly, weekly, and monthly rates are available. ✉*108 E. 8th*

Ave., Downtown, 99501 ☎*907/868–1605* ⊕*www.extendedstay.com* ⟿*75 rooms, 14 suites* ⅃*In-room: refrigerator, DVD, Wi-Fi, kitchen. In-hotel: pool, gym, laundry service, airport shuttle, public Internet* ⊟*AE, D, MC, V* ⅃⊙⅃*CP.*

NIGHTLIFE

BARS

Anchorage doesn't shut down when it gets dark. Bars here—and throughout Alaska—open in the morning and close as late as 3 AM on weekends. Smoking in bars and bingo parlors is now illegal, thanks to a recent extension of the smoking ban (first passed in 2001) that originally covered only restaurants. The "Play" section in Friday editions of the *Anchorage Daily News,* as well as the free weekly *Anchorage Press,* provides entertainment listings.

FodorśChoice
★

Anchorage's favorite martini bar, **Bernie's Bungalow Lounge** (⊠*626 D St., Downtown* ☎*907/276–8909*), is a hip spot, with retro furnishings, splashy art, and a DJ most weekends. Take a taxi to **Chilkoot Charlie's** (⊠*2435 Spenard Rd., Spenard* ☎*907/272–1010*) for a taste of Anchorage's untamed side. Known as Koot's among locals, it's not to be missed if you're in the mood for a uniquely Alaskan party. This rockin', and at times very crowded, club in Anchorage has stages for rock, swing, DJs, and local Alaskan bands. Get a drink at one of the 11 bars, make your way past the three dance floors, find a tree stump or an empty beer keg to sit on, and enjoy the show.

DANCE CLUBS

Fans of salsa, merengue, and other music crowd the dance floor at the downtown **Club Soraya** (⊠*333 W. 4th Ave., Downtown* ☎*907/276–0670*). Anchorage's favorite singles bar, **Humpy's Great Alaskan Alehouse** (⊠*610 W. 6th Ave., Downtown* ☎*907/276–2337* ⊕*www.humpys. com*), serves up rock, blues, and folk nightly, along with dozens of microbrews (including more than 40 beers on tap) and surprisingly tasty pub grub. It's noisy and always packed. **Rumrunners** (⊠*501 W. 4th Ave., Downtown* ☎*907/278–4493*) is right across from old City Hall in the center of town. A pub-grub menu brings the lunch crowd, but the big dance floor gets packed nightly as DJs spin tunes.

SHOPPING

BOOKS

Title Wave Books (⊠*1360 W. Northern Lights Blvd., Spenard* ☎*907/278–9283 or 888/598–9283* ⊕*www.wavebooks.com*) fills a sprawling store at the other end of the REI strip mall. The shelves are filled with new and used titles, including a large selection of Alaska special interest books, and the staff is very knowledgeable.

MARKETS

Every weekend from mid-May to early September, Anchorage's **Saturday and Sunday markets** (☎*907/272–5634* ⊕*www.anchoragemarkets.com*) fill the parking lot at 3rd Avenue and E Street from 10 to 6. Dozens of vendors sell Alaskan-made crafts, fine arts, fresh produce, toys, and finger food. The markets are popular with both locals and tourists, and should not be missed if you're in Anchorage on a weekend.

NATIVE CRAFTS

In-the-know locals go to the gift shop at the **Alaska Native Medical Center** (⊠ *4315 Diplomacy Dr. at Tudor Centre, University* ☎ *907/563–2662*) for authentic native crafts and artwork. The shop is only open 10 to 2 during the week and 11 to 2 the first and third Saturday of the month, and doesn't take credit cards, but the

inconvenience is well worth the effort, as here you can buy directly from the artist. **Oomingmak** (⊠ *Corner of 6th Ave. and H St., Downtown* ☎ *907/272–9225 or 888/360–9665* ⊕ *www.qiviut.com*), a native-owned cooperative, sells items made of qiviut, the warm undercoat of the musk ox. Also well worth a look is **Artic Rose Gallery** (⊠ *420 L St., Downtown* ☎ *907/279–3911*), located in the same building as the popular Simon and Seafort's restaurant. **Artique Ltd.** (⊠ *314 G St., Downtown* ☎ *907/277–1663* ⊕ *www.artiqueltd.com*) sells some of the finest examples of paintings, prints, and jewelry by prominent Alaskan artists.

SEAFOOD

New Sagaya's City Market (⊠ *900 W. 13th Ave., Midtown* ☎ *907/274–6173 or 800/764–1001*) sells an excellent selection of fresh seafood. Frozen seafood and smoked fish are available from **10th and M Seafoods** (⊠ *1020 M St., Midtown* ☎ *907/272–3474 or 800/770–2722* ⊕ *www.10thandmseafoods.com*). Both places will also ship seafood for you.

SEATTLE

Seattle has much to offer: a beautiful setting, sparkling arts and entertainment, great restaurants, friendly residents, and Pike Place Market, which provides a wonderfully earthy focal point right in the heart of downtown. Visitors to the city will almost certainly wish they had set aside more time to take in Seattle's charms.

Seattle, like Rome, is built on seven hills. As a visitor, you're likely to spend much of your time on only two of them (Capitol Hill and Queen Anne Hill), but the seven knobs are indeed the most definitive element of the city's natural and spiritual landscape. Years of largely thoughtful building practices have kept tall buildings from obscuring the lines of sight, maintaining vistas in most directions and around almost every turn. The hills are lofty, privileged perches from which residents are constantly reminded of the beauty of the forests, mountains, and waters lying just beyond the city—that is, when it stops misting long enough for you to see your hand in front of your face.

VISITOR INFORMATION

In the heart of downtown Seattle's bustling retail core, the **Seattle Convention and Visitors Bureau** (⊠7th & Pike, main floor, Washington State Convention and Trade Center ☎206/461–5888 ⊕www.seeseattle. org) offers ticket sales, reservation services, dining suggestions, and a handy visitor information packet.

ON THE MOVE

GETTING TO THE PORT

Ships from Norwegian Cruise Line and Celebrity Cruises dock at the Bell Street Pier Cruise Terminal (Pier 66). Pier 66 is within walking distance of downtown attractions, and the Waterfront Streetcar provides trolley service along the shoreline to the cruise terminal. Holland America Line, Princess Cruises, and Royal Caribbean dock at the Terminal 30 Cruise Facility at the south end of the downtown waterfront near the baseball stadium. Terminal 30 is a taxi or city bus ride from downtown.

ARRIVING BY AIR

The major gateway is Seattle–Tacoma International Airport (Sea-Tac).

🛈**Seattle–Tacoma International Airport (Sea-Tac)** (☎ 206/433–5388 ⊕ www. portseattle.org/seatac).

AIRPORT TRANSFERS

Sea-Tac is about 15 mi south of downtown on I–5. It usually takes about 30–45 minutes to ride between the airport and downtown. Metered cabs make the trip for $25–$30. Shuttle Express has the only 24-hour door-to-door service, a flat $20 from the airport to downtown (including the cruise-ship piers). You can make arrangements at the Shuttle Express counter upon arrival. Gray Line Airport Express provides service to downtown hotels for $10.

🛈**Gray Line Airport Express** (☎206/624–5077 or 800/426–7532 ⊕www. graylineofseattle.com).

ARRIVING BY TRAIN

Amtrak provides daily train service north to Vancouver; south to Portland, Oakland, and Los Angeles; and east to Spokane, Chicago, and other cities. Amtrak's King Street Station is just south of downtown at 3rd Avenue South and South King Street.

🛈**Amtrak** (☎206/382–4125 or 800/872–7245 ⊕www.amtrak.com).

PUBLIC TRANSPORTATION

Between 6 AM and 7 PM, rides on the Metro bus are free within downtown. Outside downtown, rides cost between $1.50 and $2. The Seattle Monorail quickly and conveniently links downtown and the Seattle

Center. The 1-mi journey takes 2 minutes and departs every 10 minutes 7:30 AM–11 PM on weekdays and 9 AM–11 PM weekends. The round-trip fare is $4.

🚍Metro bus (☎ *206/553-3000, 206/287-8463 for automated schedule line* ⊕ *transit.metrokc.gov).* **Seattle Monorail** (☎ *206/905-2620* ⊕ *www.seattle-monorail.com).*

TAXIS
Rides are about $2 per mile, and it's always easier to call for a taxi (no fee) than to hail one on the street. This is not a major means for transportation in Seattle, aside from late-night partying and airport trips. There are no surcharges for late-night pickups. Taxis are readily available at most hotels.

🚕**Orange Cab** (☎ *206/522-8800).* **Red Top Cab** (☎ *206/789-4949).* **Yellow Cab** (☎ *206/622-6500).*

EXPLORING SEATTLE

The Elliott Bay waterfront is Seattle's crown jewel. Pike Place Market, the Seattle Aquarium, and the Maritime Discovery Center stretch along its densely packed shore. Just south of downtown is the historic Pioneer Square area, and a short distance north of downtown lies the Seattle Center, a civic gathering place that's home to the Space Needle, Experience Music Project, the Science Fiction Museum, the Children's Museum, and the Pacific Science Center.

DOWNTOWN & PIONEER SQUARE

❸ **Odyssey Maritime Discovery Center.** Cultural and educational maritime ☾ exhibits on Puget Sound and ocean trade are the focus of this waterfront attraction. Learn all about the Northwest's fishing traditions with hands-on exhibits that include kayaking over computer-generated waters, loading a container ship, and listening in on boats radioing one another on Elliott Bay just outside. The adjacent Bell Street Conference Center hosts major local events. You can also shop the on-site fish market, dine on the catch of the day at the seafood restaurant, or spy on boaters docking at the marina and cruise ships putting into port. ✉ *2205 Alaskan Way, Pier 66, Belltown* ☎ *206/374-4000* ⊕ *www.ody.org* ☜ *$7* ☾ *Wed. and Thurs. 10–3, Fri. 10–4, weekends 11–5.*

❺ **Pike Place Market.** At this market vendors purvey handmade crafts, ☾ homemade goodies, and fresh food—from fresh-caught salmon and
Fodor'sChoice shellfish to fruits, veggies, and flowers—and waterside restaurants serve ★ meals reflecting the Northwest's bounty. The market dates from 1907, when the city issued permits allowing farmers to sell produce from wagons parked at Pike Place. Urban renewal almost killed the market, but residents rallied and voted it a historical asset in 1973, and it remains a point of pride among Seattleites. Although the market is slightly less freewheeling today than it was in yesteryear, the cobblestones of Pike Place still reverberate with the banter of fishmongers, farmers, and craftspeople. Because the market is along a bluff, the main arcade stretches down the hill for several stories; many shops are below street

level. ✉*Pike Pl. at Pike St., west of 1st Ave., Downtown* ☏*206/682–7453* ⊕*www.pikeplacemarket.org* ⊗*Stall hours vary. First level shops Mon.–Sat. 10–6, Sun. 11–5; underground shops, daily 11–5.*

❼ ★ Pioneer Square District. On the southern edge of downtown, Seattle's oldest neighborhood is a round-the-clock hub of activity. Cafés, galleries, and boutiques fill elegantly renovated, turn-of-the-20th-century redbrick buildings, and leafy trees line the narrow streets surrounding the central square. Pioneer Square can be accessed from downtown via Metro bus, taxi, or on foot. The district's most unique structure, the 42-story **Smith Tower** on 2nd Avenue and Yesler Way, was the tallest building west of the Mississippi when it was completed in 1914. The ornate iron-and-glass **pergola** on 1st Avenue and Yesler Way marks the site where the pier and sawmill owned by Henry Yesler, one of Seattle's first businessmen, once operated. Today's Yesler Way was the original "Skid Row," where in the 1880s timber was sent to the sawmill on a skid of small logs laid crossways and greased so that the cut trees would slide down to the mill. The area later grew into Seattle's first commercial center.

❽ Klondike Gold Rush National Historical Park. A redbrick building with wooden floors and soaring ceilings contains a small museum illustrating Seattle's role in the 1897–98 gold rush in northwestern Canada's Klondike region. Displays show antique mining equipment, and the walls are lined with photos of gold diggers, explorers, and the hopeful families who followed them. Film presentations, gold-panning demonstrations, and rotating exhibits are scheduled throughout the year. Other sectors of this park are in southeast Alaska. ✉*117 S. Main St., Pioneer Square* ☏*206/553–7220* ⊕*www.nps.gov/klse/index.htm* ☐*Free* ⊗*Daily 9–5.*

❹ ⟳ ★ Seattle Aquarium. From its cylindrical tank, an octopus welcomes you to the aquarium, whose darkened rooms and large, lighted tanks brilliantly display Pacific Northwest marine life. The Tide Pool re-creates Washington's rocky coast and sandy beaches, complete with a 6,000-gallon wave that sweeps over the ecosystem. Huge glass windows provide underwater views of seals and sea otters; go up top to watch them play in their pools. Kids love the Discovery Lab, where they can touch starfish, sea urchins, and sponges, then peek through microscopes at baby barnacles and jellyfish. ✉*Pier 59 off Alaskan Way, Downtown* ☏*206/386–4320* ⊕*www.seattleaquarium.org* ☐*$12.50, $25.50 with a one-hour, narrated harbor cruise* ⊗*Memorial Day–Labor Day, daily 9:30–6.*

❻ Seattle Art Museum. Postmodern architect Robert Venturi designed this five-story museum to be a work of art in itself: large-scale vertical fluting adorns the building's limestone exterior, accented by terra-cotta, cut granite, and marble. Sculptor Jonathan Borofsky's several-stories-high *Hammering Man* pounds away outside the front door. The extensive collection surveys Asian, Native American, African, Oceanic, and pre-Columbian art. Among the highlights are the anonymous 14th-century Buddhist masterwork *Monk at the Moment of Enlightenment* and

Fodor's Choice ★

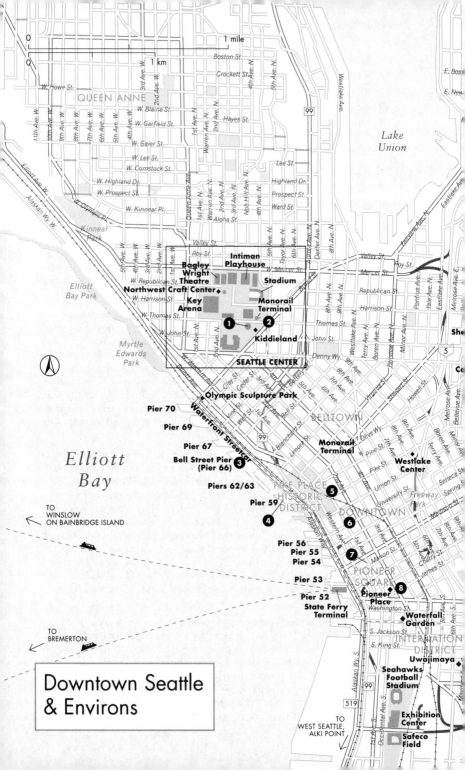

Downtown Seattle
& Environs

3

E. Lynn St.

E. Blaine St.

E. Newton St.

Boyer St. E.

oston St.

ewton St.

Broadway E.

Ave. E.

11th Ave. E.

16th Ave. E.

E. Howe St.

**Boren
Park**

**Interlaken
Park**

Interlaken Blvd. E.

E. Blaine St.

E. Garfield St.

**Lakeview
Cemetery**

E. Garfield St.

E. Highland St.

Grandview PL. E.

Auburn Pl. E.

E. Galer St.

Lakeview Blvd. E.

E. Highland St.

E. Highland St.

24th Ave. E.

**Volunteer
Park**

CAPITOL HILL

Belmont Ave. E.

Harvard Ave. E.

Federal Ave. E.

E. Prospect St.

**Seattle Asian
Art Museum**

E. Prospect St.

E. Ward St.

E. Aloha St.

18th Ave. E.

19th Ave. E.

20th Ave. E.

21st Ave. E.

22nd Ave. E.

Bellevue Ave. E.

Summit Ave. E.

Boylston Ave. E.

Broadway E.

10th Ave. E.

11th Ave. E.

13th Ave. E.

14th Ave. E.

15th Ave. E.

16th Ave. E.

12th Ave. E.

E. Roy St.

E. Mercer St. E.

23rd Ave. E.

24th Ave. E.

E. Republican St.

**Broadway
Shopping District**

E. Thomas St.

E. Thomas St.

E. John St.

E. John St.

**Seattle
Central
Community
College**

**Broadway
Playfield**

E. Denny Wy.

E. Howell St.

Summit Ave.

Belmont Ave.

Boylston Ave.

Harvard Ave.

Broadway E.

Nagle Pl.

12th Ave. E.

E. Madison St.

E. Olive St.

E. Olive St.

E. Pine St.

10th Ave.

11th

E. Pike St.

**Pike-Pine
Corridor**

E. Pike St.

16th Ave.

E. Union St.

E. Union St.

Boylston Ave.

Summit Ave.

13th Ave.

14th Ave.

15th Ave.

E. Spring St.

**Seattle
University**

E. Marion St.

20th Ave.

21st Ave.

22nd Ave.

23rd Ave.

24th Ave.

25th Ave.

E. Columbia St.

**FIRST
HILL**

E. Cherry St.

E. James St.

E. Jefferson St.

Jefferson St.

Terrace St.

Alder St.

10th Ave.

11th Ave.

14th Ave.

15th Ave.

16th Ave.

17th Ave.

18th Ave.

19th Ave.

E. Terrace St.

E. Alder St.

E. Spruce St.

**CENTRAL
AREA**

E. Fir St.

**Pratt
Park**

Yesler Wy.

Yesler Wy.

Yesler Wy.

S. Main St.

S. Jackson St.

22nd Ave. S.

S. King St.

S. Weller St.

NAL

8th Ave. S.

S. Lane St.

S. Dearborn St.

24th Ave. S.

25th Ave. S.

26th Ave. S.

S. Rainier Ave.

S. Charles St.

90

Hawthorne Pl. S.

Bradner Pl. S.

S. Plummer
St.

**TO
MUSEUM
OF FLIGHT**

Rainier Ave. S.

S. Judkins St.

Jackson Pollock's *Sea Change*. A ticket includes a free visit to the Seattle Asian Art Museum if used within a week. A ticket to the latter is good for $3 off admission here within the same period. ✉ *100 University St., Downtown* ☏*206/654–3255* ⊕*www.seattleartmuseum.org* ✉*$7, free 1st Thurs. of month* ⊙*Tues.–Sun. 10–5 (Thurs. until 9).*

SEATTLE CENTER

Located a few blocks north of downtown at the base of Queen Anne Hill, Seattle Center is a legacy of the 1962 World's Fair. Today, the 74-acre site is home to a multitude of attractions that encompass a children's museum, an opera hall, a science museum, a monorail, a basketball arena, and much more. For more information, call ☏206/684–7200 or check out ⊕www.seattlecenter.com.

> **GETTING AROUND**
>
> Get here from downtown by hopping aboard the **Monorail** (☏*206/905-2620* ⊕*www. seattlemonorail.com*) at Westlake Center (5th and Pine streets).

❷ **Experience Music Project.** Seattle's most controversial architectural statement is a 140,000-square-foot interactive museum celebrating American popular music—and the city's many contributions to rock-and-roll history. Architect Frank Gehry drew inspiration from electric guitars to achieve the building's "swoopy" design. Funded by Microsoft cofounder Paul Allen, it's a fitting home for the world's largest collection of Jimi Hendrix memorabilia; the guitar god was a native Seattleite. Other exhibits house guitars, clothing, and other artifacts once owned by Bob Dylan, Hank Williams, Kurt Cobain, and the bands Pearl Jam, Soundgarden, and the Kingsmen. Experiment with instruments and recording equipment in the interactive Sound Lab, or attend music performances, workshops, and private events in the Sky Church concert hall, JBL Theater, Liquid Lounge bar, or Turntable Restaurant. ✉*5th Ave. between Broad St. and Thomas St., Queen Anne* ☏*206/367–5483* ⊕*www.emplive.org* ✉*$19.95* ⊙*May 25–Sept. 3, Mon. and Wed.–Sun. 10–5; rest of year, daily 10–8.* The same building also houses the **Science Fiction Museum.** This interactive multimedia museum truly takes you "out there" with spaceship rooms and a science-fiction heroes hall of fame. The Fantastic Voyages exhibit focuses on time travel, Them! illustrates the fear of aliens, and Brave New Worlds explores the future. ✉*5th Ave. between Broad St. and Thomas St., Queen Anne* ☏*206/724–3284* ⊕*www.sfhomeworld.org* ✉*$12.95* ⊙*May 25–Sept. 3, Mon. and Wed.–Sun. 10–5; rest of year, daily 10–8.*

❶ **Space Needle.** The distinctive exterior of the 520-foot-high Space Needle is visible throughout downtown—but the view from the inside out is even better. A 42-second ride up to the observation deck yields 360-degree vistas of the Olympic Mountains, Elliott Bay, Queen Anne Hill, the University of Washington, and the Cascade Range. The Needle was built just in time for the World's Fair in 1962, but has since been refurbished with educational signs, interactive stations, and the glass-enclosed SpaceBase store and Pavilion spiraling around the tower's

Fodor'sChoice ★

base. If you dine at the exclusive, revolving SkyCity on the top floor, admission to the observation deck is free. Or, just enjoy views from the coffee bar. ⊠ *5th Ave. and Broad St., Queen Anne* ☎ *206/—905–2100* ⊕ *www.spaceneedle.com* ⌁ *$15* ⊙ *Sun.–Thurs. 9 AM–11 PM, Fri. and Sat. 9 AM–midnight.*

WHERE TO EAT

Downtown is a good area for lunch; but in the evening the action centers around hotel restaurants and a handful of watering holes. Pioneer Square and Belltown, on the other hand, come alive nightly with music and other entertainment. Pioneer Square features bars and restaurants that cater to baseball fans en route to Safeco Field, while Belltown's many chic restaurants and bars are packed with hipsters and urbanites.

DOWNTOWN

$$$–$$$$
★ ✕**Dahlia Lounge.** Romantic Dahlia started the valentine-red walls trend and it's still working its magic on Seattle couples. It's cozy and then some, but the food plays its part, too. Crab cakes, served as an entrée or an appetizer, lead an ever-changing regionally oriented menu. Other standouts are seared ahi tuna, near-perfect gnocchi, and such desserts as coconut-cream pie and fresh fruit cobblers. Seattle's most energetic restaurateur, chef-owner Tom Douglas also owns Etta's Seafood in Pike Place Market, and the excellent Palace Kitchen on 5th Avenue. But Dahlia is the one that makes your heart go pitter-pat. ⊠ *2001 4th Ave., Downtown* ☎ *206/682–4142* ⊕ *www.tomdouglas.com/dahlia* ⌁ *Reservations essential* ⊟ *AE, D, DC, MC, V* ⊙ *No lunch weekends.*

$$–$$$$ ✕**Campagne.** The white walls, picture windows, snowy linens, fresh flowers, and candles at this urbane restaurant overlooking Pike Place Market and Elliott Bay evoke Provence. So does the robust French country fare, with starters such as seafood sausage, and calamari fillets with ground almonds. Main plates include panfried scallops with a green-peppercorn and tarragon sauce, cinnamon-roasted quail served with carrot and orange essence, and Oregon rabbit with an apricot-cider and green-peppercorn sauce. Campagne is open only for dinner, but the adjacent Café Campagne serves breakfast, lunch, and dinner daily. ⊠ *Inn at the Market, 86 Pine St., Downtown* ☎ *206/728–2800* ⊕ *www.campagnerestaurant.com* ⌁ *Reservations essential* ⊟ *AE, DC, MC, V* ⊙ *No lunch.*

$$–$$$ ✕**Place Pigalle.** Large windows look out on Elliott Bay in this cozy spot tucked behind a meat vendor in Pike Place Market's main arcade. In nice weather, open windows let in the fresh salt breeze. Flowers brighten each table, and the staff is warm and welcoming. Despite its name, this restaurant only has a few French flourishes on an otherwise American/Pacific Northwest menu. Go for the rich oyster stew, the Dungeness crab (in season), or the fish of the day. Local microbrews are usually on tap, and the wine list is thoughtfully compact. ⊠ *81 Pike Pl. Market, Downtown* ☎ *206/624–1756* ⊟ *AE, MC, V* ⊙ *Closed Sun.*

$–$$ ✕**Pink Door.** With its Post Alley entrance and meager signage, many enjoy the Pink Door's speak-easiness almost as much as the savory

Italian food. In warm months patrons partake on the deck shaded by a grape arbor while enjoying the stunning view of Elliott Bay. The roasted garlic and tapenade are eminently sharable appetizers; spaghetti *alla puttanesca* (with anchovies, capers, and tomatoes), and cioppino are standout entrées, though nothing stands too far out—people come here mostly for the atmosphere. The whimsical bar is often crowded, the staff is saucy and irreverent, and cabaret acts regularly perform on a small corner stage. There's no place quite like it. ⊠*1919 Post Alley, Downtown* ☎*206/443–3241* ⊕*www.thepinkdoor.net* ⌑*Reservations essential* ⊟*AE, MC, V* ⊙*No lunch Sun.*

¢–$$ ✕ **Il Fornaio.** This Italian restaurant is the cornerstone of the Pacific Place mall that houses it. When shopping, there seems to be an opportunity to stop for a bite at Il Fornaio at every turn. There's a casual café on the street level, then an even more casual espresso counter on the mall's first level, and finally the elegant full-service dining room upstairs. Though the fresh breads and wood-fired pizzas are widely acclaimed, the entire menu has much to offer, most notably the seasonal antipasti, vegetarian minestrone, handmade ravioli stuffed with Swiss chard, and the rosemary-scented rotisserie chicken. ⊠*600 Pine St., Downtown* ☎*206/264–0994* ⊟*AE, DC, MC, V.*

$ ✕ **Copacabana.** Much of the strategy that preserved Pike Place Market in the 1960s was hatched at this small Bolivian café. The food served here includes such tasty fare as spicy shrimp soup, *saltenas* (savory meat-and-vegetable pies), paella, and *pescado à la Español* (halibut in a saffron-tomato-onion sauce). Tasty food, cold beer, and great views are good reasons to linger. ⊠*1520 1st Ave., Downtown* ☎*206/622–6359* ⌑*Reservations not accepted* ⊟*AE, D, MC, V* ⊙*No dinner weekdays and Sun.*

$ ✕ **Emmett Watson's Oyster Bar.** This unpretentious spot can be hard to find—it's in the back of Pike Place Market's Soames-Dunn Building, facing a small flower-bedecked courtyard. But for those who know their oysters, finding this place is worth the effort. Not only are the oysters very fresh and the beer icy cold, but both are inexpensive and available in any number of varieties. If you don't like oysters, try the salmon soup or the fish-and-chips—flaky pieces of fish with very little grease. ⊠*1916 Pike Pl., Downtown* ☎*206/448–7721* ⌑*Reservations not accepted* ⊟*No credit cards* ⊙*No dinner Sun.*

¢–$ ✕ **FareStart.** The homeless men and women who operate this café, a project of the FareStart job-training program, prepare an American-style lunch of sandwiches, burgers, and fries during the week. Reservations are essential for the $25 Thursday dinner, prepared by a guest chef from a restaurant such as Ray's Boathouse or the Metropolitan Grill. The cuisine changes with the chef. Whenever you go, you're assured a great meal for a great cause and a real taste of Seattle's community spirit. ⊠*700 Virginia St., Downtown* ☎*206/443–1233* ⊕*www.farestart.org* ⊟*D, MC, V* ⊙*No lunch weekends. No dinner Fri.–Wed.*

BELLTOWN

$$–$$$ ✕ **Brasa.** This has long been a Seattle favorite. The outstanding menu
★ is prone to change, but the paella and roast suckling pig seem to be getting all the praise these days. More traditional, but equally tooth-

some and carefully prepared, are the beef tenderloin and wild king salmon. Tip: If you don't want to shell out the big bucks for dinner, join in on one of the city's most popular happy hours. The lounge serves tapas, small plates, pizzas, and sandwiches. The dimly lighted space is a good place to sample the chichi Belltown scene in an established restaurant that isn't just style over substance. ✉2107 3rd Ave., Belltown ☎206/728–4220 ⚲Reservations essential 🖃AÉ, DC, MC, V ⊘No lunch.

$$–$$$
Fodor'sChoice
★

✕**Restaurant Zoë.** Reservations are sought after at this chic eatery on a high-trafficked corner. Its tall windows, lively bar scene, and charming waitstaff add to the popularity, which comes mainly from its inspired kitchen. The talents of chef-owner Scott Staples can be seen in his house-smoked hanger steak served with mashed potatoes, parsnips, and veal jus and his pan-seared sea scallops served over asparagus herb risotto with smoked bacon and blood-orange vinaigrette. Zoë is a great representative of the kind of fine dining experience that Seattle excels at, wherein a sleek, urban space, upscale cooking, and a hip crowd that enjoys people-watching come together to create not a pretentious, overblown, and overpriced spectacle, but a place that is unfailingly laid-back, comfortable, and satisfying. Reservations are recommended. ✉2137 2nd Ave., Belltown ☎206/256—2060 ⊕www.restaurantzoe. com 🖃AE, D, MC, V ⊘No lunch.

$$–$$$
✕**Shiro's.** Willfully unconcerned with atmosphere, this simple spot is a real curiosity amid Belltown's chic establishments. The focus is entirely on the exceptional menu of authentic Japanese eats. Seaweed becomes a haute-cuisine dish at this formal but friendly café, and a sure hand guides the sushi bar, where Shiro himself often holds court. ✉2401 2nd Ave., Belltown ☎206/443–9844 🖃AE, MC, V ⊘Closed Sun.

$–$$$
✕**Etta's Seafood.** Tom Douglas's restaurant near Pike Place Market has a sleek and slightly whimsical design and views of Victor Steinbrueck Park. Try the Dungeness crab cakes in season or the various Washington oysters on the half shell. Brunch, served on weekends, always includes zesty seafood omelets, but the chef also does justice to French toast, eggs and bacon, and Mexican-influenced breakfast dishes. ✉2020 Western Ave., Belltown ☎206/443–6000 🖃AE, D, DC, MC, V.

$–$$$
✕**Palace Kitchen.** The star of this chic yet convivial Tom Douglas eatery (he's also responsible for Dahlia Lounge, Etta's, Lola, and Serious Pie) may be the 45-foot bar, but the real show takes place in the giant open kitchen at the back. Sausages, sweet-pea ravioli, salmon carpaccio, and a nightly selection of exotic cheeses vie for your attention on the ever-changing menu of small plates. There are also always a few entrées, 10 fantastic desserts, and a rotisserie special from the apple-wood grill. ✉2030 5th Ave., Belltown ☎206/448–2001 🖃AE, D, DC, MC, V ⊘No lunch.

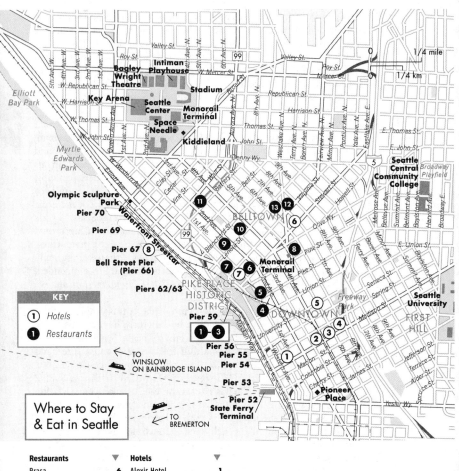

Where to Stay & Eat in Seattle

KEY

① Hotels

① Restaurants

Restaurants ▼	Hotels ▼
Brasa **6**	Alexis Hotel **1**
Campagne **2**	Edgewater **8**
Copacabana **1**	Executive Hotel Pacific **4**
Dahlia Lounge **10**	
Emmett Watson's Oyster Bar **3**	Fairmont Olympic Hotel **5**
Etta's Seafood **7**	Hotel Max **6**
FareStart **12**	Hotel Monaco **2**
Il Fornaio **8**	Pensione Nichols **7**
Palace Kitchen **13**	W Seattle **3**
Pink Door **5**	
Place Pigalle **4**	
Restaurant Zoë **9**	
Shiro's **11**	

WHERE TO STAY

$$$$ ▥**Alexis Hotel.** The Alexis occupies two historic buildings near the waterfront. It's a fine place to stay, with a focus on art (including a rotating collection of paintings in the corridor between wings); subdued colors, imported Italian and French fabrics, and antiques can be found in the standard rooms and public spaces. It is, however, starting to look a little worn around the edges in some places, and it's really the specialty theme suites that set this property apart. Spa suites, which include in-room spa services from the Aveda spa downstairs, are a good choice if you can't splurge on a specialty suite. A few rooms have restricted water views; book early to secure one of those. Downstairs, the Library bistro is one of the city's favorite lunchtime hideaways and bars. ⊠*1007 1st Ave., Downtown 98104* ☏*206/624–4844 or 888/850–1155* ⊕*www.alexishotel.com* ⇱*73 rooms, 36 suites* ♿*Inroom: refrigerator, Wi-Fi. In-hotel: restaurant, room service, bar, gym, spa, concierge, laundry service, public Wi-Fi, parking (fee), some pets allowed, no-smoking rooms* ▤*AE, D, DC, MC, V.*

$$$$ ▥**Edgewater.** Raised high on stilts above Elliott Bay—with the waves
★   lapping right underneath it—Seattle's only hotel on the water affords spectacular west-facing views of ferries and sailboats, seals and sea birds, and the distant Olympic Mountains. The whole hotel has a rustic-chic, elegant hunting lodge look, with plaid rugs and fabrics and peeled-log furnishings. Note that there is a significant price jump between the Waterfront rooms and the Waterfront Premium rooms and the upgrade is not necessarily worth it unless you want a little more space. There's also an enormous, party-style Beatles Suite (room 272), where the famous Brits stayed in 1964. The elegant Six Seven restaurant is set to an indoor-outdoor bay vista. ⊠*Pier 67, 2411 Alaskan Way, Pier 67, Belltown, 98121* ☏*206/728–7000 or 800/624–0670* ⊕*www. edgewaterhotel.com* ⇱*213 rooms, 10 suites* ♿*In-room: refrigerator, Wi-Fi. In-hotel: restaurant, room service, bar, gym, bicycles, concierge, laundry service, public Wi-Fi, parking (fee), no-smoking rooms* ▤*AE, D, DC, MC, V.*

$$$$ ▥**Fairmont Olympic Hotel.** The grande dame of Seattle hotels seems to
Fodor'sChoice   occupy its own corner of the universe, one that feels more old New
★   York or European than Pacific Northwest. The lobby of the elegant Renaissance Revival–style historic property has intricately carved wood paneling, graceful staircases that lead to mezzanine lounge areas, and plush couches occupied by men in suits and well-dressed older ladies—not a fleece jacket or pair of Birkenstocks in sight. Guest rooms, though lovely, are not quite as impressive as the lobby; however, major renovations, to be completed by early 2008, may change that—everything from fabrics to TVs is being replaced. Note that executive suites are kind of small for suites; deluxe rooms are nearly the same and slightly cheaper. Though it's hard to imagine kids being truly comfortable here, the hotel does its best to accommodate families. ⊠*411 University St., Downtown, 98101* ☏*206/621–1700 or 800/441–1414* ⊕*www. fairmont.com/seattle* ⇱*232 rooms, 218 suites* ♿*In-room: safe, refrigerator, DVD (some), Ethernet. In-hotel: 3 restaurants, room service,*

bar, pool, gym, concierge, laundry service, public Wi-Fi, parking (fee)
⊟*AE, D, DC, MC, V.*

$$$$ ⊞**Hotel Monaco.** The Hotel Monaco is the pet-friendliest hotel in town:
★   not only are pets catered to with special events like doggie fashion
shows, but anyone who had to leave the pets at home can opt to have
a goldfish (who comes with an adorable "hello my name is" type introduction card) to keep them company. The hotel is full of other fun
touches, like bright raspberry-and-cream striped wallpaper, gold sun-
burst decorations, and animal prints. Guests wishing to have a more
low-key experience will be able to do so; they, however, should opt
for a room with blue and white walls—the eclectic decor is a little
easier on the eye in these than in the ones with the raspberry striped
wallpaper. ⊠*1101 4th Ave., Downtown, 98101* ☎*206/621–1770 or
800/945–2240* ⊕*www.monaco-seattle.com* ⇗*144 rooms, 45 suites*
⅁*In-room: refrigerator, DVD, Ethernet, Wi-Fi. In-hotel: restaurant,
room service, bar, gym, spa, concierge, laundry service, public Wi-Fi,
airport shuttle, parking (fee), no-smoking rooms, some pets allowed*
⊟*AE, D, DC, MC, V.*

$$$$ ⊞**W Seattle.** The W set the bar for Seattle's trendy hotels, and it's still
★   an outstanding choice for hip yet reliable luxury. Candlelight and custom-designed board games encourage lingering around the lobby fireplace on deep couches strewn with throw pillows, and the hotel's bar
is popular with guests and locals alike. Decorated in black, brown,
and French blue, guest rooms would almost be austere if they didn't
have the occasional geometric print to lighten things up a bit. Floor-
to-ceiling windows maximize striking views of the Sound and the city.
⊠*1112 4th Ave., Downtown, 98101* ☎*206/264–6000 or 877/946–
8357* ⊕*www.whotels.com* ⇗*419 rooms, 16 suites* ⅁*In-room: safe,
refrigerator, DVD, Ethernet. In-hotel: restaurant, room service, bar,
gym, concierge, laundry service, public Internet, public Wi-Fi, parking
(fee), some pets allowed, no-smoking rooms* ⊟*AE, D, DC, MC, V.*

$$–$$$ ⊞**Hotel Max.** Fans of minimalism, travelers interested in cutting-edge
★   local artists, and anyone who wants to feel like a rock star will be
very happy with the Max, a superstylish hotel that swears it's created
a new design aesthetic, "Maximalism." The hallway of each floor is
dedicated to a different local photographer and giant black and white
photos cover each door; scenes range from Americana to live concert
shots from Seattle's grunge heyday (5th floor). The beds are huge and
heavenly—a surprising bit of substance from a hotel that prides itself
on appearance. The only downside to the Max is that some of the
rooms are on the small side—owing more to the constraints of being in
a historic building than to tenets of minimalism—and bathrooms have
very little counter space. A few rooms, however, are large enough to
include black leather couches. ⊠*620 Stewart St., Downtown, 98101*
☎*206/728–6299 or 866/833–6299* ⊕*www.hotelmaxseattle.com*
⇗*163 rooms* ⅁*In-room: safe, refrigerator, Wi-Fi check on DVDs in
rooms. In-hotel: restaurant, room service, gym, laundry service, concierge, public Wi-Fi, parking (fee), no-smoking rooms* ⊟*AE, D, DC,
MC, V.* ⅋⊙⅂*CP*

$–$$ ☆ **Executive Hotel Pacific.** This 1929 property maintains a low profile in a neighborhood filled with fancy hotels. Its 4th Avenue entrance is through a coffee shop, and its Spring Street entrance is marked only by a small awning. Location (it's across the street from the public library), skilled management, and the fair price make this one of the best lodging bargains downtown. Guest beds have tan leather headboards, sage green spreads, and flat screen TVs. Note that because this is an older building, rooms are small, but they all have city views. ☒*400 Spring St., Downtown, 98104* ☎*206/623–3900 or 888/398–3932* ⊕*www. executivehotels.net/seattle* ➳*159 rooms* ☖*In-room: refrigerator, dial-up. In-hotel: restaurant, gym, concierge, public Internet, parking (fee), some pets allowed, no-smoking rooms* ☰*AE, D, DC, MC, V.* ⦿*CP*

¢–$ ☆ **Pensione Nichols.** One of the few affordable options downtown is also a unique and endearing place. Proprietor Lindsey Nichols attends to her guests with great enthusiasm and humor—this is a place where you can just kick back, relax, and be yourself. It could be called a hostel for grown-ups, or one for young people who want more privacy and style than a hostel can provide. The bed and breakfast is in a historic building, so the rooms are a mixed bag of sizes and layouts, but most have wrought iron furnishings and all have new beds. Breakfast is served in the light-filled common area overlooking Elliott Bay. ☒*1923 1st Ave., Downtown, 98101* ☎*206/441–7125* ⊕*www.pensionenichols. com* ➳*8 rooms with shared bath, 2 suites with bath* ☖*In-room: no phone, no TV, Wi-Fi. In-hotel: no elevator, public Wi-Fi, some pets allowed* ☰*AE, D, DC, MC, V* ⦿*CP.*

NIGHTLIFE

The grunge rock legacy of Nirvana and Pearl Jam reverberates in local music venues, which showcase up-and-coming pop, punk, heavy metal, and alternative bands, along with healthy doses of other genres.

Two free papers, the *Stranger* and *Seattle Weekly* (distributed on Thursday) provide detailed music, art, and nightlife listings. Friday editions of the *Seattle Times* and the *Seattle Post-Intelligencer* have pullout sections detailing weekend events.

Bars and clubs stay open until 2 AM. Cabs are abundant and buses run until around midnight. After the witching hour, cabs are the only option for those not willing to hoof it.

Pioneer Square—home to a plethora of rock, jazz, and electronic music clubs—features a joint cover charge of $10 that covers admission to eight bars; simply pay the cover at the first club you visit, get a hand stamp, and roam at will.

BARS

Dimitriou's Jazz Alley (☒*2033 6th Ave., Downtown* ☎*206/441–9729* ⊕*www.jazzalley.com*) is where Seattleites dress up to see nationally known jazz artists. The cabaret-style theater, where intimate tables for two surround the stage, runs smoke-free shows nightly except Monday. Those with reservations for cocktails or dinner, served during the first set, receive priority seating and $2 off the combined meal-and-show ticket. **The Fenix** (⊠*1700 1st Ave., Pioneer Square* ☎*206/382–7877*) is, fittingly, the club that won't die. The original club was demolished by a 2001 earthquake but reopened hotter than ever. It then closed again only to reappear in the cavernous warehouse space that once held the Premier. The huge space offers a variety of dance music styles to choose from; there are often performances from rock, ska, and punk bands, too. The mix of music means you can find a more interesting mix of partyers than at the cheesy clubs in Pioneer Square. **Umi Sake House** (⊠*2230 1st Ave., Belltown* ☎*206/374–8717* ⊕*www.umisakehouse. com*) offers a great selection of sake and sake-based cocktails in a space designed to look like someone shoehorned a real *izakaya* (a sake house that also serves substantial snacks like a tapas bar or gastropub) into a Belltown building—there's even an enclosed patio, which they refer to as the "porch" and a tatami room that can be reserved for larger parties. The sushi is yummy and there's a long happy hour offered at one of the bar areas. Despite its chic interior, Umi is less of a meat market than some Belltown spots—unless you're here late on a Friday or Saturday night. **SEE Sound Lounge** (⊠*115 Blanchard St., Belltown* ☎*206/374–3733*) is a super-swanky nightspot in Belltown. Pulsating techno provides the soundtrack, and hypnotic ambient images are displayed on a massive flat screen. Top-notch furnishings and a delectable menu of dance-enabling appetizers and desserts keep this club's ultra-stylish crowd coming back time and again.

SHOPPING

Seattle's retail core might feel business-crisp by day, but it's casual and arts-centered by night, and the shopping scene reflects both these moods. Within a few square blocks—between 1st Avenue on the west and Boren Avenue on the east, and from University Street to Olive Way—you can find department store flagships, a trio of high-gloss vertical malls, dozens of upper-echelon boutiques, and elite retail chains. One block closer to Elliott Bay, on Western Avenue, several high-end home-furnishings showrooms make up an informal "Furniture Row." The Waterfront, with its small kitschy stores and open-air restaurants, is a great place to dawdle. ■TIP➔ Seattle's best shopping is found in the small neighborhood made up of 4th, 5th, and 6th avenues between Pine and Spring streets, and 1st Avenue between Virginia and Madison streets.

ART GALLERIES

★ **Foster/White Gallery.** One of the Seattle art scene's heaviest hitters, Foster/White has digs as impressive as the works it shows: a century-old building with high ceilings and 7,000 square feet of exhibition space. Internationally acclaimed glass artist Dale Chihuly, and paintings, sculpture, and drawings by Northwest masters Kenneth Callahan, Mark Tobey, and George Tsutakawa are on permanent exhibit. There's another equally impressive branch in Rainier Square at 5th Avenue and Union Street. ⊠*220 3rd Ave. S, Pioneer Square* ☎*206/622–2833* ⊕*www.fosterwhite.com* ▱*Free* ☉*Tues.–Sat. 10–6.* **Grover/Thurston Gallery.** Twenty Northwest artists are represented in this historic space.

Shows, which can be either solo or group exhibitions are often fun, as many of the artists create wry pieces, many of which seem more like fine art imitating folk art. ⊠ *309 Occidental Ave. S, Pioneer Square* ☎*206/223–0816* ⊕*www.groverthurston.com* ⊑*Free* ⊘*Tues.–Sat.*

William Traver Gallery. A classic gallery space with white walls and creaky, uneven wood floors, William Traver is like a little slice of Soho in Seattle—without the attitude. Light pours in from large picture windows; until the new Four Seasons is completed, the second-story space has glimpses of Elliott Bay. The focus is on high-priced (tens of thousands of dollars) glass art from local and international artists. Pieces are exquisite—never too whimsical or gaudy—and the staff is extremely courteous to those of us who can only enjoy this place as a museum and not a shop. After you're done tiptoeing around the gallery, head back downstairs and around the corner to **Vetri,** which sells glass art and objects from emerging artists at steep but much more reasonable prices. ⊠ *110 Union St., Downtown* ☎*206/587–6501* ⊕*www.travergallery. com* ⊑*Free* ⊘*Tues.–Fri. 10–6, Sat. 10–5, Sun. noon–5.*

GIFT SHOPS

Made in Washington (⊠*1530 Post Alley, Downtown* ☎*206/467–0788* ⊕*www.madeinwashington.com*) in Pike Place Market features hundreds of quality products from local artists and small businesses. There's also a branch in downtown's Westlake Center. **Pike & Western Wine Shop.** (⊠*1934 Pike Pl., Downtown* ☎*206/441–1307*) Pike & Western is one of the two best wine shops in the city (the other is McCarthy & Schiering in Queen Anne). It has a comprehensive stock of wines from the Pacific Northwest, California, Italy, and France—and expert advice from friendly salespeople to guide your choice. **Sur La Table** (⊠*84 Pine St., Downtown* ☎*206/448–2244*), in the Pike Place Market, has been a culinary aficionados' haven since 1972. It's packed to the rafters with kitchen stuff—some 12,500 items, give or take, including an exclusive line of copper cookware. Check the schedule of in-store demonstrations.

MALLS

★ **Pacific Place.** (⊠*600 Pine St., Downtown* ☎*206/405–2655* ⊕*www. pacificplaceseattle.com*) Shopping, dining, and an excellent movie multiplex are wrapped around a four-story, light-filled atrium, making this a cheerful destination even on a stormy day. The mostly high-end shops include Cartier, Tiffany & Co., MaxMara, Coach, and Brookstone, though you can find some old standards here like Victoria's Secret and Eddie Bauer. A third-floor skybridge provides a rainproof route to Nordstrom. One of the best things about the mall is its parking garage, which is surprisingly affordable given its location and has valet parking for just a few bucks more. **Westlake Center** (⊠*1601 5th Ave., Downtown* ☎*206/467–1600* ⊕*www.westlakecenter.com*) is a busy place. Roughly 60 stores and food vendors draw crowds to a four-story glass pavilion that's also the downtown link for the Monorail to Seattle Center. Fill a basket with locally produced specialty foods and crafts at Made in Washington, splurge on a fabulous writing instrument from Montblanc, or find quirky gifts and jewelry at Fireworks.

VANCOUVER, BRITISH COLUMBIA

Cosmopolitan Vancouver has a spectacular setting. Tall fir trees stand practically downtown, the Coast Mountains tower close by, the ocean laps at the doorstep, and people from every corner of the earth create a youthful and vibrant atmosphere.

Vancouver is a young city, even by North American standards. It was not yet a town in 1871, when British Columbia became part of the Canadian confederation. The city's history, such as it is, remains visible to the naked eye: eras are stacked east to west along the waterfront like some century-old archaeological dig—from cobblestone, late-Victorian Gastown to shiny postmodern glass cathedrals of commerce grazing the sunset.

Long a port city in a resource-based province, Vancouver is relatively new to tourism and, for that matter, to its famous laid-back West Coast lifestyle. Most locals mark Expo '86, when the city cleaned up old industrial sites and generated new tourism infrastructure, as the turning point. Another makeover is in the works now, as Vancouver, with Whistler, prepares to host the 2010 Winter Olympics.

The mild climate, exquisite natural scenery, and relaxed outdoor lifestyle continually attract new residents, and the number of visitors is increasing for the same reasons. People often get their first glimpse of Vancouver when catching an Alaskan cruise, and many return at some point to spend more time here. Note that Vancouver is usually the first or last stop on a cruise, unless you're sailing on a longer cruise that begins in Los Angeles or San Francisco.

Vancouver has a lot to offer so it's worth spending as much time as you can here before, or after, your cruise. Since much of your embarkation day will be spent actually embarking, try to allow at least an extra full day or two to see the city.

There is much to see and do in Vancouver, but when time is limited (as it usually is for cruise-ship passengers), the most popular options are a stroll through Gastown and Chinatown, a visit to Granville Island, or a driving or biking tour of Stanley Park.

If you have more time, head to the Museum of Anthropology, on the University of British Columbia campus; it's worth a trip.

VISITOR INFORMATION

For maps and information, stop at the **Vancouver Tourist InfoCentre** (✉ *200 Burrard St.* ☎ *604/683–2000*). It's across the street from Canada Place and next door to the Fairmont Waterfront Hotel.

ON THE MOVE

GETTING TO THE PORT

Arriving in Vancouver makes a scenic finish to an Alaska cruise. Entering Burrard Inlet, ships pass the forested shores of Stanley Park and sail beneath the graceful sweep of the Lions Gate Bridge. Most ships calling at Vancouver dock at the Canada Place cruise-ship terminal on the downtown waterfront, a few minutes' walk from the city center. Its rooftop of dramatic white sails makes it instantly recognizable.

A few vessels depart from the Ballantyne cruise-ship terminal, which is a 10- to 15-minute, C$10 to C$12 cab ride from downtown. Your hotel or cruise line may provide shuttle service to Ballantyne.

Ballantyne cruise ship terminal (⊠ *655 Centennial Rd.* ☎ *604/665–9000 or 888/767–8826* ⊕ *www.portvancouver.com.* **Canada Place cruise ship terminal** (⊠ *999 Canada Place Way* ☎ *604/665–9000 or 888/767–8826* ⊕ *www. portvancouver.com).*

ARRIVING BY AIR

Vancouver International Airport is 22 km (14 mi) south of downtown off Highway 99. It takes 30 to 45 minutes to get downtown from the airport.

Vancouver International Airport (☎ *604/207–7077* ⊕ *www.yvr.ca).*

AIRPORT TRANSFERS

The Vancouver Airporter Service bus leaves the domestic and international terminals approximately every 20 minutes, stopping at major downtown hotels and at the Canada Place cruise-ship terminal. It's C$13 one-way and C$20 round-trip. Taxi stands are in front of the terminal building; the fare downtown is about C$30 (about C$35 to Ballantyne Pier). Local cab companies include the reliable Black Top Cabs and Yellow Cabs, both of which serve the whole Vancouver area. Limousine service from LimoJet Gold costs about C$56 one-way.

To travel downtown by public transit, take any TransLink bus marked Airport Station from the stop on Level 1 of the international terminal, then transfer at Airport Station to a Burrard Station Bus 98, which stops at Waterfront Station, about a block from the Canada Place cruise ship terminal. To return to the airport, take a Richmond Centre Bus 98 and transfer at Airport Station. The adult fare is C$3.25 and you'll need exact change.

Black Top Cabs (☎ *604/681–2181).* **LimoJet Gold** (☎ *604/273–1331 or 800/278–8742* ⊕ *www.limojetgold.com).* **TransLink** (☎ *604/953–3333* ⊕ *www. translink.bc.ca).* **Vancouver Airporter Service** (☎ *604/946–8866 or 800/668–3141* ⊕ *www.yvrairporter.com).* **Yellow Cabs** (☎ *604/681–1111).*

ARRIVING BY CAR

From the south, I–5 from Seattle becomes Highway 99 at the U.S.–Canada border. Vancouver is a three-hour drive (226 km [140 mi]) from Seattle. It's best to avoid border crossings during peak times such as holidays and weekends. Highway 1, the Trans-Canada Highway, enters Vancouver from the east. To avoid traffic, arrive after rush hour (8:30 AM).

Vancouver's evening rush-hour traffic starts early—about 3 PM on weekdays. The worst bottlenecks outside the city center are the North Shore bridges, the George Massey Tunnel on Highway 99 south of Vancouver, and Highway 1 through Coquitlam and Surrey. Delays can occur anytime as Vancouver is undergoing a great deal of roadwork in preparation for the 2010 Winter Olympic Games. The BC Ministry of Transportation, at 800/550–4997 or www.drivebc.ca, has updates.

Citipark offers secure underground parking in a two-level garage at Canada Place. Rates are C$16 per day for cruise-ship passengers; reservations, by phone or Web, are recommended. The entrance is at the foot of Howe Street. Cruisepark has a secured uncovered lot five minutes away from Canada Place and offers a free shuttle service to and from Canada Place and Ballantyne cruise-ship terminals. Reservations via Web or phone are recommended. Rates start at C$110 per week.

Citipark (✉ *999 Canada Place Way* ☎ *604/684–2251 or 866/856–8080* ⊕ *www. canadaplaceparking.ca*). **Cruisepark** (✉ *455 Waterfront Rd.* ☎ *800/665–0050 or 604/331–7233* ⊕ *www.cruisepark.com*).

EXPLORING VANCOUVER

Vancouver is easy to navigate. The heart of the city—which includes the downtown area, the Canada Place cruise-ship terminal, Gastown, Chinatown, Stanley Park, and the West End high-rise residential neighborhood—sits on a peninsula hemmed in by English Bay and the Pacific Ocean to the west; by False Creek, the inlet home to Granville Island, to the south; and by Burrard Inlet, the working port of the city, to the north, past which loom the North Shore mountains.

DOWNTOWN & GASTOWN

Many sights of interest are steps from the Canada Place cruise-ship terminal, in Vancouver's downtown core, and a few blocks east in the historic district of Gastown. Gastown is where Vancouver originated after "Gassy" Jack Deighton canoed into Burrard Inlet in 1867 and built a saloon. In 1885, when the Canadian Pacific Railway announced that Burrard Inlet would be the terminus for the new transcontinental railway, the little town—called Granville Townsite at the time—saw its population boom. But on June 13, 1886, two months after Granville's incorporation as the City of Vancouver, a clearing fire got out of control and burned down the entire town. It was rebuilt by the time the first transcontinental train arrived, in May 1887, and Vancouver then became a transfer point for trade with the Far East and was soon crowded with hotels, warehouses, brothels, and saloons. The Klondike gold rush encouraged further development, but the area began to decline after about 1912. In 1971, Gastown, along with Chinatown, was declared a historic district; the area has since been revitalized, and is home to boutiques, cafés, loft apartments, and souvenir shops.

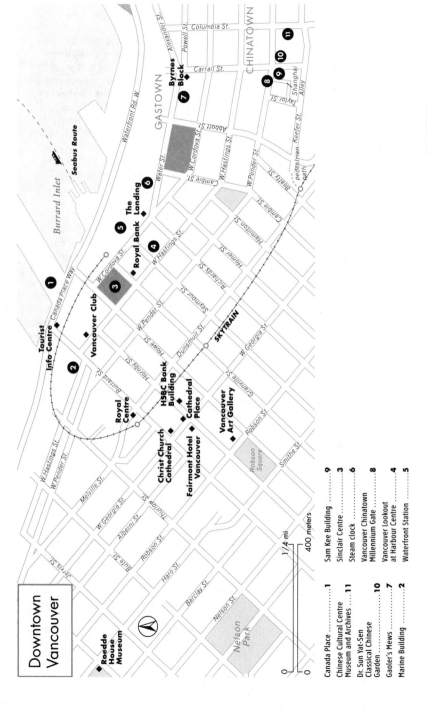

Downtown Vancouver

GASTOWN

CHINATOWN

Burrard Inlet

Seabus Route

Nelson Park

Robson Square

Byrnes Block 7

The Landing 5

Royal Bank 4

Vancouver Club 3

Tourist Info Centre 1

Royal Centre

HSBC Bank Building

Christ Church Cathedral

Cathedral Place

Vancouver Art Gallery

Fairmont Hotel Vancouver

Roedde House Museum

SKYTRAIN

1/4 mi

400 meters

GETTING THERE

A stroll from Canada Place into Gastown will take less than 15 minutes each way; allow an additional 30 minutes for the Vancouver Lookout at Harbour Centre. Note that the area just to the south of Gastown (roughly east of Cambie and south of Cordova) is one of Vancouver's roughest neighborhoods. Although Gastown itself (along Water Street) is busy with tourists and quite safe during the day, you may want to avoid walking through the area after dark.

> **DID YOU KNOW?**
>
> Gastown is where Vancouver originated after "Gassy" Jack Deighton canoed into Burrard Inlet in 1867 with his wife, some whiskey, and a few amenities. The smooth-talking Deighton convinced local mill workers into building him a saloon in exchange for a barrel of whiskey. (It didn't take much convincing; his saloon was on the edge of lumber-company land, where alcohol was forbidden.)

WHAT TO SEE

① Canada Place. When Vancouver hosted the Expo '86 world's fair, this former cargo pier was transformed into the Canadian pavilion. Extending four city blocks north into Burrard Inlet, the complex mimics the style and size of a luxury ocean liner, with exterior promenades and open deck space. The teflon-coated fiberglass roof, shaped like five sails, has become a Vancouver skyline landmark. Home to Vancouver's main cruise-ship terminal, Canada Place can accommodate up to three luxury liners at once. It's also home to the luxurious **Pan Pacific Hotel,** and, for the time being, the **Vancouver Convention and Exhibition Centre** (a new convention center, due to open in 2008, is under construction next door). You can stroll the exterior promenade and admire views of Burrard Inlet, Stanley Park, and the North Shore mountains; plaques posted at intervals offer historical information about the city and its waterfront. At the **Port Authority Interpretive Centre** (☎604/665–9179 ☐Free ☉Weekdays 9–4) you can catch a video about the workings of the port, see some historic images of Vancouver's waterfront, or try your hand at a virtual container loading game. The IMAX Theatre (☎604/682–4629 ☐C$11.50, higher prices for some films) shows films on a five-story-high screen. ☒999 Canada Place Way, Downtown ☎604/775–7200 ⊕www.canadaplace.ca.

❼ Gaoler's Mews. This brick-paved courtyard and the mews leading off it resemble a hidden slice of Victorian England. Once the site of the city's first civic buildings—the constable's cabin, customhouse, and a two-cell log jail—the mews today are home to architectural offices, a café, and an Irish pub. ☒Behind 12 Water St., Gastown.

❷ Marine Building. Bas-reliefs depicting the history of transportation, such as airships, steamships, locomotives, and submarines, as well as Maya and Egyptian motifs and images of marine life adorn this art deco structure erected in 1930. Step inside for a look at the beautifully restored interior, and then walk to the corner of Hastings and Hornby streets for the best view of the building. ☒355 Burrard St., Downtown.

3 Sinclair Centre. Vancouver architect Richard Henriquez knitted four government office buildings into Sinclair Centre, an office-retail complex that takes up an entire city block between Cordova and Hastings streets, and Howe and Granville streets. Inside are designer clothing shops, federal government offices, and fast-food outlets. The two Hastings Street buildings—the 1910 **Post Office,** which has an elegant clock tower, and the 1911 **Winch Building**—are linked with the 1937 **Post Office Extension** and the 1913 **Customs Examining Warehouse** to the north. In 1986 a meticulous restoration involved moving the post office facade to the Granville Street side of the complex. The original clockwork from the old clock tower is now on display inside on the upper level of the arcade. ⊠*757 W. Hastings St., Downtown.*

6 Steam clock. The world's first steam clock was built in 1977, although the design dates back to 1875. It's now said to be the most photographed structure in Vancouver. On every quarter hour a steam whistle rings out the Westminster chimes; on the hour a huge cloud of steam spews from the clock. ⊠*Corner of Cambie and Water Sts., Gastown.*

4 Vancouver Lookout at Harbour Centre. The lookout looks like a flying saucer stuck atop a high-rise. At 553 feet high, it affords one of the best views of Vancouver. A glass elevator whizzes you up 50 stories to the circular observation deck, where knowledgeable guides point out the sights. On a clear day you can see Vancouver Island and Mount Baker in Washington State. Tickets are good all day, so you can visit in daytime and return to see the city lights after dark. A rotating restaurant above the Lookout makes one complete revolution per hour; the elevator ride up is free for diners. ⊠*555 W. Hastings St., Downtown* ☎*604/689–0421 Lookout, 604/669–2220 restaurant* ⊕*www.vancouverlookout.com* ☞*C$13* ⊙*May–mid-Oct., daily 8:30 AM–10:30 PM; mid-Oct.–Apr., daily 9–9.*

5 Waterfront Station. This former Canadian Pacific Railway passenger terminal was built between 1912 and 1914 as the western terminus for Canada's transcontinental railway. After Canada's railways merged, the station became obsolete, but a 1978 renovation transformed it into an office-retail complex. It also serves as a depot for SkyTrain, SeaBus, and West Coast Express passengers. In the main concourse, panels near the ceiling depict the scenery travelers once saw on journeys across Canada. Here you can catch a 13-minute SeaBus trip across the harbor to the waterfront public market at Lonsdale Quay in North Vancouver. ⊠*601 W. Cordova St., Downtown* ☎*604/953–3333 SeaBus and SkyTrain, 604/488–8906 West Coast Express.*

CHINATOWN

Vancouver's Chinatown, declared a historic district in 1971, is one of the oldest and largest such areas in North America. Chinese immigrants were among the first to recognize the possibilities of Vancouver's setting and have played an important role here since the 18th century. Many came to British Columbia during the 1850s seeking their fortunes in the Cariboo gold rush. Thousands more arrived in the 1880s, recruited as laborers to build the Canadian Pacific Railway. Though much of Vancouver's Chinese community has now moved to suburban Richmond, Chinatown is still a vital neighborhood. The style of architecture in Vancouver's Chinatown is patterned on that of Guangzhou (Canton).

GETTING THERE

Although Chinatown is less than a mile from the Canada Place cruise-ship terminal, it's best to get there by cab or bus to avoid walking through the city's rough skid-row neighborhood. You can get a taxi at the stand in front of Canada Place or take the SkyTrain to Stadium Station and walk east a few blocks along Keefer or Pender streets.

WHAT TO SEE

⓫ Chinese Cultural Centre Museum and Archives. This Ming Dynasty–style facility is dedicated to promoting an understanding of Chinese-Canadian history and culture. A compelling permanent exhibit on the first floor traces the history of Chinese Canadians in British Columbia. The art gallery upstairs hosts traveling exhibits by Chinese and Canadian artists. A Chinese-Canadian military museum is also on-site. A monument across Columbia Street commemorates the community's contribution to the city, province, and country. ⊠ *555 Columbia St., Chinatown* ☎ *604/658–8880* ⊕ *www.cccvan.com* ⌨ *C$2, Tues. by donation* ☉ *Tues.–Sun. 11–5.*

⓾ ★ Dr. Sun Yat-Sen Classical Chinese Garden. The first authentic Ming Dynasty–style garden constructed outside China, this garden was built in 1986 by 52 artisans from Suzhou, China. It incorporates design elements and traditional materials from several of Suzhou's centuries-old private gardens. As you walk along the paths, remember that no power tools, screws, or nails were used in the construction. Guided tours, which are helpful in understanding the symbolism involved in the garden, are included in the price of admission. They're conducted on the hour between mid-June and the end of August (call for times the rest of the year). A concert series, including classical, Asian, world, jazz, and sacred music, plays every Friday evening in July, August, and September. The free public Dr. Sun Yat-Sen Park, next door, is also in the style of a traditional Chinese garden. ⊠ *578 Carrall St., Chinatown* ☎ *604/662–3207* ⊕ *www.vancouverchinesegarden.com* ⌨ *C$8.75* ☉ *May–mid-June and Sept., daily 10–6; mid-June–Aug., daily 9:30–7; Oct., daily 10–4:30; Nov.–Apr., Tues.–Sun. 10–4:30.*

❾ Sam Kee Building. *Ripley's Believe It or Not!* recognizes this structure, dating from about 1913, as the narrowest office building in the world. In 1913 when the city confiscated most of merchant Chang Toy's land to widen Pender Street, he built in protest on what he had left—just 6 feet. These days the building houses an insurance agency whose employees make do with the 4-foot-10-inch-wide interior. ⊠ *8 W. Pender St., Chinatown.*

❽ Vancouver Chinatown Millennium Gate. This brightly painted, three-story-high arch spanning Pender Street was erected in 2002 to commemorate the Chinese community's role in Vancouver's history. The gate incorporates both Eastern and Western symbols, and both traditional and

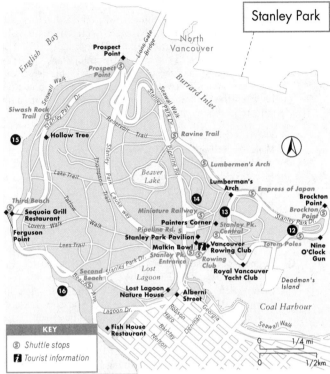

Stanley Park

3

modern Chinese themes. Just east of the gate is the entrance to **China-town Heritage Alley,** the site of Vancouver's first Chinese settlement. At the end of the alley is a replica of the West Han Dynasty Bell, a gift to Vancouver from the city of Guangzhou, China. Surrounding the bell are a series of panels relaying some of the area's early history. ✉ *Pender at Taylor St., Chinatown* ☎ *No phone* 🖭 *Free.*

FodorśChoice **STANLEY PARK**

★ A morning or afternoon in Stanley Park gives you a capsule tour of Vancouver that includes beaches, the ocean, Douglas fir and cedar forests, and a view of the North Shore mountains. One of the most popular ways to see the park is to walk, rollerblade, or cycle along Vancouver's famous Seawall Walk, a 9-km (5½-mi) seaside pathway around the park's circumference. The seawall extends an additional mile east past the marinas, cafés, and waterfront condominiums of Coal Harbour to Canada Place downtown, so you could start your walk or ride from there.

> **TOURING TIP**
>
> A more whimsical option is a ride with Stanley Park Horse-Drawn Tours (☎ *604/681—5115* ⊕ *www. stanleypark.com*), the $C26.50 fare includes a free bus ride from the Canada Place cruise-ship terminal to Stanley Park.

GETTING THERE

To get to the park by public transit, take Stanley Park Bus 19 from the corner of Pender and Howe, downtown. It's possible to see the park by car, entering at the foot of Georgia Street and driving counterclockwise around the one-way Stanley Park Drive. An even better option is to take the free Stanley Park Shuttle (☎ *604/257–8400* ⊕ *www.vancouver.ca/parks/*), which provides frequent transportation between the park entrance and all the major sights daily from mid-June to mid-September.

WHAT TO SEE

⑭ **Miniature Railway and Children's Farmyard.** A child-size train takes youngsters and adults on a ride through the woods of Stanley Park. Just next door is a farmyard full of tame, pettable critters, including goats, ponies, rabbits, and pigs. ⊠ *Off Pipeline Rd., Stanley Park* ☎ *604/257–8531* ✆ *Each site C$5.50, adults accompanying children C$2.75* ⊙ *Mid-May to late June, train and farmyard daily 11–4; late June to early Sept., train daily 10:30–5, farmyard daily 11–4; call for hrs at other times.*

⑯ **Second Beach.** In summer the main draw is the 50-meter pool with water slides and lifeguards. The shallow end fills up on hot days, but there's usually plenty of room in the lap-swimming section. A sandy beach, a playground, and covered picnic sites are nearby. ⊠ *Stanley Park Dr., Stanley Park* ☎ *604/257–8371 pool (summer only)* ⊕ *www.city.vancouver.bc.ca/parks* ✆ *Beach free, pool C$4.85* ⊙ *Pool open daily in summer, call for hrs.*

⑮ **Siwash Rock.** Legend tells of a young First Nations man who, about to become a father, bathed persistently to wash his sins away so that his son could be born pure. For his devotion he was blessed by the gods and immortalized in the shape of Siwash Rock. The rock is visible from the seawall; however, if you're driving you'll need to park and take a short path through the woods. A sign marks the trail, though at press time the trail was closed due to fallen trees.

⑫ **Totem poles.** These eight poles, all carved in the latter half of the 20th century, include replicas of poles originally brought to the park from the north coast in the 1920s, as well as poles carved specifically for the park by First Nations artists. The several styles of poles represent a cross section of British Columbia native groups, including the Kwakwaka'wakw, Haida, and Nisga'a. The combination of carved animals, fish, birds, and mythological creatures represents clan history. An information center near the site houses a snack bar, a gift shop, and information about British Columbia's First Nations.

⑬ **Vancouver Aquarium.** Pools with windows below the water level let you come face to face with beluga whales, dolphins, sea otters, sea lions, and harbor seals at this research and educational facility. In the Amazon rain-forest gallery you can walk through a jungle setting populated with sloths, tortoises, tropical birds, and, in summer, hundreds of free-flying butterflies. Other displays, many with hands-on features for children, show the underwater life of coastal British Columbia and the Canadian Arctic. A Tropic Zone exhibit is home to exotic fresh and saltwater life, including moray eels, and black-tip reef sharks. Beluga whale, sea lion, and dolphin shows, as well as dive shows (where divers swim with aquatic life—including sharks) are held daily. For an extra fee, you can help the trainers feed and train otters, belugas, and sea lions. Be prepared for lines on weekends and school holidays. ⊠ *845 Avison Way, Stanley Park* ☎*604/659–3474* ⊕*www.vanaqua.org* ⊠*C$19.95* ⊗*July–Labor Day, daily 9:30–7; day after Labor Day– June, daily 9–5.*

3

★ **GRANVILLE ISLAND**

This 35-acre peninsula in False Creek, just south of downtown Vancouver, is home to one of North America's most successful urban-redevelopment schemes. Once a derelict industrial site, Granville Island is now a vibrant urban park, with a bustling public market, several theaters, galleries, crafts shops, and artisans' studios.

GETTING THERE

To reach Granville Island, take a 15-minute walk from downtown Vancouver to the south end of Hornby Street. Aquabus Ferries (☎*604/689–5858* ⊕*www.theaquabus.com*), depart from here about every five minutes and deliver passengers (and bicycles) across False Creek at the Granville Island Public Market, which has a slew of food and other stalls. False Creek Ferries (☎*604/684–7781* ⊕*www. granvilleislandferries.bc.ca*) leave every five minutes for Granville Island from a dock behind the Vancouver Aquatic Centre, on Beach Avenue, and deliver passengers between Bridges Pub and the public market. Still another option is to take a 20-minute ride on a TransLink bus; from Waterfront Station or stops on Granville Street, take False Creek South Bus 50 to the edge of the island. On summer weekend afternoons, you can hop aboard the **Downtown Historic Railway** (⊕*www.trams.bc.ca*), a tram line that runs to the island from stops around False Creek. The market is a short walk from the bus, ferry, or tram stop. If you drive, a limited amount of parking is free for up to three hours, and paid parking is available in garages on the island.

WHAT TO SEE

℃ **Granville Island Museums.** Here you can find two museums under one roof. The **Model Ships Museum** displays exquisitely detailed replicas of early-20th-century military and working vessels and an excellent collection of model submarines. The **Model Trains Museum** has the world's largest toy-train collection on public display, including a diorama of the Fraser Canyon and the Kettle Valley that involves 1,000 feet of track and some large-scale (3-foot-high) model trains. ⊠*1502 Duranleau St., Granville Island* ☎*604/683–1939* ⊕*www. granvilleislandmuseums.com* ⊠*Both museums C$7.50* ⊗*May–Oct., daily 10–5:30; Nov.–Apr., Tues.–Sun. 10–5:30.*

Fodor'sChoice **Granville Island Public Market.** Because no chain stores are allowed in
★ this 50,000-square-foot building, each outlet here is unique. Dozens of stalls sell locally grown produce direct from the farm; others sell crafts, chocolates, cheeses, fish, meat, flowers, and exotic foods. In summer,

market gardeners sell fruit and vegetables from trucks outside. On the west side of the market you can pick up a snack, espresso, or fixings for lunch on the wharf. The Market Courtyard, on the waterside, is a good place to catch street entertainers. Weekends can get madly busy here. ⊠*1689 Johnston St., Granville Island* ☎*604/666–6477* ⊕*www. granvilleisland.com* ☉*Daily 9–7.*

OUTSIDE DOWNTOWN

FodorsChoice **Museum of Anthropology.** Set on a cliff top overlooking the Pacific, the ★ MOA houses one of the world's leading collections of Northwest Coast First Nations art. The Great Hall displays dramatic cedar poles, bentwood boxes, and canoes adorned with traditional Northwest Coast painted designs; exquisite carvings of gold, silver, and argillite (black shale) are also on display. The museum's collection also includes tools, textiles, masks, and other artifacts from around the world, as well as a gallery of European ceramics. Behind the museum are two Haida houses, set on the cliff over the water. Free guided tours—given twice daily in summer, usually at 11 and 2 (call to confirm times)—are very informative. The museum is about 30 minutes, or a C$25 taxi ride, from Canada Place. ⊠*University of British Columbia, 6393 N.W. Marine Dr., Point Grey* ☎*604/822–3825 or 604/822–5087* ⊕*www. moa.ubc.ca* ☜*C$9, C$5 Tues. 5–9* ☉*Memorial Day–mid Oct., Tues. 10–9, Wed.–Mon. 10–5; early Oct.–Memorial Day, Tues. 11–9, Wed.– Sun. 11–5.*

WHERE TO EAT

A diverse gastronomic experience awaits you in cosmopolitan Vancouver. A wave of Asian immigration and tourism has brought a proliferation of upscale Asian eateries. Cutting-edge restaurants currently perfecting and defining Pacific Northwest fare—including such homegrown regional favorites as salmon and oysters, accompanied by British Columbia wines—have become some of the city's leading attractions.

You're also spoiled for choice when it comes to casual and budget dining. Good choices include Asian cafés or any of the pubs listed in the Nightlife section; many have both an adults-only pub and a separate restaurant section where kids are welcome. A bylaw bans smoking indoors in all Vancouver restaurants, bars, and pubs.

Vancouver dining is fairly informal. Casual but neat dress is appropriate everywhere. A 15% tip is expected. A 6% Goods and Services Tax (GST) is added to the food portion of the bill and a 10% liquor tax is charged on wine, beer, and spirits. Some restaurants build the liquor tax into the price of the beverage, but others add it to the bill.

$$$$ ✕**C Restaurant.** Save your pennies, fish fans—this seafood hotspot is the place to try such sustainably harvested regional fare as Skeena River Hawkshaw salmon or Nordic Spirit sablefish from Northern British Columbia. Start with shucked oysters from the raw bar, or try one of the multicourse menu tastings. Both the chic, ultramodern interior and

the waterside patio overlook False Creek. ✉2–1600 Howe St., Downtown ☎604/681–1164 ⊟AE, DC, MC, V ☾No lunch Oct.–Apr.

$$$ ✗**Sequoia Grill at the Teahouse.** The former officers' mess in Stanley Park is perfectly poised for watching sunsets over the water. The Pacific Northwest menu includes such specialties as pear and spinach salad, grilled ahi tuna, and seasonally changing treatments of venison, B.C. salmon, and rack of lamb. In summer you can dine on the patio and sample from the small plates menu offered each afternoon. ✉On Stanley Park Dr., Ferguson Point, near Third Beach Stanley Park ☎604/669–3281 or 800/280–9893 ⊟AE, MC, V.

$$–$$$ ✗**Aqua Riva.** This lofty modern room, replete with dramatic art deco murals and an open kitchen, is yards from the Canada Place cruise-ship terminal. A wall of windows affords striking views over the harbor and the North Shore mountains. Food from the wood-fired oven, rotisserie, and grill includes thin-crust pizzas with innovative toppings, roasted wild salmon, and spit-roasted chicken. Lunch brings a good selection of salads, pizzas, sandwiches, and salmon dishes. A microbrew and martini list rounds out the menu. ✉200 Granville St., Downtown ☎604/683–5599 ⊟AE, DC, MC, V ☾No lunch weekends.

$$–$$$ ✗**Imperial Chinese Seafood.** This Cantonese restaurant in the art deco Marine Building is a good choice for dim sum, which is served daily 11 AM to 2:30 PM. At dinner, any dish with lobster, crab, or shrimp from the live tanks is recommended. ✉355 Burrard St., Downtown ☎604/688–8191 ⊟DC, MC, V.

$$–$$$ ✗**Water Street Café.** The tables at this casual tourist-friendly Gastown bistro spill out onto the sidewalk for front-row views of the steam clock across the street. Tall windows on two sides of the lofty red-and-gold interior take in the Gastown streetscape. It's tempting to pick one of the 15 varieties of pasta, but the crab chowder, West Coast crab cakes, and the Fanny Bay oysters also are good choices. Although the basics are done well here, don't expect culinary innovation. ✉300 Water St., Gastown ☎604/689–2832 ⊟AE, DC, MC, V.

$$ ✗**Cassis Bistro.** French home-cooking meets downtown chic at this good-value bistro, where the high ceilings and rough wooden floors give it a stripped-down, loftlike feel. The highlights of the French regional menu, where most dishes are less than C$20, are garlicky bouillabaisse brimming with fresh fish, salade niçoise updated with thinly sliced tuna carpaccio, and a classic daube de boeuf. ✉420 W. Pender St., Downtown ☎604/605–0420 ⊟MC, V ☾No lunch weekends.

$$ ✗**Incendio.** The hand-flipped thin-crust pizzas, with innovative toppings including Asiago cheese, prosciutto, roasted garlic, and sun-dried tomatoes, and the mix-and-match pastas and sauces (try the hot smoked-duck sausage, artichoke, and tomato combination or the broccoli and pine nuts in a creamy Gorgonzola cheese sauce) draw crowds to this Gastown eatery. The room, in a circa-1900 heritage building, with exposed brick, local artwork, and big curved windows, has plenty of atmosphere. ✉103 Columbia St., Gastown ☎604/688–8694 ⊟AE, MC, V ☾No lunch weekends.

$$ ✗**Irish Heather.** This two-story Gastown hideaway, with its brick-lined interior, sunny conservatory, and cobblestone courtyard, brings the

gastropub concept (the idea that pub food can be good) to Vancouver. Everything is made from scratch, from the hand-cut chips and whiskey-cured salmon to the bread, pasta, and even the ice cream. Try the hand-made bangers and mash, the steak-and-Guinness potpie, or any of the daily salads. Catch, if you can, the live Celtic music played every Thursday evening. The same owner also runs a **Shebeen,** or whiskey house, serving about 160 whiskies in a carriage house across the courtyard, as well as the **Salty Tongue** (⊠*213 Carrall St.* ☎*604/915–7258*), a deli, and a good spot for high-end picnic fixings, next door. **Salt Tasting Room** (⊠*Blood Alley* ☎*604/633–1912*), around the corner, offers artisanal cheeses, small-batch cured meats, and local wines by the glass. ⊠*217 Carrall St., Gastown* ☎*604/688–9779* ▭*AE, MC, V.*

¢–$$ ✕**Hon's Wun-Tun House.** Mr. Hon has been keeping Vancouverites in Chinese comfort food since the 1970s. The best bets on the 300-item menu are the wonton and noodle dishes, any of the Chinese vegetables, and anything with barbecued meat. The Robson Street outlet has a separate kitchen for vegetarians and an army of fast-moving waitresses. The original Keefer Street location is in the heart of Chinatown. ⊠*1339 Robson St., Downtown* ☎*604/685–0871* ⊠*268 Keefer St., Chinatown* ☎*604/688–0871* ▭*MC, V.*

¢–$ ✕**Go Fish.** If the weather's fine, head for this little seafood stand on the
★ docks near Granville Island. The menu is short—highlights include fish-and-chips, grilled salmon or tuna sandwiches, and oyster po'boys—but the quality is first-rate, and the accompanying Asian-flavored slaw leaves ordinary coleslaw in the dust. There are just a few (outdoor) tables, so go early or be prepared to wait. To get here, walk along the waterfront path from Granville Island; by car, drive east from Burrard on 1st Avenue until it ends at the docks. The restaurant will be on your right. ⊠*1505 W. 1st Ave., Fisherman's Wharf, Kitsilano* ☎*604/730–5039* ▭*MC, V* ⊗*Closed Mon. No dinner.*

¢–$ ✕**Lupo Caffé Bar.** The deep-red walls and upholstered bar stools give this Italian-style café an expensive feel, but the light meals are moderately priced. In the morning you can stop in for an espresso or homemade waffles with berries and maple syrup. Midday, the menu includes panini, salads, and homemade soups, and several pasta dishes. Tapas are served in the evening. ⊠*1014 W. Georgia St., Downtown* ☎*604/685–1131* ▵*Reservations not accepted* ▭*MC, V* ⊗*Closed Sun. No dinner.*

WHERE TO STAY

Accommodations in Vancouver range from luxurious waterfront hotels to neighborhood B&Bs and basic European-style pensions. Many of the best choices are in the downtown core, either in the central business district or in the West End near Stanley Park. The chart in the Port Essentials section shows high-season prices, but from mid-October through May, rates throughout the city can drop as much as 50%. Many Vancouver hotels are completely no-smoking in both rooms and public areas.

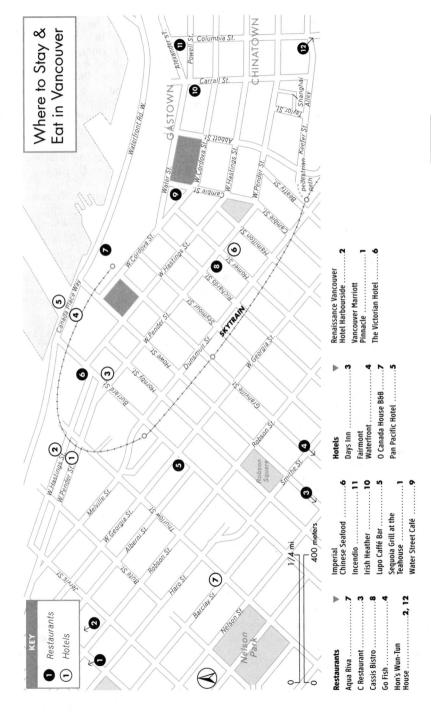

Where to Stay &
Eat in Vancouver

KEY
1 Restaurants
1 Hotels

Restaurants ▶

Aqua Riva **7**
C Restaurant **3**
Cassis Bistro **8**
Go Fish **4**
Hon's Wun-Tun
House **2, 12**

Imperial
Chinese Seafood **6**
Incendio **11**
Irish Heather **10**
Lupo Caffè Bar **5**
Sequoia Grill at the
Teahouse **1**
Water Street Café **9**

Hotels ▶

Days Inn **3**
Fairmont
Waterfront **4**
O Canada House B&B ... **7**
Pan Pacific Hotel **5**

Renaissance Vancouver
Hotel Harbourside ... **2**
Vancouver Marriott
Pinnacle **1**
The Victorian Hotel ... **6**

$$$$ ⌂ **Fairmont Waterfront.** This striking 23-story hotel is directly across the street from the Canada Place cruise-ship terminal (it's also accessible via an underground mall). But it's the floor-to-ceiling windows with ocean, park, and mountain views from most of the guest rooms that really make this hotel. The light-filled rooms are adorned with blond-wood furniture, warm earth-toned or blue-and-apricot fabrics, and contemporary Canadian artwork; each has a window that opens. Next to the mountain-view pool is a rooftop herb garden, an aromatic retreat open to guests. Two hotel dogs are on hand for petting, pampering, and taking for strolls. Ask about cruise packages, which include accommodation, a full breakfast, and porterage to the Canada Place cruise-ship terminal. ⊠*900 Canada Place Way, Downtown* ☎*604/691–1991* ⊕*www.fairmont.com/waterfront* ⧉*489 rooms, 29 suites* ⧉*In-room: safes (some), Ethernet. In-hotel: restaurant, room service, bar, pool, gym, laundry service, concierge, executive floor, public Internet, public Wi-Fi, parking (fee), some pets allowed, no-smoking rooms* ⊟*AE, D, DC, MC, V.*

$$$$ ⌂ **Pan Pacific Hotel.** Canada Place, Vancouver's main cruise-ship termi-
★   nal, is also home to this luxurious 23-story hotel. The rooms are large and modern, with bird's-eye maple wood throughout, marble vanities, Italian linens, and some of the city's best ocean, mountain, or skyline views. The suites, some with a private steam room, sauna, or baby grand piano, are popular with visiting celebrities. A 26-room, Roman bath–theme spa, and a state-of-the-art health and fitness center add to the pampering. Pre- and post-cruise packages include breakfast, early or late checkout, and seamless transfers to or from your ship—just an elevator ride away. ⊠*300–999 Canada Pl., Downtown* ☎*604/ 662–8111, 800/663–1515 in Canada, 800/937–1515 in U.S.* ⊕*www. panpacific.com* ⧉*465 rooms, 39 suites* ⧉*In-room: safe, kitchen (some), Ethernet. In-Hotel: 2 restaurants, room service, bar, pool, gym, spa, public Internet, public Wi-Fi, parking (fee), some pets allowed, no-smoking rooms* ⊟*AE, DC, MC, V.*

$$$–$$$$ ⌂ **O Canada House B&B.** This beautifully restored 1897 Victorian, within walking distance of downtown, is where the first version of "O Canada," the national anthem, was written, in 1909. Each bedroom is appointed in late-Victorian antiques; modern comforts such as bathrobes help make things homey. The top-floor room is enormous, with two king beds and a private sitting area. A separate one-room coach house in the garden is a romantic option. Breakfast, served in the dining room, is a lavish affair, and a guest pantry, with soft drinks and fresh baking, is always open. Smoking is permitted outdoors only. ⊠*1114 Barclay St., West End* ☎*604/688–0555 or 877/688–1114* ⊕*www. ocanadahouse.com* ⧉*7 rooms* ⧉*In-room: no a/c, refrigerator, DVD (some), VCR (some), Wi-Fi. In-hotel: no elevator, public Wi Fi, parking (no fee), no kids under 12, no-smoking rooms* ⊟*MC, V* ⧉*BP.*

$$–$$$$ ⌂ **Renaissance Vancouver Hotel Harbourside.** An indoor pool and play area, direct access to a waterside park, big rooms, and a kids' menu in the casual restaurant make this no-smoking high-rise a good choice for families. It's also handy to the cruise-ship terminal and central business district. The modern rooms are all at least 350 square feet and

have either step-out or full-size glassed-in balconies. Bathroom floors are heated. ✉*1133 W. Hastings St., Downtown* ☎*604/689–9211 or 800/905–8582* ⊕*www.renaissancevancouver.com* ⤳*426 rooms, 12 suites* ♿*In-room: safe (some), Ethernet, Wi-Fi. In-hotel: 2 restaurants, room service, bars, pool, gym, laundry service, concierge, executive floor, public Internet, public Wi-Fi, parking (fee), some pets allowed, no-smoking rooms* ☰*AE, D, DC, MC, V.*

$$–$$$$ 🏨**Vancouver Marriott Pinnacle.** The soaring 50-foot-high atrium lobby makes a striking entrance to this 38-story hotel a few blocks from the cruise-ship terminal and central business district. Decorated in modern pale woods and neutral tones, each room has almost a full wall of windows and many rooms offer expansive views of Burrard Inlet and the North Shore Mountains or the city skyline. The hotel's ShowCase restaurant and bar serves West Coast cuisine with global influences. The hotel is completely no-smoking. ✉*1128 W. Hastings St., Downtown* ☎*604/684–1128 or 800/207–4150* ⊕*www.vancouvermarriottpinnacle. com* ⤳*424 rooms, 10 suites* ♿*In-room: safe, Ethernet. In-hotel: restaurant, room service, bar, pool, gym, laundry service, concierge, executive floor, public Internet, public Wi-Fi, parking (fee), some pets allowed, no-smoking rooms* ☰*AE, D, DC, MC, V.*

$–$$$ 🏨**Days Inn.** Two blocks from the Canada Place cruise-ship terminal, this moderately priced, well-secured boutique hotel operates a free shuttle to any downtown location, including Vancouver's train and bus station. Rooms in this 1918 eight-story building (with an elevator) are small and lack views but are freshly renovated with checked duvets, pine furniture, and crown moldings. The two-bedroom, one-bathroom corner units are a good value for groups and families. This hotel is entirely no-smoking. ✉*921 W. Pender St., Downtown* ☎*604/681–4335 or 877/681–4335* ⊕*www.daysinnvancouver.com* ⤳*80 rooms, 5 suites* ♿*In-Room: safe, refrigerator, Ethernet, Wi-Fi. In-hotel: restaurant, bars laundry facilities, laundry service, public Internet, public Wi-Fi, parking (fee), no-smoking rooms* ☰*AE, D, DC, MC, V.*

¢–$ 🏨**The Victorian Hotel.** Budget hotels can be beautiful, too, as proven by the hardwood floors, high ceilings, and chandeliers at this prettily restored 1898 European-style pension. Offering some of Vancouver's best value accommodations, guest rooms in the two connecting three-story buildings have down duvets and oriental rugs; some have bay windows or mountain views. Some of the private bathrooms are outfitted with marble tiles and granite countertops, and even the shared baths are spotlessly clean and nicely appointed. The entire hotel is no-smoking. ✉*514 Homer St., Downtown* ☎*877/681–6369 or 604/681–6369* ⊕*www.victorian-hotel.com* ⤳*40 rooms, 20 with bath* ♿*In Room: no a/c, kitchen (some), Ethernet. In-hotel: no elevator, laundry service, public Internet, public Wi Fi, parking (fee), some pets allowed, no-smoking rooms* ☰*MC, V* ⦿*CP Nov.–Feb. only.*

NIGHTLIFE

For information on events, pick up a free copy of the *Georgia Straight*, available at cafés and bookstores around town, or look in the entertainment section of the *Vancouver Sun* (Thursday's paper has listings).

For tickets, book through **Ticketmaster** (☎*604/280–4444* ⊕*www.ticketmaster.ca*). You can pick up half-price tickets on the day of the event, as well as full-price advance tickets, at **Tickets Tonight** (✉*200 Burrard St., Downtown* ☎*604/684–2787* ⊕*www.ticketstonight.ca*), at the Vancouver Tourist Info Centre.

BARS, PUBS & LOUNGES

A massive deck with expansive False Creek views is the big draw at **Bridges** (✉*1696 Duranleau St., Granville Island* ☎*604/687–4400*), near the public market. There's a cozy pub and a restaurant at the same site. A seaside patio, casual Pacific Northwest restaurant, and house-brewed beer make the **Dockside Brewing Company** (✉*Granville Island Hotel, 1253 Johnston St., Granville Island* ☎*604/685–7070*) a popular hangout. For a pint of properly poured Guinness and live traditional Irish music every Thursday night, try **Irish Heather** (✉*217 Carrall St., Gastown* ☎*604/688–9779*). Out back, in an atmospheric coach house, a **Shebeen,** or whiskey house, serves about 160 whiskies. Harbor views, pub food, and traditionally brewed beer are the draws at **Steamworks Brewing Company** (✉*375 Water St., Gastown* ☎*604/689–2739*), a multilevel, brick-lined brewpub on the edge of Gastown; a coffee bar and a restaurant open to all ages are also on-site.

COMEDY

The **Vancouver TheatreSports League** (☎*604/738–7013* ⊕*www.vtsl.com*), a hilarious improv troupe, performs Wednesday through Saturday at the New Revue Stage (✉*1601 Johnston St.*) on Granville Island. Stand-up comedians perform Tuesday to Saturday evenings at **Yuk Yuk's** (✉*1015 Burrard St., Downtown* ☎*604/696–9857* ⊕*www.yukyuks.com*) in the Century Plaza Hotel.

DANCE CLUBS

The **Commodore Ballroom** (✉*868 Granville St., Downtown* ☎*604/739–7469* ⊕*www.hob.com/venues/concerts/commodore*), a 1929 art deco dance hall with a massive sprung dance floor, hosts bands six nights a week. The luminous, postmodern **Shine** (✉*364 Water St., Gastown* ☎*604/408–4321* ⊕*www.shinenightclub.com*) draws a trendy crowd to its hip-hop, R&B, and funk nights.

SHOPPING

Unlike many cities where suburban malls have taken over, Vancouver is full of individual boutiques and specialty shops. Antiques stores, ethnic markets, art galleries, gourmet-food shops, and high-fashion outlets abound, and you can find strong Asian and First Nations influences in crafts, home furnishings, and foods. Store hours are generally 10–6 Monday, Tuesday, Wednesday, and Saturday; 10–9 Thursday and Friday; and 11–6 Sunday.

SALES TAXES

You'll pay both 7% Provincial Sales Tax (PST) and 6% Goods and Services Tax (GST) on most purchases.

SHOPPING DISTRICTS

Robson Street, stretching from Burrard to Bute, is the city's main fashion-shopping and people-watching artery. Gap and Banana Republic have their flagship stores here, as do Canadian fashion outlets Club Monaco and Roots. Souvenir shops and cafés line the way; west of Bute, Asian food shops, video outlets, and cheap noodle bars abound. Shops in and near **Sinclair Centre** (⊠ *757 W. Hastings St., Downtown*) cater to sophisticated and pricey tastes. Bustling **Chinatown**—centered on Pender and Main streets—is at its most lively on weekend evenings in summer, when the Chinatown Night Market, an Asian-style outdoor street market, sets up along Keefer Street. There's an even bigger Asian-style nighttime market, also on summer weekends, south of Vancouver at the **Richmond Night Market** (⊠ *12631 Vulcan Way, off Bridgeport Rd. at Sweden Way, Richmond* ☎ *604/244–8448*). **Granville Island** has a lively public market and a wealth of galleries, crafts shops, and artisans' studios. **South Granville,** along Granville Street between Broadway and 16th Avenue, is lined with high-end fashion, home decor, art galleries, and specialty food shops. Treasure hunters should check out the 300 block of **West Cordova Street,** near Gastown, where offbeat shops sell curios, vintage clothing, and locally designed fashions. **Yaletown,** a gentrified former warehouse district centered on Davie and Hamilton streets, is home to chic fashion and housewares shops.

MALLS

Pacific Centre Mall (⊠ *700 W. Georgia St., Downtown* ☎ *604/688–7236*), on two levels and mostly underground, takes up three city blocks in the heart of downtown. Mid-price, mainstream clothing stores predominate on the lower level; chicer, pricier items can be found on the upper floor.

ART GALLERIES

Gallery Row along Granville Street between 5th and 15th avenues has about a dozen high-end contemporary art galleries. Gastown has the city's best selection of First Nations and Inuit galleries.

Buschlen Mowatt Gallery (⊠ *1445 W. Georgia St., West End* ☎ *604/682–1234*) exhibits the works of contemporary Canadian and international artists. **Hill's Native Art** (⊠ *165 Water St., Gastown* ☎ *604/685–4249*) has Vancouver's largest selection of First Nations art. The **Inuit Gallery of Vancouver** (⊠ *206 Cambie St., Gastown* ☎ *604/688–7323 or 888/615–8399*) exhibits Northwest Coast and Inuit art.

CLOTHES

Dream (⊠ *311 W. Cordova St., Gastown* ☎ *604/683–7326*) is where up-and-coming local designers sell their wares. Men's and women's fashions by Versace, Dior, Prada, and others are available at **Leone** (⊠ *757 W. Hastings St., Downtown* ☎ *604/683–1133*) in Sinclair Centre. You'll find more affordable, North American fashions—and an Italian café—at **L2** on Leone's lower floor. For outdoorsy clothes that double as souvenirs (many sport maple-leaf logos), check out the sweatshirts, leather jackets, and other cozy casuals at **Roots** (⊠ *1001 Robson St., West End* ☎ *604/683–4305*).

Ports of Call

WORD OF MOUTH

"We saw humpbacks cooperative feeding in the mouth of Glacier Bay and a grizzly bear swimming across one of the smaller arms. It was amazing. Plus calving glaciers and beautiful scenery. It was trip I won't soon forget!"

—jcasale

"I have been on an Alaskan cruise twice now and by far the most incredible excursion I've ever taken was the dog sled/glacier helicopter trip out of Juneau. It's pricey but worth every single penny. Absolutely amazing. We actually rode with dogs who had run the Iditarod. Landing on the glacier was breathtaking. We also enjoyed our 6 hour jeep excursion in Skagway."

—LuvToGo

THERE'S NEVER A DULL DAY on an Alaskan cruise, and whether your ship is scheduled to make a port call, cruise by glaciers, or glide through majestic fjords, you'll have constant opportunities to explore the culture, wildlife, history, and amazing scenery that make Alaska so unique. Most port cities are small and easily explored on foot, but if you prefer to be shown the sights, your ship will offer organized shore excursions at each stop along the way. Popular activities include city tours, flightseeing, charter fishing, river rafting, and visits to native communities. You can also, for the sake of shorter trips and/or more active excursions, readily organize your own tour through a local vendor.

The ports visited and the amount of time spent in each vary depending on the cruise line and itinerary, but most ships stop in Ketchikan, Juneau, and Skagway—the three big draws in Southeast Alaska. Some ports, such as Homer and Metlakatla, are visited by only a couple of the small-ship cruise lines, while other adventure ships head out to explore the wild places in the Bering Sea. Each town has its highlights. For example, Ketchikan has a wealth of native artifacts, Skagway has lots of gold rush history, Sitka has a rich Russian and native heritage, and Juneau has glacier trips. There are also ample shopping opportunities in most ports (less so in Wrangell), but beware of tacky tourist traps. All Southeast towns, but especially Haines, Sitka, and Ketchikan, have great art galleries.

PORT ESSENTIALS

RESTAURANTS & CUISINE

Not surprisingly, seafood dominates most menus. In summer, salmon, halibut, crab, cod, and prawns are usually fresh. Restaurants are informal and casual clothes are the norm; you'll never be sent away for wearing jeans in an Alaskan restaurant.

WHAT IT COSTS			
$	$$	$$$	$$$$
ALASKAN PORTS	under $9	$9–$15	$16–$25	over $25
CANADIAN PORTS	under C$15	C$15–C$27	C$28–C$40	over C$40

*Per person for a main course at dinner.

OUTDOOR ACTIVITIES

There are hikes and walks in or near every Alaska port town. Well-maintained trails are easily accessible from even the largest cities; lush forests and wilderness areas, port and glacier views, and mountaintop panoramas are often within a few hours' walk of downtown areas. More adventurous travelers will enjoy paddling sea kayaks in the protected waters of Southeast and South Central Alaska; companies in most ports rent kayaks and give lessons and tours. Fishing enthusiasts from all over the world come to Alaska for a chance to land a trophy salmon or halibut. Cycling, glacier hikes, flightseeing, or bear-viewing shore excursions in some ports also offer cruise passengers an oppor-

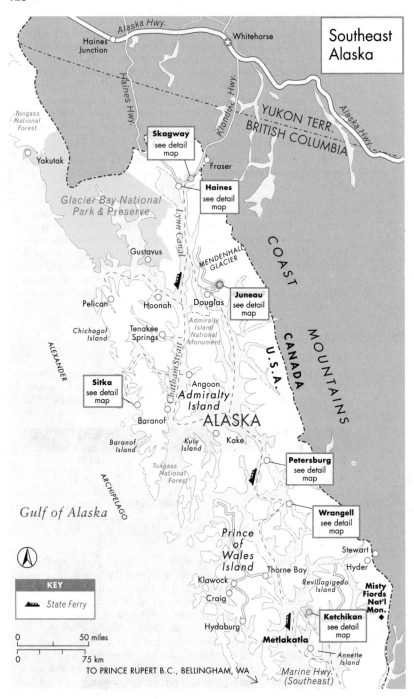

Southeast Alaska

Alaska Hwy.

Haines Junction

Whitehorse

Haines Hwy.

Klondike Hwy.

Alaska Hwy.

Tongass National Forest

Yakutat

YUKON TERR.

BRITISH COLUMBIA

Skagway
see detail map

Fraser

Haines
see detail map

Glacier Bay National Park & Preserve

Lynn Canal

Gustavus

MENDENHALL GLACIER

Pelican

Hoonah

Douglas

Juneau
see detail map

Chichagof Island

Tenakee Springs

Admiralty Island National Monument

COAST

MOUNTAINS

U.S.A.

CANADA

ALEXANDER

Chatham Strait

Sitka
see detail map

Angoon

Admiralty Island

ALASKA

Baranof

Baranof Island

Kuiu Island

Kake

Tongass National Forest

Petersburg
see detail map

Gulf of Alaska

ARCHIPELAGO

Wrangell
see detail map

Prince of Wales Island

Stewart

Hyder

Thorne Bay

Klawock

Revillagigedo Island

Misty Fiords Nat'l Mon.

Craig

Hydaburg

Metlakatla

Ketchikan
see detail map

Annette Island

KEY

State Ferry

0 — 50 miles

0 — 75 km

TO PRINCE RUPERT B.C., BELLINGHAM, WA

Marine Hwy. (Southeast)

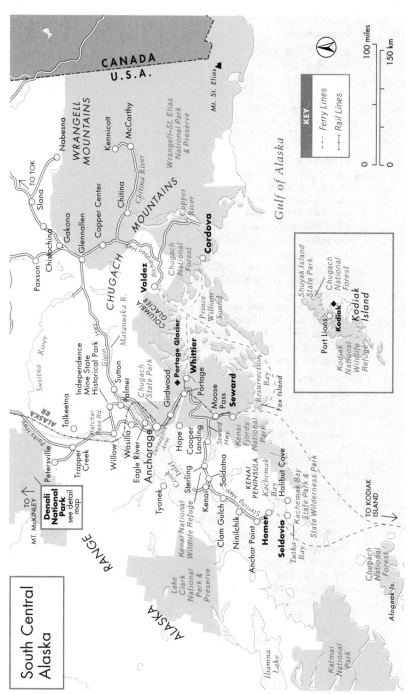

South Central Alaska

KEY
- - - Ferry Lines
—⊢— Rail Lines

100 miles
150 km

CANADA
U.S.A.

WRANGELL MOUNTAINS

Nabesna

Kennicott
McCarthy

Wrangell–St. Elias
National Park
& Preserve

Mt. St. Elias

TO TOK

Slana
Chistochina
Gakona
Glennallen
Copper Center
Chitina
Chitina River
Copper River

Paxson
Chistochina

CHUGACH MOUNTAINS

Gulf of Alaska

Cordova

Chugach
National
Forest

Valdez

Richardson Hwy

COLUMBIA GLACIER

Prince William Sound

Matanuska R.

Glenn Hwy

Susitna River

Independence Mine State Historical Park
Sutton
Palmer
Chugach State Park
Hatcher Pass Rd.

Talkeetna

ALASKA RR
Parks Hwy

Girdwood
◆ **Portage Glacier**
Whittier
Portage
Moose Pass
Seward

Resurrection Bay

Kenai Fjords National Park

Fox Island

Willow
Wasilla
Eagle River
Anchorage
Turnagain Arm
Hope
Cooper Landing
Seward Hwy

Shuyak Island State Park
Chugach National Forest

Port Lions
Kodiak
◆ Kodiak
Kodiak Island

Kodiak National Wildlife Refuge

MT. McKINLEY
TO

Denali National Park
see detail map

RANGE

ALASKA

Petersville
Trapper Creek

Susitna River

Tyonek

Cook Inlet

Sterling
Soldotna
KENAI PENINSULA
Kenai
Sterling Hwy
Kenai National Wildlife Refuge

Clam Gulch
Ninilchik
Anchor Point
Homer
Seldovia

Kachemak Bay
Halibut Cove
Kachemak Bay State Park & State Wilderness Park

Tutka Bay

TO KODIAK ISLAND

Chugach National Forest

Lake Clark National Park & Preserve

Iliamna Lake

Katmai National Park

Afognak Is.

4

tunity to engage with Alaska's endless landscape.

BARS & SALOONS

Shooting the breeze at a bar or saloon can be a delightfully colorful contrast to barstool-surfing the cruise-ship lounge areas. There isn't really a difference between saloons and bars; some saloons offer a setting that lets travelers pretend they've gone back in time to the gold rush, but other places that call themselves bars (such as the Alaskan Bar in Juneau) can be equally historic and interesting. High-volume watering holes in the busiest ports (such as the Red Dog in Juneau and the Red Onion in Skagway) serve food in addition to drinks. Generally, most bars are busiest at night and on the weekends when locals and independent travelers stop in. Pubs in Canadian ports are similar, though they often have an Irish or British, rather than gold rush, theme; all serve food and many even brew their own beer. Listed under the individual ports of call are some favorite gathering places.

> ### NAVIGATING THIS CHAPTER
>
> To help you plan your trip, we've compiled a list of the most worthwhile excursions available in each port of call (keep in mind that these lists aren't comprehensive; your cruise line may offer other options). Also look out for "Best Bets" boxes in each port of call section; these highlight each port's top experiences so you don't shell out for a flightseeing trip in one place, for example, when the experience would be better elsewhere. *For in-depth information on outdoor activities all around Alaska, see Chapter 5, Sports & Wilderness Adventures.*

SHOPPING

Alaskan native handicrafts range from Tlingit totem poles—a few inches high to more than 30 feet tall—to Athabascan beaded slippers and fur garments. Traditional pieces of art (or imitations thereof) are found in gift shops up and down the coast: Inupiat spirit masks, Yupik dolls and dance fans, Tlingit button blankets and silver jewelry, and Aleut grass baskets and carved wooden items. Salmon, halibut, crab, and other frozen fish are very popular souvenirs (shipped home to meet you, of course) and make great gifts. Most towns have at least one local company that packs and ships fresh, smoked, or frozen seafood.

To ensure authenticity, buy items tagged with the state-approved AUTHENTIC NATIVE HANDCRAFT FROM ALASKA "Silverhand" label, or look for the polar bear symbol indicating products made in Alaska. Although these symbols are designed to ensure authentic Alaskan and native-made products, not all items lacking them are inauthentic. This applies in particular to native artists who may or may not go through the necessary paperwork to obtain the Silverhand labels. Before buying something—particularly an expensive piece—ask questions to ensure its authenticity. Better prices are found in the more remote villages where you buy directly from the artisan, in museum shops, or in crafts fairs such as Anchorage's downtown Saturday Market.

SHORE EXCURSIONS

Shore excursions arranged by the cruise line are a convenient way to see the sights, but you'll pay extra for this convenience. Before your cruise, you'll receive a booklet describing the shore excursions your cruise line offers. A few lines let you book excursions in advance; all sell them on board during the cruise. If you cancel your excursion, you may incur penalties, the amount varying with the number of days remaining until the tour. Because these trips are specialized, many have limited capacity and are sold on a first-come, first-served basis.

WORD OF MOUTH

"We prefer doing our own shore excursions. We get to see exactly what we want to see, for exactly how long we want to see it, without having to waste time herding people on and off a bus, and waiting for stragglers."

–abram

CORDOVA

Cordova is decidedly and delightfully off the beaten path, and only passengers on Cruise West's four-night "Glacier Wonderland" cruise visit during their voyage around Prince William Sound. If you're one of the lucky few, you'll enjoy the real thing: a peaceful, coastal Alaskan town with no roads to the outside and some marvelous sights.

A small town with the spectacular backdrop of snowy Mt. Eccles, Cordova is the gateway to the Copper River delta—one of the great birding areas of North America. Perched on Orca Inlet in eastern Prince William Sound, Cordova began life early in the 20th century as the port city for the Copper River–Northwestern Railway, which was built to serve the Kennicott copper mines 191 mi away in the Wrangell Mountains. With the mines and the railroad shut down since 1938, Cordova's economy now depends heavily on fishing. Attempts to develop a road along the abandoned railroad line connecting to the state highway system were dashed by the 1964 earthquake, so Cordova remains isolated. Access to the community is limited to airplane or ferry.

COMING ASHORE

TRANSPORTATION & TOURS

FROM THE PIER

Cruise ships dock at the boat harbor, and Cordova is a short walk uphill from here.

Tour buses from **Copper River & Northwest Tours** (☎ *907/424–5279*) meet ships, or you can catch a cab.

CITY TOURS

Cordova Taxi Cab (☎ *907/424–5151*) provides half-hour tours of town for $15 per person, with a maximum of four people per cab.

VISITOR INFORMATION
Pick up maps and tour brochures from the **Cordova Chamber of Commerce Visitor Center** ⊠*401 1st St.* ☎*907/424–7260* ⊕*www.cordovachamber. com.*

EXPLORING CORDOVA

Cruise-ship visitors to Cordova only have enough time for a brief glimpse of the area's most fascinating sight, the **Copper River delta.** Tour buses stop 10 mi out on the 48-mi Copper River Highway, providing a view into this spectacular 700,000-acre wetland that is home to countless shorebirds, waterfowl, and other bird species. The Copper River salmon runs are world famous. When the red and king salmon hit the river in spring, there's a frantic rush to net the tasty fish and rush them off to waiting markets and restaurants all over the country.

The **Cordova Museum** emphasizes native artifacts as well as pioneer, mining, and fishing history. Displays tell of native culture, early United States exploration of the area, episodes from the Copper River Northwestern Railway and Kennicott Mine era, and the growth of the commercial fishing industry. Afternoon video programs and an informative brochure outline a self-guided walking tour of the town's historical buildings. Monthly evening programs and art exhibits are sponsored by the historical society. Evening programs and regional art exhibits such as *Fish Follies* and *Bird Flew* are sponsored by the Historical Society. The gift shop sells local postcards, gifts, and history books. ⊠*622 1st St.* ☎*907/424–6665* ⊕*www.cordovamuseum.org* 🎟*$1* ⊗*Memorial Day–Labor Day, Mon.–Sat. 10–6, Sun. 2–4; Labor Day–Memorial Day, Tues.–Fri. 10–5, Sat. 1–5.*

> ### CORDOVA BEST BETS
>
> **Copper River delta sightseeing.** Rent a car and drive the 50-mi road across the delta. Stop to watch birds and scan for wildlife at the roadside viewing areas, and end the trip at the Million Dollar Bridge and the Childs Glacier Recreation Area.
>
> **Take in a festival.** Cordova has several noteworthy activities that are well worth looking into if you're nearby at the right time. The Shorebird festival is in May, the Copper River Salmon Festival takes place in July, and for winter visitors, there's the Iceworm Festival (yes, there really is such a creature), in early February.

SHOPPING

Orca Book & Sound Co. (⊠*507 1st St.* ☎*907/424–5305*), closed Sunday, is much more than a bookstore; it also sells music, art supplies, children's toys, and locally produced art. The walls often double as a gallery for local works or traveling exhibits, and the store specializes in old, rare, out-of-print, and first-edition books, especially Alaskan. In the back is an espresso bar with Internet access (including Wi-Fi).

WHERE TO EAT

$–$$$ ✕**Killer Whale Café.** Located directly across from the bookstore, this bright and colorful café features breakfast omelets, lunchtime burgers and sandwiches, plus local seafood and nightly dinner specials. ✉*504 1st St.* ☎*907/424–7733* ▭*MC, V* ☉*Closed Sun. No dinner.*

DENALI NATIONAL PARK & PRESERVE

Although it isn't technically a port of call, Denali National Park and Preserve is one of the most popular land extensions to an Alaska cruise. Anchorage, 240 mi south of the mark, serves as a point of departure to this spectacular park. It's a fine place to see wildlife, including bear, caribou, moose, and wolves. Nowhere in the world is there more stunning background scenery to these wildlife riches, with 20,320-foot Mt. McKinley looming above forested valleys, tundra-topped hills, and the glacier-covered peaks of the Alaska Range.

GEOLOGY & TERRAIN

The park's most prominent geological feature is the Alaska Range, a 600-mi-long crescent of summits that separates South Central Alaska from the interior. These peaks are all immense, but the truly towering ones are Mt. Hunter (14,573 feet), Mt. Foraker (17,400 feet), and Mt. McKinley (20,320 feet). Mt. McKinley's granite heart is covered with glacial ice, which is hundreds of feet thick in places. Glaciers, in fact, are abundant along the entire Alaska Range, and a few are visible from the park road. Muldrow Glacier is only 5 mi from the road, near Mile 67.

WILDLIFE

Nearly every wild creature that walks or flies in South Central and interior Alaska inhabits the park. Thirty-eight species of mammals reside here, from wolves and bears to little brown bats and pygmy shrews that weigh a fraction of an ounce. The park also has a surprisingly large avian population in summer, when some 160 species have been identified. Most of the birds migrate in fall, leaving only two dozen year-round resident species, including ravens, boreal chickadees, and hawk owls. Some of the summer birds travel thousands of miles to nest and breed in subarctic valleys, hills, and ponds. The northern wheatear comes here from southern Asia, warblers fly here from Central and South America, and the arctic tern annually travels 24,000 mi while seasonally commuting between Denali and Antarctica.

The most sought-after species among visitors are the large mammals: grizzlies, wolves, Dall sheep, moose, and caribou. All inhabit the forest or tundra landscape that surrounds Denali Park Road. While traveling the park road you can expect to see Dall sheep finding their way across high meadows, grizzlies and caribou frequenting stream bottoms and tundra, moose in the forested areas both near the park entrance and deep in the park, and the occasional wolf or fox that may dart across the road. Keep in mind that, as one park lover put it, "this ain't no zoo." You might hit an off day and have few viewings, but you can

4

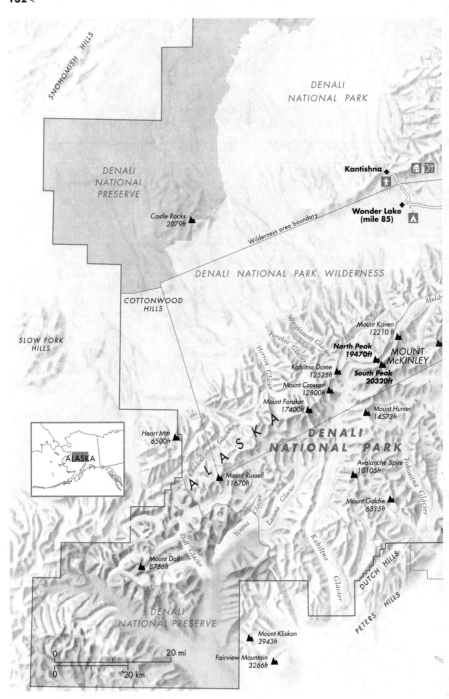

SNOHOMISH HILLS

DENALI NATIONAL PARK

DENALI NATIONAL PRESERVE

Kantishna

Castle Rocks
2079ft

**Wonder Lake
(mile 85)**

Wilderness area boundary

DENALI NATIONAL PARK WILDERNESS

COTTONWOOD HILLS

Muldr

SLOW FORK HILLS

Straightaway Glacier

Foraker Glacier

Mount Koven
12210 ft

Herron Glacier

**North Peak
19470ft**

MOUNT McKINLEY

Kahiltna Dome
12525ft

**South Peak
20320ft**

Mount Crosson
12800ft

Mount Foraker
17400ft

Mount Hunter
14573ft

Heart Mtn
6500ft

Chedolothna Glacier

A L A S K A

DENALI NATIONAL PARK

ALASKA

Avalanche Spire
10105ft

Tokositna Glacier

Mount Russell
11670ft

Yentna Glacier

Lacuna Glacier

Mount Goldie
6315ft

Dall Glacier

Kahiltna Glacier

DUTCH HILLS

Mount Dall
8756ft

DENALI NATIONAL PRESERVE

PETERS HILLS

Mount Kliskon
3943ft

0   20 mi

0   20 km

Fairview Mountain
3266ft

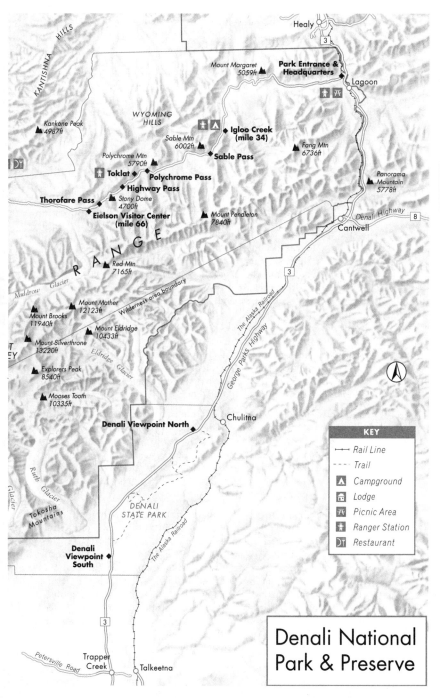

Healy

Mount Margaret
5059ft

Park Entrance &
Headquarters

Lagoon

KANTISHNA HILLS

Kankone Peak
4987ft

WYOMING
HILLS

Sable Mtn
6002ft

Igloo Creek
(mile 34)

Fang Mtn
6736ft

Polychrome Mtn
5790ft

Toklat

Polychrome Pass

Sable Pass

Panorama
Mountain
5778ft

Highway Pass

Thorofare Pass

Stony Dome
4700ft

Eielson Visitor Center
(mile 66)

Mount Pendleton
7840ft

Denali Highway

8

Cantwell

R A N G E

Red Mtn
7165ft

Muldrow Glacier

Wilderness area boundary

Mount Mather
12123ft

The Alaska Railroad

Mount Brooks
11940ft

Mount Eldridge
10433ft

Mount-Silverthrone
13220ft

Eldridge Glacier

George Parks Highway

Explorers Peak
8540ft

Mooses Tooth
10335ft

Denali Viewpoint North

Chulitna

Ruth Glacier

Tokosha
Mountains

DENALI
STATE PARK

The Alaska Railroad

Denali
Viewpoint
South

KEY

— Rail Line

---- Trail

▲ Campground

🏠 Lodge

🍴 Picnic Area

🚶 Ranger Station

🍽 Restaurant

3

Petersville Road

Trapper
Creek

Talkeetna

Denali National
Park & Preserve

enjoy the surroundings anyway. Under no circumstances should you feed the animals or birds (a mew gull or ground squirrel may try to share your lunch).

EXPLORING DENALI

You can take a tour bus or the Alaska Railroad from Anchorage to the Denali National Park entrance. Both Princess and Holland America attach their own railcars behind these trains for a more luxurious experience. Most cruise passengers stay one or two nights in hotels at a riverside settlement called Denali Park, just outside the park entrance. Shuttle buses provide transportation from your hotel to the park's busy visitor center where you can watch slide shows on the park, purchase maps and books, or check the schedule for naturalist presentations and sled-dog demonstrations. Access to the park itself is by bus on day tours. If you aren't visiting Denali as part of your cruise package, make reservations for a bus tour (usually between $62.05 and $93.75 per person, including a snack or box lunch and hot drinks). All the major hotels in the Denali Park area have good restaurants on the premises, and most travelers choose to dine there.

> **MT. MCKINLEY**
>
> Also commonly known by its Athabascan Indian name, Denali—"The High One"—North America's highest mountain is the world's tallest when measured from base to top: the great mountain rises more than 18,000 feet above surrounding lowlands. Unfortunately for visitors with little time to spend in the area, McKinley is wreathed in clouds on average two days of every three in summer, so cross your fingers and hope for a clear day when you visit.

The 90-mi Denali Park Road winds from the park entrance to Wonder Lake and Kantishna, the historic mining community in the heart of the park. Public access along this road is limited to tour and shuttle buses that depart from the Wilderness Access Center. The Park Road is paved for the first 14 mi and gravel the rest of the way. Bus drivers aren't in a hurry (the speed limit is 35 mph) and make frequent stops to view wildlife or to explain Denali's natural history.

Your narrated park tour will probably last around six hours round-trip and will include Polychrome Pass and the visitor center at Eielson (66 mi), which has been completely rebuilt, and is scheduled to reopen in 2008. Long trips to Wonder Lake (11 grueling hours round-trip) provide a better chance to see Mt. McKinley and more of the park but may not be available unless you spend an additional night in the Denali area. Check with your cruise line to see if these more expensive options are available. The Eielson–to–Wonder Lake stretch is particularly beautiful from mid-August to early September, when the tundra is ablaze with autumn's yellows, reds, and oranges.

The Wilderness Access Center near the park's entrance (at Mile 237 of the Parks Highway) is the transportation hub, with bus and campsite reservations, along with a fine film about Denali called "Across Time and Tundra." The adjacent Backcountry Information building has hiking details for those heading into the wilderness, including current data on animal sightings, river-crossing conditions, weather, and closed areas.

At Mile 1.2 of the park road (directly across from the train station), the Denali Visitor Center contains exhibits on the park's natural and cultural history. Two short hiking trails are nearby, and you can check out the naturalist presentations and sled-dog demonstrations by park rangers. An adjacent bookstore stocks titles on Denali's animals, wildflowers, and geology, and a food court is also here.

Contact: *Box 9, Denali National Park 99755 ☎907/683–2294 year-round, 907/683–1266 in summer, 800/622–7275 or 907/272–7275 shuttle bus (in Alaska), 907/272–7275 or 800/622–7275 bus tour reservations ⊕www.nps.gov/dena for park info or www.reservedenali.com for bus tour info.* **Entrance Fees:** *Park: $10 per person or $20 per family. Shuttle bus: round-trip fares $19.50 to Toklat River at Mile 53; $43.25 to Kantishna at Mile 91, the end of the road.*

OUTDOOR ACTIVITIES

HIKING

Day hiking can be amazing in Denali. A system of forest and tundra trails starts at the park entrance. These trails range from easy to challenging and are suitable for visitors of all ages and hiking abilities. Get hiking information and trail maps—along with bear and moose safety tips—from the Wilderness Access Center. Rangers lead hikes daily in summer.

RAFTING

Several rafting companies operate along the Parks Highway near the entrance to Denali and offer daily trips in the fairly placid stretches of the Nenana River and through the white water of Nenana River canyon. Gear and a courtesy pickup from your hotel are included.

Denali Outdoor Center (☎907/683–1925 or 888/303–1925 ⊕www.denalioutdoorcenter.com) takes adventuresome people on guided trips down the Nenana River rapids in inflatable rafts and kayaks. **Denali Raft Adventures** (☎907/683–2234 or 888/683–2234 ⊕www.denaliraft.com) launches its rafts several times daily on a variety of scenic and white-water Nenana River raft trips. **Nenana Raft Adventures** (☎907/683–7238 or 800/789–7238 ⊕www.raftdenali.com) runs four- and six-hour rafting trips along the Nenana River.

GLACIER BAY NATIONAL PARK & PRESERVE

Fodor's Choice ★ Cruising Glacier Bay is like revisiting the Little Ice Age—it's one of the few places in the world where you can approach such a variety of massive tidewater glaciers. You can witness a spectacular process called "calving," foreshadowed by a cannon-blast-like sound, in which bergs the size of 10-story office buildings come crashing down from the side of a glacier. Each cannon-blast signifies another step in the glacier's steady retreat. The calving iceberg sends tons of water and spray sky-

Continued on page 140

DID YOU KNOW?

The blue glow of a glacier is caused by the light-absorbing properties of glacial ice. Ice readily absorbs long-wavelength frequencies of light (associated with the color red) but reflects short-wavelength frequencies, which, you guessed it, are blue.

ALASKA'S GLACIERS
NOTORIOUS LANDSCAPE ARCHITECTS

(opposite) Facing the Taku Glacier challenge outside of Juneau (top) River of ice

Glaciers—those massive, blue-hued tongues of ice that issue forth from Alaska's mountain ranges—perfectly embody the harsh climate, unforgiving terrain, and haunting beauty that make this state one of the world's wildest places. Alaska is home to roughly 100,000 glaciers, which cover almost 5% of the state's land.

Frozen Giants

A glacier occurs where annual snowfall exceeds annual snowmelt. Snow accumulates over thousands of years, forming massive sheets of compacted ice. (Southeast Alaska's Taku Glacier, popular with flightseeing devotees, is one of Earth's meatiest: some sections measure over 4,500 feet thick.) Under the pressure of its own weight, the glacier succumbs to gravity and begins to flow downhill. This movement results in sprawling masses of rippled ice (Alaska's Bering Glacier, at 127 miles, is North America's longest). When glaciers reach the tidewaters of the coast, icebergs calve, or break off from the glacier's face, plunging dramatically into the sea.

THE RAPIDLY RETREATING GLACIERS IN KENAI FJORDS NATIONAL PARK

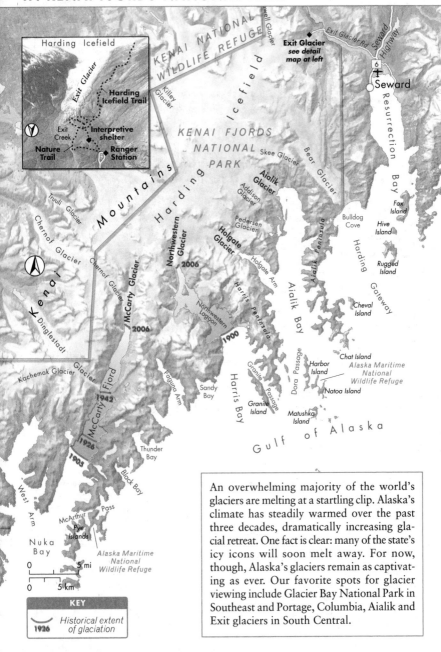

Harding Icefield

Exit Glacier

Harding Icefield Trail

Exit Creek

Interpretive shelter

Nature Trail

Ranger Station

Exit Glacier
see detail map at left

Exit Glacier Rd

Seward Highway

Seward

6

KENAI NATIONAL WILDLIFE REFUGE

Killey Glacier

Lowell Glacier

KENAI FJORDS NATIONAL PARK

Skee Glacier

Bear Glacier

Resurrection Bay

Fox Island

Bulldog Cove

Hive Island

Rugged Island

Harding Gateway

Aialik Glacier

Addison Glacier

Pedersen Glacier

Holgate Glacier

Holgate Arm

Harris Peninsula

Aialik Peninsula

Aialik Bay

Cheval Island

Northwestern Glacier

2006

Northwestern Lagoon

1900

Truuli Glacier

Chernof Glacier

Chernof Glacier

McCarty Glacier

2006

Dinglestadt Glacier

Kachemak Glacier

McCarty Fjord

1942

1926

1905

Poguna Arm

Sandy Bay

Harris Bay

Granite Passage

Granite Island

Dora Passage

Harbor Island

Chat Island

Natoa Island

Matushka Island

Alaska Maritime National Wildlife Refuge

Gulf of Alaska

Thunder Bay

Black Bay

West Arm

McArthur Pass

Pye Islands

Nuka Bay

Alaska Maritime National Wildlife Refuge

Harding Mountains

Kenai Mountains

0   5 mi
0   5 km

KEY

1926   Historical extent of glaciation

An overwhelming majority of the world's glaciers are melting at a startling clip. Alaska's climate has steadily warmed over the past three decades, dramatically increasing glacial retreat. One fact is clear: many of the state's icy icons will soon melt away. For now, though, Alaska's glaciers remain as captivating as ever. Our favorite spots for glacier viewing include Glacier Bay National Park in Southeast and Portage, Columbia, Aialik and Exit glaciers in South Central.

Icy Blue Hikes & Thunderous Boating Excursions

Glaciers enchant us with their size and astonishing power to shape the landscape. But let's face it: nothing rivals the sheer excitement of watching a bus-size block of ice burst from a glacier's face, creating an unholy thunderclap that resounds across an isolated Alaskan bay.

Most frequently undertaken with a seasoned guide, glacier trekking is becoming increasingly popular. Many guides transport visitors to and from glaciers (in some cases by helicopter or small plane), and provide ski excursions, dogsled tours, or guided hikes on the glacier's surface. Striding through the surreal landscape of a glacier, ice crunching underfoot, can be an otherworldly experience. Whether you're whooping it up on a dogsled tour, learning the fundamentals of glacier travel, or simply poking about on a massive field of ice, you're sure to gain an acute appreciation for the massive scale of the state's natural environment.

You can also experience glaciers via boat, such as the Alaska Marine Highway, a cruise ship, a small chartered boat, or even your own bobbing kayak. Our favorite out of Seward is the ride with Kenai Fjords Tours. Don't be discouraged by rainy weather. Glaciers often appear even bluer on overcast days. When piloting your own vessel, be sure to keep your distance from the glacier's face.

■ TIP→ **For more information about viewing Alaska's glaciers,** *see* **Chapter 5: Sports & Wilderness Adventures.**

Taking in the sights at Mendenhall Glacier

DID YOU KNOW?

What do glaciers and cows have in common? They both *calve*. While bovine calving refers to actual calf-birth, the word is also used to describe a tidewater glacier's stunning habit of rupturing icebergs from its terminus. When glacier ice meets the sea, steady tidal movement and warmer temperatures cause these frequent, booming deposits.

GLACIER-VIEWING TIPS

■ The most important rule of thumb is never to venture onto a glacier without proper training or the help of a guide.

■ Not surprisingly, glaciers have a cooling effect on their surroundings, so wear layers and bring gloves and rain gear.

■ Glaciers can powerfully reflect sunlight, even on cloudy days. Sunscreen, sunglasses, and a brimmed hat are essential.

■ Warm, thick-soled waterproof footwear is a must.

■ Don't forget to bring a camera and binoculars (preferably waterproof).

ward, propelling mini–tidal waves outward from the point of impact. Johns Hopkins Glacier calves so often and with such volume that large cruise ships can seldom come within 2 mi of its face.

Although the Tlingit have lived in the area for 10,000 years, the bay was first popularized by naturalist John Muir, who visited in 1879. Just 100 years before, the bay had been completely choked with ice. By 1916, though, the ice had retreated 65 mi—the most rapid glacial retreat ever recorded. To preserve its clues to the world's geological history, Glacier Bay was declared a national monument in 1925 and became a national park in 1980. Today Muir's namesake glacier, like others in the park, continues to retreat dramatically. Its terminus is now scores of miles farther up the bay from the small cabin he built at its face during his time there.

> ### GETTING TO GLACIER BAY
>
> Competition for entry permits into Glacier Bay is fierce. To protect the humpback whale, which feeds here in summer, the Park Service limits the number of ships that can call. Check your cruise brochure to make sure Glacier Bay is included in your sailing. Most ships that do visit spend at least one full day exploring the park. There are no shore excursions or landings in the bay—the steep-sided and heavily forested fjords aren't conducive to pedestrian exploration—but a Park Service naturalist boards every cruise ship.

Your experience in Glacier Bay will depend partly on the size of your ship. Ocean liners tend to stay mid-channel, while small yachtlike ships spend more time closer to shore. Smaller ships give you a better view of the calving ice and wildlife, but on a big ship you can get a loftier perspective. Both come within ¼ mi of the glaciers themselves.

For more info, check out: ⊕*www.nps.gov/glba*.

GLACIER RUNDOWN

The most frequently viewed glaciers are in the west arm of Glacier Bay. Ships linger in front of five glaciers, giving you ample time to admire their stunning and ever-changing faces. First, most ships stop briefly at Reid Glacier, which flows down from the Brady Icefield, before continuing on to Lamplugh Glacier—one of the bluest in the park—at the mouth of Johns Hopkins Inlet. Next, at the end of the inlet, is the massive Johns Hopkins Glacier, where you're likely to see a continuous shower of calving ice. (Sometimes there are so many icebergs in the inlet that ships must avoid the area.) Farther north, near the end of the western arm, is Margerie Glacier, which is also quite active. Adjacent is Grand Pacific Glacier, the largest glacier in the park.

HAINES

It's hard to imagine a more beautiful setting—a heavily wooded peninsula with magnificent views of Portage Cove and the snowy Coast Range—or a more perfectly charming coastal Alaskan town. Haines's popularity

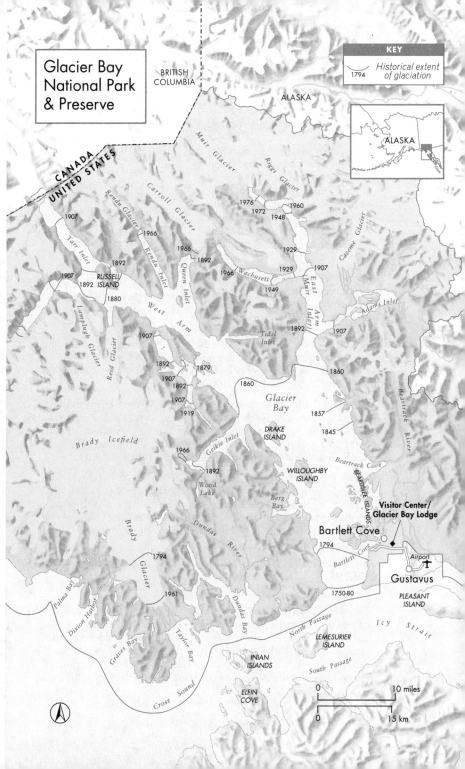

as a stop for cruise ships both large and small is growing, especially as travelers look for an alternative to the crowds at Skagway.

Nestled on the collar of the Chilkat Peninsula—a narrow strip of land that divides the Chilkat and Chilkoot Inlets, Haines encompasses an area that has been occupied by Tlingit peoples for centuries. Missionary S. Hall Young and famed naturalist John Muir were intent on establishing a Presbyterian mission in the area, and with the blessing of local chiefs, they chose the site that later became Haines.

Haines has always been a well-balanced community; its history contains equal parts enterprising gold rush boom town and regimented military outpost. The former is evidenced by Jack Dalton, who, in the 1890s, maintained a toll route from the settlement of Haines into the Yukon, charging $1 for foot passengers and $2.50 per horse. His Dalton Trail later provided access for miners during the 1897 gold rush to the Klondike.

The town's military roots are visible at Fort William Henry Seward, at Portage Cove just south of town. For 17 years (1923–39) prior to World War II, the post, renamed Chilkoot Barracks in commemoration of the gold rush route, was the territory's only military base. The fort's buildings and grounds are now a National Historic Landmark.

Today, the community is recognized for the native dance and art center at Fort Seward, the Haines Public Library (which, in 2005, was named Best Small Library in the United States), and for the superb fishing, camping, and outdoor recreation to be found at Chilkoot Lake, Portage Cove, Mosquito Lake, and Chilkat State Park. Northwest of the city is the Alaska Chilkat Bald Eagle Preserve.

> ### HAINES BEST BETS
>
> ■ **Float the Chilkat River.** Running through one of Alaska's most stunning mountain ranges, the mellow Chilkat caters more to sightseers than to thrill-seekers.
>
> ■ **Pound the pavement.** Haines has a delightfully funky vibe welcoming to visitors; Mountain Market, Sheldon Bookstore, and the public library are favorite local hangouts.
>
> ■ **Hit the road.** The Haines Highway is one of the nation's most beautiful roads. Whether you enlist a local tour operator or a rental car, a drive up this highway is an unforgettable experience.

COMING ASHORE

SHORE EXCURSIONS

Chilkat Bald Eagle Preserve Float Trip. A raft trip through the Chilkat Bald Eagle Preserve introduces you to some eagles and—if you're lucky—a moose or a bear. The trip starts with a 30-minute guided van tour through Chilkat Valley to the heart of the preserve. Then you board rafts for a gentle, scenic float trip down the Chilkat River (no children under age seven). In October, the trees are filled with some 3,000 bald eagles. ⊙ *3½ hrs* ✉ *$100.*

Chilkoot Bicycle Adventure. This easy half-day drive-and-bike tour starts with a van ride to Lutak Inlet. From there, you can hop on a mountain bike for a 6-mi jaunt along this picturesque bay, which boasts a backdrop of mountains and glaciers. Eagles are a common sight, and brown bears an occasional one. ⊙*3 hrs* 🎟*$85.*

4

Chilkat Rain Forest Nature Hike. Explore a lush Alaskan rain forest on this 3-mi guided hike along Chilkoot Inlet, which focuses on the area's plant, animal, and bird life. The path is easy and well maintained, and spotting scopes are provided to watch for bald eagles, mountain goats, and other wildlife along the way. ⊙*3 hrs* 🎟*$64–$79.*

Deluxe Haines Highlights. This bus tour includes a visit to Fort Seward and the Sheldon Museum before venturing out to Letnikof Cove (on the Chilkat Peninsula) for a view across the mighty Chilkat River to Rainbow Glacier. Back in town, you can tour a one-of-a-kind re-created salmon cannery. ⊙*3 hrs* 🎟*$34–$51.*

Offbeat Haines. Embark on a small group adventure to visit three of Haines's most unusual and out-of-the-way attractions. The trip includes time at the delightfully eclectic Hammer Museum (the only museum in the world devoted to hammers), Extreme Dreams Art Studio, downtown Haines, Fort Seward, and Dalton City. The last of these was created for the Walt Disney film *White Fang,* and is now home to the Haines Brewing Company and other local businesses. ⊙*2 hrs* 🎟*$30.*

Pilot's Choice Flightseeing to Glacier Bay National Park. Join an experienced local pilot for a memorable bush plane flight over the spectacular glaciers and towering mountains of Glacier Bay National Park. Beach landings may be made at the pilot's discretion. ⊙*2 hrs* 🎟*$270.*

TRANSPORTATION & TOURS

FROM THE PIER
Cruise ships and catamaran ferries dock in front of Fort Seward, and downtown Haines is just a short walk away (about ½ mi). Some cruise lines provide complimentary shuttle service to downtown. Taxi service is available; hour-long taxi tours of the town cost $20 per person. A one-way trip between the pier and town costs $10. For a pickup or tour call **Haines Shuttle and Tours** (☎*907/766–3138*). The Haines ferry terminal is 4½ mi northwest of downtown, and the airport is 4 mi west.

GETTING HERE ON YOUR OWN
If your cruise ship only stops in Skagway, you can catch a fast catamaran to Haines for a delightful day away from the crowds. **Chilkat Cruises** (☎*907/766–2100 or 888/766–2103* ⊕*www.chilkatcruises.com*) pro-

vides a passenger catamaran ferry between Skagway and Haines ($54 round-trip, and 35 minutes each way), with several runs a day in summer. **Alaska Fjordlines** (☎*907/766–3395 or 800/320–0146* ⊕*www.alaskafjordlines.com*) operates a high-speed catamaran from Skagway and Haines to Juneau and back, stopping along the way to watch whales and other marine mammals in Lynn Canal. The morning catamaran leaves Haines at 8:45 AM and the connecting bus from Auke Bay arrives in Juneau at noon. Passengers are back in Haines by 7:30 PM.

VISITOR INFORMATION
You can pick up walking-tour maps at the **Haines Convention and Visitors Bureau** (☎*907/766–2234 or 800/458–3579* ⊕*www.haines.ak.us*) on 2nd Avenue near Willard Street.

EXPLORING HAINES

② Celebrating Haines's location in the "Valley of the Eagles" is the **American Bald Eagle Foundation.** The main focus here is on bald eagles and associated fauna of the Chilkat Preserve, explored in lectures, displays, and videos. A taxidermy-heavy diorama shows examples of local animals, and the gift shop sells natural-history items. The foundation also sponsors bald-eagle research cooperatively with the University of Alaska. ✉*Haines Hwy at 2nd Ave.* ☎*907/766–3094* ⊕*www.baldeagles.org* 🖾*$3* ⊙*May–Nov., daily 8–6, and whenever cruise ships are in port.*

④
★ Circle the sloping parade ground of **Fort William H. Seward National Historic Landmark,** Alaska's first U.S. Army post, where clapboard structures stand against a mountain backdrop. The Haines Convention and Visitors Bureau provides a walking-tour brochure of the fort.

⑤ **Alaska Indian Arts,** a nonprofit organization dedicated to the revival of Tlingit art forms, is housed in the former fort hospital, on the south side of the parade ground. You can watch artists carve totem poles and silversmiths at work. ✉*Fort Seward parade ground* ☎*907/766–2160* ⊕*www.alaskaindianarts.com* 🖾*Free* ⊙*Weekdays 8–5, Sat. 9–5, and whenever cruise ships are in port.*

③ In Fort Seward, wander past the huge, gallant, white-columned **Hotel Halsingland,** a former commanding officers' home, and now a part of the hotel on Officers' Row.

① The **Sheldon Museum and Cultural Center,** near the foot of Main Street, houses a collection that was first established by Steve Sheldon in the 1880s. Today, the Sheldon family's personal collection anchors an impressive array of Native artifacts, including an 18th-century carved ceremonial hat from the Murrelet Clan, Chilkat blankets, and a model of a Tlingit tribal house. ✉*11 Main St.* ☎*907/766–2366* ⊕*www.sheldonmuseum.org* 🖾*$3* ⊙*Mid-May–mid-Sept., weekdays 10–5, weekends 1–4, and when cruise ships are in port.*

⑥ A pair of parks is often included in bus tours of the area. **Chilkat State Park** on Chilkat Inlet has beautiful views of both the Davidson and

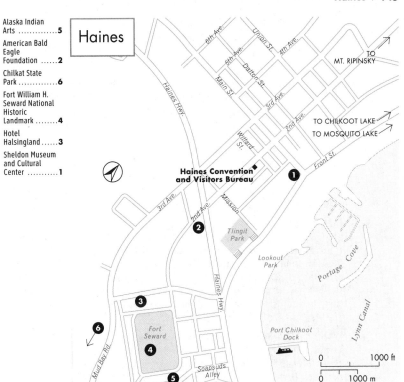

4

Rainbow glaciers. The Seduction Point trail, about 7 mi one way, takes hikers to the very tip of the peninsula upon which Haines sits. Also well worth visiting is **Chilkoot State Recreation Site,** home to the turquoise waters of Chilkoot Lake, and a river where you might spot black bears when the salmon are running.

OUTDOOR ACTIVITIES

Battery Point Trail is a fairly level path that hugs the shoreline for 2½ mi, and provides fine views across Lynn Canal. The trail begins at Portage Cove Campground (1 mi east of Haines). For other hikes, pick up a copy of "Haines Is for Hikers" at the **visitor center** (✉*112 2nd Ave.* ☎*907/766–2234 or 800/458–3579* ⊕*www.haines.ak.us*). A few doors up the street from the visitor center, **Mountain Flying Service** (☎*907/766–3007 or 800/954–8747* ⊕*www.flyglacierbay.com*) leads flightseeing trips to nearby Glacier Bay National Park.

WHERE TO EAT

$–$$$ ✕**Bamboo Room.** Pop culture meets greasy spoon in this unassuming coffee shop with red vinyl booths. The menu doesn't cater to light appetites—it includes sandwiches, burgers, fried chicken, chili, and halibut fish-and-chips—but the place really is at its best for an all-American breakfast (available until 3 PM). The adjacent bar has pool, darts, a big-screen TV, and a jukebox. ⊠*2nd Ave. near Main St.* ☎*907/766–2800* ⊟*AE, D, DC, MC, V.*

$–$$$　×**Mosey's.** The fare at this Mexican restaurant a block from the cruise-ship dock tends to be spicy. Each year owner Martha Stewart (yes, that's her real name) brings back bushels of roasted green chilis—the signature ingredient in many dishes—from New Mexico. If your taste buds can handle the kick, you'll be handsomely rewarded: the food is bursting with flavor, the service is speedy, and the atmosphere is a cheery south-of-the-border alternative to the rest of Haines's more mainstream offerings. Order lunch at the counter or sit down at a table for dinner. ⊠*Soap Suds Alley, Fort Seward* ☎*907/766–2320* ⊟*MC, V.*

$–$$　×**Mountain Market.** Meet the locals over coffee (including espresso in all its variations) and a fresh-baked pastry at this busy corner natural-foods store, deli, café, and wine-and-spirits shop. It's the town's de-facto meeting hall and hitching post—if they added Wi-Fi you wouldn't ever need to leave. But Mountain Market is also great for lunchtime sandwiches, wraps, soups, and salads. Friday is pizza day, but get here early since those pies are often gone by early afternoon. ⊠*3rd Ave. and Haines Hwy.* ☎*907/766–3340* ⊟*MC, V.*

WHERE TO DRINK

Locals might rule the pool tables at **Fogcutter Bar** (⊠*122 Main St.* ☎*907/766–2555*), but they always appreciate a little friendly competition. (Like many bars in Southeast Alaska, the Fogcutter sells drink tokens that patrons often purchase for their friends; you'll often notice folks sitting at the bar with a small stack of these tokens next to their beverage. The Fogcutter's embossed metal tokens are among the Southeast's most ornate. Purchase one for a keepsake—or for later use.) **Haines Brewing Company** (⊠*108 Whitefang Way* ☎*907/766–3823*), a microbrewery among the Dalton City buildings at the fairgrounds, sells sample trays for $5. Commercial fisherfolk gather nightly at **Harbor Bar** (⊠*Front St. at Harbor* ☎*907/766–2444*), a bar and restaurant dating from 1907. You might catch some live music here in summer. Inside one of the oldest buildings in town (it was once a brothel), the **Pioneer Bar** (⊠*2nd Ave. near Main St.* ☎*907/766–3443*) has historical photographs on the walls, a big-screen television for sports, and occasional bands.

HOMER

It's a shame that of the hundreds of thousands of cruise passengers who visit Alaska each year, only a very few get to see Homer. Its scenic setting on Kachemak Bay, surrounded by mountains, spruce forest, and glaciers, makes Homer unique even in Alaska. Homer lies at the base of a 4-mi-long sandy spit that juts into Kachemak Bay and provides beautiful bay views. Founded just before the turn of the 20th century as a gold-prospecting camp, this community was later used as a coal-mining headquarters. Today, Homer is a funky fishing port famous for its halibut and salmon fishing and serves as a base for bear-viewing flights. It's also one of the top arts communities in Alaska, with several first-rate galleries, a theater company, and an active music-and-dance scene.

COMING ASHORE

TRANSPORTATION & TOURS

FROM THE PIER

Ships and Alaska Marine Highway ferries dock at the end of the Homer Spit where you can find charters, restaurants, and shops. You can also take a taxi to town to visit local galleries and have a meal. A one-way ride from the Spit into town with **Chux Cab** (☎ *907/235–2489*) will cost you $12. The **Homer Trolley** (☎ *907/235–8624*), which connects the Spit and downtown, costs $5.

VISITOR INFORMATION

In the Homer Chamber of Commerce's **Visitor Information Center,** brochures from local businesses and attractions fill racks. ⊠ *Homer Bypass at Main St.* ☎ *907/235–7740* ⊕ *www.homeralaska.org* ⊙ *Memorial Day–Labor Day, weekdays 9–7, weekends 10–6.*

EXPLORING HOMER

FodorsChoice ★ Protruding into Kachemak Bay, the **Homer Spit** provides a sandy focal point. A paved path stretches most of the 4 mi, providing a delightful biking or walking option, and at the end are restaurants and hotels, a harbor filled with commercial-fishing boats, charter-fishing businesses, sea-kayaking outfitters, art galleries, and on-the-beach camping spots. Fly a kite, walk the beaches, drop a line in the fishing hole, or just wander through the shops looking for something interesting.

★ The **Islands and Oceans Visitor Center** houses fascinating interactive exhibits detailing the Alaska Maritime National Wildlife Refuge, which encompasses some 2,500 islands along the coast of Alaska. The 37,000-square-foot facility is a must-see for anyone interested in wild places. The first stop is the theater, where a film takes you along on a voyage of the Fish and Wildlife Service's research ship, the MV *Tiglax*. A path leads along Beluga Slough to Bishops Beach, a favorite place for a low-tide beach walk. ⊠ *95 Sterling Hwy.* ☎ *907/235–6961* ⊕ *www.islandsandocean.org* ▣ *Free* ⊙ *Memorial Day–Labor Day, daily 9–6; Labor Day–Memorial Day, call or check Web site.*

Kachemak Bay abounds in wildlife. Shore excursions or local tour operators take you to bird rooker-

HOMER BEST BETS

■ **Charter a fishing boat.** Nothing beats wrestling a monster halibut out of the icy depths.

■ **People-watch on the Spit.** Homer is home to a thriving arts community and makes for an interesting cultural mix.

■ **Cruise to a waterfront restaurant.** Crossing the bay to the Saltry for a meal is another favorite experience.

ies in the bay or to gravel beaches for clam digging. Most charter-fishing trips include an opportunity to view whales, seals, sea otters, porpoises, and seabirds close up. The bay supports a large population of bald eagles, gulls, murres, puffins, and other birds.

> **BIRD-WATCHING**
>
> Bird lovers love Homer. Sandpipers, Aleutian Terns, and Murrelets nest here throughout the year. For extensive information about bird-watching in the area, visit ⊕ www. birdinghomeralaska.org.

Directly across Kachemak Bay from the end of the Homer Spit, **Halibut Cove** is a small community of people who make their living on the bay or by selling handicrafts. There are several art galleries and a restaurant that serves local seafood. The cove itself is lovely, especially during salmon runs, when fish leap and splash in the clear water.

Central Charter Booking Agency (☎ *907/235–7847 or 800/478–7847* ⊕ *www.centralcharter.com*) runs frequent boats to the cove from Homer.

☾ For an outstanding introduction to Homer's history—both human and ★ natural—visit the **Pratt Museum,** where you can see a saltwater aquarium and exhibits on pioneers, flora and fauna, Native Alaskans, and the 1989 *Exxon Valdez* oil spill. Spy on wildlife with robotic video cameras set up on a seabird rookery and at the McNeil River Bear Sanctuary. In 2005 the Pratt was presented with the National Award for Museum Service, the highest national honor for museums. Outside are a wildflower garden and a short nature trail. The museum also leads 1½-hour walking tours of the harbor for $5 per person several times a week. ⊠ *Bartlett St. off Pioneer Ave.* ☎ *907/235–8635* ⊕ *www. prattmuseum.org* ▦ *$6* ⊙ *Mid-May–mid-Sept., daily 10–6.*

Seldovia, isolated across the bay from Homer, retains the charm of an earlier Alaska. The town's Russian heritage is evident in its onion-dome church and its name, derived from a Russian place-name meaning "herring bay." Those who fish use plenty of herring for bait, catching salmon, halibut, and king or Dungeness crab. You can find excellent fishing whether you drop your line into the deep waters of Kachemak Bay or cast into the surf for silver salmon on the shore of Outside Beach, near town. Self-guided hiking and berry picking in late July are other options. Stroll through town and along the slough, where frame houses rest on pilings.

OUTDOOR ACTIVITIES

BIKING

The **Seldovia Boardwalk Hotel** (☎ *907/234–7816*) rents bikes, an ideal way to see Seldovia.

BEAR-WATCHING

Homer is a favorite departure point to view Alaska's famous brown bears in coastal Katmai National Park. **Emerald Air Service** (☎ *907/235–6993* ⊕ *www.emeraldairservice.com*) is one of several companies offering all-day trips for around $560 per person. **Hallo Bay Wilderness** (☎907/235–2237 ⊕*www.hallobay.com*) has a comfortable day camp popular for day bear-viewing trips. These cost $450 for a five-hour trip and $575 for an eight-hour trip.

FISHING

Homer is both a major commercial fishing port (especially for halibut) and a very popular destination for sport anglers in search of giant halibut or feisty king and silver salmon. Quite a few companies offer charter fishing in summer, for around $190 per person per day (including bait and tackle). Several booking agencies set up fishing charters, including **Central Charter Booking Agency** (☎907/235–7847 or
★ 800/478–7847 ⊕*www.centralcharter.com*) and **Homer Ocean Charters** (☎800/426–6212 ⊕*www.homerocean.com*). Also try **Inlet Charters** (☎907/235–6126 or 800/770–6126 ⊕*www.halibutcharters.com*).

SEA KAYAKING

Several local companies offer guided sea-kayaking trips to protected coves within Kachemak Bay State Park and nearby islands. **True North Kayak Adventures** (☎907/235–0708 ⊕*www.truenorthkayak.com*) has a range of such adventures, including a six-hour paddle to Elephant Rock for $120 and an all-day boat and kayak trip to Yukon Island for $139 (both trips include round-trip water taxi to the island base camp, a guide, all kayak equipment, and a bakery lunch). Based in Seldovia, **Kayak'Atak** (☎907/234–7425 ⊕*www.alaska.net/~kayaks*) guides sea-kayak trips of the area. You can visit isolated beaches and look for eagle nests, fossils, and sea otters.

SHOPPING

Art by the town's residents can be found in the galleries on and around Pioneer Avenue. The **Bunnell Street Gallery** (✉*Corner of Main St. and Bunnell Ave.* ☎907/235–2662 ⊕*www.bunnellstreetgallery.org*), on the first floor of a historic trading post, displays innovative and contemporary Alaskan art, and hosts workshops, lectures, musical performances, and community events. **Ptarmigan Arts** (✉*471 E. Pioneer Ave.* ☎907/235–5345) is one of Alaska's three cooperative galleries, with photographs, paintings, pottery, jewelry, woodworking, and other pieces by local artisans. **Nomar** (✉*104 E. Pioneer Ave.* ☎907/235–8363 or 800/478–8364 ⊕*www.nomaralaska.com*) creates Polar fleece garments and other rugged Alaskan outerwear, plus duffel bags, rain gear, and children's clothing. The company also manufactures equipment and clothing for commercial fishermen, so you know their gear

---

COMPETE!

Anyone heading out on a halibut charter is advised to buy a $10 ticket for the **Homer Jackpot Halibut Derby** (☎907/235–7740 ⊕ www.homerhalibutderby.com); first prize for the largest halibut is more than $40,000. Every year, local papers publish sob stories about people who decided to save the 10 bucks and wound up catching a fish that would have won them thousands—don't be that guy!

is durable and well made. **Alaska Wild Berry Products** (✉ *528 E. Pioneer Ave.* ☎ *907/235–8858* ⊕ *www.alaskawildberryproducts.com*) sells chocolate-covered candies, jams, jellies, sauces, and syrups, as well as Alaskan-theme gifts and clothing. Drop by for free samples of the chocolates. Homer is famous for its halibut, salmon, and Kachemak Bay oysters. In addition to selling fresh fish, **Coal Point Trading Company** (☎ *907/235–3877* ⊕ *www.welovefish.com*) on the spit will package and ship fish that you caught.

WHERE TO EAT

$$$ ✕ **Café Cups.** It's hard to miss this place as you head down Pioneer Avenue—look for the huge namesake cups on the building's facade. A longtime Homer favorite, Cups makes the most of the local seafood, boasts a terrific wine list, and is one of the few small restaurants in Alaska to include vegetarian dishes on the menu. The outside deck is a fine place to enjoy a lazy morning while savoring your eggs Florentine. ✉ *162 W. Pioneer Ave.* ☎ *907/235–8330* ▭ *MC, V* ⊘ *Closed Sun.*

$$–$$$ ✕ **Saltry Restaurant.** On a hill overlooking Halibut Cove, this is a wonderful place to soak up a summer afternoon. Local seafood is prepared in everything from curries and pastas to sushi. For libations, you can choose from a wide selection of imported beers. The restaurant is small, and although the tables aren't exactly crowded together, you'll definitely feel cozy. When weather permits, sit on the deck. Dinner seatings are at 6 and 7:30; before or after dinner, you can stroll around the boardwalks at Halibut Cove and visit the art galleries or just relax on the dock. Sea otters often play just offshore. Reservations are essential for the ferry (at a reduced $28 round-trip), which leaves Homer Spit at 5 PM. A noon ferry ($48; $25 children) will take you to Halibut Cove for lunch (¢–$), stopping along the way for wildlife viewing. ✉ *Halibut Cove* ☎ *907/235–7847, 800/478–7847 Central Charters* ⌂ *Reservations essential* ▭ *D, MC, V* ⊘ *Closed Labor Day–Memorial Day.*

$–$$ ✕ **Two Sisters Bakery.** Two Sisters fills with a mixed crowd of fishermen, writers, and local businesspeople drinking espresso, talking politics, and sampling pastries, a block from Bishops Beach. Focaccia sandwiches, savory Danish pastries, and deep-dish pizza are also on the menu. The wraparound deck has tables for warm summer afternoons. ✉ *233 E. Bunnell Ave.* ☎ *907/235–2280* ⊕ *www.twosistersbakery.net* ▭ *MC, V.*

WHERE TO DRINK

The Spit's infamous **Salty Dawg Saloon** (☎ *907/235–9990*) is a tumbledown lighthouse of sorts, sure to be frequented by a carousing fisherman or two, and half the tourists in town. The ceilings are low, the pool table is usually busy, and wood chips cover the floors. The Dawg's walls are covered with business cards, signed dollar bills, and bras.

JUNEAU

Juneau, Alaska's capital and third-largest city, is on the North American mainland but can't be reached by road. The city owes its origins to two colorful sourdoughs (Alaskan pioneers)—Joe Juneau and Dick Harris—and to a Tlingit chief named Kowee, who led the two men to rich reserves of gold at Snow Slide Gulch, the drainage of Gold Creek around which the town was eventually built. That was in 1880, and shortly thereafter, a modest stampede resulted in the formation of a mining camp, which quickly grew to become the Alaska district government capital in 1906. The city may well have continued under its original appellation—Harrisburg, after Dick Harris—were it not for Joe Juneau's political jockeying at a miners' meeting in 1881.

JUNEAU BEST BETS

■ **Walk South Franklin Street.** Juneau's historic downtown still retains much of its hardscrabble mining feel. While away hours in the saloons and shops of this charming district.

■ **Ride the Mt. Roberts Tram.** On Juneau's favorite attraction, enjoy panoramic views of the area's stunning scenery from 1,800 feet above town.

■ **Marvel at the Mendenhall Glacier.** With an otherworldly blue hue and a visitor center that answers all your glacier questions, Alaska's most accessible—and most popular—glacier is a must-see.

For nearly 60 years after Juneau's founding, gold remained the mainstay of the economy. In its heyday, the Alaska Juneau gold mine was the biggest low-grade-ore mine in the world. Then, during World War II, the government decided it needed Juneau's manpower for the war effort, and the mines ceased operations. After the war, mining failed to start up again, and the government became the city's principal employer. Juneau's mines leave a rich legacy, though; the AJ mine alone produced more than $80 million in gold.

Today tourism is equally important to the local economy. Juneau is an obligatory stop on the Inside Passage cruise and ferry circuit and a port of embarkation for many small cruise ships. On summer days several cruise ships anchor along the downtown docks, sending thousands of travelers off to explore this small city.

COMING ASHORE

SHORE EXCURSIONS

ADVENTURE

Exploring Glaciers by Helicopter and Dog Sled. Fly deep into the Juneau Icefield by helicopter on this high-adventure excursion. A guide greets you when you land, explains dogsledding, then takes you on a sled ride across the snow-covered glacier. Return to Juneau by helicopter, with additional flightseeing en route. ⊙ *3 hrs* 🖳*$445.*

Mendenhall River Rafting. Starting on Mendenhall Lake, this professionally guided trip takes you down the Mendenhall River through alternating stretches of calm water and gentle rapids. Rubber rain boots, protective clothing, and life jackets are provided. Children love this one (the minimum age is six). ⊙ *3½ hrs* 🚌 *$100–$110.*

Photo Safari by Land and Sea. A professional photographer guides you to Juneau "photo hot spots," while sharing picture-taking tips and techniques. The first part of the tour takes place on land, and includes Mendenhall Glacier and the colorful downtown area. Next you board a covered 32-foot boat for a journey to Juneau's Channel Islands to photograph marine wildlife. Your photographer guide will help you take full advantage of the conditions and opportunities of the day. ⊙ *4½ hrs* 🚌 *$170.*

Pilot's Choice Helicopter Flightseeing. One of Alaska's most popular helicopter tours includes a landing on the Juneau Icefield for a walk on a glacier. Boots and rain gear are provided. ⊙ *3 hrs* 🚌 *$378.*

Tram and Guided Alpine Walk. You start with a short tour of downtown Juneau, then ride up the Mt. Roberts Tramway on this very popular trip. Once you reach the top—1,800 feet over the city—a guide takes you through pristine rain forest and alpine meadows. The hike is ½ mi over gravel and boardwalk trails and is conducted in all weather conditions. Sturdy, comfortable walking shoes and warm, waterproof clothing are advised. If you'd rather relax than hike, the tram complex has lots of shops and a restaurant called the Timberline Bar & Grill. You can return via the tram at any time. ⊙ *2 hrs* 🚌 *$55.*

SCENIC

Gold Mine Tour and Gold Panning. Former miners lead three-hour tours of the historic A.J. Gold Mine south of Juneau. A gold-panning demonstration is included, and you spend approximately 45 minutes of the tour inside the old tunnels. Tours depart from downtown by bus. This trip is highly recommended for an authentic look into Juneau's rich mining history. ⊙ *1½ hrs* 🚌 *$60.*

Grand Tour of Juneau. Take this bus excursion to see Mendenhall Glacier, spawning salmon at the Macaulay Salmon Hatchery, and the Glacier Gardens rain forest. ⊙ *5 hrs* 🚌 *$90.*

TASTES OF ALASKA

Floatplane Ride and Taku Glacier Lodge Salmon Bake. Fly over the Juneau Icefield to rustic Taku Glacier Lodge, where you can dine on outstanding barbecued salmon. Hole-in-the-Wall Glacier is directly across the inlet from the lodge. Nature trails wind through the surrounding country, where black bears and bald eagles are frequently sighted. Afterward, explore the virgin rain forest or relax in the lodge. This tour consistently gets rave reviews. ⊙ *3½ hrs* 🚌 *$240.*

Gold Creek Salmon Bake. Alaska wild salmon barbecued over an open fire is included at this all-you-can-eat outdoor meal. After dinner, you can walk in the woods, explore abandoned Wagner mine, or pan for gold. ◷ *1½–2 hrs* ⌂ *$35.*

TRANSPORTATION & TOURS

FROM THE PIER

Most cruise ships dock on the south

> **TIP**
>
> Several sights outside downtown—including Mendenhall Glacier, Glacier Gardens, and the Macaulay Salmon Hatchery—are too far to walk to. You can catch a tour bus or a taxi from Marine Park.

edge of town between the **Marine Park** and the **A.J. Dock.** Several ships can tie up at once; others occasionally anchor in the harbor. Juneau's downtown shops are a pleasant walk from the docks. A shuttle bus ($2 all day) runs from the A.J. Dock to town whenever ships are in port.

CITY TOURS

Juneau Trolley Car Company (☎ *907/586–7433 or 877/774–8687* ⊕ *www. juneautrolley.com*) conducts narrated tours, stopping at several of Juneau's historic and shopping attractions. An all-day pass is $19. **Mighty Great Trips** (☎ *907/789–5460* ⊕ *www.mightygreattrips.com*) leads bus tours that include a visit to Mendenhall Glacier. The **Juneau Steamboat Company** (☎ *907/723–0372* ⊕ *www.juneausteamboat.com*) offers scenic tours of Gastineau Channel aboard an authentic wood-fired steam launch, similar to those used around Juneau in the late 1800s and early 1900s. Tours come with entertaining narration that focuses on the historic mines of the Juneau area.

VISITOR INFORMATION

Pick up maps, bus schedules, charter-fishing information, and tour brochures at the small kiosks on the pier at Marine Park and in the cruise-ship terminal on South Franklin Street. Both are staffed when ships are in port.

The **Centennial Hall Visitor Center** has details on local attractions and nature trails. ✉ *101 Egan Dr.* ☎ *907/586–2201 or 888/581–2201* ⊕ *www. traveljuneau.com* ◷ *May–Sept., weekdays 8:30–5, weekends 9–5.*

EXPLORING JUNEAU

Downtown Juneau is compact enough that most of its main attractions are within walking distance of one another. Note, however, that the city is very hilly, so your legs will get a real workout. Look for the 20 signs around downtown that detail Juneau's fascinating history.

❺ At the corner of Seward and 4th streets is the **Alaska State Capitol,** completed in 1931 and remodeled in 2006, with pillars of southeastern Alaska marble. It houses the governor's office, and hosts state legislature meetings in winter, placing it at the epicenter of Alaska's increasingly animated political discourse. Pick up a self-guided tour pamphlet as you enter. ☎ *907/465–2479* ◷ *Weekdays 8–5.*

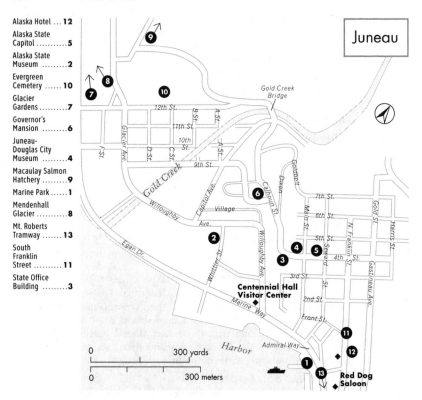

The **Alaska State Museum** is one of Alaska's best, with exhibits covering the breadth of the state's history, native cultures, wildlife, industry, and art. Be sure to visit the cramped gift shop with its extraordinary selection of native art, including baskets, carvings, and masks. ✉*395 Whittier St.* ☎*907/465–2901* ⊕*www.museums.state.ak.us* 🎫*$5* ☻*Mid-May–mid-Sept., daily 8:30–5:30.*

Evergreen Cemetery is where many Juneau pioneers are buried. Joe Juneau (1836–99), a Canadian by birth, died in Dawson City, Yukon, but his body was returned to the city that bears his name. Dick Harris (1833–1907), whose name can be found on downtown's Harris Street, died in Juneau. A meandering gravel path leads through the graveyard, and at the end of it is the monument commemorating the cremation spot of Chief Kowee.

Spread over 50 acres of rain forest 8 mi north of Juneau, **Glacier Gardens Rainforest Adventure** contains ponds, waterfalls, hiking paths, and gardens. The roots of fallen trees, turned upside down and buried in the ground, act as bowls to hold planters that overflow with begonias, fuchsias, and petunias. Guided tours (on covered golf carts) carry you along the 4 mi of paved paths to a dramatic mountainside overlook.

✉*7600 Glacier Hwy.* ☎*907/790–3377* ⊕*www.glaciergardens.com* 🎫*$22 including guided tour* ⊙*Daily 9–6.*

❻ Completed in 1912, the **Governor's Mansion,** a stately, white, three-level, colonial-style home, overlooks downtown Juneau. With 14,400 square feet, six bedrooms, and 10 bathrooms, it's no miner's cabin. Out front is a totem pole that tells three tales: the history of man, the cause of ocean tides, and the origin of Alaska's ubiquitous mosquitoes. Alaska's first female governor, Sarah Palin, currently lives there with her husband ("First Dude" Todd Palin) and their children. Unfortunately, tours of the residence are not permitted. ✉*716 Calhoun Ave.*

❹ Two fine totem poles flank the entrance to the **Juneau-Douglas City Museum,** a favorite among local residents. Inside, the city's history is relayed through memorabilia, gold-mining exhibits, and videos. ✉*114 W. 4th St., at Main St.* ☎*907/586–3572* ⊕*www.juneau.org/parksrec/museum* 🎫*$4* ⊙*Weekdays 9–5, weekends 10–5.*

❶ **Marine Park** is a little urban oasis on the dock where the cruise ships tie up. It's a great place for an outdoor meal purchased from one of Juneau's many street vendors, and, on Friday evenings during summertime, it features live performances by Juneau musicians. A visitor kiosk is staffed according to cruise-ship schedules.

⓭
★ For a bird's-eye view of the harbor and your cruise ship, take the **Mt. Roberts Tramway** to an observation deck 1,800 feet above Juneau. Walking paths radiate from the mountaintop visitor center, which also houses retail shops, a restaurant and bar, a nature center, and an auditorium that shows a film on Tlingit native culture. You can catch the tram from the base terminal downtown. The tram and all facilities are wheelchair accessible. (Energetic visitors may choose the 6-mi round-trip hike to Mt. Roberts, 3,819-foot summit.) ✉*490 S. Franklin St.* ☎*907/463–3412 or 888/461–8726* ⊕*www.goldbelttours.com* 🎫*$25* ⊙*May–Sept., daily 9–9.*

⓫ Cruise ships dock along busy **South Franklin Street** near the Mt. Roberts tram. The buildings here (and on neighboring Front Street), are among the oldest and most inviting structures in the city, house curio and crafts shops, snack shops, and two salmon shops. The small **Alaskan Hotel** (✉*167 S. Franklin St.* ☎*907/586–1000 or 800/327–9347*) was called "a pocket edition of the best hotels on the Pacific Coast" when it opened in 1913. The building, which has been lovingly restored with period trappings, operates as an active hotel, and still gives visitors a taste of Juneau's whiskey-rich history. The barroom's massive, mirrored oak bar, accented by Tiffany lamps and panels, is a particular delight. Topped by a wood-shingled turret, the **Alaska Steam Laundry Building** (✉*174 S. Franklin St.*), circa 1901, now houses a great collection of photos from Juneau's past, a popular espresso shop (Heritage Coffee Co. ☎*907/586–1752*), and several stores.

❸ At the **State Office Building** you can have a picnic lunch with the state workers on the eighth-floor patio facing Gastineau Channel and Douglas Island. On most Fridays at noon, concerts inside the four-story atrium feature a grand old theater pipe organ, a veteran of the silent-movie era. Also here is the historic old witch totem pole, the Alaska State Library, with a fine collection of historical photos, plus computers with public Internet access. If you're having trouble finding it, just ask for the "S.O.B."—the locals are fond of acronyms. ⊠*4th and Calhoun Sts.*

GETTING THERE

Mendenhall Glacier Tours
(☎ *907/789-5460* ⊕ *www.might-ygreattrips.com*) provides direct bus transport between downtown and the glacier for $12 round-trip or tours that include time at the glacier for $30 per person.

OUTSIDE TOWN

❾ Located 3 mi north of downtown, **Macaulay Salmon Hatchery** is a fine place to learn about salmon and commercial fishing. An underwater window lets you watch as salmon fight their way up a 450-foot fish ladder, and the gift shop sells salmon products. It's about a $5 cab ride from downtown. ⊠*2697 Channel Dr.* ☎*907/463–4810 or 877/463–2486* ⊕*www.dipac.net* 🖾*Admission and tour $3.25* ⊙*Weekdays 10–6, weekends 10–5.*

❽ One of Juneau's most popular sights, **Mendenhall Glacier,** is 12 mi from
Fodor'sChoice downtown. Like many other Alaskan glaciers, it is retreating up the
★ valley, losing more than 100 feet a year as massive chunks of ice calve off into a small lake. The visitor center has educational exhibits, videos, and natural-history walks. Nearby hiking trails offer magnificent views of the glacier itself. A visit to the glacier is included in most Juneau bus tours. ☎*907/789–0097* ⊕*www.fs.fed.us/r10/tongass* 🖾*Visitor center $3* ⊙*May–Sept., daily 8–7:30.*

OUTDOOR ACTIVITIES

HIKING

Gastineau Guiding (☎*907/586–8231* ⊕*www.stepintoalaska.com*) leads hikes from the visitor center on the top of the Mt. Roberts tram, as well as a variety of other treks along local rain-forest trails.

MOUNTAIN BIKING

Driftwood Lodge (⊠*435 Willoughby Ave.* ☎*907/586–2280* ⊕*www.driftwoodalaska.com*) has basic mountain bikes for rent.

ROCK CLIMBING

While it isn't technically an *outdoor* activity, Juneau's indoor climbing gym, the **Rock Dump** (⊠*1310 Eastaugh Way* ☎*907/586–4982* ⊕*www.rockdump.com*), is one of the finest in Alaska, and it's near where most cruise ships dock. The Dump has climbing walls for all abilities from beginner to expert; day passes are $10, and rental equipment is available.

WHALE-WATCHING

Several companies lead whale-watching trips from Juneau. **Four Seasons Marine** (☎*907/790–6671 or 877/774–8687* ⊕*www.4seasonsmarine.com*) combines whale-watching with an hour at Orca Point Lodge on

Colt Island where guests are served a grilled salmon lunch. The boat departs from Auke Bay after a free shuttle from Juneau. **Juneau Sportfishing & Sightseeing** (☎907/586–1887 ⊕*www.juneausportfishing.com*) has been around for many years, and its boats carry a maximum of six passengers, providing a personalized trip.

SHOPPING

Annie Kaill's Fine Art and Craft Gallery (✉244 *Front St.* ☎907/586–2880) displays a whimsical mix of original prints, trinkets, jewelry, and ceramics from Alaskan artists. Prints from one of Alaska's best-known artists, Rie Muñoz, are sold at **Decker Gallery** (✉233 *S. Franklin St.* ☎907/463–5536 *or* 800/463–5536). Her works use stylized designs and bright swirls of colors and often feature Native Alaskans. The **Raven's Journey** (✉435 *S. Franklin St.* ☎907/463–4686), across from the tram, specializes in high-quality Alaskan native masks, grass baskets, carvings, dolls, and ivory pieces.

At **Taku Smokeries** (✉550 *S. Franklin St.* ☎907/463–5033 *or* 800/582–5122), on the south end of town near the cruise-ship docks, you can view the smoking process through large windows and then purchase packaged fish in the deli-style gift shop. It can also ship fish home for you. A fun place to browse is the **Wm. Spear Designs Gallery** (✉174 *S. Franklin St.* ☎907/586–2209 ⊕*www.wmspear.com*) above Heritage Coffee. Spear's colorful enameled pins are witty, creative, amusing, and sometimes simply perverse.

WHERE TO EAT

$$$$　✕**Gold Creek Salmon Bake.** Trees, mountains, and the rushing water of Salmon Creek surround the comfortable, canopy-covered benches and tables at this authentic salmon bake. Fresh-caught salmon is cooked over an alder fire and served with a succulent sauce. For $35 there are all-you-can-eat salmon, pork spareribs, and chicken along with baked beans, rice pilaf, salad bar, corn bread, and blueberry cake. Wine and beer are extra. After dinner you can pan for gold in the stream, wander up the hill to explore the remains of the Wagner gold mine, or roast marshmallows over the fire. A round-trip bus ride from downtown is included. ✉1061 *Salmon Lane Rd.* ☎907/789–0052 *or* 800/323–5757 ▤*AE, MC, V* ⊗*Closed Oct.–Apr.*

$$–$$$　✕**Hangar on the Wharf.** This Juneau hot spot, which occupies the building where Alaska Airlines started business, has expansive views of Gastineau Channel and Douglas Island, plus a menu with locally caught halibut or salmon, jambalaya, filet mignon, and great burgers. The Hangar has one of the largest selections of draft beers in Southeast Alaska, with two dozen brews available. On Friday and Saturday nights, jazz or rock bands take over the stage. ✉2 *Marine Way, Merchants Wharf Mall* ⊕*www.hangaronthewharf.com* ☎907/586–5018 ▤*AE, D, MC, V.*

$$–$$$　✕**Twisted Fish.** Juneau's liveliest downtown eatery serves up creative Pan-Asian seafood and Alaskan classics. Housed in a log-frame water-

front building adjacent to the Taku Store and the base of the Mt. Roberts tram, Twisted's fish is as fresh as you can find anywhere. (The attitude here is fresh, too, in a good way.) Grab a seat on the deck for prime-time Gastineau Channel–gazing and a bowl of Captain Ron's chowder, a local favorite. Inside, you can find a well-appointed dining room complete with a roaring river-rock hearth and flame-painted salmon, porpoises, marlin, and tuna decorating the walls. ⊠ *550 S. Franklin St.* ☎ *907/463–5033* ⊟ *AE, D, MC, V.*

$–$$$ ✕ **Wild Spice.** In addition to a full menu with sandwiches, soups and salads, seafood entrées, and an extensive wine list, this trendy downtown eatery also offers a Mongolian-style barbecue, where customers assemble their own entrées from an assortment of meats, vegetables, rice, noodles, and sauces, then hand them over to the chef to cook on an open, circular flat-top grill. Quick and (usually) delicious, this is a good mid-walk lunch or dinner stop. ⊠ *140 Seward St.* ☎ *907/523–0444* ⊟ *AE, MC, V.*

WHERE TO DRINK

Juneau is one of the best saloon towns in all of Alaska. Alaskan Amber, Frontier Beer, and Pale Ale are brewed and bottled in Juneau at the **Alaskan Brewing Company** (⊠ *5429 Shaune Dr.* ☎ *907/780–5866* ⊕ *www.alaskanbeer.com* ☾ *Mon.–Sat. 11–5; tours every ½ hr*), where you can take a tour and sample its award-winning beers. Alaska Brewing Company is several miles from downtown, so you'll need to take a taxi or join one of the tours that include a visit to the brewery. Keep in mind that this is no designer brewery; there's no upscale café/bar attached, but the gift shop sells T-shirts and beer paraphernalia. The Victorian-style **Alaskan Hotel Bar** (⊠ *167 S. Franklin St.* ☎ *907/586–1000 or 800/327–9347*) is about as funky a place as you can find in Juneau, with flocked-velvet walls, antique chandeliers above the bar, and vintage Alaskan-frontier brothel decor. The atmosphere, however, is anything but dated, and the bar's live music and open mike night draw high-spirited crowds.

The frontier quarters of the **Red Dog Saloon** (⊠ *278 S. Franklin St.* ☎ *907/463–3658*), Alaska's best-known saloon, have housed the once infamous, but now rather touristy Juneau watering hole since 1890. Every conceivable surface in this two-story bar is cluttered with life preservers, business cards, and memorabilia, including a pistol that reputedly belonged to Wyatt Earp, who failed to reclaim the piece after checking it at the U.S. Marshal's office on June 27, 1900. When tourist season hits, a little atmospheric sawdust covers the floor as well. Bands pump out dance tunes when cruise ships are docked.

KETCHIKAN

Famous for its colorful totem poles, rainy skies, steep–as–San Francisco streets, and lush island setting, Ketchikan is a favorite stop. Some 13,000 people call it home, and in summer, cruise ships crowd the shoreline, floatplanes depart for Misty Fiords National Monument, and salmon-laden commercial fishing boats head home to Tongass

Narrows. Ketchikan has a rowdy, blue-collar heritage of logging and fishing, somewhat softened by the loss of many timber industry jobs and the dramatic rise of cruise ship tourism. With a little effort, though, visitors can still glimpse the rugged frontier spirit that once permeated this hardscrabble cannery town.

Ketchikan is at the foot of 3,000-foot Deer Mountain, near the southeast corner of Revillagigedo (locals shorten it to Revilla) Island. Prior to the arrival of white miners and fishermen in 1885, the Tlingit used the site, at the mouth of Ketchikan Creek, as a summer fish camp. Gold discoveries just before the turn of the 20th century brought more immigrants, and valuable timber and commercial fishing resources spurred new industries. By the 1930s the town bragged it was the "salmon-canning capital of the world." You'll still find some of the Southeast's best salmon fishing here.

> ## KETCHIKAN BEST BETS
>
> ■ **Exploring Creek Street.** No visit to Ketchikan would be complete without a stroll along this elevated wooden boulevard, once the site of the town's rip-roaring bordellos.
>
> ■ **Totem gazing at Saxman Native Village.** View one of the best totem collections in all of Southeast Alaska at this must-see stop.
>
> ■ **Rainforest Canopy Tours.** Zip through the towering trees of Ketchikan's coastal rain forest, experiencing the majesty of this unique ecosystem from a bird's-eye view.

COMING ASHORE

SHORE EXCURSIONS

ADVENTURE

Alaska Canopy Adventures. Featuring a series of zip lines, nature trails, and suspension bridges, canopy tours provide an up-close view of the coastal forests. A course at the Alaska Rainforest Sanctuary, 16 mi south of town ⊕www.alaskacanopyadventures.com, has the longest of the tour's eight zip lines, stretching over 800 feet and whisking you along some 130 feet off the ground. (Book online or with your cruise line.) ⊘3¼ hrs ▨$165–$180.

Misty Fiords by Floatplane. Aerial views of granite cliffs that rise 4,000 feet from the sea, waterfalls, rain forests, and wildlife are topped off with a landing on a high wilderness lake. ⊘2 hrs ▨$220–$225.

Misty Fiords Wilderness Cruise and Flight. See this beautiful area from the air and sea on a 20-minute floatplane trip and a 2¾-hour cruise. The plane lands in the heart of the wilderness where you climb onboard a small boat for the narrated voyage back to Ketchikan. ⊘4 hrs ▨$260–$270.

Sportfishing. Cast your line for Alaska king and silver salmon or halibut along the Inside Passage. All equipment is provided, and you can buy your license on board. Group size is limited. Fish will be cleaned, and arrangements can be made to have your catch frozen or smoked and shipped home. ⊙*5 hrs* ⊠*$170–$185.*

Tatoosh Islands Sea Kayaking. A scenic drive to Knudson Cove is followed by a boat ride to Tatoosh Islands, where you board an easy-to-paddle sea kayak for a whale's-eye view of a remote part of Tongass National Forest. The minimum age is seven. ⊙*4½ hrs* ⊠*$115–$130.*

CULTURAL

Saxman Native Village. Learn about the Tlingit culture in this native village with more than 20 totem poles. You can watch totem-pole carvers and a theatrical production in the Beaver Clan House. ⊙*2½ hrs* ⊠*$50.*

Totem Bight and Ketchikan City Tour. Visit the bustling center of Ketchikan and Totem Bight State Park to the north, where totem poles and a native clan house face the salt water. ⊙*2½ hrs* ⊠*$35–$40.*

TRANSPORTATION & TOURS

FROM THE PIER

Most ships dock or tender passengers ashore directly across from the Ketchikan Visitors Bureau on Front and Mission streets, in the center of downtown. A new dock, several blocks north on the other side of the tunnel, is still within easy walking distance of most of the town's sights. Walking-tour signs lead you around the city. For panoramic vistas of the surrounding area—and a wee bit of exercise—climb the stairs leading up several steep hillsides.

To reach sights farther from downtown, hire a cab or ride the local buses. Metered taxis meet the ships right on the docks and also wait across the street. Rates are $3.50 for pick-up and $3.50 per mi. Local buses run along the main route through town and south to Saxman. The fare is $1.

VISITOR INFORMATION

Ketchikan Visitors Bureau. The helpful visitors' bureau is right next to the cruise-ship docks. Half the space is occupied by day-tour, flightseeing, and boat-tour operators. ⊠*131 Front St., 99901* ☎*907/225–6166 or 800/770–3300* ⊕*www.visit-ketchikan.com* ⊙*May–Sept., daily 8–5, 6–6 when cruise ships are docked.*

EXPLORING KETCHIKAN

❿ The Deer Mountain Hatchery and Eagle Center lead into the small but charming **City Park,** which has picnic tables, a fountain, and paved paths. Ketchikan Creek runs through it. ⊠*Park and Fair Sts.*

⓰ Ketchikan's infamous red-light district once existed on **Creek Street.**
★ During Prohibition, it was home to numerous speakeasies, and in the early 1900s, more than 30 houses of prostitution operated here. Today the small colorful houses, built on stilts over the creek waters, have been restored as trendy shops. Sea kayakers often paddle up the creek at high tide.

6 Stand over Ketchikan Creek on **Creek Street Footbridge** for good salmon viewing when the fish are running. In summer, you can see coho, king, pink, and chum salmon, along with smaller numbers of steelhead and rainbow trout heading upstream to spawn. ■ **TIP→ Keep your eyes peeled for sea lions snacking on the incoming fish.**

11 Tens of thousands of king and coho (silver) salmon are raised at **Deer Mountain Hatchery and Eagle Center** on Ketchikan Creek. Midsummer visitors can view both natural spawning in the creek by pink and chum salmon and workers collecting and fertilizing the salmon eggs for the hatchery. Tanks hold young salmon and those old enough to head out to the ocean, and a video details the fascinating life cycle of salmon. Owned by the Ketchikan Indian Corporation, the hatchery has exhibits on traditional native fishing. Also here is a nesting pair of injured bald eagles. Although both are unable to fly, you may see them catching salmon that swim into their enclosure. ⊠ *429 Deermount St.* ☎ *907/228–4941 or 800/252–5158* ⊕ *www.kictribe.org/hatchery/hatchery.htm* ⊠ *$9* ⊙ *Early May–Sept., daily 8–4:30.*

17 Formerly owned by the inimitable Dolly Arthur, **Dolly's House** is the steep-roofed home that once housed Creek Street's most famous brothel. The house has been preserved as a museum, complete with furnishings, beds, and a short history of the life and times of Ketchikan's best-known madam. ⊠ *Creek St.* ☎ *907/225—6329 (summer only)* ⊠ *$5* ⊙ *Daily whenever cruise ships are in port, 8–4.*

8 At one time virtually all of Ketchikan's walkways and streets were made from wooden trestles, but now **Grant Street Trestle** is the only one of these handsome wooden streets that remains, constructed in 1908.

14 Twenty-one native students created **Return of the Eagle,** a colorful mural on a wall of the Robertson Building on the Ketchikan campus of the University of Alaska–Southeast. ⊠ *Stedman St.*

3 Built in 1903, **St. John's Church** is the oldest remaining house of worship in Ketchikan. Its interior is formed from red cedar cut in the native-operated sawmill in nearby Saxman. ⊠ *Mission St.* ☎ *907/225–3680.*

7 Get out your camera and set it for fast speed at **Salmon Falls**—a series of pools arranged like steps that allow fish to travel upstream over a dam or falls. When the salmon start running in midsummer, from June onward, thousands leap the falls (or take the easier fish-ladder route) to spawn in Ketchikan Creek's waters farther upstream. Many can also be seen in the creek's eddies, both above and below the falls. The falls, fish ladder, and a large carving of a jumping salmon are just off Park Avenue on Married Man's Trail. (The trail was once used by mar-

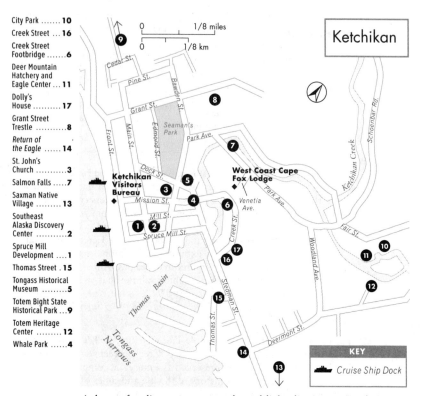

ried men for discreet access to the red-light district on Creek Street.)
⊠ *Married Man's Trail off Park Ave.*

❷ The **Southeast Alaska Discovery Center** features museum-quality exhibits—including one on the rain forest—that focus on the resources,
native cultures, and ecosystems of Southeast Alaska. The U.S. Forest Service and other federal agencies provide information on Alaska's
public lands, and a large gift shop sells natural-history books, maps,
and videos about the sights in Ketchikan and the Southeast. The multi-
media show "Mystical Southeast Alaska" is shown every half hour in
summer in the center's theater. ⊠ *50 Main St.* ☎ *907/228–6220* 💲 *$5*
🕙 *May–Sept., daily 8:30–5.*

❶ The attractive **Spruce Mill Development** is modeled after 1920s-style cannery architecture. Spread over 6½ acres along the waterfront—much of
it built out over the waters of Tongass Narrows—five buildings contain
a mix of retail stores, souvenir shops, galleries, and restaurants. Cruise
ships moor a few steps away, filling the shops with tourists all summer
long. ⊠ *Spruce Mill and Front Sts.*

❶⓯ From **Thomas Street** you can see Thomas Basin, the most accessible of
Ketchikan's four harbors and home port to pleasure and commercial
fishing boats. Old buildings, including the maroon-fronted Potlatch Bar,

sit atop pilings, and you can walk out to the breakwater for a better view of busy Tongass Narrows.

5 Native artifacts and pioneer relics revisit the mining and fishing eras at **Tongass Historical Museum,** this somewhat ho-hum museum in the same building as the library. Exhibits include a big, brilliantly polished lens from Tree Point Lighthouse and a well-presented collection of Native tools and artwork. Other exhibits change periodically but always include Tlingit native items. ⊠*629 Dock St.* ☎*907/225–5600* *$2* ⊙*May–Sept., daily 8–5.*

> **GREAT VIEWS**
>
> For the town's best harbor views and one of Southeast Alaska's most luxurious lobbies, head to **WestCoast Cape Fox Lodge.** Walk to the top of steep Venetia Avenue or take the funicular ($2) up from Creek Street. ⊠*800 Venetia Way* ☎*907/225–8001 or 800/426–0670* ⊕*www. capefoxlodge.com.*

12 ★ Gathered from native villages, many of the authentic native totems in **Totem Heritage Center**'s rare collection are well over a century old—a rare age for cedar carvings, which, because of the Southeast's exceedingly wet climate, are frequently lost to decay. The center also features guided tours and a video about the preservation efforts. Outside are several more poles carved in the three decades since this center opened. ⊠*601 Deermount St.* ☎*907/225–5900* *$5* ⊙*May–Sept., daily 8–5.*

4 The small **Whale Park,** in a traffic island across from St. John's Church, is the site of the Chief Kyan Totem Pole, now in its third incarnation. The original was carved in the 1890s, but over the decades it deteriorated and was replaced in the 1960s. The current replica was erected in 1993 with the 1960s version now housed in the Totem Heritage Center.

OUTSIDE TOWN

13 A 2½-mi paved walking path–bike trail parallels the road from Ketchikan to **Saxman Native Village,** named for a missionary who helped Native Alaskans settle here before 1900. The totem park in Saxman's center has poles moved from abandoned village sites in the 1930s. Saxman's Beaver Clan tribal house is said to be the largest in the world, and residents still practice traditional carving techniques; you can observe their craft in the adjacent shed, which is free and open whenever someone's working. You can get to the park on foot, by taxi, or by city bus. You're free to explore on your own, but to visit the tribal house and theater you must take a tour. Two-hour tours, which include an educational video, along with dancing, totem stories, and local legends, are generally part of a shore excursion package, but may also be purchased from the gift shop across from the totems. ⊠*S. Tongass Hwy., 2 mi south of town* ☎*907/225–4846* ⊕*www.capefoxtours.com.*

9 Most of Ketchikan's totem poles are 60-year-old replicas of older totem poles brought in from outlying villages as part of a federal-works cultural project during the late 1930s. Along with its many totem poles, **Totem Bight State Historical Park** has a hand-hewn native tribal house and sits on a scenic spit of land facing the waters of Tongass Narrows.

Most bus tours of Ketchikan include Totem Bight in their itinerary, but there is no public transportation to the site. ✉ *N. Tongass Hwy., 10 mi north of town* ☎ *907/247–8574* ⊕ *www.alaskastateparks.org* ☞ *Free* ☉ *Daily dawn–dusk.*

OUTDOOR ACTIVITIES

We don't recommend it if you're looking for authenticity, but the **Great Alaskan Lumberjack Show** is a 60-minute lumberjack contest providing a Disneyesque taste of old-time woodsman skills, including ax throwing, buck-sawing, springboard chopping, log-rolling duels, and a 50-foot tree climb that ends in a free fall. Shows take place in a covered grandstand directly behind the Spruce Mill Development and go on, rain or shine, all summer. ✉ *50 Main St.* ☎ *907/225–9050 or 888/320–9049* ⊕ *www.lumberjackshows.com* ☞ *$34* ☉ *May–Sept., 2–5 times daily; hrs vary.*

FISHING

Salmon are so plentiful in these waters that the town has earned the nickname of "Salmon Capital of the World." The **Ketchikan Visitors Bureau** (✉ *131 Front St., 99901* ☎ *907/225–6166 or 800/770–3300* ⊕ *www.visit-ketchikan.com*) has a full list of charter companies, or sign up for a sportfishing adventure at your shore excursion desk.

FLIGHTSEEING

The dramatic fjords and isolated alpine lakes of the 2.3 million acre Misty Fiords National Monument don't exactly lend themselves to pedestrian exploration. But thanks to flightseeing services like **Island Wings Air Service** (☎ *907/225–2444 or 888/854–2444* ⊕ *www.islandwings.com*), the sublime splendor of this region doesn't go unseen. Island Wings offers a popular two-hour tour that includes a 35-minute stopover at one of the Monument's many lakes or fjords.

SEA KAYAKING

Southeast Exposure (☎ *907/225–8829* ⊕ *www.southeastexposure.com*) rents kayaks and mountain bikes and guides kayaking trips. **Southeast Sea Kayaks** (☎ *907/225–1258 or 800/287–1607* ⊕ *www.kayakketchikan.com*) leads tours of Ketchikan's historic waterfront and provides kayak rentals, along with guided trips to Misty Fiords.

> **DID YOU KNOW?**
>
> Expect rain at some time during the day, even if the sun is shining when you dock: the average annual precipitation is more than 150 inches. Ketchikan receives so much rainfall that the wet stuff is often measured in feet, not inches—and in 1949, the town received a record 16.8 feet of precipitation. Residents take the rain in stride, though; it's often referred to as "Liquid Sunshine." (There's even a concrete testimony to this tongue-in-cheek attitude: the Liquid Sunshine Gauge is located on the cruise-ship dock adjacent to the Ketchikan Visitors Bureau.)

SHOPPING

■TIP➜ Because artists are local, prices for Native Alaskan crafts are sometimes lower in Ketchikan than at other ports. The **Saxman Village** gift shop has some Tlingit wares.

Saxman Arts Co-op, one block downhill from the Saxman Village, (☎907/225–4166), has baskets, button blankets (traditional wool blankets, usually bright red, with designs made from ivory-color buttons sewn into the fabric), moccasins, wood carvings, and jewelry that are all locally made. **Creek Street** has several attractive boutiques.

Parnassus Books (⊠5 Creek St. ☎907/225–7690 ⊕www.ketchikanbooks. com), is a book-lover's bookstore, with creaking floors, cozy quarters, many Alaskan titles, and a knowledgeable staff.

The same building houses **Soho Coho Contemporary Art and Craft Gallery** (☎907/225–5954 or 800/888–4070 ⊕www.trollart.com), headquarters for artist Ray Troll, Alaska's well-known producer of all things weird and fishy.

For some of the Southeast's best canned, smoked, or frozen salmon and halibut, along with crab and clams, try **Salmon Etc.** on Mission St. **Simply Salmon,** its sister store, is on Creek Street. ⊠322 Mission St. ☎907/225–6008 or 800/354–7256 ⊠10 Creek St. ☎907/225–1616 ⊕www.salmonetc.com.

WHERE TO EAT

$$–$$$$ ✕**Annabelle's Famous Keg and Chowder House.** Nestled into the ground floor of the historic Gilmore Hotel, this unpretentious Victorian-style restaurant serves a hearty array of seafood and pastas, including several kinds of chowder and steamer clams. Prime rib on Friday and Saturday evenings is a favorite, and the lounge with a jukebox adds a friendly vibe. Be sure to order a slice of peanut-butter pie. ⊠326 Front St. ☎907/225–6009 ⊕www.gilmorehotel.com ⊟AE, D, DC, MC, V.

$$–$$$$ ✕**Heen Kahidi Dining Room.** Located within Cape Fox Lodge, this hilltop restaurant is accessible via a small funicular car just off Creek Street. The hotel here is one of the finest in Southeast Alaska, with a big lobby accented by Tlingit and Haida artwork, an interesting collection of museum-quality artifacts, and a roaring fire. Heen Kahidi Dining Room serves three meals a day, with seafood, pasta, chicken, and steaks highlighting the dinner menu. Be sure to reserve one of the window tables that overlook Ketchikan. ⊠800 Venetia Way, 99901 ☎907/225–8001 ⊟AE, D, DC, MC, V.

$$–$$$$ ✕**Steamers.** Anchoring Ketchikan's Spruce Mill Mall, this lively, noisy, and spacious restaurant is popular with cruise passengers, and features an extensive menu of fresh seafood (including king crab and steamer clams), pasta, and steaks. Vegetarian choices are also available, and the servings are certain to fill you up. The bar pours 125 draft beers, including a number of Alaskan brews, along with a substantial wine list and 300 different liquors. Tall windows face Ketchikan's busy water-

front, where cruise ships and floatplanes vie for your attention. ✉76 *Front St.* ☎907/225–1600 ▭*AE, D, MC, V.*

WHERE TO DRINK

Ketchikan has quieted down in recent years as the economy shifted away from logging into tourism, but remains something of a party town, especially when crews stumble off fishing boats with cash in hand. You won't have any trouble finding something going on at several downtown bars. **First City Saloon** (✉*830 Water St.* ☎907/225–1494) is the main dance spot, with live music throughout the summer. **Potlatch Bar** (✉*126 Thomas Basin* ☎907/225–4855) delivers up music on weekends as well. You can glimpse the maroon facade from across Thomas Basin.

KODIAK ISLAND

On the second-largest island in the United States (Hawaii's Big Island is the largest), the town of Kodiak is the least touristy of all the Alaska port towns. It's an out-of-the-way destination for smaller cruise ships and Alaska state ferries, and despite its small population (just over 6,000 people), there's a lot of "big" stuff here: Kodiak is home to a very large commercial fishing fleet, and is almost always one of the top two or three in the country for tonnage of fish brought in. It's also home to the country's largest Coast Guard base, and the world-famous Kodiak brown bear, billed as the largest land carnivore in the world.

Russian explorers discovered the island in 1763, and Kodiak served as Alaska's first capital until 1804, when the government was moved to Sitka. Situated as it is in the northwestern Gulf of Alaska, Kodiak has been subjected to several natural disasters. In 1912 a volcanic eruption on the nearby Alaska Peninsula covered the town site in knee-deep drifts of ash and pumice. A tidal wave resulting from the 1964 earthquake destroyed the island's large fishing fleet and smashed Kodiak's low-lying downtown area.

Today commercial fishing is king in Kodiak. A clearinghouse for fish caught by islanders throughout the Kodiak archipelago—about 15,000 people are scattered among the islands—the city is among the busiest fishing ports in the United States. The harbor is also an important supply point for small communities on the Aleutian Islands and the Alaska Peninsula.

COMING ASHORE

SHORE EXCURSIONS

ADVENTURE

Kodiak Bear Viewing by Floatplane. Weather permitting, you can fly over Kodiak's lush green hills and remote backcountry waterways, then spend at least two hours on the ground watching the world's largest carnivores in their natural habitat. During the flight out and back the pilot will also point out marine and terrestrial mammals and other points of interest. ⊘4½ *hrs* ⊠*$650.*

Halibut fishing. From picturesque St. Paul Harbor, you can thread your way through the commercial fishing fleet and into the icy waters of the Gulf of Alaska in pursuit of the wily and tasty Pacific halibut. Be prepared to work for your food, though—the state record halibut weighed 459 pounds, and 100- to 200-pound fish are common. Along the way you can spot marine mammals such as seals, sea lions and sea otters, and numerous seabirds as well. All bait and tackle is supplied, and local fish processors can arrange to clean, package, and ship your catch for you. ⊘6 *hrs* ⊠*$275.*

SCENIC

Waterfront and Wildlife Cruise. Take a cruise along the waterfront, and view the fishing fleet, canneries, the Russian Orthodox church and seminary, and the abandoned World War II defense installation. Chances of seeing seabirds and marine mammals such as sea lions and sea otters are excellent. ⊘1½ *hrs* ⊠*$190.*

TRANSPORTATION & TOURS

FROM THE PIER

Most cruise ships dock at Pier 2, ½ mi south of downtown Kodiak. Some ships offer shuttles into town, but if yours doesn't, it's a 15-minute walk. You can catch a cab ride from **A&B Taxi** (☎*907/486–4343*).

AREA TOURS

Kodiak Island Charters (☎*907/486–5380 or 800/575–5380* ⊕*www.ptialaska.net/~urascal*) operates boat tours for fishing, hunting, and sightseeing aboard the 43-foot *U-Rascal*. They'll take you on a combined halibut and salmon trip, with sightseeing and whale-watching thrown in as well.

VISITOR INFORMATION

Pick up maps, details on kayaking trips, bear-viewing flights, marine tours, and more from the **Kodiak Island Convention & Visitors' Bureau** (⊠*100 Marine Way* ☎*907/486–4782*), which is staffed whenever cruise ships are in port.

KODIAK BEST BETS

■ **Visit the world's largest bears.** Join one of the local flight operators and spend the day watching these animals devour amazing quantities of salmon.

■ **Relax, have a brew.** Stop by the local brewery for a tasting session and tour, and stock up on fresh local beer for your stay.

■ **Walk off those calories.** Pick up a map of the Kodiak hiking trails at the Visitors' Bureau and head for the hills. Chances are you won't be eaten by a bear.

4

EXPLORING KODIAK

The **Alutiiq Museum and Archaeological Repository** is home to one of the largest collections of Eskimo materials in the world and contains archaeological and ethnographic items dating back 7,500 years. Museum displays include harpoons, masks, dolls, stone tools, seal-gut parkas, grass baskets, and pottery fragments. The museum store sells native arts. ⊠*215 Mission Rd.* ☎*907/486–7004* ⊕*www.alutiiq-museum.org* ✉*$3 donation requested* ۞*Memorial Day–Labor Day, weekdays 9–5, Sat. 10–5, Sun. by appointment.*

The **Baranov Museum** presents artifacts from the area's Russian origins. Built in 1808 by Alexander Baranov to warehouse precious sea-otter pelts, the museum is in one of the oldest Russian buildings in North America. On display are samovars, Russian Easter eggs, native baskets, and other relics from the early Native Koniags and the later Russian settlers. In 2008, the museum will be celebrating the 200th year of the building with a series of lectures, Russian dancing classes, and an illustrated book. Contact the museum for a calendar of events. ⊠*101 Marine Way* ☎*907/486–5920* ⊕*www.baranov.us* ✉*$3* ۞*May–Sept., daily 10–4.*

As part of America's North Pacific defense in World War II, Kodiak was the site of an important naval station, now occupied by the Coast Guard fleet that patrols the surrounding fishing grounds. Part of the old military installation has been incorporated into **Fort Abercrombie State Park,** 3½ mi north of Kodiak on Rezanof Drive. The land is carpeted with spruce trees and trails lead past old concrete bunkers and gun emplacements to magnificent shores. You can even see nesting puffins on the cliffs here. ⊠*Mile 3.7, Rezanof Dr.* ✑*Alaska State Parks, Kodiak District Office, 1400 Abercrombie Dr., Kodiak 99615* ☎*907/486–6339* ⊕*www.dnr.state.ak.us/parks.*

One of the chief attractions in the area is the 1.6-million-acre **Kodiak National Wildlife Refuge,** which lies partly on Kodiak Island and partly on Afognak Island to the north and where spotting the enormous Kodiak brown bears is the main goal of a trip. Seeing the Kodiak brown bears, which weigh a pound at birth but up to 1,500 pounds when fully grown, is worth the trip to this rugged country. ■TIP➜ **The bears are spotted easily in July and August, feeding along salmon-spawning streams.** Charter flightseeing trips are available to the area, and exaggerated tales of encounters with these impressive beasts are frequently heard. ⊠*1390 Buskin River Rd., Kodiak 99615* ☎*907/487–2600* ⊕*www. r7.fws.gov/nwr/kodiak.*

OUTDOOR ACTIVITIES

BEAR-WATCHING

Access to Kodiak bears from the road system is almost nonexistent. To see them requires traveling by boat or plane to remote streams where bears feed on the abundant salmon runs. Here are a few of the local outfits that offer the service. **Harvey Flying Service** (☎*907/487–2621*

⊕*www.harveyflyingservice.com*); **Andrew Airways** (☎*907/487–2566*
⊕*www.andrewairways.com*); **Kodiak Treks** (✉*11754 S. Russian Creek
Rd., Kodiak 99615* ☎*907/487–2122* ⊕*www.kodiaktreks.com*).

SHOPPING

Shopping in Kodiak is limited, but the town does have a downtown
gift shop–gallery called **Norman's Fine Alaskan Gifts and Jewelry,** (✉*414
Marine Way, Kodiak 99615* ☎*907/486–3315*). They have some works
by local artisans. The Alutiiq Museum store also sells native arts and
educational materials.

WHERE TO EAT

$$–$$$$ ✕**Henry's Great Alaskan Restaurant.** Henry's is a boisterous, friendly, and
smoky downtown spot. The menu is the biggest in town and ranges
from fresh local seafood to barbecue to pastas and even some Cajun
dishes. A long list of appetizers, salads, and tasty desserts rounds out
the choices. The bar is popular with sports enthusiasts. ✉*512 Marine
Way* ☎*907/486–8844* ▭*AE, MC, V.*

$$–$$$ ✕**Old Powerhouse Restaurant.** Enjoy fresh sushi, sashimi, and other Japa-
nese specials made with local seafood while watching the procession of
fishing boats glide past on their way to catch or deliver your next meal.
Keep your eyes peeled for sea otters, seals, sea lions, and eagles, too.
There's even occasional live music. ✉*516 E. Marine Way* ☎*907/481–
1088* ▭*MC, V.*

$$ ✕**El Chicano.** This unexpectedly authentic Mexican restaurant dishes up
all the traditional favorites, from chiles rellenos to homemade tama-
les. There are large servings at reasonable prices. ✉*103 Center St.*
☎*907/486–6116* ▭*AE, D, MC, V.*

$ ✕**Monk's Rock Coffee House.** Run by the St. Herman of Alaska Brother-
hood, a splinter group of the Russian Orthodox Church, this unusual
little gathering spot is a pleasant place for coffee, tea, smoothies, fresh-
squeezed juices, freshly baked breads, and ice cream. Books are for
sale, and the back room doubles as a chapel. ✉*202 E. Rezanof Dr.*
☎*907/486–0905* ▭*No credit cards.*

WHERE TO DRINK

The **Kodiak Island Brewing Co.** (✉*338 Shelikof Ave.* ☎*907/486–2537*
⊕*www.kodiakbrewery.com*) sells fresh-brewed, unfiltered beer in a
variety of styles and sizes of containers, from 20-ounce bottles up to
full kegs. Brewer Ben Millstein will also give you a tour of the facility
on request. It's open from noon to 7 daily in summer, and from noon to
6 Monday to Saturday in winter. Due to a recent change in state liquor
laws, some on-premise sales and consumption are now allowed.

METLAKATLA

The village of Metlakatla—whose name translates roughly to "salt water passage"—is on Annette Island, just a dozen miles by sea from busy Ketchikan but a world away culturally. A visit to this quiet native community offers visitors the chance to learn about small-town life in the Inside Passage. Local taxis can take you to other sights around the island, including Yellow Hill and the old air force base.

People in most Southeast native villages are of Tlingit or Haida heritage. Metlakatla is the exception; here most folks are Tsimshian. They moved to the island from British Columbia in 1887, led by William Duncan, an Anglican missionary from England. The new town grew rapidly and soon included dozens of buildings laid out on a grid of streets—a cannery, a sawmill, and a church that could seat 1,000 people. Congress declared Annette Island a federal Indian reservation in 1891, and it remains the only reservation in Alaska today. Father Duncan continued to control life in Metlakatla for decades, until the government finally stepped in shortly before his death in 1918.

During World War II the U.S. Army built a major air base 7 mi from Metlakatla that included observation towers for Japanese subs, airplane hangars, gun emplacements, and housing for 10,000 soldiers. After the war it served as Ketchikan's airport for many years, but today the long runways are virtually abandoned save for a few private flights.

COMING ASHORE

Cruise ships dock at the Metlakatla dock adjacent to town. Buses from **Metlakatla Tours** (☎ *907/886–8687* ⊕ *tours.metlakatla.net*) meet all ships and provide a standard shore excursion that includes a bus tour of town taking in most of the beautifully carved totem poles and a dance performance at the longhouse.

EXPLORING METLAKATLA

Metlakatla's religious heritage still shows through today. The clapboard **William Duncan Memorial Church,** topped with two steeples, burned in 1948 but was rebuilt several years later. It's one of nine churches in tiny Metlakatla. **Father Duncan's Cottage** is maintained to appear exactly as it would have in 1891, and includes original furnishings, personal items, and a collection of turn-of-the-century music boxes. ⊠ *Corner of 4th Ave. and Church St.* ☎ *907/886–8687* 🖃 *$2* ☉ *When cruise ships are in port.*

Father Duncan worked hard to eliminate traditional Tsimshian beliefs and dances, so he probably wouldn't have approved of recent efforts to relearn the old ways. Today the people of Metlakatla proudly perform these old dances and stories. The best place to catch these performances is at the traditional **longhouse** (known as "Le Sha'as" in the Tsimshian dialect), which faces Metlakatla's boat harbor. Three totem poles stand on the back side of the building, and the front is covered with a Tsimshian design. Inside are displays of native crafts and a model of the fish traps that were once common throughout the Inside Passage. Just down from the longhouse is an Artists' Village, a simple covered market where booths display locally made arts and crafts. The village and longhouse open when groups and tours are present.

MISTY FIORDS NATIONAL MONUMENT

Fodor'sChoice
★
In the past, cruise ships bypassed Misty Fiords on their way up and down the Inside Passage. But today more and more cruise passengers are discovering its unspoiled beauty as ships big and small feature a day of scenic cruising through this protected wilderness. At the southern end of the Inside Passage, Misty Fiords is usually visited just before or after a call at Ketchikan. The attraction here is the wilderness—3,500 square mi of it—highlighted by waterfalls and cliffs that rise 3,000 feet. Small boats enable close-up views of breathtaking vistas. Traveling on these waters can be an almost mystical experience, with the greens of the forest reflected in waters as still as black mirrors. You may find yourself in the company of a whale, see bears fishing along the shore, or even pull in your own salmon for an evening meal. Park rangers may kayak out to your cruise ship to help point out wildlife and explain the geology of the area. ■TIP→Keep in mind that the name Misty refers to the weather you're likely to encounter in this rainy part of Alaska.

GETTING HERE ON YOUR OWN

The dramatic fjords and isolated alpine lakes of the 2.3-million-acre Misty Fiords National Monument don't exactly lend themselves to pedestrian exploration. But thanks to flightseeing services like **Island Wings Air Service** (☎907/225–2444 or 888/854–2444 ⊕ *www.island-wings.com*), the sublime splendor of this region doesn't go unseen. Based in Ketchikan, Island Wings offers a popular two-hour tour that includes a 35-minute stopover at one of the Monument's many lakes or fjords.

NOME

Nome is visited by Cruise West and Clipper Cruise Lines adventure ships as part of their Bering Sea trips, which include Homer, Kodiak, Dutch Harbor, the Pribilofs, and Siberia. More than a century has passed since a great stampede for gold put a speck of wilderness called Nome on the Alaska map, but gold mining and noisy saloons are still mainstays in this frontier community on the icy Bering Sea. Only 165 mi from the coast of Siberia, Nome is considerably closer to Russia than either Anchorage or Fairbanks. Mainly a collection of ramshackle houses and low-slung commercial buildings, Nome looks like a vintage gold-mining camp or the neglected set of a western movie—raw-boned, rugged, and somewhat shabby. What the town lacks in appearance is made up for with a cheerful hospitality and colorful history.

Nome's golden years began in 1898, when three prospectors known as the Lucky Swedes struck rich deposits on Anvil Creek, about 4 mi from what became Nome. The news spread quickly. When the Bering Sea ice parted the next spring, ships from Puget Sound, down by Seattle, arrived in Nome with eager stampeders. An estimated 15,000 people landed in Nome between June and October of 1900. Among the gold-rush luminaries were Wyatt Earp, the old gunfighter from the O.K. Corral, who mined the gold of Nome by opening a posh saloon; Tex Rickard, the boxing promoter, who operated another Nome saloon; and Rex Beach, the novelist.

A network of 250 mi or so of gravel roads around the town leads to creeks and rivers for gold panning or fishing for trout, salmon, and arctic grayling. You may also see reindeer, bears, foxes, and moose on the back roads that once connected early mining camps and hamlets.

COMING ASHORE

TRANSPORTATION & TOURS

FROM THE PIER

Cruise ships dock a mile south of Nome at the city dock. Taxis are available to downtown for $5.

AREA TOURS

Most travelers take a tour of the area through **Nome Discovery Tours** (☞ *Box 2024, Nome 99762* ☎ *907/443–2814*), in which former Broadway showman Richard Beneville emphasizes Nome's gold rush and the region's Inupiat history.

VISITOR INFORMATION

For exploring downtown, stop at the **Nome Convention and Visitors Bureau** (✉ *301 Front St.* ☎ *907/443–6624, 800/478–1901 in Alaska* ⊕ *www. nomealaska.org/vc*) for a historic-walking-tour map, a city map, and information on local activities from flightseeing to bird-watching.

EXPLORING NOME

Nome's only museum, the **Carrie M. McClain Memorial Museum** showcases the history of the Nome gold rush, from the Lucky Swedes' discovery in 1898 to Wyatt Earp's arrival in 1899 and the stampede of thousands of people into Nome in 1900. There are exhibits on the lifestyles and art of the Bering Strait Inupiat Eskimos, plus historic photos and stories about the Nome Kennel Club and its All-Alaska Sweepstakes of the early 1900s. ✉ *223 Front St.* ☎ *907/443–6630* ☞ *Free* ☾ *June–early Sept., daily 9–5:30.*

WHERE TO EAT

$$–$$$ ✗ **Fat Freddie's Restaurant.** This popular family-style eatery overlooking the Bering Sea serves New York steak and prime rib, plus notable burgers and chowder. ✉ *50 Front St.* ☎ *907/443–5899* ⊟ *AE, D, MC, V.*

$$–$$$ ✕ **Polar Café.** American diner food, from omelets to steak, fills the menu here. Locals like to linger over coffee, making it a good place to eavesdrop on residents discussing area issues, or just to gaze out at the Bering Sea. With its sea views, good prices, and friendly service, the Polar Café is a great place for an early-morning breakfast. ⊠*205 W. Front St., downtown* ☎*907/443–5191* ⊟*AE, MC, V.*

WHERE TO DRINK

Since its establishment more than a century ago, Nome has always been a place where drinking is a major focus. Because all the surrounding native villages are dry, many folks come here to drink to excess.

The town's most famous bar is **Board of Trade Saloon** (⊠*211 Front St.* ☎*907/443–2611*), which was originally owned by Wyatt Earp (when it was called the Dexter Saloon). Nowadays it has live music a few nights a week. The **Gold Dust Lounge** (⊠*315 W. Front St.* ☎*907/443–5101*) at Nugget Inn has big windows facing Norton Sound, making it a good spot for a drink.

SHOPPING

Nome is one of the best places to buy ivory, because many of the Eskimo carvers from outlying villages come to Nome first to offer their wares to dealers. The Marine Mammals Protection Act permits the purchase of walrus-ivory goods from Native Alaskans. The **Arctic Trading Post** (⊠*Bering and Front Sts.* ☎*907/443–2686*) has an extensive stock of authentic Eskimo ivory carvings and other Alaskan artwork, jewelry, and books. **Chukotka–Alaska** (⊠*514 Lomen Ave.* ☎*907/443–4128*) sells both Native Alaskan and Russian artwork and handicrafts as well as books, beads, and furs.

PETERSBURG

Getting to Petersburg is a heart-quickening experience. Only ferries and the smallest cruise ships can squeak through Wrangell Narrows, with the aid of more than 50 buoys and markers along the 22-mi passage. The inaccessibility of Petersburg is part of its charm, for unlike several other Southeast communities, this one is never overwhelmed with hordes of cruise-ship passengers.

At first sight Petersburg invokes the spirit of Norway; tidy white homes and storefronts line the streets, bright-color swirls of leaf and flower designs (called rosemaling) decorate a few older homes, and row upon row of sturdy fishing vessels pack the harbor. The Scandinavian feel is no accident—this prosperous fishing community was founded by Norwegian Peter Buschmann in 1897.

COMING ASHORE

SHORE EXCURSIONS

LeConte Glacier Flightseeing. One of the best flightseeing tours in Alaska takes you to the southernmost calving glacier in North America, which is backed by one of the Southeast's most beautiful collections of mountain peaks, including the Devil's Thumb. ⊙*45 mins* ⊠*$170.*

Little Norway. Here's a chance to explore this pretty fishing town by bus and watch a Scandinavian dance performance at the Sons of Norway Hall. Some tours also include a Norwegian-style smorgasbord. ⊙*2 hrs* ⊠*$30.*

Waterfront Walking Tour. A guide will relate the history and fishing heritage of Petersburg as you explore the old part of town on foot. ⊙*1½ hrs* ⊠*$15.*

> ### PETERSBURG BEST BETS
>
> ■ **Soak up the Scandinavian heritage.** Little Norway's cultural history is readily accessible at landmarks like the Clausen Memorial Museum and the Sons of Norway Hall.
>
> ■ **Cycle to Sandy Beach.** Rent a bike and pedal up to Sandy Beach, where you can find killer views of Frederick Sound and the Coast Mountains beyond.
>
> ■ **Stroll the harbor docks.** Petersburg is one of Alaska's most prosperous fishing communities, and the variety of seacraft is enormous. You can see small trollers, big halibut vessels, and sleek pleasure craft.

TRANSPORTATION & TOURS

FROM THE PIER

Five cruise companies include stops at Petersburg: American Safari Cruises, American West Steamboat Company, Cruise West, Glacier Bay Cruiseline, and Lindblad Expeditions. All of these are smaller, adventure-oriented ships. The ships dock in the South Harbor, which is about a ½-mi walk from downtown.

CITY TOURS

If you want to learn about the local history, the commercial fishing industry, and the Tongass National Forest, you can take a guided tour with Viking Travel (*see Outdoor Activities, below*).

VISITOR INFORMATION

The **Petersburg Visitor Information Center,** within walking distance of the harbor, is a good source for local information, including details on tours, charters, and nearby outdoor recreation opportunities. ⊠*1st and Fram Sts.* ☎*907/772–4636* ⊕*www.petersburg.org.*

EXPLORING PETERSBURG

One of the most pleasant things to do in Petersburg is to roam among the fishing vessels tied up at dockside. This is one of Alaska's busiest, most prosperous fishing communities, and the variety of boats is enormous. You can see small trollers, big halibut vessels, and sleek pleasure craft. Wander, too, around the fish-processing structures (though beware of the pungent aroma). Just by watching shrimp, salmon, or halibut catches being brought ashore, you can get a real appreciation for this industry and the people who engage in it.

③ At 2nd and Fram streets you can find the **Clausen Memorial Museum** and the bronze *Fisk* (Norwegian for "fish") sculpture. Not surprisingly, the museum devotes a lot of space to fishing and fish processing. There's an old "iron chink," used in the early days for gutting and cleaning fish, as well as displays on several types of fishing boats. On exhibit are a 126½-pound king salmon, the largest ever caught (it came out of a fish trap on Prince of Wales Island in 1939), and the world's largest chum salmon—a 36-pounder. ⊠*203 Fram St.* ☎*907/772–3598* ⊠*$3* ☉*Mon.–Sat. 10–5.*

❶ In the center of town, walk through **Hammer Slough,** a narrow inlet lined with weathered houses built on stilts, where the town's bachelors used to live. (You're sure to recognize some traces of Ketchikan's Creek Street here.) It makes for a postcard-perfect picture, and at high tide the slough fills with salt water and measures 100 feet bank to bank. The large, white, barnlike structure that borders the slough is the Sons of Norway Hall, where descendants of Norwegian settlers keep the traditions and culture of the old country alive.

❹ The best place to watch for America's national bird is the appropriately named **Eagle's Roost Park,** along the shore north of the Petersburg Fisheries cannery. At low tide you may see more than two dozen eagles diving for live fish or carrion here. Three pioneer churches—Catholic, Lutheran, and Presbyterian—are nearby at Dolphin and 3rd streets, Excel and 5th streets, and on Haugen Street between 2nd and 3rd streets, respectively. Of the three, the 50-year-old Lutheran church is the oldest. It is said that boys would bring dirt loads by the wheelbarrow for landscaping around the foundation. Their compensation? Ice-cream cones. The enticement was so successful that, after three years of ice-cream rewards, it was necessary to bring in a bulldozer to scrape off the excess dirt.

❷ **Petersburg Marine Mammal Center.** Visitors to this nonprofit research and learning center can share and gather information on marine mammal sightings, pick up reference material, and have fun with the interactive educational kiosk. ⊠*Gjoa St. and Sing Lee Alley, behind Viking Travel* ☎*907/772–4170 summer only* ⊕*www.psgmmc.org* ⊠*Free* ☉*Mid-June–Aug. 9–5 Mon.–Sat.*

The peaks of the Coastal Range behind the town mark the border between Canada and the United States; the most striking is Devil's Thumb, at 9,077 feet. About 25 mi east of Petersburg lies spectacular **LeConte Glacier,** the continent's southernmost tidewater glacier and one of its most active ones. It often happens that so many icebergs have calved into the bay that the entrance is carpeted bank to bank with the floating bergs. LeConte Glacier is accessible only by water or air; contact **Kaleidoscope Cruises** (☎*907/772–3736 or 800/868–4373* ⊕*www.petersburglodgingandtours.com*) to schedule a five-hour trip.

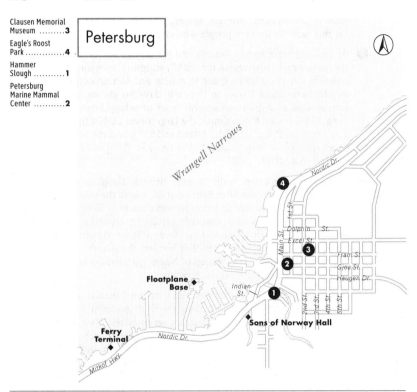

Petersburg

Wrangell Narrows

Nordic Dr.

4

1st St.

Dolphin St.
Excel St.

Main St.

3

Fram St.

2

Gjoa St.

Haugen Dr.

Floatplane
Base

Indian
St.

1

2nd St.
3rd St.
4th St.
5th St.

Ferry
Terminal

Nordic Dr.

Sons of Norway Hall

Mitkof Hwy.

OUTDOOR ACTIVITIES

Viking Travel (✉*101 Nordic Dr.* ☎*907/772–3818 or 800/327–2571* ⊕*www.alaskaferry.com*) is a full-service travel agency that specializes in custom Alaska tours, and can book whale-watching, glacier, sea-kayaking, and other charters with local and regional operators.

CYCLING
Renting a bicycle is an especially pleasant way to see the sights. Ride along the coast on Nordic Drive, past the lovely homes, to the boardwalk and the city dump, where you might spot some bears. Coming back to town, take the interior route and you'll pass the airport and some pretty churches before returning to the waterfront.

LITTLE NORWAY FESTIVAL

Petersburg's Nordic heritage is gradually being submerged by the larger American culture, but you may still occasionally hear Norwegian spoken, especially during the Little Norway Festival, held here each year. The party should be extra-huge in 2008, the 50th anniversary of the festival. Festivities are planned from May 15 to 18. If you're in town during the festival, be sure to partake in one of the fish feeds that highlight the Norwegian Independence Day celebration. You won't find better folk dancing and beer-batter halibut outside Norway.

Bikes are available from **Petersburg Cyclery** (⊠*1216 S. Nordic Dr.* ☎*907/772–3929*).

PICNICS

For a scenic hike, hop in a taxi for the 3-mi drive to Sandy Beach (on Nordic Drive, north of town), one of Petersburg's favorite spots for picnics, recreation, and eagle-viewing. There's even a petroglyph that's exposed at low tide.

SHOPPING

At **Tonka Seafoods** (⊠*Sing Lee Alley* ☎*907/772–3662 or 888/560–3662* ⊕*www.tonkaseafoods.com* ✉*Free; tours $15* ☉*June–Aug., daily 8–5; Sept.–May, Mon.–Sat. 8–5; tours at 1* PM *[Minimum 5 people]*), across the street from the Sons of Norway Hall, you can tour the plant and sample smoked or canned halibut and salmon. Off an alley in a beautiful big white house that served as a boardinghouse to fishermen and schoolteachers, **Sing Lee Alley Books** stocks books on Alaska, best sellers, cards, and gifts. ⊠*Sing Lee Alley* ☎*907/772–4440.*

WHERE TO EAT

$ ✕**Coastal Cold Storage Fish Market.** This busy little seafood deli in the heart of Petersburg serves daily lunch seafood specials, including fish chowders and halibut beer bits (a local favorite), along with grilled chicken wraps, steak sandwiches, and breakfast omelets and waffles. It's a great place to stop in for a quick bite en route to your next adventure; there isn't much seating in the shop's cramped interior. Live or cooked crab is available for takeout, and the shop can process your sport-caught fish. ⊠*306 N. Nordic Dr.* ☎*907/772–4171 or 877/257–4746* ▭*AE, D, DC, MC, V.*

$ ✕**Helse Restaurant.** Locals flock to this modest mom-and-pop place for lunch. It's the closest thing to home cooking Petersburg has to offer, and most days it's open 8–5, even in winter. A couple dozen sandwiches grace the menu, as do rotating soups and homemade bread. The daily specials are a good bet, and the gyros are decent as well. Helse also doubles as an ice-cream and espresso stand. ⊠*13 Sing Lee Alley* ☎*907/772–3444* ▭*MC, V.*

WHERE TO DRINK

The **Harbor Bar** (⊠*310 N. Nordic Dr.* ☎*907/772–4526*), with ships' wheels, ship pictures, and a mounted red snapper, is true to the town's seafaring spirit. A separate outside entrance leads to the bar's

> **LOCAL TREATS**
>
> One of the Southeast's gourmet delicacies is Petersburg pink salad shrimp. Small (they're seldom larger than half your pinky finger), tender, and succulent, they're much treasured by Alaskans, who often send them "outside" as thank-you gifts. You can find the little critters fresh in meat departments and canned in gift sections at food stores throughout the Panhandle. Also, be sure to taste the white king salmon—it's an especially flavorful type of Chinook that locals swear by.

liquor store. Sample the brew and blastingly loud music at the smoky **Kito's Kave** (✉ *Sing Lee Alley* ☎ *907/772–3207*); it's a classic Southeast bar—rough around the edges, but full of vim and vigor, and a perfect place for rowdy local fisherman to congregate. La Fonda, a Mexican restaurant, leases space inside the bar.

PRINCE RUPERT, BRITISH COLUMBIA

Just 40 mi (66 km) south of the Alaskan border, Prince Rupert is the largest community on British Columbia's north coast. Set on Kaien Island at the mouth of the Skeena River and surrounded by deep green fjords and coastal rain forest, Prince Rupert is rich in the culture of the Tsimshian, people who have been in the area for thousands of years.

As the western terminus of Canada's second transcontinental railroad and blessed with a deep natural harbor, Prince Rupert was, at the time of its incorporation in 1910, poised to rival Vancouver as a center for trans-Pacific trade. This didn't happen, partly because the main visionary behind the scheme, Grand Trunk Pacific Railroad president Charles Hays, went down with the *Titanic* on his way back from a financing trip to England. Prince Rupert turned instead to fishing and forestry. A port of call for both BC and Alaska ferries, but relatively new to cruise ships, this community of 15,000 retains a laid-back, small-town air. ■ TIP → Note that some cruise ships dock here, but don't stop long enough for passengers to disembark. Check before booking if this isn't clear on your cruise itinerary.

> ### PRINCE RUPERT BEST BETS
>
> ■ **Looking for wildlife?** The Khutzeymateen Grizzly Bear Sanctuary is North America's largest concentration of humpbacks and a strong population of orcas.
>
> ■ **Short on time?** Pay a visit to the excellent Museum of Northern British Columbia, followed by a stroll around the funky **Cow Bay** neighborhood.
>
> ■ **Want something different?** If you have a little extra time, hit the North Pacific Historic Fishing Village.

COMING ASHORE

SHORE EXCURSIONS

Wilderness Jet Boat Adventure. A jet boat ride into the wilderness is the highlight of a trip that also includes a guided walk through an old growth forest and a salmon barbecue on the banks of a pristine river. ⏱ *4½ hrs* 🎟 *$164.*

Khutzeymateen Grizzly Bear Watch. Travel by boat to see one of North America's highest concentrations of grizzly bears, passing stunning scenery and two First Nations villages en route. Eagles, porpoises, and whales may also be spotted. Since boats are not permitted to land at the sanctuary, you'll watch the bears from a safe distance offshore. Viewing is best between mid-May and late July; trips may not be offered in August and September. ⊘ *5 hrs* 🖃*About $199.*

TIP

Public transport is limited, so an organized excursion is the best way to get to the Fishing Village.

Ancient Village, Petroglyphs & Rainforest Discovery. Join First Nations guides on a visit to traditional Tsimshian lands, follow trails through old growth forest, see archaeological sites, and enjoy a traditional salmon barbecue. ⊘ *4 hrs* 🖃*$96.*

North Pacific Historic Fishing Village. Travel by bus to this national historic site, built in 1889 at the mouth of the Skeena River. Staff lead tours and demonstrations about the canning process and the unique culture of cannery villages. A seafood meal in the original cannery mess is included. ⊘ *3 hrs* 🖃*$80.*

Mysteries & Traditions of the Northcoast Native People. Learn about the life and history of the Tsimshian people at the Museum of Northern British Columbia, then enter a Tsimshian longhouse to join in a feast with dancing, stories, and songs. ⊘ *2½ hrs* 🖃*$47.*

TRANSPORTATION

FROM THE PIER

Large cruise ships calling at Prince Rupert dock at the **Northland Cruise Terminal** while smaller ships tie up at **Atlin Terminal** next door. Both terminals are at the city's historic Cow Bay district, steps from the Museum of Northern British Columbia and about five blocks from the central business district. The terminals for both British Columbia and Alaska ferries as well as the VIA Rail train station are grouped together about 2 km (1 mi) from town.

Most points of interest are within walking distance of the cruise-ship terminals. **Far West Bus Lines** (☎*250/624–6400*) buses have service around town. For a taxi, contact **Skeena Taxi** (☎*250/624–2186*).

VISITOR INFORMATION

Prince Rupert's **Visitor Information Centre** (☎*250/624–5637 or 800/ 667–1994*) is at the Atlin Terminal. **Tourism Prince Rupert** ⊕www. tourismprincerupert.com has a useful Web site.

TIME

■TIP➔ If you're coming from Alaska, remember to adjust your watch. British Columbia is on Pacific Time, one hour ahead of Alaska Time.

EXPLORING PRINCE RUPERT

Home to both of Prince Rupert's cruise-ship terminals, **Cow Bay** is a historic waterfront area of shops, galleries, seafood restaurants, yachts, canneries, and fishing boats. Cow Bay takes its name seriously; lampposts, benches, and anything else stationary is painted Holstein-style. While here, you can stop for a coffee or seafood lunch, shop for local crafts, or watch fishermen bring in their catch.

★ The **Museum of Northern British Columbia,** in a longhouse-style facility overlooking the waterfront, has one of the province's finest collections of coastal First Nations art, with artifacts portraying 10,000 years of Northwest Coast history. Artisans work on totem poles in the carving shed nearby and, at the longhouse, you can catch performances of Tsimshian storytelling, song, and dance twice daily between mid-May and mid-October. In summer, museum staff also offer a variety of museum and city tours and operate the **Kwinista Railway Museum,** a five-minute walk away on the waterfront. ⊠*100 1st Ave. W* ☎*250/624–3207* ⊕*www.museumofnorthernbc.com* ☒*C$5* ⊙*Late May–Aug., daily 9–5; Oct.–May, Mon.–Sat. 9–5.*

SHOPPING

Prince Rupert has a great selection of locally made crafts and First Nations artwork. Look for items carved in argillite, a kind of slate unique to this region. The **Cow Bay Gift Galley** (⊠*24 Cow Bay Rd.* ☎*250/627–1808*) has gifts, souvenirs, and local art. The **Northern Cooperative Ice House Gallery** (⊠*At the Atlin Cruise Ship Terminal* ☎*250/624–4546*) has paintings, jewelry, weaving, pottery and more, all by local artists.

WHERE TO EAT

$$ ✕**OPA Sushi.** An historic net loft makes a suitably nautical setting for this popular Cow Bay sushi spot, and the patio out back is a prime spot for eagle watching. Locals and visitors flock here for nigiri, sashimi, and maki rolls made with wild, local British Columbian salmon, prawns, octopus, and other treats from the sea. Donburi rice dishes, miso soup, sake cocktails, and green tea ice cream round out the menu. ⊠*34 Cow Bay Rd., Cow Bay* ☎*250/627–4560* ☐*AE, MC, V* ⊙*Closed Sun. and Mon.*

$–$$ ✕**Cow Bay Café.** Local seafood and creative vegetarian dishes shine at this tiny waterfront café, where the friendly chef-owner makes almost everything (including breads and desserts) from scratch. What's on the chalkboard menu depends on what's fresh that day but could include curries, Mexican dishes, or the popular crab cakes. The solariumlike room with floor-to-ceiling ocean-view windows only seats 35, so reservations are highly recommended. ⊠*205 Cow Bay Rd., Cow Bay* ☎*250/ 627–1212* ☐*AE, MC, V* ⊙*Closed Mon. No dinner Tues. and Sun.*

$ ✕**Cowpuccino's Coffee House.** When Rupertites want to while away a wet afternoon, they flock to this cozy meeting place in Cow Bay. You can curl up on the sofa with an espresso and a magazine, strum on the café's guitar, or pull up a chair for homemade soup, sandwiches, crepes, and luscious house-made desserts (try the cow patty: a chocolate-macaroon concoction). Hearty breakfasts are served here, too. Tables on the patio are a great place to watch eagles gathering across the street. ⊠*25 Cow Bay Rd., Cow Bay* ☎*250/627–1395* ☐*MC, V.*

PRINCE WILLIAM SOUND

Every Gulf of Alaska cruise visits Prince William Sound. Along its shoreline are quiet bays, trickling waterfalls, and hidden coves. In addition to hosting brown and black bears, gray wolves, and Sitka blacktail deer, the sound thrives with a variety of birds and all manner of marine life, including salmon, halibut, humpback and killer whales, sea otters, sea lions, and porpoises. Bald eagles often soar overhead or perch in tall trees. The sound made worldwide headlines in 1989, when the *Exxon Valdez* hit a reef and spilled 11 million gallons of North Slope crude. Vast sections of the sound appear pristine today, with abundant wildlife, but the oil has sunk into the beaches below the surface. The lasting effects on the area of this lurking oil—sometimes uncovered after storms and high tides—are still being studied.

4

EXPLORING PRINCE WILLIAM SOUND

The major attraction in Prince William Sound on most Gulf of Alaska cruises is the day spent in **College Fjord.** Dubbed "Alaska's newest Glacier Bay" by one cruise line, this deep finger of water is ringed by 16 glaciers, each named after one of the colleges that sponsored early exploration of the fjord.

A visit to **Columbia Glacier,** which flows from the surrounding Chugach Mountains, is included on many Gulf of Alaska cruises. Its deep aquamarine face is 5 mi across, and it calves new icebergs with resounding cannonades. This glacier is one of the largest and most readily accessible of Alaska's coastal glaciers.

The three largest Prince William Sound communities—Valdez, Whittier, and Cordova—are all visited by cruise ships, but none are major destinations. Valdez (pronounced val-*deez*) and Cordova are visited only by the smaller, expedition-style cruise ships. Whittier has replaced Seward as a terminus for many sailings by Princess Cruises, Radisson Seven Seas Cruises, Carnival Cruise Lines, and some from Norwegian Cruise Line (although passengers actually fly into Anchorage and take transportation provided by the cruise line to Whittier). Unless you book a shore expedition such as sea kayaking, fishing, or a Sound cruise, you won't see much of Whittier (not that you'll be missing anything). In addition, Cruise West has a special Prince William Sound tour.

SEWARD

Seward is one of Alaska's oldest and most scenic communities and you shouldn't miss it in your haste to get to Anchorage, set between high mountain ranges on one side and Resurrection Bay on the other. One of the Kenai Peninsula's major communities, it lies at the south end of the Seward Highway, which connects with Anchorage and is the southern terminus of the Alaska Railroad. The city was named for U.S. Secretary of State William H. Seward, who was instrumental in arranging the purchase of Alaska from Russia in 1867. Resurrection Bay was named in 1791 by Russian fur trader and explorer Alexander Baranof. The town was established in 1903 by railroad surveyors as an ocean terminal and supply center. The biggest event in Seward's history is the 1964 Good Friday earthquake—the strongest ever recorded in North America. The tsunami that followed the quake devastated the town; fortunately, most residents saw the harbor drain almost entirely, knew the wave would follow, and ran to high ground. Since then the town has relied heavily on commercial fishing, and its harbor is important for shipping coal to Asia.

Historic downtown Seward retains its small-town atmosphere. Many of its early-20th-century buildings survived the 1964 earthquake or were rebuilt. Modern-day explorers can enjoy wildlife cruises, sportfishing, sailing, and kayaking in the bay or investigating the intricacies of marine biology at the Alaska SeaLife Center. If you're in Seward on July 4, you'll have the chance to see—and perhaps join—the second-oldest footrace in North America. Each year participants race straight up 3,022-foot Mt. Marathon from downtown. Seward also is the launching point for excursions into Kenai Fjords National Park, where you can spy calving glaciers, sea lions, whales, and otters.

SEWARD BEST BETS

■ **Get your sea legs.** Seward's main claims to fame and most notable draws are Resurrection Bay and Kenai Fjords National Park.

■ **Landlubber?** Visit the park at Exit Glacier north of town, any of the numerous trails in the area, or shop at one of the stores near the small boat harbor or in the downtown business district.

■ **Rainy day?** The Sealife Center is not to be missed. It's a combination aquarium, rescue facility for marine animals, and research center. If the seas are too rough or the rain too bothersome, there's interesting stuff here for all ages.

COMING ASHORE

SHORE EXCURSIONS

ADVENTURE

Fox Island Sea Kayaking. At the entrance to Resurrection Bay, Fox Island contains a mix of rain forest, sculpted cliffs, protected coves, and pebbled beaches. This tour includes a guided wilderness paddle around Fox Island, boat transportation to and from the Island, and a salmon bake lunch. ⏲ *8 hrs* 💲*$200.*

Godwin Glacier Dog Sled Tour. These outstanding tours begin with a 15-minute helicopter flight to remote Godwin Glacier. Here you step onto the ice and learn about mushing from an Iditarod veteran, meet the dogs, and head out across the glacier by dog sled. ⏲ *1½ hrs* 💲*$430.*

SCENIC

Portage Glacier. Passengers disembarking in Seward often take advantage of the chance to see Portage Glacier while en route to Anchorage.

The drive along Turnagain Arm to Portage Glacier is one of Alaska's most beautiful. A boat transports you to the glacial face, which has receded dramatically in recent years. ⊘ *1-hr boat tour* ⚏ *$40.*

Resurrection Bay Cruise. Boats depart from the Seward harbor and cruise near Bear Glacier and past playful sea otters, a sea lion rookery, and nesting seabirds (including puffins). Whales are commonly sighted, too. ⊘ *3½ hrs* ⚏ *$75.*

TRANSPORTATION & TOURS

FROM THE PIER

Cruises officially start in Seward, but transportation is included from (or to) Anchorage. Cruise ships dock approximately ½ mi from downtown.

AREA TOURS

Kenai Fjords Tours (☎ *907/224–8068 or 800/478–8068* ⊕ *www.kenaifjords.com*) has a very good half-day cruise of the bay with a stop for a salmon bake on Fox Island ($139 before taxes for an eight-hour cruise).

Major Marine Tours (☎ *907/274–7300 or 800/764–7300* ⊕ *www.majormarine.com*) conducts half-day and full-day cruises of Resurrection Bay and Kenai Fjords National Park. Park cruises are narrated by a National Park Ranger, and meals featuring salmon and prime rib are an option.

Renown Charters and Tours (☎ *907/272–1961 or 800/655–3806* ⊕ *www.renowncharters.com*) is the only outfit that operates tours into Resurrection Bay. Cruises include a four-hour whale-watching tour (March 31 through May 18) and a six-hour Kenai Fjords trip, which runs from May 19 through September 16. The latter trip is onboard a speedy and stable catamaran.

VISITOR INFORMATION

The Seward Chamber of Commerce has a visitor information center at the cruise-ship dock that is staffed when ships are in port. The **Kenai Fjords National Park visitor center** (☎ *907/224–7500* ⊘ *Daily 8–7*) is within walking distance: turn left as you leave the pier, then left again onto 4th Avenue; the center is two blocks ahead. Ask here about visiting scenic Exit Glacier, which is 13 mi northwest of Seward. The Alaska National Historical Society operates a book and gift store in the Park Service center. The Chugach National Forest Ranger

---

MARITIME EXPLORATIONS

The protected waters of the bay provide the perfect environment for sailing, fishing, sea kayaking, and marine wildlife watching. There are numerous tours to choose from—just check out the boardwalk area adjacent to the docks. Half-day tours include Resurrection Bay, while all-day tours also allow you to view parts of spectacular Kenai Fjords National Park. The more adventurous trips venture out of the bay and into the Gulf of Alaska when the notoriously fickle weather permits visits to the more distant glaciers and attractions.

District office is at 334 4th Avenue. They have maps and information on local trails, cabins, and wildlife.

EXPLORING SEWARD

Ⓒ The **Alaska SeaLife Center** is a world-class research and visitor facility
Fodor's Choice complete with massive cold-water tanks and outdoor viewing decks.
★ The center performs cold-water research on fish, seabirds, and marine mammals, including harbor seals and sea lions (the main attraction). It also rehabilitates injured marine wildlife and provides educational experiences for the general public and school groups. The center was partially funded with reparations money from the *Exxon Valdez* oil spill. Films, hands-on activities, a gift shop, and behind-the-scenes tours ($15 and up) complete the offerings. ✉ *301 Railway Ave.* ☎ *907/224–6300 or—888/378–2525* ⊕ *www.alaskasealife.org* 🔲 *$15* ⊗ *Mid-Apr.–mid-Sept., daily 8–7.*

The first mile of the historic original **Iditarod Trail** runs along the beach and makes for a nice, easy stroll, as does the city's printed walking tour—available at the visitors' bureau, the converted railcar at the corner of 3rd Avenue and Jefferson Street, or the Seward Chamber of Commerce Visitor Center at Mile 2 on the Seward Highway.

Seward is the gateway to the 670,000-acre **Kenai Fjords National Park.** This is spectacular coastal parkland incised with sheer, dark slate cliffs, ribboned with white waterfalls, and tufted with deep-green spruce. Kenai Fjords presents a rare opportunity for an up-close view of blue tidewater glaciers as well as some remarkable ocean wildlife, but access is quite limited unless you charter a boat or airplane, or arrange for a tour with one of the local companies. If you take a day trip on a tour boat out of Seward, you can be pretty sure of seeing sea otters, crowds of Steller's sea lions lazing on the rocky shelves along the shore, a porpoise or two, bald eagles soaring overhead, and tens of thousands of seabirds. Humpback whales and orcas are also sighted occasionally, and mountain goats frequent the seaside cliffs. Tours range in length from 4 to 10 hours.

One of the park's chief attractions is **Exit Glacier,** which can be reached only by the one road that passes into Kenai Fjords. Trails inside the park lead to an overlook of the vast **Harding Icefield.** ✉ *Box 1727, Seward 99664* ☎ *907/224–7500* ⊕ *www.nps.gov/kefj.*

If you're looking for history, check out the **Seward Museum,** which has exhibits on the 1964 earthquake, the Iditarod Trail (the route of the 1925 diphtheria serum run from Seward to Nome, now commemorated by an annual 1,100-mi dogsled race), and Native history. ✉ *336 3rd Ave., at Jefferson St.* ☎ *907/224–3902* 🔲 *$3* ⊗ *Mid-May–Sept., daily 9–5.*

OUTDOOR ACTIVITIES

FISHING

For several weeks in August the **Seward Silver Salmon Derby** attracts hundreds of competitors for the $10,000 top prize. Get details from the **Fish House** (⊠*Small-boat harbor* ☎*907/224–3674 or 800/257–7760* ⊕*www.thefishhouse.net*), Seward's oldest booking agency for deep-sea fishing.

HIKING

The strenuous **Mt. Marathon** trail starts at the west end of Lowell Canyon Road and runs practically straight uphill. An easier and more convenient hike is the **Two Lakes Trail,** a loop of footpaths and bridges on the edge of town. A map is available from the **Seward Chamber of Commerce** (⊠*2001 Seward Hwy.* ☎*907/224–8051* ⊕*www.sewardak.org*).

SHOPPING

♻ Several places display and sell fine art in Seward, but of particular note is **Resurrect Art Coffeehouse Gallery** (⊠*320 3rd Ave.* ☎*907/224–7161*), located in a building that was originally a Lutheran church. Today the old church provides a fine spot to enjoy a latte and pastry while checking out works by regional artisans. The **Ranting Raven** (⊠*224 4th Ave.* ☎*907/224–2228*) is a combination gift shop, bakery, and lunch spot, adorned with raven murals on the side of the building. You can indulge in fresh-baked goods, espresso drinks, and daily lunch specials such as quiche, focaccia, and homemade soups while perusing the packed shelves of Russian handicrafts and artwork, native crafts, and jewelry. A browser's dream across from the small-boat harbor, **Bardarson Studio** (☎*907/224–5448 or 800/354–0141* ⊕*www.bardarsonstudio.com*) sells everything from prints and watercolors to sculpture and beaded earrings. There's a kiddie cave for children and a video-viewing area with Alaska programs for nonshoppers. Owner Dot Bardarson is a talented watercolorist whose paintings are prized by local collectors.

WHERE TO EAT

$$–$$$$ ✗**Christo's Palace.** Serving a menu of Greek, Italian, Mexican, pizzas, and seafood meals, this ornately furnished downtown restaurant is a surprisingly elegant hidden treasure. The nondescript facade belies the high, beamed ceilings, dark-wood accents, ornate chandeliers, and large, gorgeous mahogany bar reputed to have been built in the mid-1800s and imported from San Francisco. There's an extensive wine list to complement the menu, a decent selection of wines by the glass, and salads for those looking for lighter fare. For those less concerned with counting calories, meal portions are very generous, desserts are tempting, and there's a small selection of after-dinner cognacs. ⊠*133 4th Ave.* ☎*907/224–5255* ▭*MC, V.*

$$–$$$$ ✗**Harbor Dinner Club.** Don't let the name deter you—it's not a private club. The dining room is broken up into small sections, and lots of green plants contribute to the intimate feel. Alaskan artwork, mostly

with a nautical theme, adorns the walls. The large menu, complete with multipage wine list, features local seafood, fresh whenever possible (it's frozen during the off-season), as well as steaks. ⊠220 5th Ave. 🕾907/224 3012 ⌷AE, D, DC, MC, V.

$–$$$$ ✕**Chinooks Waterfront Restaurant.** On the waterfront in the small-boat harbor, Chinooks has a dazzling selection of fresh seafood items, an extensive wine list, and a great view from the upstairs window seats. It's marine-themed, with fish photos and carvings, antique fishing tackle, and mounted fish on the walls. Pasta dishes and a few beef specialties round out the menu. ⊠1404 4th Ave. 🕾907/224–2207 ⊕*www. chinookswaterfront.com.*

$$–$$$ ✕**Ray's Waterfront.** True to its name, this dining spot has views of the bay and small-boat harbor. Sea otters and sea lions have occasionally been known to swim right past the large picture windows. Seafood is the specialty here; the seafood chowder is a must-try. The walls are lined with stuffed and mounted fish so you can point to the kind you'd like to eat. ⊠*Small-boat harbor* 🕾907/224–5606 ⊟*AE, D, DC, MC, V.*

$ ✕**Railway Cantina.** This little hole-in-the-wall near the small-boat harbor is a local favorite. A wide selection of burritos, quesadillas, and tacos incorporates local seafood and is supplemented by an array of hot sauces, many contributed by customers who bring back exotic items from their travels. Feel free to add to the collection. ⊠*1401 4th Ave.* 🕾*907/224–8226* ⊟*MC, V.*

WHERE TO DRINK

The **New Seward Saloon** (⊠*209 5th Ave.* 🕾*907/224–3095*) is the best bet for Seward nightlife. They've got a carved-wood bar and a great bar menu of oysters, seafood, appetizers, soups, and a large beer selection. You can check your e-mail here or play a game of pool. Weekends in summer they have a DJ and outdoor seating (with heaters—this is Alaska, after all).

SITKA

Sitka was the home to the Kiksadi Clan of the Tlingit people for centuries prior to the 18th-century arrival of the Russians, who, under the direction of territorial governor Alexander Baranof, coveted the Sitka site for its beauty, mild climate, and economic potential. In 1799, Baranof established an outpost that he called Redoubt St. Michael, 6 mi north of the present town, and moved a large number of his Russian and Aleut sea otter and seal hunters there from Kodiak Island.

The Tlingits attacked Baranof's people and burned his buildings in 1802, but Baranof returned in 1804 with formidable strength, including shipboard cannons. He attacked the Tlingits at their fort near Indian River (site of the present-day, 105-acre Sitka National Historical Park) and drove them to Chichagof Island, 70 mi northwest of Sitka. The Tlingits and Russians made peace in 1821, and eventually the capital of Russian America was shifted from Kodiak to Sitka.

Today Sitka is known for its beautiful setting and some of Southeast Alaska's most famous landmarks: the onion-dome Saint Michael's church; the Alaska Raptor Center, where you can come up close to ailing and recovering birds of prey; and Sitka National Historical Park, where you can see some of the oldest and most skillfully carved totem poles in the state.

COMING ASHORE

SHORE EXCURSIONS

ADVENTURE

Sea Life Discovery **Semi-Submersible.** Large underwater windows on this vessel let you see Sitka Sound's kelp forests, fish, and crab. Just outside the boat, divers capture underwater camera images that are then displayed on the boat's video monitor. ☉*2 hrs* 🚌*$80.*

Sitka Bike and Hike Tour. This guided, three-hour hike-and-bike excursion takes you out of town for a 5-mi ride over gently rolling terrain. Stop at Thimbleberry Creek for a short hike that crosses a picturesque waterfall and resume your bike ride to Whale Park. End at Theobroma Chocolate Factory where you can enjoy a locally made chocolate bar before taking the bus back to town. ☉*3 hrs* 🚌*$65–$70.*

> ### SITKA BEST BETS
>
> ■ **Take in the Totems.** Just east of downtown, Sitka National Historical Park features a workshop, interpretive center, and 15 topnotch totem poles spread along a meandering, waterfront, wooded trail.
>
> ■ **Visit the Alaska Raptor Center.** Alaska's only full-service avian hospital lets you get face-to-beak with more than 100 injured and rehabilitating bald eagles, hawks, owls, and other raptors.
>
> ■ **Stroll Around.** Sitka's oceanfront setting, picturesque streets, and rich, varied history make it one of the Southeast's best walking towns.

Sitka by Sea Kayak. Kayak Sitka's coastline against the backdrop of the Mt. Edgecumbe volcano. ☉*3 hrs* 🚌*$95–$100.*

Sportfishing. Try for the abundant salmon and halibut in these waters. All equipment is provided; you buy your license on board. Your catch can be frozen and shipped. ☉*4 hrs* 🚌*$180–$185.*

CULTURAL

Best of Sitka. Let a Native Alaskan guide you on this informative grand-slam bus tour of Sitka, with time at Sitka National Historic Park, the Alaska Raptor Center, and a performance by the Naa Kahidi Dancers in a traditional-style clan house. ☉*3½ hrs* 🚌*$135.*

History and Nature Walking Tour. A guided walk through Sitka details its political and natural history. This tour includes all the major sites plus a visit to the Sitka National Historic Park for a stroll through the rain forest, and time at the Alaska Raptor Center. Return downtown by van. ☉*2½ hrs* 🚌*$45–$50.*

Russian-America Tour. Stops at Castle Hill, the Russian Cemetery, St. Michael's Cathedral, and Sitka National Historic Park are included in this bus-and-walking tour of Sitka's rich Russian heritage. The finale is a Russian-style folk-dance performance by the New Archangel Dancers, local women who have mastered the timing and athletic feats required for this traditional style of dance. ⏱ 2½ *hrs* 🎫$35–$40.

SCENIC

Sea Otter Quest. This search for the sea otter and other Sitka wildlife is a cruise passenger favorite. Creatures that you're likely to see from the boat include whales, eagles, puffins, and more. ⏱*3 hrs* 🎫$105–$110.

Tongass Forest Nature Hike. This 4-mi hike provides an excellent introduction to the rain forests that surround Sitka. The hike covers a mix of boardwalk and gravel trails through tall spruce forests and open muskeg, and then loops back via the shore. Children under the age of 10 are not allowed to participate, and hikers need to be in good physical condition. ⏱*3 hrs* 🎫$58–$60.

TRANSPORTATION & TOURS

FROM THE PIER

Only the smallest excursion vessels can dock at Sitka. Ocean liners must drop anchor in the harbor and tender passengers ashore near **Harrigan Centennial Hall.** You can recognize the hall by the big Tlingit war canoe to the side of the building. Sitka is an extremely walkable town, and the waterfront attractions are all fairly close to the tender landing.

VISITOR INFORMATION

Also housed in Harrigan Centennial Hall is an information desk for the **Sitka Convention and Visitors Bureau** (☎907/747–5940 ⊕*www.sitka. org*), where you can get a list of local charter-fishing operators.

EXPLORING SITKA

It's hard not to like Sitka, with its eclectic blend of Native, Russian, and American history and its dramatic and beautiful setting. ■**TIP**→ This is one of the best Inside Passage towns to explore on foot.

 ⑥ ★ One of Sitka's most interesting attractions is the **Alaska Raptor Center,** where injured bald eagles and other wild birds, such as raptors, hawks, and owls, are nursed back to health. The primary attraction is a 20,000-square-foot flight training center, built to replicate the rain forest. In this enormous enclosed space, injured eagles relearn survival skills, including flying and

HISTORY & A VIEW

For one of the best views in town, turn left on Harbor Drive and head for Castle Hill, where Alaska was handed over to the United States on October 18, 1867, and where the first 49-star U.S. flag was flown, on January 3, 1959, signifying the spirit of Alaska's statehood. Take the first right off Harbor Drive; then look for the entrance to Baranof Castle Hill State Historic Site. Make a left on the paved path (it's wheelchair accessible), which takes you to the top of the hill overlooking Crescent Harbor.

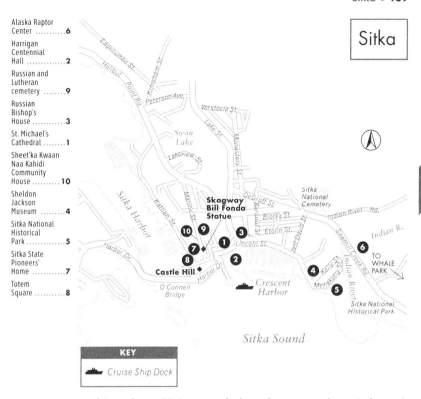

Sitka

Sitka Sound

KEY

Cruise Ship Dock

catching salmon. Visitors watch through one-way glass windows. A large deck out back faces an open-air enclosure for eagles and other raptors whose injuries prevent them from returning to the wild. The gift shop sells all sorts of eagle paraphernalia, the proceeds from which fund the Center's programs. ■ **TIP→** If you're heading here, you may want to consider taking a taxi. ⊠*1000 Raptor Way, off Sawmill Creek Rd.* ☎*907/747–8662 or 800/643–9425* ⊕*www.alaskaraptor.org* ☎*$12* ⊙ *Mid-May–Sept., daily 8–4.*

❷ Inside **Harrigan Centennial Hall,** you can find a volunteer-staffed information desk provided by the Sitka Convention and Visitors Bureau, an auditorium for New Archangel Dancers performances, which take place when cruise ships are in port, and the **Sitka Historical Museum,** which includes a scale model of Sitka from 1867 in its collection of Tlingit, Russian, and American historical artifacts. ⊠*330 Harbor Dr.* ☎*907/747–6455 museum, 907/747–5940 visitors bureau* ⊕*www. sitka.org/historicalmuseum* ☎*Free* ⊙*Museum mid-May—mid-Sept., daily 8–5.*

❾ Reached from Marine Street above Seward Street, the most distinctive grave in the **Russian and Lutheran cemetery** marks the final resting place of Princess Maksoutoff, one of the most well-known members of the Russian royal family buried on Alaskan soil. ■ TIP→ **Because of its wooded location, this cemetery requires a bit of exploring to find.**

❸ Several blocks past St. Michael's Cathedral on Lincoln Street and facing the harbor is the **Russian Bishop's House.** Constructed in 1842, this is one of the few remaining Russian log structures in Alaska. The Park Service has carefully restored the building, using original Russian furnishings and artifacts. In several places, portions of the house's interior have been peeled away to expose 19th-century Russian construction techniques. Park Service rangers lead guided tours of the second floor, which houses the residential quarters and a chapel. ⊠ *501 Lincoln St.* ☎ *907/747–6281* ⊕ *www.nps.gov/sitk* ⊠ *$5* ۞ *May–Sept., daily 9–5.*

❶
★ Sitka's most photographed sight—and one of Southeast Alaska's best-known landmarks—**St. Michael's Cathedral** was originally a frame-covered log structure built in the 1840s. In 1966 the church burned in a fire that swept through the business district. Using original blueprints, an almost exact replica of St. Michael's was built and dedicated in 1976. ⊠ *Lincoln St.* ☎ *907/747–8120* ⊠ *$2 donation* ۞ *May–Sept., daily 8:30–4.*

❹ The state-run **Sheldon Jackson Museum,** built in 1895 (Alaska's oldest concrete building), contains priceless Native American items collected by Dr. Sheldon Jackson, a Presbyterian missionary and the first General Agent for Education in Alaska, during his travels to remote regions of Alaska in the late 19th century. Carved masks, Chilkat blankets, dogsleds, kayaks—even the helmet worn by Chief Katlian during the 1804 battle between the Sitka Tlingits and the Russians—are displayed here. The museum's gift shop, operated by the Friends of the Sheldon Jackson Museum, carries handicrafts created exlusively by Alaska native artists. ⊠ *104 College Dr.* ☎ *907/747–8981* ⊕ *www.museums.state.ak.us* ⊠ *$4 mid-May–mid-Sept., $3* ۞ *Mid-May–mid-Sept., daily 9–5.*

❺
★ At the main building of the **Sitka National Historical Park,** audiovisual programs and exhibits of Native and Russian artifacts give an overview of Southeast Alaskan cultures both old and new. Native artists and craftspeople are on hand to demonstrate and interpret traditional crafts of the Tlingit people, such as silversmithing, weaving, and basket making. Don't be afraid to strike up conversation; the artists are happy to talk about their work. A self-guided forest trail (maps available at the visitor center) leading to the site of the Tlingit Fort passes by exquisitely carved totem poles; several of these 15 poles were carved for the 1904 St. Louis World's Fair. ⊠ *106 Metlakatla St.* ☎ *907/747–6281* ⊕ *www. nps.gov/sitk* ⊠ *$3* ۞ *Mid-May–Sept., daily 8–5.*

❼ The **Sitka State Pioneers' Home** is hard to miss with its yellow paint and red roof. It was built in 1934 as the first of several retirement and medical facilities for elder Alaskans, and is still in operation today. The imposing 14-foot statue in front was modeled after an authentic prospector, William "Skagway Bill" Fonda. It portrays a determined gold hunter with pack, pick, rifle, and supplies, headed for gold country. ⊠ *Lincoln and Katlian Sts.* ☎ *907/747–3213.*

8 Three old anchors, believed to be from 19th-century British ships, mark **Totem Square**, across the street from the Pioneers' Home. Notice the double-headed eagle of czarist Russia on the park's totem pole.

10 Just up the street from the Pioneers' Home is the **Sheet'ka Kwaan Naa Kahidi Community House** (⊠ *200 Katlian St.* ☎*888/270–8687* ⊕*www.sitkatribal. com*), which schedules demonstrations and performances by members of the Sitka tribe.

SHOPPING

Across the street from St. Michael's Cathedral, **Fairweather Wearable Art & World Crafts** (⊠ *209 Lincoln St.* ☎*907/747–8677* ⊕*www. fairweatherprints.com*) sells beautifully printed "wearable art" with Alaskan designs. **Fishermen's Eye Fine Art Gallery** (⊠ *239 Lincoln St.* ☎*907/747–6080* ⊕*www.fishermenseye.com*) is a tasteful downtown gallery with art prints and limited editions from Southeast Alaskan artists, including Evon Zerbetz and Rie Muñoz. Stop by **Old Harbor Books** (⊠ *201 Lincoln St.* ☎*907/747–8808* ⊕*www.oldharborbooks. com*) for a wall-to-wall selection of photography and coffee-table books, guides and maps, fiction, poetry, and prose about Alaska or by Alaskans, as well as books on Alaska's natural history, art, and culture, both native and contemporary. And don't miss the ever-popular Backdoor Café, which sits at the rear of the bookstore. Housed within an 1895 home, **Sitka Rose Gallery** (⊠ *419 Lincoln St.* ☎*907/747–3030 or 888/236–1536* ⊕*www.sitkarosegallery.com*) is the town's most charming shop, and has two small galleries with Alaskan paintings, sculptures, native art, and jewelry. Next door is **WinterSong Soap Company** (⊠ *419 Lincoln St.* ☎*907/747–8949 or 888/819–8949* ⊕*www. wintersongsoap.com*), which sells colorful and scented soaps that are handcrafted on the premises.

WHERE TO EAT

$–$$$$ ✕**Ludvig's Bistro.** This convivial and remarkably creative eatery used to escape detection by most tourists (much to the pleasure of Sitkans). It's now almost always packed with food lovers from all corners of the globe, so be prepared for a bit of a wait—but rest assured that Ludwig's is well worth it. The interior evokes an Italian bistro, with rich yellow walls and copper-topped tables. Seafood (particularly king salmon and scallops) is a centerpiece, and organic ingredients are used whenever possible. You can also find Caesar salads, vegetarian specials, prime rib, and one of the best wine lists in the state. From 2 to 5 PM, the café serves Spanish-style tapas with house wine for $13–$17. ✉ *256 Katlian St.* ☎☎ *907/966–3663* ⊟ *AE, MC, V.*

$$–$$$ ✕ **Little Tokyo.** Sitka probably isn't the first place you might expect to find Japanese food, but Little Tokyo delivers first-rate rolls and nigiri. The atmosphere is nothing fancy, but this small restaurant does have a sushi bar where you can watch chefs preparing all the standards, plus Alaska rolls (cream cheese, smoked salmon, and avocado). Udon noodle soups are popular on rainy afternoons, and bento box dinners—complete with katsu entrées, California rolls, tempura, pot stickers, miso soup, and salad—are a real bargain at $11. ✉ *315 Lincoln St.* ☎ *907/747–5699* ⊟ *MC, V.*

WHERE TO DRINK

As far as the locals are concerned, a spot in one of the green-and-white-vinyl booths at **Pioneer Bar** (✉ *212 Katlian St.* ☎ *907/747–3456*), across from the harbor, is a destination unto itself. It's vintage Alaska, with hundreds of pictures of local fishing boats, rough-hewn locals clad in Carhartt and Xtra-Tuff boots, occasional live music, and pickup pool games.

SKAGWAY

Skagway is an amazingly preserved artifact from Alaska's early gold-rush days, when scores of dreamers and hooligans passed through town while headed north toward the Yukon. Most of the downtown district forms part of the Klondike Gold Rush National Historical Park, which is dedicated to commemorating and interpreting the frenzied stampede that extended to Dawson City in Canada's Yukon. Although the town feels a little like a Disney theme park in spots, when you walk down Broadway, the scene isn't appreciably different from what the prospectors saw in 1898, except the street is now paved to make your exploring easier. Old false-front stores, saloons, and brothels have been restored, repainted, and refurnished by the federal government and Skagway's citizens.

Skagway had only a single cabin when the Yukon gold rush began. At first, the argonauts, as they liked to be called, swarmed to Dyea and the Chilkoot Trail, 9 mi west of Skagway. Skagway and its White Pass Trail didn't seem as attractive until a dock was built in town. Then it mushroomed overnight into the major gateway to the Klondike, supporting a wild mixture of legitimate businesspeople, con artists (among the most notorious was Jefferson "Soapy" Smith), stampeders, and curiosity seekers. Much of the disorder ended with a shoot-out one pleasant July evening in 1898. Good guy Frank Reid (the surveyor who laid out Skagway's streets so wide and well) faced down bad guy Soapy Smith on a dock downtown near the present ferry terminal. After a classic exchange of gunfire, Smith lay dead and Reid lay dying.

When the gold rush played out after a few years, the town of 20,000 dwindled to 700. The White Pass & Yukon Railroad kept the town alive until 1982, when it began to run in summer only. By this time,

Continued on page 196

GOLD! GOLD! GOLD!

At the end of the 19th Century, scoundrels and starry-eyed gold seekers alike made their way from Alaska's Inside Passage to Canada's Yukon Territory, with high hopes for heavy returns.

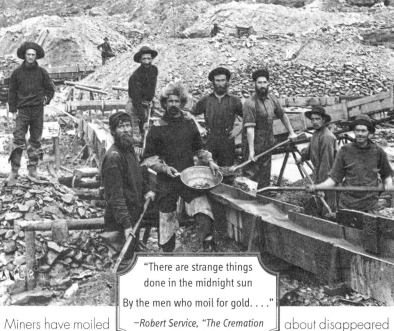

> "There are strange things done in the midnight sun By the men who moil for gold. . . ."
>
> *−Robert Service, "The Cremation of Sam McGee"*

Miners have moiled for gold in the Yukon for many centuries, but the Klondike Gold Rush was a particularly strange and intense period of history. Within a decade, the towns of Skagway, Dyea, and Dawson City appeared out of nowhere, mushroomed to accommodate tens of thousands of people, and just about disappeared again. At the peak of the rush, Dawson City was the largest metropolis north of San Francisco. Although only a few people found enough gold even to pay for their trip, the rush left an indelible mark on the nation's imagination.

An 1898 photograph shows bearded miners using a gold pan and sluice as they search for riches.

A Great Stampede

Historians squabble over who first saw the glint of Yukon gold. All agree that it was a member of a family including "Skookum" Jim Mason (of the Tagish tribe), Kate and George Carmack, and Dawson Charlie, who were prospecting off the Klondike River in 1896. Over the following months, word spread and claims were quickly staked. When the first boatload of gold reached Seattle in July 1897, gold fever ignited with the *Seattle Post-Intelligencer's* headline: "GOLD! GOLD! GOLD! Sixty-Eight Rich Men On the Steamer Portland." Within six months, 100,000 people had arrived in Southeast Alaska, intent upon making their way to the untold riches.

Skagway had only a single cabin standing when the gold rush began. Three months after the first boat landed, 20,000 people swarmed its raucous hotels, saloons, gambling houses, and dance halls. By spring 1898, the town was labeled "little better than a hell on earth." When gold was discovered in Nome the next year and in Fairbanks in the early 1900s, Skagway's population dwindled to 700 souls.

Rush hour on Broadway, Skagway, 1898.

A Gritty Reality

To reach the mining hub of Dawson City, prospectors had to choose between two risky routes from the Inside Passage. From Dyea, the Chilkoot Trail was steep and bitterly cold. The longer, bandit-ridden White Pass Trail from Skagway killed so many pack animals that it earned the nickname Dead Horse Trail. After the mountains, there were still over 500 mi to travel. For those who arrived, dreams were quickly washed away, as most promising claims had already been staked by the Klondike Kings. Many ended up working as labor. The disappointment was unbearable.

KLONDIKE KATE

The gold rush was profitable for clever entrepreneurs. Stragglers, outfitters, and outlaws took advantage of every opportunity to make a buck. Klondike Kate, a brothel keeper and dance-hall gal, had an elaborate song-and-dance routine that involved 200 yards of bright red chiffon.

Bowers

"Soapy" Smith's Saloon

Peiser *Skaguay Alaska.*   *Jeff Smith.*   *Flashlight 1 P.M.*   *Larss & Duclos 1898. 2126.*

TWO ENEMIES DIE IN A SKAGWAY SHOWDOWN

CON ARTIST "SOAPY" SMITH

Claim to Fame: Skagway's best-known gold-rush criminal, Soapy was the de facto leader of the town's loosely organized network of criminals and spies.

Cold-Hearted Snake: Euphemistically referred to as "colorful," he ruthlessly capitalized on the naïveté of prospectors.

Famous Scheme: Soapy charged homesick miners $5 to wire a message home in his counterfeit Telegraph Office (the wires ended in a tangled pile behind a shed).

Shot Through the Heart: In 1898, just days after he served as grand marshal of Skagway's 4th of July parade, Soapy barged in on a meeting set up by his rival, Frank Reid. There was a scuffle, and they shot each other.

Famous Last Words: When he saw Reid draw his gun, Soapy shouted, "My God, don't shoot!"

R.I.P.: Soapy's tombstone was continually stolen by vandals and souvenir seekers; today's grave marker is a simple wooden plank in Skagway's Gold Rush Cemetery.

GOOD GUY FRANK REID

Claim to Fame: Skagway surveyor and all-around good fellow, Frank Reid was known for defending the town against bad guys.

The Grid Man: A civil engineer, Reid helped to make Skagway's streets wide and gridlike.

Thorn in My Side: Reid set up a secret vigilante meeting to discuss one very thorny topic: Soapy Smith.

In Skagway's Honor: Reid killed Soapy during the shootout on the city docks, breaking up Soapy's gang and freeing the town from its grip.

Dyin' Tryin': Reid's heroics cost him his life—he died some days later from the injuries he sustained.

R.I.P.: The town built a substantial monument in Reid's memory in the Gold Rush Cemetery, which you can visit to this day; the inscription reads: HE GAVE HIS LIFE FOR THE HONOR OF SKAGWAY.

(above) Soapy Smith (front), so named for his first con, which involved selling "lucky soap," stands with five friends at his infamous saloon.

4

GOLD! GOLD! GOLD!

however, tourism revenue was sufficient to compensate for any economic loss suffered as a result of the railroad's more limited schedule.

COMING ASHORE

SHORE EXCURSIONS

ADVENTURE

Heli-Hike Glacier Trek. The helicopter flight that begins this popular trip is followed by a 4-mi hike to Laughton Glacier. Return to Skagway on the famous White Pass & Yukon Route Railway. Participants must be in strong physical condition. ⊙ *5½ hrs* 🚌 *$320.*

Hike and Float the Chilkoot Trail. This trip opens with a guided van tour to the historic gold-rush townsite of Dyea, start of the historic Chilkoot Trail. From here you hike 2 mi along the Taiya River, then board rafts for an easy 40-minute float back to Dyea. No children under seven are allowed. ⊙ *4¼ hrs* 🚌 *$100–$105.*

Klondike Bicycle Tour. Ride a van to the top of the Klondike Pass and then bike 15 mi downhill, taking in the spectacular views of White Pass and Alaska's scenery along the way. Stops are made to take photographs of the area's glaciers, coastal mountains, and waterfalls. ⊙ *2½ hrs* 🚌 *$80.*

CULTURAL/SCENIC

Haines Highlights and Lynn Fjord Cruise. Escape the crowds in Skagway on a fast ferry that crosses Lynn Fjord to the scenic town of Haines. Tour historic Fort Seward and the Sheldon Museum; visit a restored fish canning line from the 1950s; and ride up the Chilkat River valley. Return by ferry to Skagway in time to catch your ship. ⊙ *6 hrs* 🚌 *$100.*

Skagway Streetcar. Ride in the Skagway Streetcar Company's vintage 1930s cars through town to the Gold Rush Cemetery and Reid Falls, accompanied by a knowledgeable tour guide dressed in Victorian-style costume. ⊙ *2 hrs* 🚌 *$40.*

White Pass & Yukon Railroad. The 20-mi trip in vintage railroad cars skims along the edge of granite cliffs, climbs to 2,865 feet at White Pass Summit, and zigzags through dramatic scenery—including the actual Trail of '98, worn into the mountainside a century ago. Alternate routes take you as far as Fraser, British Columbia (where bus connections are available for the trip back to Skagway), or Carcross, Yukon. ⊙ *3½ hrs* 🚌 *$100.*

SKAGWAY BEST BETS

■ **Ride the White Pass & Yukon Route.** Wending upward through unparalleled scenery and steep-sided gorges to the breathtaking summit of White Pass, the route remains an engineering marvel.

■ **Explore the Klondike Gold Rush National Historical Park.** This marvelous collection of museums and landmarks spread throughout downtown will immerse you in the rough-and-tumble spirit of yesteryear.

■ **Score a find.** From scrimshaw to silver, Skagway's shops offer huge collections of art, jewelry, and craftworks.

TRANSPORTATION & TOURS

FROM THE PIER

Skagway is a major stop for cruise ships in Alaska, and this little town sometimes has four large ships in port at once. Some dock a short stroll from downtown, others ½ mi away at the Railroad Dock, where city buses are waiting to provide transportation to the center of town. The charge is $1.50 one-way.

Virtually all the shops and gold-rush sights are along Broadway, the main strip that leads from the visitor center through the middle of town. It's a nice walk from the docks up through Broadway, but you can also take tours with horse-drawn surreys, antique limousines, and modern vans.

AREA TOURS

Fodor's Choice
★

Visitors to Skagway can travel at least part of the way along the gold-rush route aboard the **White Pass & Yukon Route** (WP & YR) narrow-gauge railroad. The historic diesel locomotives tow vintage viewing cars up the route's steep inclines, hugging the walls of precipitous cliff sides and providing views of craggy peaks, plummeting waterfalls, lakes, and forests. Two or three times daily, the WP & YR leaves Skagway for a three-hour, round-trip excursion to the White Pass summit. Sights along the way include Bridal Veil Falls, Inspiration Point, and Dead Horse Gulch. Longer trips into the Yukon, special steam excursions, and a Chilkoot Trail hikers' service are also offered. ☎*907/983–2217 or 800/343–7373* ⏲ *Mid-May–late Sept., daily.*

VISITOR INFORMATION

You can't help but notice the Arctic Brotherhood Hall—just up Broadway between 2nd and 3rd avenues—with its curious driftwood-mosaic facade. Inside is the **Skagway Convention and Visitors Bureau** (☎*907/983–2854, 888/762–1898 message only* ⊕*www.skagway.com*), along with public restrooms. From the pier you can see the large maroon-and-yellow building that houses the **Klondike Gold Rush National Historical Park** (☎*907/983–2921* ⊕*www.nps.gov/klgo*), a museum and visitor center displaying historical photographs, artifacts, and films. Rangers lead guided walks through town and can provide details on nearby hiking trails (including the famous Chilkoot Trail). Next door to the visitor center is the White Pass & Yukon Route Depot, the departure point for Skagway's most popular shore excursion.

EXPLORING SKAGWAY

Skagway is perhaps the easiest port in Alaska to explore on foot. The town is flat, and nearly all the historic sights are within a few blocks of the cruise ship and ferry dock, so you can take all the time you want. Just walk up and down Broadway, detouring here and there into the

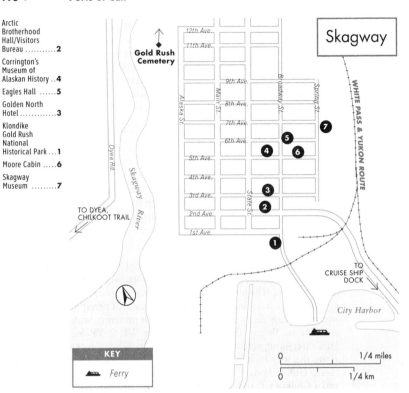

side streets. Keep an eye out for the humorous architectural details and advertising irreverence that mark the Skagway spirit.

2 **Arctic Brotherhood Hall.** The Arctic Brotherhood was a fraternal organization of Alaskan and Yukon pioneers. To decorate the exterior false front of their Skagway lodge, members of the Brotherhood built the (now renovated) building's false front out of 8,883 pieces of driftwood and flotsam gathered from local beaches. The AB Hall now houses the **Skagway Convention and Visitors Bureau,** along with public restrooms. ⊠*Broadway, between 2nd and 3rd Aves., Box 1029, 99840* ☎*907/983–2854, 888/762–1898 message only* ⊕*www.skagway.org* ⊗*May–Sept., daily 8–6; Oct.–Apr., weekdays 8–noon and 1–5.*

4 **Corrington's Museum of Alaskan History** is a private collection of exquisitely carved ivory pieces. There's also a gift shop. ⊠*5th Ave. and Broadway* ☎*907/983–2579* ⊡*Free* ⊗*When cruise ships are in port.*

5 Since 1927 locals have performed a six-act musical called *The Days of '98 with Soapy Smith* at **Eagles Hall.** If you stop in for the evening show, you can enjoy a few warm-up rounds of mock gambling with Soapy's money. ⊠*Broadway and 6th Ave.* ☎*907/983–2545* ⊡*$16* ⊗*Mid-May–mid-Sept., daily at 10:30, 2:30, and 8.*

❸ Built during the 1898 gold rush, the **Golden North Hotel** was—until closing in 2002—Alaska's oldest hotel. Despite the closure, the building has been lovingly maintained, and still retains its gold-rush-era appearance, with a golden dome topping the corner cupola. The hotel is now occupied by shops. ✉*3rd Ave. and Broadway.*

❶
★ **Klondike Gold Rush National Historical Park.** Housed in the former White Pass & Yukon Route Depot, this wonderful museum contains exhibits, photos, and artifacts from the White Pass and Chilkoot trails. Films, ranger talks, and walking tours are offered. Special free Robert Service poetry performances by Buckwheat Donahue—a beloved local character and head of the Skagway Convention and Visitors Bureau— occasionally take place at the visitor center. ✉*2nd Ave. at Broadway* ☎*907/983–2921 or 907/983–9224* ⊕*www.nps.gov/klgo* 🎟*Free* ⊙*May–Sept., daily 8–6; Oct.–Apr., weekdays 8–5.*

❻ Built in 1887 by Captain William Moore and his son Ben, the tiny **Moore Cabin** was the first structure built in Skagway. An early homesteader, Captain Moore prospered from the flood of miners. Next door, the larger Moore House (1897–98) contains interesting exhibits on the Moore family. Both structures are maintained by the Park Service, and the main house is open daily in summer. The Moore Cabin was under renovation at press time, so call before you go. ✉*5th Ave. between Broadway and Spring St.* ☎*907/983–2921* 🎟*$2 suggested donation* ⊙*Memorial Day–Labor Day, daily 10–5.*

❼ In the granite-fronted **Skagway Museum** you can see documents relating to Soapy Smith and Frank Reid, native artifacts, and a healthy collection of contemporary local art and post–gold rush history exhibits. The museum shares a building with the Skagway City Hall, one block off Broadway. ✉*7th Ave. and Spring Sts.* ☎*907/983–2420* ⊕*www. skagwaymuseum.org* 🎟*$2* ⊙*Mid-May–Sept., weekdays 9–5, weekends 10–4.*

OUTDOOR ACTIVITIES

Real wilderness is within a stone's throw of the docks, which makes this an excellent hiking port. Try the short jaunt to beautiful Lower Dewey Lake. Start at the corner of 4th Avenue and Spring Street, go toward the mountain, cross the footbridge over Pullen Creek, and follow the trail uphill. It's a 20-minute climb to the lake.

A less-strenuous hike is the trip through Gold Rush Cemetery, where the epitaphs offer strange but lively bits of social commentary. Infamous villain Soapy Smith has a simple marker; hero Frank Reid has a much larger monument. To get to the cemetery, take the city bus to 23rd Avenue, where a dirt road leads to the graves; it's a 10-minute walk each way. To reach 300-foot-high Reid Falls, continue through the cemetery for ¼ mi. Trail maps are available at the Skagway Convention and Visitors Bureau.

SHOPPING

Corrington's Alaskan Ivory (⊠*525 Broadway* ☏*907/983–2579*) is the destination of choice for scrimshaw seekers; it has perhaps the state's best collection of ivory art. For those in search of locally produced silver jewelry and watercolor prints, the artist-owned **Skagway Artworks** (⊠*555C Broadway* ☏*907/983–3443 or 866/728–7830* ⊕*www.skagwayartworks.com*) can't be beat.

WHERE TO EAT

$$–$$$ ✗**Olivia's at the Skagway Inn.** An upmarket restaurant in the center of the historic district, Olivia's specializes in freshly caught Alaskan seafood. For lunch there are also delicious homemade seafood, chicken, or beef potpies. Great wine and dessert selections round out the menu. The restaurant offers a special 2½-hour Alaska Garden Gourmet tour that includes time in the garden, along with a lecture and cooking demonstration. ⊠*655 Broadway* ☏*907/983–2289 or 888/752–4929* ⊕*www.skagwayinn.com* ▤*AE, D, MC, V.*

$$–$$$ ✗**Stowaway Cafe.** Always crowded, this noisy little harborside café is a few steps from the cruise-ship dock. Not surprisingly, seafood is the main attraction—including wasabi salmon and glace de poisson, but you can also choose tasty steaks, chicken, or smoked ribs. ⊠*205 Congress Way* ☏*907/983–3463* ⌖*Reservations essential* ▤*AE, MC, V.*

$–$$$ ✗**Skagway Pizza Station.** Housed in a former gas station, this year-round restaurant is known by locals for its homestyle specials, such as meat loaf or stuffed pork chops with mashed potatoes and gravy. (Friday is prime rib day.) The huge calzones are stuffed with quality ingredients and served piping hot with sides of house marinara and ranch dressing—build your own or choose one of the chef's creations, like the Chicken Hawk Squawk with pineapple and jalepeños. Or do like the Skagwegians do and wash down one of the 14-inch pizzas with a pint or two of Alaskan Summer Ale. ⊠*4th Ave., between Main and State Sts.* ☏*907/983-2200* ▤*MC, V.*

$ ✗**Glacial Smoothies and Espresso.** This local hangout is the place to go for a breakfast bagel or a lunchtime soup-and-sandwich combo. Prices are slightly steeper than some coffee shops—a 12-ounce mocha goes for $4—but the ingredients are fresh and local, and nearly everything on the menu is made on-site. Customers can cool down with a Mango Madness or Blueberry Blues smoothie, and soft-serve ice cream is available in the summer months. ⊠*3rd Ave., between Main and State Sts.* ☏*907/983-3223* ▤*MC, V* ☺*No dinner.*

> **DID YOU KNOW?**
>
> You may find it strange to see so many diamonds being sold in these small Alaska towns. The truth is that many of the jewelry shops in major ports of call, such as Skagway, Juneau, and Ketchikan, are actually owned by large cruise lines. When the Alaska cruise season ends in September, the stores are boarded up and the wares shipped down to the Caribbean for the winter season there. If you'd rather buy from a local merchant, keep your eyes peeled; year-round residents often post signs indicating their authentic status.

WHERE TO DRINK

Whereas Skagway was once host to dozens upon dozens of watering holes in its gold-rush days, the **Red Onion Saloon** (⊠*Broadway at 2nd Ave.* ☎*907/983–2222* ⊕*www.redonion1898.com*) is pretty much the sole survivor among them. The upstairs was once a brothel, and you'll find a convivial crowd of Skagway locals and visitors among the scantily clad mannequins who represent the building's former illustrious tenants. A ragtime pianist tickles the keys most afternoons, and local musicians strut their stuff on Thursday nights. The saloon closes up shop for winter.

TRACY ARM

Tracy Arm and its sister fjord, Endicott Arm, have become staples on many Inside Passage cruises. Ships sail into the arm just before or after a visit to Juneau, 50 mi to the north. A day of scenic cruising in Tracy Arm is a lesson in geology and the forces that shape Alaska. The fjord was carved by a glacier aeons ago, leaving behind sheer granite cliffs. Waterfalls continue the process of erosion that the glaciers began. Very small ships may nudge their bows under the waterfalls so crew members can fill pitchers full of glacial runoff. It's a unique Alaska refreshment. Tracy Arm's glaciers haven't disappeared, though; they've just receded, and at the very end of Tracy Arm you'll come to two of them, known as the twin Sawyer Glaciers.

VALDEZ

Valdez is the largest of the Prince William Sound communities. This year-round ice-free port was originally the entry point for people and goods going to the interior during the gold rush. Today that flow has been reversed, with Valdez harbor being the southern terminus of the trans-Alaska pipeline, which carries crude oil from Prudhoe Bay and surrounding oil fields nearly 800 mi to the north. This region, with its dependence on commercial fishing, is still feeling the aftereffects of 1989's massive oil spill. Much of Valdez looks modern because the business area was relocated and rebuilt after its destruction by the 1964 Good Friday earthquake. Even though the town is younger than the rest of "civilized" Alaska, it's gradually acquiring a lived-in look.

VALDEZ BEST BETS

■ **Tour the Sound.** Take a tour of Prince William Sound with Stan Stephens Tours, and get a seaside view of the Alyeska Pipeline terminal, where the 800-mi-long Trans-Alaska Pipeline loads oil into huge tanker ships.

■ **Visit a sea otter.** Several local companies offer sea-kayaking tours of varying lengths and degrees of difficulty.

■ **Hike on a glacier.** Worthington Glacier State Park at Thompson Pass is a roadside attraction. If you want to learn glacier travel or ice climbing, H2O Guides can hook you up.

COMING ASHORE

TRANSPORTATION & TOURS

FROM THE PIER

Ships tie up at the world's largest floating container dock. About 3 mi from the heart of town, the dock is used not only for cruise ships but also for cargo ships loading with timber and other products bound for markets "outside" (that's what Alaskans call the rest of the world). Ship-organized motor coaches meet you on the pier and provide transportation into town. Cabs and car-rental services will also provide transportation from the pier and individualized tours of the area can be arranged with the cab dispatcher. Several local ground- and adventure-tour operators meet passengers as well.

> **COMPETE!**
>
> Many Alaskan communities have summer fishing derbies, but Valdez may hold the record for the number of such contests, stretching from late May into September. The Valdez Silver Salmon Derby begins in late July and runs the entire month of August. Fishing charters abound in this area of Prince William Sound for a good reason: the fertile waters provide some of the best saltwater sport fishing in all of Alaska.

VISITOR INFORMATION

Once in town, you can find that Valdez is a very compact community. Almost everything is within easy walking distance of the Valdez Convention and Visitors Bureau (✉ *200 Fairbanks St.* ☎ *907/835–4636)* in the heart of town. Motor coaches drop passengers at the Visitors Bureau.

EXPLORING VALDEZ

Sightseeing in Valdez is mostly limited to gazing at the 5,000-foot mountain peaks surrounding the town or to visiting the **Valdez Museum** and its annex. The main building depicts the lives, livelihoods, and events significant to Valdez and surrounding regions. Exhibits include a 1907 steam fire engine, a 19th-century saloon, and a model of the pipeline terminus. ✉ *217 Egan Ave.* ☎ *907/835–2764* ⊕ *www.valdezmuseum.org* ☑ *$5* ⊙ *June–Aug.,daily 9–6.*

Remembering Old Valdez has exhibits about the 1964 quake, including an impressive replica of the old town and a seismograph showing current activity. ✉ *436 S. Hazelet St.* ☎ *907/835–5407* ☑ *Included in price of Valdez Museum* ⊙ *Daily 9–6.*

★ **Columbia Glacier** flows from the surrounding Chugach Mountains. Its deep aquamarine face is 5 mi across, and it calves icebergs with resounding cannonades. This glacier is one of the largest and most readily accessible of Alaska's coastal glaciers.

OUTDOOR ACTIVITIES

Anadyr Adventures (☎*907/835–2814 or 800/865–2925* ⊕*www. anadyradventures.com*) offers half-day sea-kayaking trips into Prince William Sound. Whether you're looking for a full-on winter backcountry heli-ski excursion or a shorter glacier experience, **H2O Guides** can hook you up. For most visitors, their day trips to Worthington Glacier State Park will suffice. The guides can set up any level of icy adventure you desire, from a half-day walk on the glacier to full-day or multiday ice-climbing trips. Their office is in the lobby of the Best Western hotel, and they can also arrange fishing, flightseeing, multiday, and multisport trips as well. ⊠*100 N. Harbor Dr.* ☎*907/835—8418 or 800/578–4354* ⊕*www.h2oguides.com.*

4

WHERE TO EAT

$$–$$$$ ✕**Alaska's Bistro.** The view of the small-boat harbor is complemented inside by the nautical theme and color scheme. Local art adorns the walls, and the two-tier dining room guarantees a view for all. The house specialty is paella for two (or more), and fresh local seafood dominates the menu. There's also a large selection of appetizers, salads, and poultry, pork, steaks, and pizza. The wine cellar includes more than 150 selections. ⊠*100 Fidalgo Dr.* ☎*907/835–5688* ▤*AE, MC, V.*

$$–$$$ ✕**Mike's Palace.** This convivial restaurant is a local favorite. The menu includes veal, terrific pizza, beer-batter halibut, steaks, and Mexican food. ⊠*201 N. Harbor Dr.* ☎*907/835–2365* ▤*MC, V.*

$–$$ ✕**Alaska Halibut House.** A very casual place: order at the counter, sit at the Formica-covered tables, and check out the photos of local fishing boats. The battered halibut is excellent—light and not a bit greasy. There are other items on the menu, including homemade clam chowder, but if you're eating at the Halibut House, why try anything else? ⊠*208 Meals Ave.* ☎*907/835–2788* ▤*MC, V.*

VICTORIA, BRITISH COLUMBIA

Although Victoria isn't in Alaska, it's a port of call for many ships cruising the Inside Passage. Victoria is the oldest city (founded 1843) on Canada's west coast and the first European settlement on Vancouver Island. It was chosen to be the westernmost trading outpost of the British-owned Hudson Bay Company in 1843 and became the capital of British Columbia in 1868. Just like the communities of Southeast Alaska, Victoria had its own gold-rush stampede in the 1800s, when 25,000 miners flocked to British Columbia's Cariboo country. Victoria has since evolved into a walkable, livable seaside town of gardens, waterfront pathways, and restored 19th-century architecture. Often described as the country's most British city, Victoria is these days—except for the odd red phone box, good beer, and well-mannered drivers—working to change that image, preferring to celebrate its combined native, Asian, and European heritage. Though it's quite touristy in summer, it's also at its prettiest then, with flowers hanging from

19th-century lampposts and strollers enjoying the beauty of Victoria's natural harbor. If you have the time, the beautiful Butchart Gardens, a short drive outside the city, are worth a trip.

COMING ASHORE

SHORE EXCURSIONS

Butchart Gardens. More than 700 varieties of flowers grow in these spectacular gardens north of town. If you're there in the evening you can witness the romantic nighttime illumination of the gardens. Some excursions include a narrated tour of Victoria en route, while others offer such add-ons as a wine and chocolate tasting at a local winery. ⊙ *3½–4 hrs* 🖼 *Gardens only: $69; with city tour: $89; with wine and chocolate tasting: $95.*

Grand City Drive and Empress High Tea. Travel by bus through Victoria's downtown, past its historic residential neighborhoods, and along a scenic ocean drive. Some tours include a stop at a viewpoint atop Mount Tolmie. The tour finishes with an elaborate afternoon tea at the historic Fairmont Empress Hotel. ⊙ *3 hrs* 🖼 *$98.*

Whale Watching. Orca (killer whales), seals, sea lions, and porpoises are abundant in the waters off Victoria. Some of the covered jet boats are equipped with hydrophones so you can hear the whales communicate. ⊙ *3 hrs* 🖼 *$120.*

VICTORIA BEST BETS

■ Most cruise ships visit Victoria in the late afternoon and evening, which is an ideal time for a stroll around the city's compact downtown or a visit to the splendid 55-acre Butchart Gardens.

■ Victoria's other main attraction is the city center itself, with its street entertainers, yachts at harbor, cafés, funky little shops, intriguing museums, and illuminated Victorian architecture.

■ A promenade around the Inner Harbour with, perhaps, a carriage ride for two (available at the corner of Belleville and Menzies streets, next to the Parliament Buildings) is a romantic option.

TRANSPORTATION & TOURS

FROM THE PIER

Only the smallest excursion vessels dock downtown in Victoria's Inner Harbour. Ocean liners tie up at the Ogden Point cruise-ship terminal (⊕ *www.victoriaharbour.org*), 2.4 km (1½ mi) from the Inner Harbour, and a few pocket cruise ships moor at Sidney, 29 km (18 mi) north of Victoria. When ships are in port, a shuttle bus makes frequent trips between Ogden Point and downtown Victoria. The $C5 fare allows you to make as many return trips as you like. The walk downtown is pleasant and will take 20 to 30 minutes.

Metered taxis also meet each ship. Taxi rates are C$2.85 for pickup, and C$1.64 per kilometer (½ mi). A cab from Ogden Point to the Inner Harbour will cost about C$7. **Bluebird Taxi** (☎ *250/382–2222*) serves the Victoria area. **Victoria Taxi** (☎ *250/383–7111*) is another reliable local company.

GETTING AROUND

Most points of interest are within walking distance of the Inner Harbour. For those that aren't, public and private transportation is readily available. The public bus system is excellent; pick up route maps and schedules at the Tourism Victoria Visitor InfoCentre. City tours by horse-drawn carriage and double-decker bus, as well as bicycle rentals and limousine service, are available at the cruise-ship terminal.

VISITOR INFORMATION

The **Tourism Victoria Visitor InfoCentre** (⊠*812 Wharf St.* ☎*250/953–2033 or 800/663–3883*) is across the street from the Empress Hotel, on the Inner Harbour.

TIME

■ TIP→ **If you're coming from Alaska, remember to adjust your watch.** British Columbia is on Pacific Time, one hour ahead of Alaska Time.

EXPLORING VICTORIA

❶ Victoria's heart is the **Inner Harbour,** always bustling with ferries, seaplanes, and yachts. In summer the waterfront comes alive with strollers and street entertainers.

❾ **Chinatown.** Founded in 1858, Victoria's Chinatown is the oldest in Canada. If you enter from Government Street, you can walk under the elaborate Gate of Harmonious Interest, made from Taiwanese ceramic tiles and decorative panels. Along the street, merchants display fragile paper lanterns, wicker baskets, and exotic groceries. Fan Tan Alley, just off Fisgard Street, holds claim not only to being the narrowest street in Canada, but also to having been the gambling and opium center of Chinatown, where games of mah-jongg, fan-tan, and dominoes were played. It's now lined with tiny shops.

❷ **Fairmont Empress Hotel.** Opened in 1908 by the Canadian Pacific Railway, the Empress is a grand château–style hotel with old-world architecture, ornate decor, and a commanding view of the Inner Harbour. Designed by Francis Rattenbury, who also designed the Parliament Buildings, the Empress, with its solid Edwardian grandeur, has become a symbol of the city. The archives, a historical photo and cartoon display on the lower level, are open to the public. Nonguests can also stop by the Empress for a traditional afternoon tea (reservations recommended), meet for a curry under the tiger skin in the Bengal Lounge, enjoy a treatment at the hotel's Willow Stream spa, sample the superb French-influenced cuisine in the Empress Room restaurant, or check out the high-end shops and galleries in the hotel's arcade. **Miniature World** (☎*250/385–9731*), a display of more than 50 doll-size dioramas, including one of the world's largest model railways, is on the Humboldt Street side of the complex. ⊠*721 Government St., entrance at Belleville and Government Sts., Downtown* ☎*250/384–8111, 250/389–2727 tea reservations* ⊕*www.fairmont.com/empress* 🖃*Afternoon tea C$56 July–Sept., C$30–C$40 Oct.–June; Miniature World C$9.*

❼ Maritime Museum of British Columbia. In Victoria's original courthouse, model ships, Royal Navy charts, photographs, uniforms, and ships' bells chronicle British Columbia's seafaring history. Among the hand-built boats on display is the Tilikum, a dugout canoe that sailed from Victoria to England between 1901 and 1904. An 1899 hand-operated cage lift, believed to be the oldest continuously operating elevator in North America, ascends to the third floor, where an 1888 Vice-Admiralty courtroom looks set for a court-martial. ⊠ *28 Bastion Sq., Old Town* 🕾 *250/385–4222* ⊕ *www.mmbc.bc.ca* ⊠ *C$8* ⊙ *Daily 9:30–4:30.*

❽ Market Square. During Victoria's late-19th-century heyday, this three-level square, originally the courtyard of an old inn, provided everything a sailor, miner, or up-country lumberjack could want. Now, beautifully restored to its original architectural, if not commercial, character, it's a traffic-free café- and boutique-lined hangout. ⊠ *560 Johnson St., Old Town* 🕾 *250/386–2441.*

❸ Parliament Buildings. Dominating the Inner Harbour, these massive stone structures, completed in 1898, were designed by Francis Rattenbury (who also designed the Fairmont Empress Hotel). Two statues flank the main doors: one of Sir James Douglas (1803–77), who chose the site upon which Victoria was built, and another of Sir Matthew Baille Begbie (1819–94), the man in charge of law and order during the gold rush. Atop the central dome is a gilded statue of Captain George Vancouver (1757–98), the first European to sail around Vancouver Island. A statue of Queen Victoria (1819–1901) stands in front of the complex. More than 3,000 lights outline the buildings at night. The interior is lavishly appointed with stained-glass windows and murals depicting scenes from the province's history. From the public gallery, when the legislature is in session you can watch British Columbian democracy at work; tradition has the opposing parties sitting 2½ sword lengths apart. Informative half-hour tours are free. ⊠ *501 Belleville St., Downtown* 🕾 *250/387–3046* ⊕ *www.legis.gov.bc.ca* ⊠ *Free* ⊙ *Mid-May–Labor Day, daily 8:30–5, first tour at 9*AM; *at least 20 tours a day. Some Fri. and Sat. evening tours may also be available in summer; call for details. Day after Labor Day–mid-May, weekdays 8:30–5, first tour at 9*AM, *last tour at 4* PM.

❹ Royal BC Museum. This excellent museum, one of Victoria's leading attractions, traces several thousand years of British Columbian history. Exhibits include a genuine Kwakwaka'wakw big house (the builders retain rights to its ceremonial use) and an extensive collection of First Nations masks and other artifacts. The Living Land, Living Sea Gallery includes a climate change exhibit, featuring thunder, lightning, and a massive Woolly Mammoth looming next to a wall of ice. In the History Gallery, a replica of Captain Vancouver's ship, the HMS *Discovery,* creaks convincingly, and a re-created early-20th-century town comes complete with cobbled streets and silent movies. The Ocean Station exhibit showcases BC's coastal marine life, Century Hall reviews British Columbia's 20th-century history, and an on-site IMAX theater shows *National Geographic* films on a six-story-high screen.

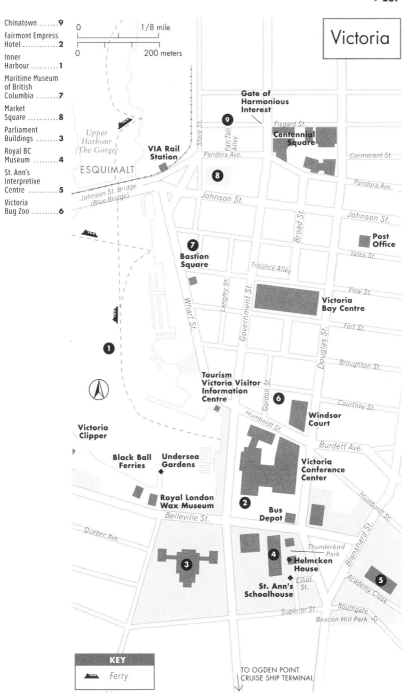

Victoria

0   1/8 mile

0   200 meters

Upper Harbour (The Gorge)

ESQUIMALT

Johnson St. Bridge (Blue Bridge)

VIA Rail Station

Store St.

Fan Tan Alley

Pandora Ave.

Gate of Harmonious Interest

Fisgard St.

Centennial Square

Cormorant St.

Pandora Ave.

Johnson St.

Broad St.

Johnson St.

Post Office

Yates St.

Bastion Square

Trounce Alley

View St.

Victoria Bay Centre

Langley St.

Government St.

Fort St.

Wharf St.

Douglas St.

Broughton St.

Courtney St.

Tourism Victoria Visitor Information Centre

Gordon St.

Humboldt St.

Windsor Court

Victoria Clipper

Black Ball Ferries

Undersea Gardens

Royal London Wax Museum

Belleville St.

Burdett Ave.

Victoria Conference Center

Humboldt St.

Quebec Ave.

Bus Depot

Thunderbird Park

Helmcken House

Blanshard St.

St. Ann's Schoolhouse

Elliot St.

Academy Close

Superior St.

Southgate St.

Beacon Hill Park

KEY
🚢 Ferry

TO OGDEN POINT CRUISE SHIP TERMINAL

4

Three more interesting sights are part of the museum complex. **Helmcken House** is one of the oldest houses in British Columbia and still on its original site. Erected in 1852 for pioneer doctor and statesman John Sebastian Helmcken, the house is a repository of interesting history, from the family's Victorian

furnishings to the doctor's collection of 19th-century medical tools. Beside Helmcken House is **Thunderbird Park,** with totem poles and Wawadit'la, a longhouse, which is still used for ceremonial purposes. Also next to Helmcken House is **St. Ann's Schoolhouse,** one of British Columbia's oldest schools (you can view the interior through the door). ⊠ *675 Belleville St., Downtown* ☎ *250/356–7226 or 888/447–7977* ⊕ *www.royalbcmuseum.bc.ca* ⊠ *C$14, IMAX theater C$10.50, combination ticket C$22.50. Rates may be higher during special exhibit periods* ☉ *Museum: June–Sept., Sun.–Thurs. 9–5, Fri. and Sat. 9 AM–10 PM; Oct.–May, daily 9–5. Theater: daily 10–8; call for showtimes. Helmcken House: June–Labor Day, daily noon–4.*

❺ St. Ann's Academy Interpretive Centre. This former convent and school, founded in 1858, played a central role in British Columbia's pioneer life. The academy's little chapel, the first Roman Catholic cathedral in Victoria, has been restored to look just as it did in the 1920s. The 6-acre grounds, with fruit trees and herb and flower gardens, are also being restored as historic landscapes. ⊠ *835 Humboldt St., Downtown* ☎ *250/953–8828* ⊕ *www.stannsacademy.com* ⊠ *By donation* ☉ *Gardens daily dawn–dusk. Chapel mid-May–mid-Oct., daily 10–4; mid-Oct.–mid-May, call for hrs.*

❻ Victoria Bug Zoo. Home to about 50 species of bugs, this offbeat, two-room minizoo houses the largest collection of live tropical insects in North America. You can even hold many of the varieties, which include walking sticks, scorpions, and millipedes. Staff members are on hand to dispense scientific information. ⊠ *631 Courtney St., Inner Harbour* ☎ *250/384–2847* ⊕ *www.bugzoo.bc.ca* ⊠ *C$8* ☉ *Mid-June–Labor Day, daily 9:30–7; Sept.–mid-June, call for hrs.*

OUTSIDE TOWN

FodorśChoice
★
Butchart Gardens. More than 700 varieties of flowers grow in the sunken, Italian, Japanese, and rose gardens of this stunning 55-acre garden, 21 km (13 mi) north of downtown Victoria. Originally a private estate and still family-run, it has drawn visitors since it was planted in a limestone quarry in 1904. From mid-June to mid-September, the gardens are illuminated at night, and musicians and other entertainers perform in the afternoons and evenings. On Saturday nights in July and August, fireworks light the sky over the gardens. You can indulge in a gelato or pastry in the Italian garden, or enjoy traditional afternoon tea in the dining room restaurant. The wheelchair-accessible site is also home to a seed-and-gift shop, two restaurants, and a coffee shop. To get to the gardens by public transit, take Bus 75 from Douglas Street downtown. ⊠ *800*

Benvenuto Ave., Brentwood Bay ☎250/652–5256 or 866/652–4422 🌐www.butchartgardens.com 🎟Mid-June–Sept. C$25; discounted rates rest of yr ⏲Mid-June–Labor Day, daily 9 AM–10:30 PM; day after Labor Day–mid-June, daily 9 AM–dusk; call for precise times.

SHOPPING

> **TIP**
>
> To get to the gardens, which are about 20 minutes north of town, a shore excursion is your best bet: a tour costs less per couple than a cab and will probably include a narrated city tour. Tours that straddle sunset are best as they allow you to see the gardens in the less-crowded afternoon hours and after dark, when thousands of tiny lights illuminate the blooms.

Victoria stores specializing in English imports are plentiful, though Canadian-made goods are usually a better buy. You'll pay both 7% Provincial Sales Tax (PST) and 6% Goods and Services Tax (GST) on most purchases.

Victoria's main shopping area is along Government Street north of the Fairmont Empress Hotel. Handmade chocolates are displayed in antique cases at **Roger's Chocolates** (*✉913 Government St. ☎250/384–7021*). At **Artina's** (*✉1002 Government St., Downtown ☎250/386–7000 or 877/386–7700*) you can find unusual Canadian art jewelry—mostly handmade, one-of-a-kind pieces. **Hill's Native Art** (*✉1008 Government St. ☎250/385–3911*) sells original West Coast native artwork. For imported linens and lace, have a look at the **Irish Linen Store** (*✉1019 Government St. ☎250/383–6812*).

Munro's Books (*✉1108 Government St. ☎250/382–2464*), in a beautifully restored 1909 building, is one of Canada's prettiest bookstores. For exotic teas, aromatherapy remedies, and spa treatments (think green tea facials) stop in at the chic and multifaceted **Silk Road** (*✉1624 Government St. ☎250/704–2688*). High-end fashion boutiques line **Trounce Alley,** a pedestrian-only lane north of View Street between Broad and Government streets. **Victoria Bay Centre** (*✉1 Victoria Bay Centre, at Government and Fort Sts., Downtown ☎250/952–5690*), a department store and mall, holds about 100 chain stores, boutiques, and restaurants. Just off Government Street, historic **Market Square** (*✉560 Johnson St., Downtown ☎250/386–2441*) offers everything from toys and music to jewelry, local arts, and new-age accoutrements.

From Government Street, turn right onto Fort Street and walk five blocks to **Antique Row,** between Blanshard and Cook streets, where dozens of antiques shops sell books, jewelry, china, furniture, artwork, and collectibles.

WHERE TO EAT

"Fresh, local, organic" has become a mantra for many Victoria chefs. Wild salmon, locally made cheeses, Pacific oysters, forest-foraged mushrooms, organic vegetables in season, local microbrews, and British Columbian wines can all be sampled here. Restaurants in the region generally are casual. A bylaw bans smoking indoors in all Victoria restaurants.

Casual but neat dress is appropriate everywhere. A 15% tip is expected. A 5% Goods and Services Tax (GST) is charged on food and a 10% liquor tax is charged on wine, beer, and spirits. Some restaurants build the liquor tax into the price of the beverage, but others add it to the bill.

★ $$ ✕**The Tapa Bar.** Chef-owner Danno Lee has re-created the fun and flavors of a Spanish tapas bar in this little pedestrians-only lane off Government Street. Small flavorful dishes run from grilled vegetables to prawns in butter, garlic, and white wine, spicy mussels, thin-crust pizzas, and hearty soups. Exposed brick and lively artwork create a casual interior; a heated patio is a choice spot on a sunny day. Just need a snack? No problem. Tapas are served all afternoon and late into the evening. ✉*620 Trounce Alley Downtown* ☎*250/383–0013* ▤*AE, MC, V.*

$–$$ ✕**The Noodle Box.** Noodles, whether Indonesian-style with peanut sauce, thick Japanese Udon noodles in teriyaki, or Thai-style chow mein, are piled straight from steaming woks in the open kitchen to bowls or cardboard take-out boxes at this local answer to fast-food chains. Malaysian, Singapore, and Cambodian-style curries tempt those who like it hot. Brick, rose, and lime walls keep things modern and high energy. ✉*818 Douglas St., Inner Harbour* ☎*250/384–1314* ✉*626 Fisgard St., Chinatown* ☎*250/360–1312* ⚑*Reservations not accepted* ▤*AE, MC, V.*

$–$$ ✕**Re-Bar Modern Food.** Bright and casual, this kid-friendly café in Bastion Square is *the* place for vegetarians in Victoria, though the almond burgers, veggie enchiladas, decadent baked goodies, and big breakfasts will keep omnivores happy as well. An extensive tea and fresh-juice selection shares space with espresso, microbrews, and British Columbian wines on the drinks list. ✉*50 Bastion Sq., Old Town* ☎*250/361–9223* ⊕*www.rebarmodernfood.com* ▤*AE, DC, MC, V* ◷*No dinner Sun.*

$ ✕**Sam's Deli.** For a quick pit stop on a stroll around the Inner Harbour, you can't beat this long-established sandwich bar catercorner to the Tourist Information Office. Thick sandwiches, salads, and big bowls of homemade soup come cheap, hearty, and cafeteria style. Patio seats are prime people-watching territory, and the ice cream is among the best in town. This is a popular breakfast stop, too. ✉*805 Government St., Inner Harbour* ☎*250/382–8424* ⚑*Reservations not accepted* ▤*AE, MC, V* ◷*No dinner Oct.–May.*

$ ✕**Willie's Bakery.** Housed in a handsome Victorian building near Market Square, this bakery serves wholesome breakfasts, rich soups, delicious sandwiches made with house-baked bread, tasty baked treats, and house-made gelato. The brick patio with an outdoor fireplace and fountain is a pleasant spot to watch the world go by. A second location is inside the Royal BC Museum. ✉*537 Johnson St., Old Town* ☎*250/381–8414* ⊕*www.isabellasbb.com/willies* ⚑*Reservations not accepted* ▤*MC, V* ◷*No dinner.*

WHERE TO DRINK

Pub culture is an important part of life in Victoria, providing a casual, convivial atmosphere for lunch, a casual dinner, or an afternoon pint. The pubs listed here all serve food and many brew their own beer. Patrons must be 19 or older to enter the pub itself, but many pubs have a restaurant section where kids are welcome, too. Smoking is banned indoors in all Victoria pubs.

★ The patio at the **Canoe Brewpub** (⊠*450 Swift St., Old Town* ☎*250/361–1940*) looks over the Gorge waterway. Inside, the former power station has been stylishly redone and has a wide range of in-house brews, top-notch bar snacks, and a restaurant that welcomes kids. Filling a two-story former bank building on Victoria's main shopping strip, **Irish Times** (⊠*1200 Government St.* ☎*250/383–7775*) offers fish-and-chips, shepherd's pie, and Irish stew, as well as stout on tap and live Celtic music every night. Worth a cab ride over the Johnson Street Bridge, **Spinnakers Gastro Brewpub** (⊠*308 Catherine St.* ☎*250/386–2739 or 877/838–2739*) has water views and some of the city's best food and beer. The restaurant welcomes all ages. **Swans Brewpub** (⊠*506 Pandora Ave., Downtown* ☎*250/361–3310*), set in a 1913 heritage building, serves its own microbrews in a room decorated with Pacific Northwest art. Live music plays every night and the no-smoking patio is open to all ages.

WRANGELL

Wrangell is on an island near the mouth of the fast-flowing Stikine River, and like much of the Southeast, has suffered in recent years from a declining resource-based economy. The town is off the typical cruise-ship track and is frequented by lines with an environmental or educational emphasis, such as Cruise West. This small, unassuming timber-and-fishing community has lived under three flags since the arrival of the Russian traders. It was known as Redoubt St. Dionysius when it was part of Russian America; then it was called Fort Stikine after the British took it over. It became Wrangell when the Americans took over in 1867; the name came from Baron Ferdinand Petrovich von Wrangell, governor of the Russian-American Company.

COMING ASHORE

TRANSPORTATION & TOURS

FROM THE PIER

Cruise ships calling in to Wrangell dock downtown, within walking distance of the museum and gift stores. Greeters welcome you and are available to answer questions. Wrangell's few attractions—the most notable being totem-filled Chief Shakes Island—are within walking distance of the pier. The Nolan Center houses an excellent museum, and Petroglyph Beach, where rocks are imprinted with mysterious prehistoric symbols, is 1 mi from the pier. Most cruise-ship visitors see it on guided shore excursions or by taxi. Call **Northern Lights Taxi** (☎907/874–4646) or **Star Cab** (☎907/874–3622).

AREA TOURS

Breakaway Adventures (☎907/874–2488 or 888/385–2488 ⊕*www. breakawayadventures.com*) leads day trips up the majestic Stikine River by jet boat, including a visit to Chief Shakes Glacier, along with time to take a dip at Chief Shakes Hot Springs. **Sunrise Aviation** (☎907/874–2319 or 800/874–2311 ⊕*www.sunriseflights.com*) is a charter-only air carrier that offers trips to the Anan Creek Wildlife Observatory, LeConte Glacier, or Forest Service cabins.

VISITOR INFORMATION

The **Wrangell Visitor Center** is housed in the Nolan Center. (☎907/874–2829 or 800/367–9745 ⊕*www.wrangell.com* ⊙*During museum hrs*). Stop by for details on local adventure options.

EXPLORING WRANGELL

⑥ On your way to Wrangell's number one attraction—Chief Shakes Island—stop at **Chief Shakes's grave site,** uphill from the Wrangell shipyard on Case Avenue. Buried here is Shakes VI, the last of a line of chiefs who bore that name. He led the local Tlingits during the first half of the 19th century. Two killer-whale totems mark the chief's burial place.

⑦ On **Chief Shakes Island,** reached by a footbridge off the harbor dock, you can see some of the finest totem poles in Alaska, as well as a tribal house constructed in the 1930s as a replica of one that was home to many of the various Shakes and their people. There are six totems on the island, two of them more than 100 years old. The original corner posts of the tribal house are in the museum. After your visit to Chief Shakes Island, wander out to the end of the dock for the view and for picture taking at the busy boat harbor and the adjacent seaplane float. ⊠*Off Shakes St.* ☎907/874–3481 ⊡*$3.50* ⊙ *When cruise ships are in port.*

② Outside the **Irene Ingle Public Library** are a couple of ancient petroglyphs, which are worth seeing if you don't plan to make the trip to Petroglyph Beach. The library offers free Internet access and has a helpful staff. ⊠*124 2nd Ave.* ☎907/874–3535.

⑤ Walking up Front Street will bring you to **Kiksetti Totem Park,** a pocket park of Alaska greenery and impressive totem poles.

④ Despite the name, **Mount Dewey** is more of a hill than a peak; it sits right behind Wrangell. Still, it's a steep 15-minute climb to the top through a second-growth forest. The trail begins from 3rd Street behind the high school, and an observation platform on top provides a viewpoint for protected waterways and quirkily named islands, including Zarembo, Vank, and Woronkofski—which derive their appellations from 19th-century lieutenants of the Russian American Company.

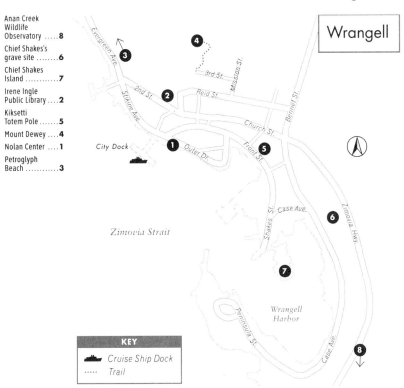

KEY

🚢 *Cruise Ship Dock*

..... *Trail*

❶ The **Nolan Center**'s exhibits provide a window on the region's rich his-
Fodor'sChoice tory. Featured pieces include decorative posts from Chief Shakes's clan
★ house (carved in the late 1700s), petroglyphs, century-old spruce-root
and cedar-bark baskets, masks, items from Russian and English settlers, gold-rush memorabilia, and a fascinating photo collection. The
building also houses the **Wrangell Visitor Center** and the town's **Civic
Center,** a 200-seat movie theater/performance space. Stop by to watch
videos on the Stikine River and the town of Wrangell. If you're spending any time in town, don't pass this up. ⊠*296 Outer Dr.* ☎*907/874–
3770* 🔊*$5* ⊘*May–Sept., Tues.–Sat. 10–5, and when ferry or cruise
ships are in port.*

❸ **Petroglyph Beach** is undoubtedly one of the more curious sights in Southeast Alaska. Scattered among other rocks along the shore are three
dozen or more large stones bearing designs and pictures chiseled by
unknown ancient artists. Most of these petroglyphs are to the right
between the viewing deck and a large outcropping of rock in the tidal
beach area. A boardwalk provides access to the beach and includes
signs describing the site, along with carved replicas of the petroglyphs.
You are welcome to use these (but not the originals) for rubbings. Most
tours provide rice paper and charcoal or crayons for this purpose. ⊠
mi north of ferry terminal off Evergreen Ave.

OUTSIDE TOWN

8 About 30 mi southeast of Wrangell in the Tongass National Forest, **Anan Creek Wildlife Observatory** is one of Alaska's premier black- and brown-bear viewing areas. Each summer, from early July to mid-August, as many as 30 to 40 black bears gather at this stream to feed on one of the Southeast's largest runs of pink salmon. On an average visit of about two hours you might spot two to four bears while strolling the ½-mi viewing boardwalk. Forest Service interpreters are on hand to answer questions. The site is accessible only by boat or floatplane. In addition to a variety of guided sea-kayak adventures, **Alaska Vistas and Stikine Wilderness Adventures** (☎*907/874–3006 or 866/874–3006* ⊕*www.alaskavistas.com*) has jet-boat trips to Anan Creek that depart from Wrangell. They also offer custom tours and itinerary planning services.

OUTDOOR ACTIVITIES

Rain Walker Expeditions (☎*907/874—2549 or 888/276-2549* ⊕*www. rainwalkerexpeditions.com*) leads natural-history tours of wild places near Wrangell. The company also rents mountain bikes, canoes, and sea kayaks if you want to head out on your own.

SHOPPING

A rocky ledge near the Stikine River is the source for **garnets** sold by local children for 25¢ to $50. The site was deeded to the Boy Scouts in 1962, and then to the Presbyteria of Alaska in 2006, so there's a strong tradition of granting only children the privilege to collect these colorful but imperfect stones. Some are as large as an inch across. At a few covered shelters near the city dock when cruise ships are in, you can buy locally crafted items or book an adventure. Local artist **Brenda Schwartz** (✉*7 Front St.* ☎*907/874-3508* ⊕*www.marineartist.com*) has created a unique style that combines marine paintings with navigational charts. Find her studio at the base of Chief Shakes Island.

WHERE TO EAT

$$–$$$ ✕ **Zak's Cafe.** Despite its spartan, no-nonsense atmosphere, Zak's is a standout among Wrangell's very limited dining choices, with good food and reasonable prices. Check out the daily specials or try their steaks, chicken, seafood, salads, and Asian-style stir-fries. At lunch, the menu includes burgers, sandwiches, fish-and-chips, and wraps. ✉*314 Front St.* ☎*907/874-3355* ▭*MC, V.*

Sports &Wilderness Adventures

WORD OF MOUTH

"When I was younger, I almost ran off with my lover to Alaska. I always wondered what I missed."
— cigalechanta

"Now that we're back from our two-week Alaska trip, I can say quite honestly that kayaking in Alaska will not disappoint you. The place is magnificent. My best advice is to bring a barrel of money and tons of time!"
— BayouGal

Updated by
Ken Marsh

DERIVED FROM AN ALEUT WORD
meaning "great land," *Alaska* has more land in parks, wilderness areas, and wildlife refuges than all the other states combined. About one-third of Alaska's 375 million acres is set aside in protected public lands.

Four great mountain ranges—the St. Elias, Alaska, Brooks, and Chugach—and more than 30 lesser chains sweep through the state. The St. Elias Mountains form the highest coastal range in the world; the Alaska Range contains North America's highest peak (Mt. McKinley, 20,320 feet); the Brooks Range roughly follows the Arctic Circle; and the Chugach arcs through Alaska's most populous region.

> **NAVIGATING THIS CHAPTER**
>
> Flip through this chapter to find tips on how best to plan your adventure; in-depth descriptions of sports, from kayaking to skiing to biking; as well as our favorite regions and guides for each sport; and finally our best wildlife-viewing advice and experiences.
> In regional chapters, we recommend even more local outfitters and guides.

Alaska's public lands are as varied as they are magnificent; recreational activities include wildlife viewing, hiking, mountain biking, kayaking, rafting, canoeing, fishing, hunting, mountaineering, skiing, and snowboarding. Limited road access (Alaska averages only 1 mi of road for every 42 square mi of land; the U.S. average ratio is 1 to 1) means that many destinations can only be reached via airplane, boat, or all-terrain vehicle.

Even the most-visited parks—Denali National Park & Preserve, Glacier Bay National Park & Preserve, Kenai Fjords National Park, and Chugach State Park—allow backpackers and kayakers abundant opportunities for remote wilderness experiences. Parks closer to roads, and to cities like Anchorage and Fairbanks, draw more visitors. Particularly remote and solitary experiences await in the state's least-visited places, such as Wood-Tikchik State Park, where only two rangers patrol 1.6 million acres, or Aniakchak National Monument & Preserve, south of Katmai, where trekkers can go days or weeks without seeing another human.

PLANNING YOUR ADVENTURE

Trips to Alaska are best planned months, or even a year, in advance, particularly to the most popular destinations, such as Denali and Glacier Bay national parks. Prime time for summer backcountry sports is June through early September. Winter sports are better enjoyed later in the season, in late February and March, when longer daylight hours return, temperatures start to rise a little, and snow conditions are unsurpassed for snowshoeing, skiing, and mushing.

Alaska's wilderness is enormous almost beyond comprehension. Visitors to the farther-flung reaches should come prepared for constantly changing and often harsh weather, difficult or impassable terrains, mosquitoes and gnats, bear encounters, and other backcountry challenges. A keen knowledge of the country, proper clothing, quality camping gear, good physical conditioning, and excellent navigation skills are vital to successful and safe trips. Visitors without extensive wilderness experience can avoid logistical headaches and hazards by hiring local tour guides to provide equipment, direction, and necessary expertise.

WELCOME TO THE 49TH

Interspersed among Alaska's great mountain ranges are canyons and waterfalls, alpine valleys, salmon-rich rivers, clear lakes, blue glaciers, temperate rain forests, and sweeping, spongy tundra plains. Adding to this wealth are thousands of miles of spectacular tidal coastline. Prepare for some unforgettable outdoor adventuring!

CHOOSING A TRIP

Opportunities for outdoor adventures sit beyond the edge of every Alaska village, port, and city. A day—or a week—of sea kayaking in Prince William Sound may begin a stone's throw from the streets of Whittier, which is a scenic hour's drive south of Anchorage. A much more complex trip, such as a 10-day navigation of the North Fork Koyukuk River, may require a commuter flight from Fairbanks to the remote community of Bettles, and from there a prearranged flight into the headwaters high in the Brooks Range. So the first question is whether an organized tour or a do-it-yourself trip is most appropriate for you.

The answer depends upon how much wilderness experience you have, what kind of physical condition you are in, how much time you have, and how much money you can afford to spend on gear and logistics. ■ TIP➔ The Alaska wilderness can be as difficult to navigate as it is beautiful; plan ahead and do not step into "the last frontier" poorly prepared. Know when to enlist the services of local guides or outfitters; allowing these professionals to provide vital gear, expertise, and direction can make your adventure safer, more comfortable, and more fulfilling.

RESOURCES With proper planning and the help of local professionals, there's an Alaska trip—and likely many—just for you, no matter your age, physical ability, or level of wilderness savvy. The first step is to obtain a list of outfitters and guides who are permitted to operate in the regions you plan to visit. Such a list is available from the staff of the refuge, forest, or park you want to go to. When contacting businesses, learn about the guides, the nature of the activities they offer, and the area you want to explore. Also be sure to determine how well the guides know the area. Make it a point to ask for references. Throughout this book you'll find in-depth information about all of Alaska's regions; contact information and insider tips are provided for every park, refuge, and wildland that we deem worthy of a visit.

Here are some top organizations to help you get started:

A state-produced *Alaska Vacation Planner* (which also contains information on ecotourism) can be obtained from the **Alaska Travel Industry Association** (☎907/929–2200, 800/862–5275 *to order vacation planners* ⊕*www.travelalaska.com*).

The **Alaska Wilderness Recreation and Tourism Association** (☎907/258–3171 ⊕*www.awrta.org*) can provide information on many businesses and activities across the state.

Recreational Equipment Inc. (☎907/272–4565 ⊕*www.rei.com*) is a great resource for equipment needs.

Larger tour companies will take care of everything if you want to just sit back and be guided through a specific part of the state doing a variety of activities. In some cases they offer shorter tours and activities for independent travelers. Ask about timing and pricing.

Gray Line of Alaska (☎206/281–3535 *or* 800/544–2206 ⊕*www.graylinealaska.com*).

Princess Cruises and Tours (☎800/426–0442 ⊕*www.princesslodges.com*).

Smaller, independent tour companies and agencies offer, you guessed it, smaller-scale tours and packages; they are good resources for tailor-made Alaska journeys. See individual sports listed in this chapter for specialized Alaska-based companies.

Alaska Bound (☎231/439–3000 *or* 888/252–7527 ⊕*www.alaskabound.com*).

Alaska Tour & Travel (☎907/245–0200 *or* 800/208–0200 ⊕*www.alaskatravel.com*).

Alaska Tours (☎907/277–3000 *or* 866/317–3325 ⊕*www.alaskatours.com*).

Viking Travel (☎907/772–3818 *or* 800/327–2571 ⊕*www.alaskaferry.com*).

MONEY MATTERS

To reserve a spot, most tour operators require a deposit, with the balance due before your start date. In most cases, if you cancel your reservation, you get at least a partial refund, but policies vary widely. ■TIP➡ **Find out how far in advance you must cancel to get a full refund, and ask whether any allowances are made for cancellations due to medical emergencies.** If cancellation insurance is available, you may want to take it. You'll receive a full refund regardless of the reason for your cancellation.

Taxes are generally not included in the quoted price and can add substantially to the cost of your trip. Depending on the program, you should inquire about which members of the tour personnel customarily get tipped and what the going rate is.

SAFETY FIRST

In choosing a guide, a primary concern should be safety. A guide should be equipped with proper technical and first-aid gear and should know how to use it.

If you have no experience in the activity, ask what sort of training you'll receive. Explain your own goals and abilities, and ask about the difficulty of the terrain; 1 mi across hilly, trail-less tundra may demand the same energy as 2 or 3 mi on a flat, maintained trail. Most guides plan trips so that you'll have time to relax and enjoy the landscape and look for wildlife, but it's a good idea to ask about the travel schedule and number of miles to be covered daily. As a general rule, hikers in good physical condition should be able to travel 2 mi an hour on maintained trails and about 1 mi per hour or less across trail-less terrain. Traveling 6 or 7 mi per day, even on trails, is likely to be tiring for a novice. Be honest with the guide regarding your level of expertise.

The amount of weight carried on your back will also influence your traveling ability, especially if you haven't carried a heavy pack before, so determine the amount of gear you'll be required to carry, particularly if you'll be hiking, backpacking, or glacier trekking.

GEAR & WEATHER

Ask what gear the company will provide. Guides normally provide group gear, such as tents and tarps, and expect you to provide your own personal equipment, such as boots, rain gear, a pack, and a sleeping bag. (Some guides rent gear such as sleeping bags and packs.)

Ask about the weather. From the temperate rain forests of the Tongass National Forest in Alaska's Southeast to the inland deserts of the Northwest, climates vary greatly. No matter what region you visit, always come prepared for cool, wet weather, even in midsummer. Insect repellent (and sometimes head nets) may be required to ward off mosquitoes, flies, and no-see-ums during all snow-free months.

> **STEP LIGHTLY**
>
> Ecotourists aim to travel responsibly. Typically, ecotourism is on a smaller scale and involves more education than traditional tourism; often, you are led by guides who know the local natural history and cultures. Itineraries allow you a closer connection to the areas explored. As one Alaska guide says, "Slow down, take a deep breath, feel where you are." The **International Ecotourism Society** (⊕ *www.ecotourism.org*) is a great resource.

LODGING

From beautiful wilderness lodges to remote campsites to spongy tundra, your lodging options are quite varied. Where will you be happiest going to sleep after a day of adventuring?

PUBLIC-USE CABINS

Not all Alaska wilderness trips require the expense of luxury lodges or the sacrifices of tent camping. For between $15 and $65 per night, backcountry travelers can have a million-dollar view and a roof over their heads at one of more than 250 public-use cabins available across the state. Cabin costs and locations depend upon which of five land-management agencies they fall under—the U.S. Forest Service, National Wildlife Refuges, National Park Service, Bureau of Land Management, or Alaska State Parks. Most cabins are remote or semiremote and must be reached by plane, boat, or trail. ■ TIP➜ **Almost all must be reserved in advance, either in person, by mail, or online; in some cases nominal service fees may be charged for cancellations.**

> ### EVERYBODY LOVES THE SUNSHINE
>
> In most parts of the state, June through August are considered prime months for summer backcountry trips. July is usually the warmest month. Hope for sunshine, but come prepared for rain, especially in August.

Accommodations are rustic; most cabins have bunks or wooden sleeping platforms, tables, heating stoves, outdoor fire pits, outhouses, and, sometimes, skiffs. Agency Web sites offer descriptions of individual cabins, including the number of bunks, types of stoves, and other amenities visitors can expect. Visitors who fly to cabins located on lakes or in coastal areas where skiffs are provided can usually rent outboards and gasoline tanks in the closest town and bring them along.

The most convenient way to shop for public-use cabins is to visit the listings posted online by the agencies that oversee them. Listings for individual cabins include notes on accessibility (you may need to charter a floatplane from the nearest community, paddle a sea kayak, hike, mountain bike, or travel in on horseback). Logbooks are provided at most cabins; check out entries from previous guests about area hikes, wildlife sightings, and fishing opportunities.

For the central **National Park Service** (⊕ *www.nps.gov/aplic/cabins*) information listing about the cabins, visit their Web site.

In order to reserve any public-use cabin, log on to ⊕ *www.recreation. gov* or call ☎ 877/444–6777.

Alaska State Parks. More than 50 cabins are maintained over a huge area between Ketchikan and Fairbanks. Some are road accessible; reservations can be made up to six months in advance. Cabins vary in size, with sleeping capacity ranging from three to 10 people. For more information or to reserve a cabin online, contact the Department of Natural Resources Public Information Center in Anchorage. ☎ 907/269–8400 ⊕ *www.dnr.state.ak.us/parks/cabins/index.htm.*

Bureau of Land Management. Several public-use cabins are in the White Mountains National Recreation Area near Fairbanks. Cabins can be booked up to 30 days in advance by mail, phone, or in person. Contact the Bureau of Land Management Land Information Center. *1150 University Ave., Fairbanks, 99709-3844* ☎*907/474-2250.*

National Park Service. Cabins are available in Kenai Fjords National Park, Wrangell–St. Elias National Park, and Yukon–Charley Rivers National Park. ☎*907/271-2737 in Kenai Fjords, 907/822-5234 in Wrangell–St. Elias, 907/547-2233 in Yukon–Charley.*

National Wildlife Refuges. Eight public-use cabins are in Kodiak National Wildlife Refuge on Kodiak Island. Cabins can be reached by floatplane or boat only. Reservations are scheduled by a lottery. Applications, which may be mailed or delivered in person, are accepted until the last business day before the drawing date. *1390 Buskin River Rd., Kodiak, 99615* ☎*907/487-2600 or 888/408-3514.*

U.S. Forest Service. The agency maintains more than 150 cabins in Southeast's Tongass National Forest, and more than 40 in the Chugach National Forest in South Central. Most cabins can be reached only by boat or plane; those accessible by trails are very popular and frequently booked months in advance. Maximum stays range from three to seven nights in the summer. Cabin reservations may be made up to six months ahead. ☎*877/444-6777, 518/885-3639 international* ⊕*www.fs.fed.us/r10.*

WILDERNESS LODGES

If your goal is to really get away from it all, consider booking a remote Alaska wilderness lodge. Some of the most popular are in the river drainages of Bristol Bay, in the secluded bays of Southeast Alaska, along the western edge of Cook Inlet, around Katmai and Lake Clark national parks, and in the Susitna Valley north of Anchorage. Most of these lodges specialize in fishing and/or bear viewing. Lodges in and near Denali emphasize opportunities to explore the wilderness as well as natural history programs. Activities can also include dog mushing, hiking, rafting, flightseeing, horseback riding, and gold panning.

Lodge stays generally include daily guided trips and all meals. Fees can be expensive (daily rates of $300–$900 per person). Study their Web sites and list your favorites. E-mail or phone (many lodge operators provide toll-free numbers) with questions regarding activities offered, prices, gratuities, and what you should expect. ■TIP➡**Some of the more popular lodges need to be booked at least a year in advance, though last-minute cancellations can create openings even late in the season.**

For listings of wilderness lodges throughout Alaska, including individual Web sites, phone numbers, and general information, visit ⊕*www.travelalaska.com* or ⊕*www.alaska.com.* As you read through this book, you'll find plenty of recommendations for great wilderness lodges. Below we've listed three options.

Denali Backcountry Lodge. It's in the very heart of Denali National Park & Preserve. Activities for overnight guests include naturalist programs; hiking; fishing; gold panning; mountain biking; and, for an extra fee, flightseeing when weather permits. Family-style meals emphasiz-

A HISTORY OF PROTECTION

Alaska's wealth of public lands is no accident. More than 100 million acres were marked for protection in 1980 when President Jimmy Carter signed into law the Alaska National Interest Lands Conservation Act (ANILCA). The act instantly doubled the size of the national park and refuge system in the United States, and tripled the amount of federal lands designated as wilderness. But the process of what many call the most significant land conservation measure in the nation's history was not simple.

When Alaska became a state in 1959, nearly all of its land mass was federally owned. Under the Statehood Act, the new state was allowed to choose 104 million acres to be managed as a revenue base. Of that, 91 million acres have been chosen. As the state began staking land, Alaska's native people argued that lands traditionally belonging to them were being taken. They pointed out that, lacking an act of Congress removing native title, the state land selections were illegal. A resolution came in 1971 when the Alaska Native Claims Settlement Act (ANCSA) granted Alaska's native peoples the right to choose 44 million acres of federal land in Alaska. So far, about 38 million acres have been selected and transferred to native ownership.

Today Alaska's protected federal lands include nearly 55 million acres of national parks, 73 million acres of national wildlife refuges, 25 wild and scenic rivers totaling nearly 2 million acres, and 5.8 million acres of wilderness areas. Along with the federally protected lands established in Alaska by the passage of ANILCA, approximately 3.2 million acres of superb lands are set aside as state parks.

ing Alaska fare are included in the room rate. ☎*907/376–1992 or 877/233–6254* ⊕*www.denalilodge.com.*

Afognak Wilderness Lodge. This rustic log lodge is set amid coastal wilderness of Afognak State Park on Afognak Island north of Kodiak. Featured activities include fishing, photography and guided wildlife viewing—including brown bear, deer, and whales and other marine wildlife. Guests stay in private, two-bedroom cabins with hot running water and other creature comforts. ☎*907/486–6442 or 800/478–6442* ⊕*www.afognaklodge.com/index.html.*

Tutka Bay Wilderness Lodge. Perched among spruces and coastal western hemlocks overlooking Kachemak Bay, the lodge is reached via plane or boat. You can spend your time sea kayaking, sportfishing, birding, bear and marine wildlife viewing, and relaxing in the open-air hot tub. ☎*907/235–3905 or 800/606–3909* ⊕*www.tutkabaylodge.com.*

CAMPING

Hundreds of campgrounds, public and private, are along Alaska's road system. They typically include sites for tent and RV camping, with fire pits, latrines, running potable water, and picnic benches. Most campsites are on a first-come, first-served basis.

and Denali, Columbia Glacier, and Prince William Sound. ☎*907/243–1595 or 800/544–2299* ⊕*www.flyrusts.com.*

Frontier Flying Service Inc. This Fairbanks-based operation serves Interior Alaska's isolated towns and villages. ☎*907/450–7200 or 800/478–6779* ⊕*www.frontierflying.com/index.shtml.*

Southeast Aviation. This Ketchikan-based operation offers floatplane tours of the glaciers and mountains of Misty Fiords National Monument. Wildlife sightings are quite common. ☎*907/225–2900 or 888/359–6478* ⊕*www.southeastaviation.com.*

Talkeetna Aero Services. These folks are located a two-hour drive north of Anchorage, in the shadow of McKinley; take a twin-engine aerial tour of the mountain. ☎*907/733–2899, 907/683–2899, or 888/733–2899* ⊕*www.talkeetna-aero.com.*

Talkeetna Air Taxi. Check out McKinley and environs, then swoop down to a glacier to test your boots. ☎*907/733–2218 or 800/533–2219* ⊕*www.talkeetnaair.com.*

★ **Wings Airways and Taku Glacier Lodge.** This Juneau-based company specializes in tours of the surrounding ice fields and the Taku Flight & Feast ride on which a salmon feast awaits you. ☎*907/586–6275* ⊕*www.wingsairways.com.*

GLACIER TREKKING

Roughly 100,000 glaciers flow out of Alaska's mountains, covering 5% of the state. These slow-moving "rivers of ice" concentrate in the Alaska Range, Wrangell Mountains, and the state's major coastal mountain chains: the Chugach, St. Elias, Coast, and Kenai ranges. Alaska's largest glacier, the Bering, covers 2,250 square mi. If you're an adventurous backcountry traveler, glaciers present icy avenues into the remote corners of premier mountain wilderness areas. ■TIP➡ For information about glaciers, flip to ⇨ *Glaciers: Notorious Landscape Architects* in Chapter 4.

> **WORD OF MOUTH**
>
> "In Juneau, we liked seeing Mendenhall Glacier, which is not far from downtown. We also enjoyed the floatplane trip over the Juneau Icefields to Taku Glacier Lodge. There they served king salmon cooked over alder logs."
>
> –sluggo

Glacier terrain includes a mix of ice, rock debris, and often-deep surface snow; sometimes frigid pools of meltwater collect on the surface. Watch out for glacier crevasses. Sometimes hidden by snow, especially in spring and early summer (a popular time for glacier trekking), these cracks in the ice may present life-threatening traps. Though some are only inches wide, others may be several yards across and hundreds of feet deep. ■TIP➡Glacier travel should be attempted only after you've been properly trained. If you haven't been taught proper glacial travel and crevasse-rescue techniques, hire a backcountry guide to provide the nec-

essary gear and expertise. Some companies offer day or half-day hikes onto glaciers that don't have the same physical demands as longer treks but that still require proper equipment and training. For instance, St. Elias Alpine Guides takes hikers of all ages and abilities on one of its glacier walks.

TOP REGIONS & EXPERIENCES

SOUTHEAST   In Southeast, visitors to the capital city of Juneau can drive or take the bus to **Mendenhall Glacier,** located on the outskirts of town. This 85-mi-long, 45-mi-wide sheet of ice provides awesome glacier trekking opportunities. Guided tour packages are a very good idea for beginners.

SOUTH CENTRAL & THE INTERIOR   The mountains outside the state's largest city have their share of glaciers. Among the most popular for trekkers of all abilities is **Matanuska Glacier,** located at Mile 103 off the Glenn Highway (about a 90-minute drive northeast of Anchorage). Anchorage-based guides often use the Matanuska as a training ground for those new to navigating glaciers.

Talkeetna, a two-hour drive north of Anchorage, is a small community famous as the jump-off point to some of the world's greatest and most challenging glacier treks. The town rests a short bush-plane hop from the foot of the Alaska Range and the base of Mt. McKinley. Miles of ice await the most intrepid and experienced trekkers. Local and Anchorage-based guide services offer training and tours into the region.

Far to the east, off the McCarthy Road between Valdez and Glennallen, are the great ice fields of the Wrangell Mountains. Experienced outfitters based in the town of McCarthy get newcomers in touch with awesome ice where few outsiders dare visit.

RESOURCES & GUIDES

Above & Beyond Alaska. If you're in the Juneau area and want to get your glacier fix, these folks offer treks to the popular Mendenhall Glacier. ☎ *907/364–2333* ⊕ *www. beyondak.com.*

Adventure Bound. Based in Juneau, these guides offer all-day summertime trips to Sawyer Glacier within Tracy Arm. ☎ *907/463–2509 or 800/228–3875* ⊕ *www.adventurebound alaska.com.*

> ### HELPFUL WEB SITES
>
> List of Alaska air taxis: ⊕ *www. flyalaska.com/directoryp.html.*
>
> National Transportation Safety Board database to check air-taxi safety records: ⊕ *www.ntsb.gov/ NTSB/query.asp.*

Alaska Mountaineering School. Whether it's on mountaineering expeditions to McKinley or less extreme treks into the Alaska Range, this Talkeetna company takes the time to train you before heading out to pristine backcountry. ☎ *907/733–1016* ⊕ *www.climbalaska.org.*

Exposure Alaska. A variety of small-group options, from ice climbing and short treks on the blue ice of the Matanuska Glacier, to more intense multiday outings from Prince William Sound to Denali, are offered through this Anchorage company. ☎ *907/761–3761 or 800/956–6422* ⊕ *www.exposurealaska.com.*

NorthStar Trekking. A Juneau-based operation specializing in helicopter glacier trekking on the Juneau Icefield, these folks accommodate a broad range of physical abilities. All trips are conducted in small groups, gear provided. Flightseeing tours are also offered. ☏907/790–4530 ⊕*www.northstartrekking.com.*

Fodor'sChoice ★ **St. Elias Alpine Guides.** Based in the town of McCarthy, within Wrangell–St. Elias National Park, these überexperienced guides conduct day hikes to nearby glaciers and extended glacier treks well beyond. ☏907/554–4445 or 888/933–5427 ⊕*www.steliasguides.com.*

> **BLISS IN BOOTS**
>
> In late June and early July, when the sun barely sets in much of Alaska, it's tempting to shoulder your pack and keep on hiking. Around 10 PM the light grows mellow and golden. The birds seem to call all night long. Your boots crunch softly over gravel bars and hillocks. This time of year Alaska rarely sleeps; there will be time for rest when summer is over.

★ **Ultima Thule Outfitters.** Based at a fly-in-only lodge on the Chitina River within Wrangell–St. Elias National Park, Ultima Thule leads guided activities in the surrounding mountains, including alpine and glacier treks. A longtime presence in these parts, they're known for family-style hospitality. ☏907/258–0636 ⊕*www.ultimathulelodge.com.*

HIKING & BACKPACKING

From Southeast's coastal rain forests and the Interior's historic Yukon River country to the high Arctic tundra, Alaska presents some of the continent's finest landscape for wilderness hiking and backpacking. Or, if remote backcountry is not your preference, it's possible to travel well-maintained and well-marked trails on the edges of Alaska's largest cities and still get a taste of the wild. Many of the trails in road-accessible parklands, refuges, and forests are well maintained and cross terrain that is easy for novice hikers, seniors, and families.

TOP REGIONS & EXPERIENCES

Below we've listed some notable exceptions to one rule: most of Alaska is pristine wilderness, with few or no trails. In such areas it's best to be accompanied by an experienced backcountry traveler who understands the challenges of trail-less wilderness: how to behave in bear country, how to navigate using map and compass techniques, and how to cross glacial streams. ■TIP➔ For information about hiking Southeast's Chilkoot Trail, flip to *Gold! Gold! Gold!* in Chapter 4.

SOUTHEAST Virtually all hiking country in the Southeast is part of the 17-million-acre Tongass National Forest, administered by the U.S. Forest Service. It can be wet and steep here, but you also will be walking through temperate rain forest—lush and gorgeous!

FROM ANCHORAGE TO DENALI **Chugach State Park,** along Anchorage's eastern edge, has dozens of trails, many of them suited for day hikes or overnight camping. Across Turnagain Arm, near Hope, hikers can step onto the **Resurrection Pass Trail** which traverses the forests, streams, and mountains of the Chugach National Forest. And though it is best known for its trail-less wilderness, **Denali National Park & Preserve** has some easy-to-hike trails near the park entrance, not to mention miles of taiga and tundra waiting to be explored. Nearby "Little Denali"—**Denali State Park**—has the 36-mi-long Kesugi Ridge Trail, within easy reach of the Parks Highway.

FAIRBANKS & THE INTERIOR
If you're in the Interior's main hub, definitely check out **Creamer's Field Migratory Waterfowl Refuge** for easy trails and great birding. Some 100 mi east of Fairbanks, the **Pinnell Mountain National Recreation Trail** offers a great three-day hike above the tree line.

RESOURCES & GUIDES

Alaska Mountaineering School. Best known for its McKinley expeditions, this Talkeetna-based company also leads custom-designed backcountry expeditions in the Alaska Range. ☎907/733–1016 ⊕www.climbalaska.org.

Fodor'sChoice ★
Alaska Nature Tours. This company in Southeast Alaska leads summer hiking trips into the Alaska Chilkat Bald Eagle Preserve near Haines. Other trips include beach walks and rain-forest hikes. ☎907/766–2876 ⊕www.kcd.com/aknature.

Alaskan Gourmet Adventures. This Anchorage-based operator offers fun hiking trips with great guides. ☎907/346–1087 ⊕www.hikealaska.com.

★ **Arctic Treks.** These wilderness hiking and backpacking trips, sometimes combined with river floats, explore areas throughout the Arctic region's Brooks Range, including Gates of the Arctic and the Arctic National Wildlife Refuge. ☎907/455–6502 ⊕www.arctictreksadventures.com.

Go North Alaska Adventure Travel Center. Since 1991, this Fairbanks business has been organizing Brooks Range tours. ☎907/479–7272 or 866/236–7272 ⊕www.paratours.net.

Fodor'sChoice ★
St. Elias Alpine Guides. For more than a quarter century, this outfitter has been leading mountain hikes, nature tours, and extended backpacking expeditions in the St. Elias and Wrangell mountain ranges. ☎888/933–5427 or 907/554–4445 ⊕www.steliasguides.com.

HORSE PACKING

To minimize a horse-packing group's impact on the environment, most are limited to 12 riders, and some to just three or four. Most outfits post at least two wranglers for 12 guests, and some bring along another person who serves as cook and/or assistant wrangler. Outfitters who operate on federal lands must have a permit.

■TIP→ It's a good idea to find out how much time is spent in the saddle each day and how difficult the riding is. Six hours is a long day in the saddle, and although some outfitters schedule that much, most keep the riding time to about four hours. Most trips move at a walk, but some trot, lope, and even gallop. As with many other guided adventures, special expertise is not required for horse packing, and guides will train you in the basics before setting out.

On trips into the wilderness, expect the food to be straightforward cowboy fare, cooked over a campfire or cookstove. Guides often pull double duty in the kitchen, and often a little help from group members is appreciated. If you have dietary restrictions, make arrangements beforehand. For lodging, don't allow yourself to be surprised: find out what the rooms are like if you're going to be staying in motels or cabins, and if the trip involves camping, ask about the campsites and the shower and latrine arrangements.

TOP REGIONS & EXPERIENCES

SOUTH CENTRAL Encompassing more than 13 million acres of mountains, glaciers, and remote river valleys, **Wrangell-St. Elias National Park & Preserve** is wild and raw. There's no better way to absorb the enormity and natural beauty of this region than on horseback. Centuries-old game trails and networks blazed and maintained by contemporary outfitters wind through lowland spruce forests and into wide-open high-country tundra. From there, horses can take you almost anywhere, over treeless ridgelines and to sheltered campsites on the shores of scenic tarns.

> **SADDLE UP!**
>
> There are no traffic jams, no overcrowded campgrounds on horse-packing vacations. The farther into the wilderness you go, the more untouched and spectacular the landscape. You can also cover a lot more ground with less effort than you can backpacking. Before you book, ask your outfitter for suggestions on appropriate clothing, footwear, and gear.

Closer to the state's population center in South Central, yet no less magnificent for horse packing, is the Kenai Peninsula. Outfitters frequently travel the well-groomed mountain trails of the **Chugach National Forest** and **Kenai Mountains.** In both regions, wildlife is abundant: moose, bear, Dall sheep, mountain goats, and wolves are frequently seen. Although overnight cabins are occasionally available, guests should come prepared to camp outdoors.

RESOURCES & GUIDES

Alaska Horsemen. This Cooper Landing–based company offers multiday pack trips into the Kenai Mountains via Crescent Lake, Resurrection, and other area trail systems. ☎*907/595–1806 or 800/595–1806 ⊕www.alaskahorsemen.com.*

Castle Mountain Outfitters. Based in Chickaloon, north of Anchorage in Matanuska Valley, this outfitter conducts a variety of trips ranging from guided hour-long horseback rides to one-week expeditions. ☎*907/745–6427 ⊕www.mtaonline.net/~cmoride/index.html.*

D & S Alaskan Trail Rides. Specializing in short rides of Denali State Park, these outfitters are right off the Parks Highway, north of Anchorage.

☎907/733–2207, 907/733–2205, or 907/745–2208 *winter months* ⊕*www.alaskantrailrides.com.*

Wrangell Outfitters. This husband-wife team from Fairbanks takes visitors on horse-packing trips into the heart of Wrangell–St. Elias National Park & Preserve. ☎907/479–5343 ⊕*www.wrangelloutfitters.com.*

RIVER RAFTING

So much of Alaska is roadless wilderness that rivers often serve as the best avenues to explore the landscape. This is especially true in several of Alaska's premier parklands and refuges. Here, as elsewhere, rivers are ranked according to their degrees of difficulty. ■ TIP➔ **Class I rivers are considered easy floats with minimal rapids; at the other extreme, Class VI rivers are extremely dangerous and nearly impossible to navigate. Generally, only very experienced river runners should attempt anything above Class II on their own.** Also be aware that river conditions change considerably from season to season and sometimes day to day, so always check on a river's current condition. The National Weather Service Alaska–Pacific River Forecast Center keeps tabs on Alaska's most popular streams. The center's Web site (⊕*aprfc.arh.noaa.gov/ak_ahps2.php*) provides the latest data on water levels and flow rates, including important flood-stage alerts.

Do-it-yourselfers would be wise to consult two books on Alaska's rivers: *Fast & Cold: A Guide to Alaska Whitewater* (Skyhouse), by Andrew Embick (though intended primarily for white-water kayakers, it has good information for rafters as well), and *The Alaska River Guide: Canoeing, Kayaking, and Rafting in the Last Frontier* (Alaska Northwest Books), by Karen Jettmar.

Fortunately you don't have to be an expert river runner to explore many of Alaska's premier waterways. Experienced rafting companies operate throughout the state. Some outfits emphasize extended wilderness trips and natural-history observations, whereas others specialize in thrilling one-day (or shorter) runs down Class III and IV white-water rapids that will get your adrenaline pumping. And some combine a little of both.

TOP REGIONS & EXPERIENCES

Never has the term "it's all good" been truer than in the context of river rafting in Alaska. With thousands of rivers to choose from, virtually every region of the state promises prime rafting. Which region and river you float depends largely upon the impetus of your trip. White-water thrill-seekers

RIOTOUS RIVERS

From the Southeast Panhandle to the far reaches of the Arctic, Alaska is blessed with an abundance of wild, pristine rivers. The federal government has officially designated more than two dozen Alaska streams as "wild and scenic rivers," but hundreds more would easily qualify. Some meander gently through forests or tundra. Others, fed by glacier runoff, rush wildly through mountains and canyons.

will find challenging streams tumbling from the mountainous areas of South Central, while rafters interested in sportfishing may choose extended float trips on the gentler salmon- and trout-rich rivers of Southwest. Birders and campers may consider the pristine rivers draining the North Slope of the Brooks Range or Northwest Alaska. Beyond your agenda, though, which river you choose to float should depend upon your rafting and backcountry skills. If there's any question at all, go with an experienced river guide.

SOUTH
CENTRAL

For those seeking the adrenaline surge of white-water rafting, South Central offers many accessible and affordable options. **Chugach National Forest's Six-Mile River,** about a 90-minute drive south of Anchorage on the Seward Highway, is relished for its Class VI and V white water and spectacular canyon scenery. Options available off the highway system north of Anchorage include the glacial **Eagle** and **Matanuska** rivers, each known for varying degrees of white water.

THE INTERIOR
& THE BUSH

North of Anchorage via the Parks Highway, the **Nenana River** flows along the eastern side of Denali National Park & Preserve, offering a variety of conditions ranging from calm to Class III and IV.

Flowing north out of the eastern Brooks Range to the Arctic Ocean, the **Kongakut** and **Hulahula** rivers promise far-flung wilderness adventures. As much as the water, trips here are about seeing the high Arctic tundra landscape and wildlife such as caribou, grizzly bears, musk ox, and thousands of nesting birds.

RESOURCES & GUIDES

Be certain that the guide gives you a safety talk before going on the water. It's important to know what you should do if you do get flipped out of the raft or if the boat overturns. Also, when arranging your trip well in advance, find out what gear and clothing are required. Ask if you'll be paddling or simply riding as a passenger. Reputable rafting companies will discuss all of this, but it never hurts to ask.

★ **Alaska Discovery.** This Juneau-based outfitter leads 9- to 12-day trips down two of North America's wildest rivers, the Tatshenshini and Alsek. The trips begin in Canada and end in Glacier Bay. Also check out the rafting/hiking trips in the Arctic National Wildlife Refuge and Gates of the Arctic. ☎*800/586–1911* ⊕*www.akdiscovery.com.*

Alaska Outdoor Adventures. South Central's Six-Mile River and Turnagain Pass are two trips offered by this Whittier-based company. ☎*907/472–2534 or 877/472–2534* ⊕*www.akadventures.com.*

Alaska Wildland Adventures. Head down the Kenai River and learn about the surroundings and wildlife with these guides. ☎*800/478–4100* ⊕*www.alaskarivertrips.com.*

Chugach Adventure Guides. Right outside of Anchorage, this company has plenty of trips on offer, from Six-Mile River to a Talkeetna four-day float. ☎*907/783–4354* ⊕*www.alaskanrafting.com.*

Chugach Outdoor Center. Head to Hope, about a 90-minute drive south of Anchorage, for a broad regional menu ranging from nearby **Six-Mile**

5

River's Class IV and V white water to the Talkeetna River north of Anchorage and Denali's **Nenana River.** Van shuttles from Anchorage are available with advance reservations. ☎*907/277–7238 or 866/277–7238* ⊕*www.chugachoutdoorcenter.com.*

Denali Raft Adventures. River trips are conducted on the glacially fed, white-water Nenana River, which skirts the eastern boundary of Denali National Park & Preserve. Trips vary from two-hour scenic floats to all-day white-water canyon trips. ☎*907/683–2234 or 888/683–2234* ⊕*www.denaliraft.com.*

FodorsChoice **Nova.** These super-experienced guides offer white-water trips down the
★ Matanuska, Chickaloon, and Talkeetna rivers in South Central Alaska; multiday float trips through Wrangell–St. Elias and part-day trips on the Kenai Peninsula's Six-Mile River. White-water ratings range from Class I to Class V. ☎*800/746–5753* ⊕*www.novalaska.com.*

SEA KAYAKING

FodorsChoice Sea kayaking can be as thrilling or as peaceful as you want. More stable
★ than a white-water kayak and more comfortable than a canoe, a sea kayak, even one loaded with a week's worth of gear, is maneuverable enough to poke into hidden crevices, explore side bays, and beach on deserted spits of sand. Don't assume, though, that if you've kayaked 10 minutes without tipping over you'll be adequately prepared to circumnavigate Glacier Bay National Park & Preserve. There's a lot to learn, and until you know your way around tides, currents, and nautical charts, you should go with an experienced guide who also knows what and how to pack and where to pitch a tent.

It's important to honestly evaluate your tolerance for cold, dampness, and high winds. Nothing can ruin a trip faster than pervasive discomfort. ■**TIP**➔ **Ask whether the outfitter stocks a variety of boats, so you can experiment until you find the kayak that best fits your weight, strength, ability, and paddling style.**

TOP REGIONS & EXPERIENCES

SOUTHEAST This largely roadless coastal region is the setting of North America's last great temperate wilderness. Sometimes called Alaska's Panhandle, this appendage of islands, mainland, and fjords is a sparsely populated, scenic paradise for sea kayaking. In deep Southeast, Ketchikan is a popular starting point for many sea kayakers. Set in the heart of the **Tongass National Forest** and well within paddling range of the **Misty Fiords National Monument,** this former logging town is home to several sea kayaking guides and rental businesses. Ketchikan is also a stop on the Alaska Marine Highway, making it convenient for travelers to simply drive or walk off the state ferry and spend a couple of days exploring local bays and fjords before boarding another ferry.

An equally popular destination for Southeast saltwater paddlers is **Glacier Bay National Park & Preserve.** The hub for this region is Juneau, where kayakers can hop a plane or ferry to the small community of Gustavus, located within the park.

SOUTH
CENTRAL

Prince William Sound, with its miles of bays, islands, forests, and glaciers is a big draw for sea kayakers. Popular ports include Whittier, Cordova, and Valdez. Of the three, Whittier and Valdez are on the state highway system, making them most accessible (Whittier is a one-hour drive south from Anchorage). Guides catering to ocean paddlers are found in all three ports.

Two Kenai Peninsula venues also lure sea kayakers. About a two-hour drive south of Anchorage, at the terminus of the Seward Highway, **Resurrection Bay** serves up awesome scenery and marine wildlife. Homer, perched over **Kachemak Bay,** at the terminus of the Sterling Highway (a five-hour drive south of Anchorage), is also an excellent spot.

RESOURCES & GUIDES

Fodor's Choice
★

Alaska Discovery. These experienced guides know Southeast Alaska intimately, and they emphasize skills and safety. Destinations include Tracy Arm, Glacier Bay, Icy Bay, Point Adolphus (for whale-watching), and Admiralty Island (with bear viewing at Pack Creek). Also check out the inn-to-inn paddling trip through the Kenai Peninsula's Kachemak Bay. ☎800/586–1911 ⊕www.akdiscovery.com.

Anadyr Adventures. Prince William Sound comes alive from a sea kayak. See for yourself with Anadyr, based in Valdez. ☎907/835–2814 or 800/865–2925 ⊕www.anadyradventures.com.

Prince William Sound Kayak Center. Operating out of Whittier since 1981, this center provides kayak rentals, introductory classes, guided day tours, and escorted trips in Prince William Sound. ☎907/276–7235 or 877/472–2452 ⊕www.pwskayakcenter.com.

Southeast Exposure. Over twenty years in the business translates into great trips with this Ketchikan outfit. Their most popular paddle is through Misty Fiords National Monument. ☎907/225–8829 ⊕www.southeastexposure.com.

Spirit Walker Expeditions. This veteran Southeast company (based in Gustavus) gives guided wilderness sea kayaking trips that combine scenery, wildlife, solitude, and paddling within the Inside Passage. Guides prepare meals, offer instruction, and provide all gear. Beginners are welcome. ☎907/697–2266 or 800/529–2537 ⊕www.seakayakalaska.com.

Sunny Cove Sea Kayaking. Extended trips in and around Kenai Fjords National Park involve paddling among icebergs, seals, and seabirds as tidewater glaciers calve in the distance. Day and overnight trips explore Resurrection Bay, near Seward. Tours include equipment, instruction, and meals. ☎907/224–8810, 800/770–9119 reservations ⊕www.sunnycove.com.

SKIING & SNOWBOARDING

Alaska is a great destination for Nordic, downhill, and extreme downhill skiing. Three of the state's largest cities—Anchorage, Fairbanks, and Juneau—have nearby ski areas, complete with equipment rentals and ski schools. Many of Alaska's towns have maintained trails for cross-country skiers. Anchorage's trail system ranks among the nation's finest and hosts world-class races.

For those who are more ambitious, Alaska's wilderness areas present plenty of opportunities, and lots of challenges. Unless you are knowledgeable in winter backcountry travel, camping techniques, and avalanche dangers, the best strategy is to hire a guide when exploring Alaska's backcountry on skis.

> ### THE STROKES
>
> Anyone who doesn't mind getting a little wet and has an average degree of fitness can be a sea kayaker. The basic stroke is performed in a circular motion with a double-bladed paddle: you pull one blade through the water while pushing forward with the other through the air. Most people pick it up with a minimal amount of instruction.

■ **TIP**➜ **Given the extremes of Alaska's winters, your primary concern should be safety: be sure your guide has had avalanche-awareness and winter-survival training.** Conditions can change quickly, especially in mountainous areas, and what begins as an easy cross-country ski trip can suddenly become a survival saga if you're not prepared for the challenges of an Alaska winter.

TOP REGIONS & EXPERIENCES

SOUTHEAST **Eaglecrest** gets high marks for excellent spring skiing. Set 12 mi outside of Juneau, ski season runs December through mid-April. This hill is rarely crowded and the views on a bright day are remarkable.

SOUTH CENTRAL & THE INTERIOR **Alyeska Resort,** located 40 mi south of Anchorage in Girdwood, is Alaska's largest and best-known downhill ski resort. It encompasses 1,000 acres of terrain for all skill levels. Ski rentals are available at the resort. Local ski and snowboard guides teach classes on the mountain and offer helicopter ski and snowboard treks into more remote venues in the nearby Chugach and Kenai ranges.

Closer to Anchorage, two much smaller ski hill operations, **Alpenglow** and **Hilltop,** offer great runs for beginners. Both are also good options when the weather occasionally rules out Alyeska.

Moose Mountain, outside of Fairbanks, is the ski and snowboard draw for visitors to the Interior. More than 1,250 feet of terrain includes everything from bunny slopes to vertical. Best of all, while the city is known for frigid winters, the mountain enjoys warmer temperatures.

RESOURCES & GUIDES

Alaska Mountaineering School. Custom cross-country ski trips of varying lengths and degrees of difficulty can be arranged, primarily through Denali national and state parks, with an emphasis on natural history. ☎907/733–1016 ⊕ *www.climbalaska.org.*

Fodor's Choice **Alaska Nature Tours.** This company in Southeast rents ski and snow-
★ board gear and conducts trips into the amazing Alaska Chilkat Bald Eagle Preserve near Haines. ☎907/766–2876 ⊕ *www.alaskanature-tours.net.*

Chugach Powder Guides. This decade-old helicopter-ski and snowcat operation focuses on backcountry skiing and snowboarding in the Chugach Range out of Girdwood and Seward; Alaska Range adventures are also featured. ☎907/783–4354 ⊕*www.chugachpowderguides.com.*

SPORTFISHING

Fodor's Choice
★
Five species of Pacific salmon (king, silver, sockeye, pink, and chum) spawn in Alaska's innumerable rivers and creeks, alongside rainbow trout, cutthroat trout, steelhead, arctic char, sheefish, Dolly Varden char, arctic grayling, northern pike, and lake trout, among other freshwater species. Salmon are also caught in saltwater, along with halibut, lingcod, many varieties of rockfish (locally called snapper or sea bass), and salmon sharks that can weigh more than 800 pounds.

> **GONE FISHIN'**
>
> Famous for streams rich in salmon, trophy-size trout and char, and sizable saltwater catches, Alaska is an angler's paradise. It's one thing to have so many fish-packed rivers to choose from; it's an added bonus that the backdrop is some of the most stunning scenery in the world.

Alaska's salmon sharks aren't the only sport fish capable of reaching huge proportions: the world-record king salmon, weighing 97¼ pounds, was caught in the Kenai River, and halibut exceeding 300—and occasionally 400—pounds are annually caught off Alaska's coasts. Even so, some anglers will tell you that bigger isn't necessarily better. Sockeyes, medium-weight salmon averaging 6 to 8 pounds, are considered by many to be the best tasting and best fighting, pound for pound, of any fish. And though the sail-finned arctic grayling commonly weighs a pound or less, its willingness to rise for dry flies makes it a favorite among fly fishermen.

■**TIP→** Sportfishing regulations vary widely from area to area. Licenses are required for both fresh- and saltwater fishing. To learn more about regulations, contact the **Alaska Department of Fish and Game** (☎907/465–4180 *sportfishing seasons and regulations, 907/465–2376 licenses ⊕www. adfg.state.ak.us*). To purchase a fishing license online, visit the state of Alaska Web site (⊕*www.admin.adfg.state.ak.us/license*).

TOP REGIONS & EXPERIENCES

Roadside fishing for salmon, trout, char, pike, and grayling is in **South Central** and **Interior Alaska.** In fact, Alaska's best-known salmon stream, the **Kenai River,** parallels the Sterling Highway. But in most of the state, prime fishing waters can be reached only by boat or air. Not surprisingly, hundreds of fishing charters and dozens of sportfishing lodges operate statewide, attracting anglers from around the world. **Southwest Alaska,** in particular, is known for its fine salmon, trout, and char fishing; many of its best spots are remote and expensive to reach, but fishing opportunities here are unparalleled.

SOUTHEAST This huge coastal region is renowned for its outstanding sportfishing for salmon, rockfish, and halibut. Charters operate out of all main ports and the action is frequently so good that catching a limit is almost a given. Splendid scenery is guaranteed—even when shrouded in misty rains, which are common. Streams offer fine angling for steelhead, cutthroat trout, rainbow trout, and Dolly Varden. The waters of **Prince of Wales Island** are especially popular among steelhead, salmon, and trout anglers, with the Karta and Thorne rivers among the favorites.

SOUTH CENTRAL & THE INTERIOR Alaska lives up to its reputation for angling excellence in South Central. From the hub of Anchorage, the Seward and Sterling highways provide access to the world-famous spots on the Kenai Peninsula. Anglers seeking rainbow trout, Dolly Varden, and salmon will do no better than the **Kenai River.** This dream stream—tinted an opaque emerald from glacial runoff—serves up fine fishing from ice-out in spring to freeze-up in late fall. The **Russian River,** a tributary which joins the upper Kenai River near Cooper Landing, is a dashing mountain stream that runs crystal-clear—except when it's chock-full of red salmon from mid-June through August. Other fine Kenai Peninsula streams include **Quartz Creek, Deep Creek,** and **Anchor River.** Many excellent trout and salmon guides are based in the Kenai River towns of Cooper Landing, Sterling, Soldotna, and Kenai.

Saltwater angling out of the ports of **Whittier, Seward,** and **Homer** is legendary for king, pink, and silver salmon as well as for rockfish, lingcod, and huge halibut. Charter operators are in all three ports, offering half-day and full-day fishing trips.

North of Anchorage, the Parks Highway courses through the **Mat-Su Valley,** a scenic piece of wilderness backed by Mt. McKinley and veined with fine streams. Five species of salmon, rainbow trout, Dolly Varden, grayling, northern pike, and lake trout are among the draws here. Some of the most popular Parks Highway streams include **Willow, Sheep, Montana,** and **Clear** creeks. Fishing guides based in Wasilla, Houston, Willow, and Talkeetna offer riverboat and fly-in trips. Remember that salmon runs are seasonal. Kings run late May through mid-July, and silvers run from mid-July through August. And don't forget the lakes; scores of them brim with trout, landlocked salmon, arctic char, and grayling. Cast for them from canoes or float tubes on calm summer afternoons.

THE BUSH The most popular bush sportfishing region is roadless **Southwest,** home of the richest salmon runs in the world. Along with huge schools of red salmon, kings, silvers, chums, and pinks, anglers will find trophy rainbow trout, Dolly Varden, arctic grayling, and arctic char. Many anglers fish with guides based out of remote fishing lodges located on rivers and lakes. Others do it themselves, arranging for bush planes to drop them off in headwater streams, then floating the river in rafts, fishing along the way until reaching a prearranged pickup point.

RESOURCES, GUIDES & CHARTERS

When hiring a guide, ask about species likely to be caught when you'll be visiting, catch limits, and any special equipment or clothing needs. Normally, all necessary fishing gear is provided and the guides will teach you the appropriate fishing techniques. In some cases, catch-and-release may be emphasized. Prime time for saltwater fishing is July through mid-August; for river trips, mid-June through September.

Alaska Fishing Online. This Web resource provides listings of fishing charter services, air-taxi operators, and angling lodges around the state. Browse listings by region, and shop around for the best price. Also, ask plenty of questions to ensure you find the outfit best suited to your needs. ⊕ *www.alaskafishing.com.*

Alaska River Adventures. These Cooper Landing–based guides take small groups fishing throughout the region, with self-professed "well-seasoned old pros." ☎ *907/595–2000 or 888/836–9027* ⊕ *www. alaskariveradventures.com.*

Alaska Wildland Adventures. From their lodge in Cooper Landing south of Anchorage, these folks provide fishing adventures on the upper and lower Kenai River. ☎ *907/783–2928 or 800/334–8730* ⊕ *www. alaskawildland.com.*

Alaskan Fishing Adventures. Anglers are guided in several areas of the Kenai Peninsula, including Resurrection Bay, Cook Inlet, and the Kenai River, home of the famous Kenai king salmon that may weigh 90 pounds. Among the other species they catch are halibut, sockeye and silver salmon, and rainbow trout. Boats have a four-person limit on rivers, six-person limit on saltwater. ☎ *800/548–3474* ⊕ *www. alaskanfishing.com.*

Central Charter Booking Agency. In Homer, this company can arrange fishing trips in outer Kachemak Bay and Lower Cook Inlet——areas known for excellent halibut fishing. Boat sizes vary considerably; some have a six-person limit, whereas others can take up to 16 passengers. ☎ *907/235–7847 or 800/478–7847* ⊕ *www.centralcharter.com.*

The Fish House. Operating out of Seward since 1974, this booking agency represents dozens of Resurrection Bay and **Kenai Peninsula** fishing charters and can hook you up for half-day or full-day charters. ☎ *907/224–3674 or 800/257–7760* ⊕ *www.thefishhouse.net.*

Great Alaska Adventure Lodge. Fishing packages are run out of this Kenai River lodge. Trips with expert guides include fly-in fish camps, river floats, and saltwater charters. Stories are traded at happy hour in the lodge. ☎ *907/262–4515 in summer, 360/697–6454 in winter, 800/544– 2261 year-round* ⊕ *www.greatalaska.com.*

ENJOYING ALASKA'S WILDLIFE

Alaska's 375 million acres support more than 800 species of mammals, birds, and fish. The 105 different mammals range from whales to shrews (Alaska's shrews are the smallest of North America's land mammals, weighing [1//10] ounce). Some 478 species of birds range from hummingbirds to bald eagles, including species found nowhere else in North America. Migrant birds come here annually from every continent and many islands to take advantage of Alaska's rich breeding and rearing grounds in its wetlands, rivers, shores, and tundra. Among the 430 different kinds of fish—including five kinds of salmon—some weigh more than 400 pounds (halibut) whereas others more commonly weigh less than a pound (arctic grayling).

The largest numbers of animals are seen during migration periods. The state is strategically positioned for creatures that migrate vast distances. Some birds fly from the southern tip of South America to nest and rear their young on sandbars in Alaska's wild rivers. Others travel from parts of Asia to thrive in Alaska's summers. The arctic tern comes all the way from Antarctica. Sea mammals congregate in great numbers in the waters of Prince William Sound, the Panhandle, the Gulf of Alaska, and the Bering, Beaufort, and Chukchi seas. Hundreds of thousands of caribou move across the Arctic, including the Porcupine herd (named after the Porcupine River), which travels between Canada and Alaska. Anadromous fish by the millions swim up Alaska's rivers, returning unerringly to the waters where they were born.

Bears live in virtually every part of the state, and though they are often solitary, it is not unusual to see a sow with cubs. In some areas bears gather in large numbers to feed upon rich runs of salmon. Several world-class bear-viewing areas from Southeast to Southwest Alaska attract visitors. Moose abound in the wetter country of the Southeast, as well as in forested portions of South Central and Interior Alaska. Caribou wander over the tundra country of the Arctic, sub-Arctic, and South Central. The coastal mountains of Southeast and South Central harbor mountain goats, and the mountains of the South Central, Interior, and Arctic regions are home to white Dall sheep. Wolves and lynx, though more rarely seen, live in many parts of the Southeast, South Central, Interior, and Arctic regions, and if you're lucky, a wolf may dash across the road in front of you, or a smaller mammal, such as a red fox or snowshoe hare, may watch you when you're rafting or even when you're traveling on wheels.

STRATEGIES FOR SPOTTING WILDLIFE

Know what you're looking for. Season and time of day are critical. Many animals are nocturnal and best viewed during twilight, which during summer in Alaska's northern regions can last all night. In the winter, large creatures such as moose and caribou can be spotted from far away, as their dark bodies stand out against the snow. It is also possible to track animals after a fresh snowfall. You have only a few hours of sunlight each day during which you can look for wildlife in winter, and in northern Alaska, there won't be any direct sunlight at all during the winter months.

Be careful. Keep a good distance, especially with animals that can be dangerous. Whether you're on foot or in a vehicle, don't get too close. A pair of good binoculars or a spotting scope is well worth the expense and extra weight. Don't get too close to or touch wildlife (and, if you're traveling with pets, keep them leashed). **Move slowly,** stop often, look, and listen. The exception is when you see a bear; let the animal know you're there with noise. Avoid startling an animal and risking a danger-

Continued on page 249

KEEPERS OF THE DEEP:
A LOOK AT ALASKA'S WHALES

It's unforgettable: a massive, barnacle-encrusted humpback breaches skyward from the placid waters of an Alaskan inlet, shattering the silence with a thundering display of grace, power, and beauty. Welcome to Alaska's coastline.

Alaska's cold, nutrient-rich waters offer a bounty of marine life that's matched by few regions on earth. Eight species of whales frequent the state's near-shore waters, some migrating thousands of miles each year to partake in Alaska's marine buffet. The state's most famous cetaceans (the scientific classification of marine mammals that includes whales, dolphins, and porpoises) are the humpback whale, the gray whale, and the Orca (a.k.a. the killer whale).

(top) A breaching humpback (left) An Orca whale

Best Regions to View Whales

Whales can be viewed throughout the world; after all, they are migratory animals. But thanks to its pristine environment, diversity of cetacean species, and jaw-dropping beauty, Alaska is perhaps the planet's best whale-watching locale.

From April through October, humpbacks visit many of Alaska's coastal regions, including the Bering Sea, the Aleutian Islands, and Prince William Sound. The **Inside Passage,** though, is the best place to see them: it's home to a migratory population of up to 600 humpbacks. Good bets for whale-viewing include taking a trip on the **Alaska Marine Highway,** spending time in **Glacier Bay National Park,** or taking a day cruise out of any of Southeast's main towns. While most humpbacks return to

Mutually curious!

Hawaiian waters in the winter, some spend the whole year in Southeast Alaska.

Gray whales favor the coastal waters of the Pacific, which terminate in the Bering Sea. Their healthy population—some studies estimate that 30,000 gray whales populate the west coast of North America—make

THE HUMPBACK: Musical, Breaching Giant

Humpbacks' flukes allow them to breach so effectively that they can propel two-thirds of their massive bodies out of the water.

Known for their spectacular breaching and unique whale songs, humpbacks are captivating. Most spend their winters in the balmy waters off the Hawaiian Islands, where females, or sows, give birth. Come springtime, humpbacks set off on a 3,000-mile swim to their Alaskan feeding grounds.

Southeast Alaska is home to one of the world's only groups of bubble-net feeding humpbacks. Bubble-netting is a cooperative hunting technique in which one humpback circles below a school of baitfish while exhaling a "net" of bubbles, causing the fish to gather. Other humpbacks then feed at will from the deliciously dense group of fish.

The Song of the Humpback

All whale species communicate sonically, but the humpback is the most musical. During mating season, males emit haunting, songlike calls that can last for up to 30 minutes at a time. Most scientists attribute the songs to flirtatious, territorial, or competitive behaviors.

QUICK FACTS:

Scientific name:
Megaptera novaeangliae

Length: Up to 50 feet

Weight: Up to 90,000 pounds (45 tons)

Coloring: Dark blue to black, with barnacles and knobby, lighter-colored flippers

Life span: 30 to 40 years

Reproduction: One calf every 2 to 3 years; calves are generally 12 feet long at birth, weighing up to 2,000 pounds (1 ton)

them relatively easy to spot in the spring and early summer months, especially around **Sitka** and **Kodiak Island** and south of the **Kenai Peninsula**, where numerous whale-watching cruises depart from Seward into **Resurrection Bay.**

Orcas populate nearly all of Alaska's coastal regions. They're most commonly viewed in the **Inside Passage** and **Prince William Sound,** where they reside year-round. A jaunt on the Alaska Marine Highway is one option, but so is a kayaking or day-cruising trip out of **Whittier** to Prince William Sound.

When embarking on a whale-watching excursion, don't forget rain gear, a camera, and binoculars!

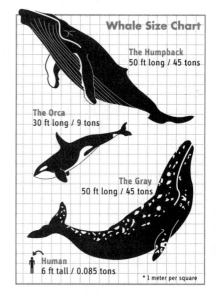

Whale Size Chart

The Humpback
50 ft long / 45 tons

The Orca
30 ft long / 9 tons

The Gray
50 ft long / 45 tons

Human
6 ft tall / 0.085 tons

* 1 meter per square

THE GRAY WHALE: Migrating Leviathan

Though the average lifespan of a gray whale is 50 years, one individual was reported to reach 77 years of age—a real old-timer.

While frequenting Alaska during the long days of summer, gray whales tend stay close to the coastline. They endure the longest migration of any mammal on earth—some travel 14,000 mi each way between Alaska's Bering Sea and their mating grounds in sunny Baja California.

Gray whales are bottom-feeders that stir up sediment on sea floor, then use their baleen—a comblike collection of long, stiff hairs inside their mouths—to filter out sediment and trap small crustaceans and tube worms.

Their predilection for near-shore regions, coupled with their easy going demeanor—some "friendly" gray whales have even been known to approach small tour boats—cements their spot on the short list of Alaska's favorite cetacean celebrities. (Gray whales aren't always in such amicable spirits: whalers dubbed mother gray whales "devilfish" for the fierce manner in which they protected their young.)

QUICK FACTS:

Scientific name:
Eschrichtius robustus

Length: Up to 50 feet

Weight: Up to 90,000 pounds (45 tons)

Coloring: Gray and white, usually splotched with lighter growths and barnacles

Life span: 50 years

Reproduction: One calf every 2 years; calves are generally 15 feet long at birth, weighing up to 1,500 pounds (3/4 ton)

An Age-Old Connection

Nearly every major native group in Alaska has relied on whales for some portion of their diet. The Inupiaq and Yup'ik counted on whales for blubber, oil, meat, and intestines to survive. Aleuts used whale bones to build their semisubterranean homes. Even the Tlingit, for whom food was perennially abundant, considered a beached whale a bounty.

Subsistence whaling lives on in Alaska: although gray-whale hunting was banned in 1996, the Eskimo Whaling Commission permits the state's native populations to harvest 50 bowhead whales every year.

Other Alaskan whale species:

Bowhead, northern right, minke, fin, and beluga whales also inhabit Alaskan waters.

barnacles

BARNACLES These ragged squatters of the sea live on several species of whales, including humpbacks and gray whales. They're conspicuously absent from smaller marine mammals, such as Orcas, dolphins, and porpoises. The reason? Speed. Scientists theorize that barnacles are only able to colonize the slowest-swimming cetacean species, leaving the faster swimmers free from their unwanted drag.

THE ORCA: Conspicuous, Curious Cetacean

Why the name killer whale? Perhaps for this animal's skilled and fearsome hunting techniques, which are sometimes used on other, often larger, cetaceans.

Perhaps the most recognizable of all the region's marine mammals, Orcas (also called killer whales) are playful, inquisitive, and intelligent whales that reside in Alaskan waters year-round. Orcas travel in multigenerational family groups known as pods, which practice cooperative hunting techniques.

Orcas are smaller than grays and humpbacks, and their 17-month gestation period is the longest of any cetacean. They are identified by their white-and-black markings, as well as by the knifelike shape of their dorsal fins, which, in the case of mature males, can reach 6 feet in height.

Pods generally adhere to one of three common classifications: **residents**, which occupy inshore waters and feed primarily on fish; **transients**, which occupy larger ranges and hunt sea lions, squid, sharks, fish, and whales; and **offshores**, about which little is known.

QUICK FACTS:

Scientific name: *Orcinus orca*

Length: Up to 30 feet

Weight: Up to 18,000 pounds (9 tons)

Coloring: Smooth, shiny black skin with white eye patches and chin and white belly markings

Life span: 30 to 50 years

Reproduction: One calf every 3 to 5 years; calves are generally 6 feet long at birth, weighing up to 400 pounds (0.2 ton)

ous confrontation, especially with a momma bear with cubs or a cow moose with a calf.

Be prepared to wait; patience often pays off. And if you're an enthusiastic birder or animal watcher, **be prepared to hike over some rough terrain** to reach the best viewing vantage. **Respect and protect** the animal you're watching and its habitat. Don't chase or harass the animals. The willful act of harassing an animal is punishable in Alaska by a $1,000 fine. This includes flushing birds from their nests and purposely frightening animals with loud noises.

Don't disturb or surprise the animals, which also applies to birds' eggs, the young, the nests, and such habitats as beaver dams. It's best to let the animal discover your presence quietly, if at all, by keeping still or moving slowly (except when viewing bears or moose). If you accidentally disturb an animal, limit your viewing time and leave as quietly as possible. **Don't use a tape recorder or any device** to call a bird or to attract other animals if you're in bear country, as you might call a hungry bear. And **don't feed animals,** as any creature that comes to depend on humans for food almost always comes to a sorry end. Both state and federal laws prohibit the feeding of wild animals.

TOP REGIONS & EXPERIENCES

Even those traveling by car in Alaska have abundant opportunity to spot wildlife. For those traveling by boat, the **Alaska Marine Highway,** the route plied by Alaska's state ferries, passes through waters rich with fish, sea mammals, and birds. Throughout the Southeast, ferries often provide sightings of whales, porpoises, and sea otters, and virtually always of bald eagles. In **Kenai Fjords National Park,** tour boats enable you to view sea mammals and seabirds. Smaller boats and touring vessels are found in such places as **Glacier Bay National Park & Preserve,** an especially good place to spot humpback whales, puffins, seals, shorebirds, and perhaps a black or brown bear. **Denali National Park & Preserve** is known worldwide for its wildlife; you are likely to see grizzlies, moose, Dall sheep, caribou, foxes, golden eagles, and wolves. The **Alaska Chilkat Bald Eagle Preserve** hosts the world's largest gathering of bald eagles each fall and winter. And Dall sheep that inhabit **Chugach State Park** can often be seen along the Seward Highway south of Anchorage.

You can't be absolutely sure you'll spot a grizzly bear in **Denali National Park & Preserve** (☎*907/683–2294* ⊕*www.nps.gov/dena*), but chances are better than 50–50 (especially early morning) that you'll see grizzlies digging in the tundra or eating berries. Sometimes females even nurse their cubs within sight of the park road. Talk with the staff at the visitor center near the park entrance when you arrive.

Katmai National Park (☎*907/246–3305* ⊕*www.nps.gov/katm*), on the Alaska Peninsula, has an abundance of bears, on average more than one brown bear per square mile, among the highest densities of any region in North America. In July, when the salmon are running up Brooks River, bears concentrate around Brooks River Falls, resulting in a great view of these animals as they fish, and the spectacle of hundreds of salmon leaping the falls.

Kodiak National Wildlife Refuge (☎907/487–2600 or 888/408–3514 ⊕ *kodiak.fws.gov*), on Kodiak Island, is an excellent place to see brown bears, particularly along salmon-spawning streams.

The **McNeil River State Game Sanctuary,** on the Alaska Peninsula, hosts the world's largest gathering of brown bears (as many as 70 have been counted at one time at McNeil Falls) and thus affords unsurpassed photographic opportunities. Peak season, when the local salmon are running, is early June through mid-August. Much-sought-after reservations are by a lottery conducted in March by the **Alaska Department of Fish and Game** (☎907/267–2182 ⊕ *www.wildlife.alaska.gov*).

At **Pack Creek,** on Admiralty Island in Southeast, brown bears fish for spawning salmon—pink, chum, and silver. To get here, you can fly (air charter) or take a boat from Juneau. If you time your visit to coincide with the salmon runs in July and August, you will almost surely see bald eagles. Permits are required to visit during the peak bear-viewing period; contact **Admiralty Island National Monument** (☎907/586–8790 ⊕ *www.fs.fed.us/r10/tongass/districts/admiralty/packcreek/index. shtml*).

The **Silver Salmon Creek Lodge** (☎888/872–5666 ⊕ *www.silversalmoncreek.com*) conducts a bear-viewing program along the shores of western Cook Inlet, near Lake Clark National Park, with lodging, meals, and guide services for both bear viewing and sportfishing.

BIRDS   If you come on your own, try the following sure and easily accessed bets for bird spotting. In **Anchorage,** walk around Potter Marsh or Westchester Lagoon or along the Tony Knowles Coastal Trail and keep your eye out for shorebirds, waterfowl, and the occasional bald eagle. Songbird enthusiasts are likely to see many species in town or neighboring Chugach State Park. The **Anchorage Audubon Society** (☎907/338–2473 ⊕ *www.anchorageaudubon.org*) has a bird-report recording and offers various trips, such as the Owl Prowl and Hawk Watch.

In **Juneau,** visit the Mendenhall Wetlands State Game Refuge, next to the airport, for ducks, geese, and swans (there are trails and interpretive signs). In **Fairbanks,** head for the Creamer's Field Migratory Waterfowl Refuge on College Road. If you're lucky, you'll see sandhill cranes in summer and spectacular shows of ducks and geese in spring.

The folks at **Alaska Birding & Wildlife** (☎877/424–5637 ⊕ *www.alaskabirding.com*) can take you to St. Paul Island with these folks to see the huge range of birds and get to know local Aleut culture and customs.

Alaska Discovery (☎907/780–6226 or 800/586–1911 ⊕ *www.akdiscovery.com*) offers trips to Pack Creek, including a floatplane trip, sea kayaking, and bear viewing.

With **Mariah Tours** (☎877/777–2805 ⊕ *www.alaskaheritagetours.com*) the Kenai Fjords National Park comes to life on tailor-made birding and photography boat tours.

Ouzel Expeditions (☎ *800/825–8196* ⊕ *www.ouzel.com*) offers seven-day birding float trips in Southwest Alaska and the Arctic National Wildlife Refuge. Trips are in remote fly-in locations; camping and floating quietly along rivers provides wonderful birding opportunities. Southwest birding trips begin in Anchorage; trips in Arctic National Wildlife Refuge begin in Fairbanks.

The Web site of the **University of Alaska Fairbanks** (⊕ *www.uaf.edu/ museum/bird/products/checklist.pdf*) has a checklist of Alaska's 478 bird species.

★ The owners of **Wilderness Birding Adventures** (☎ *907/694–7442* ⊕ *www. wildernessbirding.com*) are both experienced river runners and expert birders. Among their trips is a rafting, hiking, and birding expedition through one of the world's last great wilderness areas, the Arctic National Wildlife Refuge.

CARIBOU The migrations of caribou across Alaska's Arctic regions are wonderful to watch, but they are not always easy to time because of annual variations in weather and routes that the herds follow. The U.S. Fish and Wildlife Service and Alaska Department of Fish and Game will have the best guess as to where you should be and when. Or you can settle for seeing a few caribou in places such as Denali National Park & Preserve.

At **Round Island,** outside Dillingham in the Southwest, bull walruses by the thousands haul out during the summer. Part of the Walrus Islands State Game Sanctuary, Round Island can be visited by permit only. For details, contact the **Alaska Department of Fish and Game** (☎ *907/842–2334* ⊕ *www.wildlife.alaska.gov/index.cfm?adfg=refuge.rnd_is*). Access is by floatplane or, more commonly, by boat. Expect rain, winds, and the possibility of being weathered in. Rubber boots are essential, as are a four-season tent, high-quality rain gear, and plenty of food.

It's easier, but expensive (more than $1,000 for travel and tour) to visit the remote **Pribilof Islands,** where about 80% of the world's northern fur seals and 200 species of birds can be seen, but you may also encounter fog and Bering Sea storms. Tours to the Pribilofs leave from Anchorage. Contact the **Alaska Maritime National Wildlife Refuge** (☎ *907/235–6546 or 907/235–6961* ⊕ *www.r7.fws.gov/nwr/akmar/index.htm*) for information about wildlife viewing.

5

UNDERSTANDING ALASKA

NATIVE ALASKANS

Most of Alaska's Natives still reside in widely scattered communities spread across the ½-million square mi of Alaska. Unlike the Native Americans of the Lower 48 states, the Alaskan Natives have never been restricted to reservations. Many villages remain isolated, the preference of traditional villagers; others have plunged into modern life with mixed results. Recently, Alaska's Native peoples have become more enterprising in the tourist business. No longer content to let out-of-state tour operators have all the business, they are now starting to take charge of tours in their communities.

Eskimos. Most of Alaska's more than 40,000 Eskimos are found in scattered settlements along the Bering Sea and Arctic Ocean coasts, the deltas of the lower Yukon and Kuskokwim rivers in western Alaska, and on remote islands in the Bering Sea such as St. Lawrence, Nunivak, and Little Diomede. The principal Arctic and sub-Arctic Eskimo communities include Barrow, Kotzebue, Nome, Gambell, Savoonga, Point Hope, Wainwright, and Shishmaref.

The Eskimos are divided into two linguistic groups: the Inupiat of the Far North and the Yup'ik, who reside mostly along the coastal regions of the west. The Yup'ik share the same dialect as the Eskimos of Siberia. Both groups are famed for their hunting and fishing skills. They are also noted craftspeople, carving animals and creating jewelry from Native materials.

Indians. Alaska has four major Indian cultures: Tlingit, Haida, Athabascan, and Tsimshian.

Once among North America's most powerful tribes, the **Tlingits** (pronounced *klink*-its) are found mostly throughout coastal Southeast Alaska. They number about 13,000 and live in cities such as Juneau, Ketchikan, and Sitka and in villages from Hoonah, near Juneau, to Klukwan, near Haines.

Haidas are also found mainly in Southeast Alaska, as well as in British Columbia. They number only about 1,000 in Alaska. Their principal community is Hydaburg on Prince of Wales Island, near Ketchikan. The Queen Charlotte Islands of British Columbia are another Haida center. Historically, the Haidas were far-ranging voyagers and traders. Some historians credit the artistic Haidas with originating totem carving among Alaska's Natives.

Most of Alaska's 7,000 or so **Athabascan** Indians are found in the villages of Alaska's vast Interior, including Fort Yukon, Stevens Village, Beaver, Chalkyitsik, and Minto, near Fairbanks. Other Athabascans are scattered from the Kenai Peninsula–Cook Inlet area, near Anchorage, to the Copper River area near Cordova. Linguistically, the Athabascans are related to the Navajo and Apache of the American Southwest. They were driven out of Canada by Cree tribes more than 700 years ago.

The ancestral home of the **Tsimshian** (pronounced *simp*-shee-ann) Indians was British Columbia, but Tsimshian historians say their forebears roamed through much of southeastern Alaska fishing, hunting, and trading long before the arrival of the white man. The 1,000 or so Tsimshians of Alaska settled in 1887 on Annette Island, near Ketchikan, when a dissident Church of England lay missionary, William Duncan, led them out of British Columbia to escape religious persecution. The town of Metlakatla on Annette Island is their principal community. Their artwork includes wood carvings, from totem poles to ceremonial masks.

By Stanton H. Patty

FAUNA & FLORA
OF ALASKA

FAUNA

(C) Arctic Ground Squirrel (*Spermophilus parryii*): These yellowish brown, gray-flecked rodents are among Alaska's most common and widespread mammals. Ground squirrels are known for their loud, persistent chatter. They may often be seen standing above their tundra den sites, watching for grizzlies, golden eagles, and weasels.

(F) Arctic Tern (*Sterna paradisaea*): These are the world's long-distance flying champs; some members of their species make annual migratory flights between the high Arctic and the Antarctic. Sleekly beautiful, the bird has a black cap and striking blood-red bill and feet. They often can be seen looking for small fish in pond and coastal marshes.

(A) Bald Eagle (*Haliaeetus leucocephalus*): With a wingspan of 6 to 8 feet, these grand Alaska residents are primarily fish

eaters, but they will also take birds or small mammals when the opportunity presents itself. The world's largest gathering of bald eagles occurs in Southeast Alaska each winter, along the Chilkat River near Haines.

(B) Beluga Whale (*Dephinapterus leucas*): Belugas are gray at birth, blueish gray as adolescents, and white as adults (the word *byelukha* is Russian for "white"). Though they seem to favor fish, belugas' diet includes more than 100 different species, from crabs to squid. They range along much of the coast, from the Beaufort Sea to the Gulf of Alaska.

(D) Black-capped chickadee (*Parus atricapillus*): This songbird is one of Alaska's most common residents. With two close relatives, the chestnut-backed and boreal chickadees, the black-cap gets through the winters by lowering its body temper-

ature at night and shivering through the long hours of darkness.

(G) Caribou (*Rangifer tarandus*): Sometimes called the "nomads of the north," caribou are long-distance wandering mammals. They are also the most abundant of the state's large mammals; in fact, there are more caribou in Alaska than people! The Western Arctic Caribou Herd alone numbers more than 400,000 members, while the Porcupine Caribou Herd has ranged between 120,000 and 180,000 over the past decades. Another bit of caribou trivia: they are the only members of the deer family in which both sexes grow antlers. Those of bulls may grow up to 5½ feet long with a span of up to 3 feet.

(E) Common Loon (*Gavia immer*): The common loon is one of five *Gavia* species to inhabit Alaska (the others are the Arctic, Pacific, red-throated, and yellow-billed).

Common loons are primarily fish eaters. Excellent swimmers, they are able to stay submerged for up to three minutes.

Common Raven (*Corvus corax*): A popular character in Alaska native stories, the raven in traditional indigenous culture is both creator and trickster. Entirely black, with a wedge-shaped tail and a heavy bill that helps distinguish it from crows, the raven is Alaska's most widespread avian resident.

Common Redpoll (*Carduelis flammea*): Even tinier than the chickadee, the common redpoll along with its close cousin, the hoary redpoll (*Carduelis hornemanni*), are among the few birds to inhabit Alaska's Interior year-round. Though it looks a bit like a sparrow, this red-capped, black-bibbed songbird is a member of the finch family.

Dall Sheep (*Ovis dalli dalli*): One of four wild sheep to inhabit North America, the white Dall is the only to reside within Alaska. Residents of high alpine areas, the sheep live in mountain chains from the St. Elias Range to the Brooks Range. Though both sexes grow horns, those of females are short spikes, while males grow grand curls that are "status symbols" displayed during mating season.

Dolly Varden (*Salvelinus malma*): This sleek, flashy fish inhabits lakes and streams throughout Alaska's coastal regions. A member of the char family, it was named after a character in Charles Dickens's novel *Barnaby Rudge* because the brightly colored spots on its sides resemble Miss Dolly Varden's pink-spotted dress and hat. Some members of the species remain in freshwater all their life, while sea-run dollies may live in the ocean for two to five years before returning to spawn.

Golden Eagle (*Aquila chrysaetos*): With a wingspan of up to 7½ feet, this inland bird can often be spotted spiraling high in the sky, riding thermals. The bird usually nests on cliff faces and feeds upon small mammals and ptarmigan. The plumage of adult birds is entirely dark, except for a golden head. These migratory eagles spend their winters as far away as Kansas and New Mexico.

Great Horned Owl (*Bubo virginianus*): The best known of Alaska's several species of owls, the call of the great horned is a familiar one here. It is a large owl with prominent ear tufts and a white throat with barred markings. Residing in forests from Southeast Alaska to the Interior, it preys on squirrels, hares, grouse, and other birds.

Harbor Seal (*Phoca vitulina*): Inhabiting shallow marine waters and estuaries along much of Alaska's southern coast, harbor seals may survive up to 30 years in the wild, on a diet of fish, squid, octopus, and shrimp. They, in turn, may be eaten or killed by Orcas, sea lions, or humans. Solitary in the water, harbor seals love company on land, and will gather in large colonies. They weigh up to 250 pounds and range in color from black to white.

Hermit Thrush (*Catharus guttatus*): Some Alaskans argue that there is no northern song more beautiful than the flutelike warbling of the hermit thrush and its close relative, the Swainson's thrush (*Catharus ustulatus*). The two birds are difficult to tell apart, except for their songs, the hermit's reddish brown tail, and the color of their eye rings. Among the many songbird migrants to visit Alaska each spring, they begin singing in May while seeking mates and defending territories in forested regions of southern and central Alaska.

(H) Horned Puffin (*Fratercula corniculata*): Named for the black, fleshy projections above each eye, horned puffins are favorites among birders. Included in the group of diving seabirds known as alcids, puffins spend most of their life on water, coming to land only for nesting. They are expert swimmers, using their wings to "fly" underwater and their webbed feet as rudders. Horned puffins have large orange-red and yellow bills. A close relative, the tufted puffin (*Fratercula cirrhata*), is named for its yellow ear tufts.

Lynx (*Lynx canadensis*): The lynx is the only wild cat to inhabit Alaska. It's a secretive animal that depends on stealth and quickness. It may kill birds, squirrels, and mice, but the cat's primary prey

is the snowshoe hare (*Lepus americanus*), particularly in winter; its population numbers closely follow those of the hare's boom-bust cycles. Large feet and a light body help the lynx run through deep snowpack.

Moose (*Alces alces gigas*): The moose is the largest member of the deer family, with the largest bulls standing 7 feet tall at the shoulders and weighing up to 1,600 pounds. The peak of breeding occurs in late September. Females give birth to calves in late May and early June; twins is the norm. Bulls enter the rut in September, with the most dominant engaging in brutal fights. Though most commonly residents of woodlands, some moose live in or just outside Alaska's cities.

Mountain Goat (*Oreamnos americanus*): Sometimes confused with Dall sheep, mountain goats inhabit Alaska's coastal mountains. As adults, both males and females have sharp-pointed horns that are short and black (sheep have buff-colored horns). They also have massive chests and comparatively small hindquarters, plus bearded chins.

Musk Ox (*Ovibos moschatus*): The musk ox is considered an Ice Age relic that survived into the present at least partly because of a defensive tactic: they stand side by side and form rings to fend off predators such as grizzlies and wolves. Unfortunately for the species, that tactic didn't work very well against humans armed with guns. Alaska's last native musk oxen were killed in 1865. Musk oxen from Greenland were reintroduced here in 1930; they now reside on Nunivak Island. The animal's most notable physical feature is its long guard hairs, which form "skirts" that nearly reach the ground. Inupiats called musk ox *oomingmak*, meaning "bearded one." Beneath those coarser hairs is fine underfur called qiviut, which can be woven into warm clothing.

Pacific Halibut (*Hippoglossus stenolepis*): The halibut is the largest of the flatfish to inhabit Alaska's coastal waters, with females weighing up to 500 pounds. Long-lived "grandmother" halibut may survive 40 years or more, producing millions of eggs each year. Bottom dwellers that feed on fish, crabs, clams, and squid, they range from the Panhandle to Norton Sound. Young halibut generally stay near shore, but older fish have been found at depths of 3,600 feet.

(I) Pacific Salmon (*Oncorhynchus*): Five species of Pacific salmon spawn in Alaska's waters, including the king, silver, sockeye, pink, and chum. Hundreds of millions of salmon return to the state's streams and lakes each summer and fall, after spending much of their lives in saltwater. They form the backbone of Alaska's fishing industry and draw sportfishers from around the world.

Rainbow Trout (*Salmo gairdneri*): A favorite of anglers, the rainbow trout inhabits streams and lakes in Alaska's coastal regions. The Bristol Bay region is best known for large 'bows, perhaps because of its huge returns of salmon. Rainbows feed heavily on salmon eggs as well as the deteriorating flesh of spawned-out salmon. Sea-run rainbows, or steelhead, grow even larger after years spent feeding in ocean waters. The state record for steelhead/rainbow trout is 42 pounds, 3 ounces.

FAUNA & FLORA OF ALASKA

Red Fox (*Vulpes vulpes*): Though it's called the red fox, this species actually has four color phases: red, silver, black, and cross (with a cross pattern on the back and shoulders). An able hunter, the red fox preys primarily on voles and mice, but will also eat hares, squirrels, birds, insects, and berries.

Sandhill Crane (*Grus canadensis*): The sandhill's call has been described as "something between a French horn and a squeaky barn door." Though others may dispute that description, few would disagree that the crane's calls have a prehistoric feeling. And, in fact, scientists say the species has changed little in the 9 million years since its earliest recorded fossils. Sandhills are the tallest birds to inhabit Alaska; their wingspan reaches up to 7 feet. The gray plumage of adults is set off by a bright red crown. Like geese, they fly in Vs during migratory journeys.

(K) Sea Otter (*Enhydra lutris*): Sea otters don't depend on blubber to stay warm. Instead, hair trapped in their dense fur keeps their skin dry. Beneath their outer hairs, the underfur ranges in density from 170,000 to one million hairs per square inch. Not surprisingly, the otter takes good care of its coat, spending much of every day grooming. Otters also spend a lot of time eating. In one study, researchers found that adult otters consumed 14 crabs a day, equaling about one-fourth of their body weight.

Sitka Blacktailed Deer (*Odocoileus hemionus sitkensis*): The Panhandle's rain forest is the primary home of this deer, though it has been transplanted to Prince William Sound and Kodiak. Dark gray in winter, and reddish brown in summer, it's stockier than the whitetails found in the Lower 48. The deer stay at lower elevations during the snowy months of win-

ter, then move up to alpine meadows in summer.

(L) Snowy Owl (*Nyctea scandiaca*): Inhabiting the open coastal tundra, the snowy owl is found from the western Aleutian Islands to the Arctic. Adults are largely white (though females have scattered light brown spots) though immature birds are heavily marked with brown. Their numbers rise and fall with swings in the population of lemmings, their primary prey. Rather than hoots, the snowy emits loud croaks and whistles.

(Q) Steller's Sea Lion (*Eumetopias jubatus*): Its ability—and tendency—to roar is what gives the sea lion its name. Because they can rotate their rear flippers and lift their bellies off the ground, sea lions can get around on land much more easily than seals can. They are also much larger, with males reaching up to 9 feet and weighing up to 1,500 pounds. They feed pri-marily on fish, but will also eat sea otters and seals. They have been designated an endangered species because their populations north of the Panhandle have suffered huge declines.

(P) Walrus (*Odobenus rosmarus*): The walrus's ivory tusks can be dangerous weapons; there are stories of walruses killing polar bears when attacked. Weighing up to 2 tons, the walrus's primary food—which it detects in water with the help of a bristled muzzle—includes clams, mussels, snails, crabs, and shrimp.

(O) Willow Ptarmigan (*Lagopus lagopus*): One of three species of ptarmigan (the others are the rock and the white-tailed), the willow is the most widespread. It is also Alaska's state bird, as picked by schoolchildren in a statewide vote. It tends to live in willow thickets, where it both feeds and hides from a variety of predators. Aggressively protective parents, willow ptarmigan have been known to attack humans to defend their young.

Wolf (*Canis lupus*): The largest and most charismatic of the far North's wild canines, wolves roam throughout all of mainland Alaska. They form close-knit family packs, which may range from a few animals to more than 30. Packs hunt a variety of prey, from small mammals and birds to caribou, moose, and Dall sheep. They communicate with each other through body language, barks, and howls.

Wolverine (*Gulo gulo*): Consider yourself lucky if you see a wolverine, because they are among the most secretive animals of the North. They are also fierce predators, with enormous strength and endurance. Denali biologists once reported seeing a wolverine drag a Dall sheep carcass more than 2 mi; an impressive feat, since the sheep likely weighed four times what the wolverine did. They have been known to run 40 mph through snow when chased by hunters. Though they look a lot like bears and have the ferocity of a grizzly, wolverines are in fact the largest members of the weasel family.

Wood Frog (*Rana sylvatica*): One of the few amphibians to inhabit Alaska, and the only one to live north of the Panhandle, these frogs range as far north as the Arctic, surviving winters through the help of a biochemical change that keeps them in a suspended state, while frozen. Come spring, the bodies revive after thawing. Though they mate and lay eggs in water, wood frogs spend most of their lives on land.

FLORA

Balsam Poplar and Black Cottonwood (*Populus balsamifera* and *Populus trichocarpa*): These two closely related species sometimes interbreed and are difficult, if not impossible, to tell apart. Mature trees of both species have gray bark that is rough and deeply furrowed. In midsummer they produce cottony seed pods. They also have large, shiny, arrowhead-shaped leaves.

Birch (*Betula*): Ranging from Kodiak Island to the Brooks Range, birch trees are important members of Alaska's boreal forests. Deciduous trees that prefer well-drained soils, they have white bark and green heart-to-diamond-shaped leaves with sharp points and toothed edges. One species, the paper birch (*Betula papyrifera*), is easily distinguished by its peeling, paperlike bark.

(J) Blueberry (*Vaccinium*): A favorite of berry pickers, blueberries are found throughout Alaska, except for the farthest northern reaches of the Arctic. They come in a variety of forms, including head-high forest bushes and sprawling tundra mats. Pink, bell-shape flowers bloom in spring and dark blue to almost black fruits begin to ripen in July or August, depending on the locale.

(R) Cow Parsnip (*Heracleum lanatum*): Also known to some as Indian celery, cow parsnip resides in open forests and meadows. The plant may grow several feet high, with dull green leaves the size of

dinner plates; thick, hairy, hollow stalks; and clusters of white flowers. Anyone who harvests—or walks among—this species must take great care. Oils on the stalks, in combination with sunlight, can produce severe skin blistering.

(N) Devil's Club (*Echinopanax horridum*): This is a prickly shrub that may grow 4 to 8 feet high and forms dense, spiny thickets in forests ranging from the Panhandle to South Central. Hikers need to be wary of this plant: its large, maple-like leaves (which can be a foot or more across) have spines, and needles cover its pale brown trunk. In late summer, black bears enjoy its bright red berries.

(M) Salmonberry (*Rubus spectabilis*): The salmonberry canes, on which the leaves and fruits grow, may reach 7 feet tall; they grow in dense thickets. The juicy raspberrylike fruits may be either orange or red at maturity; the time of ripening is late June through August.

Spruce (*Picea*): Three species of spruce grow in Alaska. Sitka spruce (*Picea sitchensis*) is an important member of coastal rain forest communities; white spruce (*Picea glauca*) prefers dry, well-drained soils in boreal forests that stretch from South Central to the Arctic; black spruce (*Picea mariana*) thrives in wet, boggy areas.

Tall fireweed (*Epilobium angustifolium*): The fireweed is among the first plants to reinhabit burn areas and, in the proper conditions, it grows well. Found throughout much of Alaska, it's a beautiful plant, with fuchsia flowers that bloom from the bottom to the top of stalks; it's said that the final opening of flowers is a sign that winter is only weeks away. Spring fireweed shoots can be eaten raw or steamed and its blossoms can be added to salads.

A related species is dwarf fireweed (*Epilobium latifolium*); also known as "river beauty," it is shorter and bushier.

(S) Wild Prickly Rose (*Rosa acicularis*): Serrated leaves grow on prickly spines and fragrant, five-petaled flowers begin blooming in late spring. The flowers vary from light pink to dark red. Appearing in late summer and fall, bright red rose hips rich in vitamin C can be harvested for jellies, soups, or pie.

Willow (*Salix*): An estimated three dozen species of willow grow in Alaska. Some, like the felt-leaf willow (*Salix alaxensis*), may reach tree size; others form thickets; still others, like the Arctic willow (*Salix arctica*), hug the ground in alpine terrain. They often grow thickest in the sub-alpine zone between forest and tundra. Whatever the size, willows produce soft "catkins" (pussy willows), which are actually columns of densely packed flowers without petals. The plant is an important food for many animals, from moose to songbirds.

—Bill Sherwonit

ALASKA: A GEOLOGIC STORY

Most people know about Alaska's oil and gold. But did you know that the state has a desert? That camels once roamed here? That there's a fault line nearly twice as long as the San Andreas Fault? That the largest earthquake ever to hit North America struck Alaska in 1964 and affected the entire planet? That the state has 80 potentially active volcanoes and approximately 100,000 glaciers?

All these physical wonders are geological in origin and are in addition to a North Slope oil supply that accounts for 25% of U.S. production and more than 10% of U.S. consumption as well as caches of gold that fueled more than 20 rushes.

GLACIERS

Nearly all visitors will have at least one encounter with a glacier (with 29,000 square mi of them, they're hard to miss). Courtesy of the Pleistocene Ice Age, high-latitude location, and abundant moisture from the North Pacific, Alaska has approximately 100,000 of these large sheets of ice. The vast majority are in the southern and southeastern parts of the state, as these are the areas with the most moisture. How much moisture? Portions of the Chugach Mountains can gather 600 inches of snow each year, an amount that is comparable, in rain, to the annual precipitation in Seattle. In north-central Alaska, the Brooks Range contains a glacial field of approximately 280 square mi. Although small by Alaskan standards, it is larger than all the glacial fields in the rest of the United States combined, which comprise approximately 230 square mi.

There are alpine or valley glaciers, those that form high in mountain valleys and travel to lower elevations. Alaska harbors several of the great alpine glaciers in the world, found in the high country of the Alaska Range, the Talkeetna, Wrangell, Chugach, St. Elias, and Coast mountains. Some, such as the Bering Glacier, come tantalizingly close to the water. At more than 100 mi in length, and with an area of more than 2,250 square mi, the Bering is the longest and largest Alaskan glacier, its seclusion guarded by Cape St. Elias and the stormy waters of the Gulf of Alaska. Also impressive are the Hubbard, its imposing terminus dominating the head of isolated Yakutat Bay; and the Columbia, foreboding and threatening, calving icebergs that tack in line like Nelson's fleet across the mouth of Valdez Arm.

The Malaspina Glacier is an unusual piedmont glacier. Formed by the coalescence of several glaciers, this 850-square-mi mass is lobate, or fan-shape, and occupies a benchland on the northwest side of Yakutat Bay. So much of the Alaska Range, Wrangell, Chugach, St. Elias, and Coast mountains are covered by glacial ice that it is often more appropriate to talk about ice fields than individual glaciers.

Then there are the great tidewater glaciers of Prince William Sound and southeastern Alaska. Alpine glaciers that come right to the water's edge, they creak, moan, thunder, and calve off great bergs and little bergeys. The world's longest is the previously mentioned Hubbard Glacier, which, because it stretches more than 70 mi from its head in Canada to its terminus in Yakutat Bay, is both an alpine and a tidewater glacier. Sixteen tidewater glaciers can be found in Glacier Bay National Park, 20 in Prince William Sound. Some are advancing, some retreating. Hubbard has not only advanced in recent years but has surged. In 1986, a surge by Hubbard blocked the Russell Fjord at the upper end of Yakutat Bay, turning it into Russell Lake. Later that year, the portion of the glacier acting as a dam in front of Russell Lake gave way, violently releasing the backed-up water to an elevation of 83 feet above sea level. That's pretty impressive when you stop to think that the Russell Fjord is normally at sea level. Surging glaciers can move downhill hundreds of feet per day. The Hubbard's greatest surge was in September 1899, when it advanced ½ mi into the bay in just five minutes, courtesy of an earthquake.

Glaciologists are interested in knowing more about how glaciers, especially tidewater glaciers, advance and retreat. The Columbia Glacier, both an alpine and a tidewater glacier like the Hubbard, in Prince William Sound is approximately 40 mi long, covers more than 400 square mi, and flows to sea level from 10,000- to 12,000-foot peaks in the Chugach Range. Its width at the terminus can be as much as 4 mi; its ice thickness can reach 900 feet (on average 300 feet above the water and 600 feet below). It is also only 8 mi from the shipping lanes traveled by oil tankers leaving the Alaska pipeline terminal at Valdez. Columbia has been receding since the early 1980s, sending berg after berg into Prince William Sound and into the shipping lanes to Valdez, and now that it's receding, it has the potential to calve even more bergs. Although a shallow sill, or shoal, of underwater glacial deposits keeps icebergs more than 100 feet thick from entering Prince William Sound, some big bergs still make it to the shipping lanes. Columbia's calving took its toll just after midnight on March 29, 1989, when Captain Hazlewood of the *Exxon Valdez* steered too far east while trying to avoid bergs in Valdez Arm and ran aground on Bligh Reef.

You can see many glaciers from the Alaska Marine Highway. The tidewater glaciers of Glacier Bay and the Malaspina and Hubbard glaciers in Yakutat Bay are best seen by boat or ship. Sailing into Valdez Arm, you may see more of the Columbia Glacier than you want—it's often coming to see you in the form of scores of bergs and bergeys, forcing you east toward Bligh Reef. Once you are safely ashore in Valdez it's time to look at valley glaciers. You can access either the Valdez or Worthington Glacier by road. If in the Matanuska Valley, go see the Matanuska Glacier. If on the Kenai Peninsula, try either the Exit or Portage Glacier. If you are visiting Juneau, the Mendenhall Glacier is on the outskirts of town.

VOLCANOES

More than 80 volcanoes in Alaska are potentially active. Novarupta, Pavlof, Augustine, Redoubt, and Spurr are Alaskan volcanoes that are part of the "Ring of Fire," the volcanic rim of the Pacific. From Mt. Wrangell at 144° west longitude in Southeast Alaska to Cape Wrangell at 173° east longitude at the tip of the Aleutian archipelago, southern Alaska exists, to paraphrase historian Will Durant, by volcanic decree . . . subject to change.

Anchorage (and the greater Cook Inlet area) is a great place to watch volcanoes erupt. Augustine, Redoubt, and Spurr volcanoes have put on shows up and down the Cook Inlet; the Mt. Spurr eruption of August 1992 temporarily stopped air travel into and out of Anchorage. The most violent Alaskan eruption? The 2½-day eruption of Novarupta in 1912 in what is now Katmai National Park. The 2.5 cubic mi of ash deposited there has left an Alaskan legacy: the surreal Valley of Ten Thousand Smokes.

EARTHQUAKE COUNTRY

The length of a fault system and whether or not the fault is straight over great distances are of interest to geologists. Fault length is related to earthquake magnitude. Generally speaking, the longer a fault, the greater the potential magnitude. Impressed by the 600-mi length of California's San Andreas? The onshore portion of the Denali Fault System is more than 1,000 mi long. Numerous long faults around the world move horizontally. This produces some interesting results if the fault trace is not straight. A fault system such as the Denali has a large component of horizontal movement (called strike-slip motion): crustal blocks on either side move past each other, rather than up or down. If a strike-slip fault bends, one of two situations results: a gap or hole in the crust (usually filled by volcanic outbreaks and/or sediments sloughing into the hole) or a compression of the bend, resulting in vertical uplift (mountains). Which condition occurs is a function of fault motion, whether into or out of the bend. South of Fairbanks, the Denali Fault System changes trend, from northwest–southeast to north-east–southwest. The sense of horizontal motion is into the bend, resulting in vertical uplift. What mountain just happens to be in the vicinity? Mt. McKinley, at 20,320 feet the tallest mountain in North America. Moreover, its relief (difference in elevation between the base and top of the mountain), at 18,000 feet, is unsurpassed. Mt. Everest is more than 29,000 feet, but "only" 11,000 feet above the Tibetan Plateau, which forms its base.

With such big faults, it's no wonder geologists look at Alaska as big earthquake country. Seward, Valdez, Whittier, and Anchorage are just some of the more prominent names associated with the Good Friday Earthquake of 1964. Upgraded in 1977 to magnitude 9.2, the Good Friday quake is the largest on record for North America. Fifteen to thirty seconds is not unusual for ground motion in a big, destructive earthquake; Alaskans shook for three to four minutes during the Good Friday quake. The epicenter was about 6 mi east of College Fjord in Prince William Sound, some 70 mi east of Anchorage. Vertical deformation (uplift or down-dropping of the land) affected an area of 100,000 square mi. By the time the shaking had stopped, the area of Latouche Island had moved 60 feet to the southeast and portions of the Montague Island area were uplifted by as much as 30 feet. The area of Portage was down-dropped by approximately 10 feet. The largest tsunami (often misnamed a tidal wave) that hit Hilo, Hawaii, checked in

at 12½ feet; the largest at Crescent City, California, was 13 feet; and in Chenega, Alaska, native residents were never sure what rose from the sea to smite them . . . just that it was 90 feet tall. The entire planet was affected: the area in which the quake was felt by people is estimated at 500,000 square mi—South Africa checked in to report that groundwater was sloshing around in wells.

Geologists generally describe tsunamis with respect to displacement on a fault underwater. They use the more general term "seismic sea wave" when other things, such as submarine landslides, cause enormous waves. The 90-foot seismic sea wave that hit Chenega was topped by the 220-foot wave reported from the Valdez Arm area. But a few years earlier in southeastern Alaska, on the evening of July 9, 1958, an earthquake in the Yakutat area dumped an enormous landslide into the head of Lituya Bay. The result was a seiche, or splash wave, that traveled 1,740 feet up the opposite mountainside.

Impressed yet? In the last century the average recurrence interval for Alaskan earthquakes in excess of 8.0 on the Richter Scale was 10 years. The recurrence interval for earthquakes over 7.0 is just over a year. Never mind California—Alaska is the most seismically active state in the Union. Volcanic hazard? Well, Pavlof has averaged an eruption every 6 years over the last 240.

DESERT

And now about that desert. The North Slope of Alaska is 80,000 square mi of frozen, windswept desert where Inupiat Eskimos live. It's a desert from the climatological perspective that the North Slope receives less than 10 inches of precipitation each year. If you go around the west end of the Brooks Range, you can even find sand dunes—Great Kobuk, Little Kobuk, and Hunt River sand-dune fields. Temperatures during the short, cool summers are usually between 30°F and 40°F. Temperatures during the winter can average –20°F. In winter, the Arctic Ocean moderates temperatures on the North Slope, but there is nothing to moderate the wind.

ROCKS & MINERALS

The first people to come into the country came across the Bering Land Bridge from Asia, between 10,000 and 40,000 years ago. The Bering Land Bridge was a product of the Pleistocene epoch—the Great Ice Age—which lowered the sea level enough for the bridge to form. At the start of the Mesozoic era (beginning about 245 million years before the present), sandstones and conglomerates deposited in a warm, shallow sea marked the beginning of Prudhoe Bay. That abundant organic matter is now abundant oil under the North Slope. Also during the Mesozoic era, oil-bearing shales were deposited in the Cook Inlet, home of Alaska's first oil boom; copper and silver deposits were formed in what is now the Copper River country; Cretaceous swamps in South Central Alaska became the Matanuska coalfield; and gold was emplaced around present-day Fairbanks and near Nome on the Seward Peninsula.

The oldest rocks in Alaska are of Precambrian age (the "Time Before Life") and are in southwestern Alaska. They have been dated at 2 billion years of age, nearly half the age of the earth. Rocks 1 billion years old have been identified in the area of the Brooks Range south to the Yukon River. Interestingly, the 1-billion-year-old rocks are native; the 2-billion-year-old rocks are expatriates. In fact, southern and southeastern Alaska are composed of a mosaic or quilt of microplates, all much smaller than continent size. Some terranes (blocks or fragments of the Earth's crust that may vary in age, geologic character, or site of origin) arrived in Alaska from as far south as the equator.

Certain Alaskan rocks tell a tale of warm climates and seas. Evidence? Hike the Holitna River basin in Southwest Alaska and look for fossil remains of the many trilobites (those now-extinct three-lobe marine arthropods that scavenged the bottoms of warm, shallow, Cambrian seas—parents, if you don't know what they look like, ask your children). The central interior of Alaska evidently was never covered by ice but was instead a cool steppe land roamed by mammoths, bison, horses, saber-toothed cats, and camels. Yes, camels.

A GEOLOGICAL WONDER

Alaska's stunning expanse incorporates fire and ice, wind and rain, volcano, glacier, windswept tundra, towering rain forest, and mist-shrouded island. Its geologic story covers a great deal of time and distance and has produced (and is producing) some of the most exquisite land anywhere. In the north, the rocks tell a story of relative stability—geological homebodies born and raised. In the south, the patchwork terrains tell a tale of far-traveled immigrants coming into the country. Geological processes that have produced, and are still producing, both homebodies and expatriates create a land in constant flux. But the majesty of the land: that is the unchanging legacy of Alaska.

—Dr. Charles Lane

INDEX

PHOTO CREDITS